MYSTICS AND MESSIAHS

# Mystics and Messiahs

*Cults and New Religions in American History*

PHILIP JENKINS

OXFORD
UNIVERSITY PRESS

# OXFORD
## UNIVERSITY PRESS

Oxford   New York
Athens   Auckland   Bangkok   Bogotá   Buenos Aires
Cape Town   Chennai   Dar es Salaam   Delhi   Florence   Hong Kong   Istanbul
Karachi   Kolkata   Kuala Lumpur   Madrid   Melbourne   Mexico City   Mumbai
Nairobi   Paris   São Paulo   Shanghai   Singapore   Taipei   Tokyo   Toronto   Warsaw

and associated companies in
Berlin   Ibadan

Copyright © 2000 by Oxford University Press

First published by Oxford University Press, Inc., 2000
198 Madison Avenue, New York, New York 10016

First issued as an Oxford University Press paperback, 2001

Library of Congress Cataloging-in-Publication Data
Jenkins, Philip, 1952–
Mystics and messiahs : cults and new religions in American history/Philip Jenkins.
p. cm.
Includes bibliographical references and index.
ISBN 0-19-512744-7 (Cloth)
ISBN 0-19-514596-8 (Pbk.)
1. Cults—United States—History—20th Century.
2. United States—Religion—20th Century.
I. Title.
BL2525 .J46 2000
200'.973—dc21
99-028732

Book design by Adam B. Bohannon
1 3 5 7 9 10 8 6 4 2
Printed in the United States of America
on acid-free paper

# Contents

*Acknowledgments*   vii

# *Acknowledgments*

I have the great good fortune to have colleagues like Anne C. Rose, William L. Petersen, Gary Knoppers, and Wilson J. Moses, all of whom supplied helpful advice as I was writing this book. Kathryn Hume very kindly read the manuscript and made many valuable comments. I am also grateful to Cynthia Read of Oxford University Press for her advice and assistance at every stage of this project.

---

*A genuine first-hand religious experience like this*
*is bound to be a heterodoxy to its witnesses,*
*the prophet appearing as a mere lonely madman.*
*If his doctrine prove contagious enough to spread to any others,*
*it becomes a definite and labeled heresy.*
*But if it then still prove contagious enough to triumph over persecution,*
*it becomes itself an orthodoxy;*
*and when a religion has become an orthodoxy,*
*its day of inwardness is over: the spring is dry;*
*the faithful live at second hand exclusively*
*and stone the prophets in their turn.*
*The new church, in spite of whatever human goodness it may foster,*
*can be henceforth counted on as a staunch ally*
*in every attempt to stifle the spontaneous religious spirit,*
*and to stop all later babblings of the fountain from which,*
*in purer days, it drew its own supply of inspiration.*

WILLIAM JAMES, *Varieties of Religious Experience*

---

MYSTICS AND MESSIAHS

# ONE

## Overrun with Messiahs

It should be obvious to any man who is not one himself that the land
is overrun with messiahs.
  Charles W. Ferguson, *The Confusion of Tongues*

In the 1920s, like today, the American media relished a scandal that
mixed religion with sexual depravity and crime, and the newspapers
found rich pickings in the story of Benjamin Purnell, the head of
an odd messianic sect. In 1905, "King Ben" opened a colony for his
House of David at Benton Harbor in Michigan. At its peak, the settlement grew to nine hundred believers, over which Purnell reigned as a
patriarch, resplendent in his white robes and magnificent beard. But
the sect repeatedly attracted bad publicity, all the more hazardous because of the proximity to Chicago, Detroit, and other major media
centers: the site was also exposed to the gaze of curious tourists. Purnell
demanded total control over his followers' property, allowing him to
live in palatial splendor while his subjects starved, and he maintained
order with threats of death or exile. The sect became a multimillion
dollar operation, with impressive real-estate holdings. He treated the
younger female members of the group as his personal harem, and his
secret Inner Circle initiation rituals sometimes involved rape (notionally, the sect demanded celibacy). In 1923, disgruntled followers sued
Purnell for the restitution of their property and compensation for their
forced labor. He disappeared for some years and was believed dead, but
his hiding place in the settlement was revealed by a woman who was
a former member of the Inner Circle and whom the press termed a
harem girl. In 1927, Purnell faced multiple charges of statutory rape
involving perhaps twenty underage cult members, in what the press
touted as the "trial of the century."[1]

To a modern audience, the case of King Ben contains few surprises. The House of David neatly fits the image of religious cults familiar since the 1970s. In common parlance, cults are exotic religions that practice spiritual totalitarianism: members owe fanatical obedience to the group and to its charismatic leaders, who enforce their authority through mind-control techniques or brainwashing. According to the stereotype, cult members live separated from the "normal" world, sometimes socially, in the sense of being cut off from previous friends and family, and sometimes also spatially, in a special residence house or a remote compound. Other cult characteristics include financial malpractice and deceit by the group or its leaders, the exploitation of members, and sexual unorthodoxy. An extreme example of such a deviant group would be the People's Temple founded by Jim Jones, who led his followers to mass suicide at Jonestown, Guyana, in 1978.

By all these criteria, the lascivious prophet Benjamin Purnell was a typical cult leader and his followers were model cultists, but what is remarkable here is the chronology. This particular cult scandal erupted not in the 1970s, in the age of Jonestown and national controversies over cult conversions and deprogramming, but half a century before. Though modern observers tend to assume that the idea of cults is relatively modern, in fact it has deep roots in American history. Fringe groups like Purnell's were by no means unusual in the 1920s, and many attracted similar charges of exploitation and sexual misbehavior. In Purnell's case, the charges were probably justified, but in many others, they were not. Already in this era, marginal religious movements were regularly denounced as cults, and like today, the cult phenomenon was a source of public fear. Moreover, both cults and cult scares had become familiar parts of the American scene long before the Purnell trial. The specific terminology might change over time—the language of "cult" only dates from the 1890s—but there is no period, including colonial times, in which we cannot find numerous groups more or less indistinguishable from the most controversial modern movements. As Charles W. Ferguson remarked in 1928, "America has always been the sanctuary of amazing cults."[2]

## Cults in American History

A historical perspective is crucial for understanding contemporary debates over fringe movements, over modern "destructive cults" or "doomsday cults." Over the last three decades, the word "cult" has featured regularly in the news, and it has acquired ever more frightening connotations. Images of robotlike obedience were frightening enough, but that already grim picture was aggravated by incidents of extreme violence, such as the Manson Family murders and Jonestown. Notorious cult outbreaks during the 1990s included the confrontation at Waco, the violent deaths of the Heaven's Gate and Solar Temple groups, and the nerve gas attack on the Tokyo subway by the Japanese Aum Shinrikyo organization. For the media, each of these events spoke eloquently of blind fanaticism, megalomaniacal leaders, and the following of incomprehensible dogma. Even if we do not focus on the most aberrant groups, the existence of so many unorthodox fringe religions can be seen as a symptom of social malaise or fragmentation. In response, many commentators have inquired what has gone so badly wrong with the religious consciousness of their nation as to permit the emergence of such suspect movements.

All these lines of inquiry imply that the contemporary American situation is a frightening novelty, with few or no historical parallels: the unspoken assumption is that the religious landscape of fifty or a hundred years ago must have been a fairly tranquil, monochrome affair, a straightforward matter of "Protestant, Catholic, and Jew." In 1980, for instance, James and Marcia Rudin claimed that "there has never in recorded history been such a proliferation of cults. . . . Never before have religious cults been so geographically widespread. . . . Today's religious cults are unique also because of their great wealth."[3] But as cases like Ben Purnell's illustrate, this view of modern exceptionalism is misleading. If such groups had only appeared in the 1960s and 1970s, then they would have to be explained in terms of circumstances prevailing at that particular time; but far from being a novelty, cults and cultlike movements have a very long history on American soil.

Extreme and bizarre religious ideas are so commonplace in American history that it is difficult to speak of them as fringe at all. To speak of a fringe implies a mainstream, but in terms of numbers, perhaps the largest component of the religious spectrum in contemporary America remains what it has been since colonial times: a fundamentalist evangelicalism with powerful millenarian strands. The doomsday theme has never been far from the center of American religious thought. The nation has always had believers who responded to this threat by a determination to flee from the wrath to come, to separate themselves from the City of Destruction, even if that meant putting themselves at odds with the law and with their communities or families. In its earliest days, colonial New England was a refuge for those seeking to live godly lives uncontaminated by the sinful world, very much the same motivation that today drives believers into remote enclaves. We can throughout American history find select and separatist groups who looked to a prophetic individual claiming divine revelation, in a setting that repudiated conventional assumptions about property, family life, and sexuality. They were marginal groups, peculiar people, people set apart from the world: the Shakers and the Ephrata community, the communes of Oneida and Amana, the followers of Joseph Smith and Brigham Young. And most were at some point charged, fairly or otherwise, with excesses very similar to those alleged against modern cults. Ben Purnell did not exist in a social vacuum; he and others like him have always been able to attract followers, sometimes in their thousands.

Most early radical sects were avowedly Christian, but some held occult or mystical doctrines of the sort that we would today term "New Age." This occult tradition includes alchemy and astrology, together with forms of spiritual healing, all of which were already deeply rooted in colonial America. As early as the 1690s, some sects in German Pennsylvania were deeply imbued with rosicrucian and Hermetic thought, and demonstrated the same fascination with mystic numbers that would characterize fringe movements up to the present day. Though more visible in some decades than others, these esoteric traditions have never died out entirely.[4]

Magi and prophets are American productions just as characteristic as bishops and revivalists. Martin Marty has written that William Dudley Pelley, a religious activist of the 1930s, dabbled with "so many movements that [he] seemed a fictional creation: Christian Science, atheism, Rosicrucianism, Theosophy, New Thought, Spiritualism, Darwinism, the occult, the Great Pyramid, telepathy, sexology, metaphysics, Emersonianism, more of conventional Christianity than he or his enemies recognized, and science of the sort later associated with extrasensory perception."[5] Though the list of creeds is intended to make Pelley sound absurdly eclectic, the resulting picture is less that of a fictional creation than of a familiar American type. The combination of occult, mystical, Masonic, and pseudoscientific views with esoteric Christianity would have been instantly comprehensible to Americans of the 1830s, 1880s, and 1970s, while as far back as 1730, there were regions where a synthesis of this sort would have been regarded as perfectly familiar, if not already old hat. Such a package of esoteric beliefs is so persistent a theme of American religion that it constitutes a separate tradition running parallel to better known and much larger schools like liberal Protestantism, evangelical enthusiasm, or the Catholic heritage.

## Boom Years on the Religious Frontier

Some eras were particularly fertile for religious innovation and, hence, for the formation of groups a modern observer might describe as cults. The 1830s and 1840s were marked by ideas of millenarianism, perfectionism, and communitarianism, and some of the emerging movements experimented with innovative sexual relationships. From 1850 to 1880, spiritualism exercised a powerful attraction for all social classes and disseminated its technical vocabulary into everyday speech, much as consciousness-raising movements would do in the 1970s. Spiritualism also prepared the ground for the Theosophical and Asian-oriented religious ideas that have flourished since the end of the nineteenth century: Asian sects and gurus made their first impact in American life not during the presidencies of Nixon or Ford, but during those of McKinley and Theodore Roosevelt. Not only are New Age ideas long established, but the term itself has had more or less its present meaning for most of the past century. By 1900, the most active of the new sects included apocalyptic movements like the Watch Tower Society (later the Jehovah's Witnesses) and the Adventists, and metaphysical healing sects like Christian Science and the various schools of New Thought.

Though historical accounts often draw parallels between the religious excitement of the pre–Civil War years and that of the 1960s, it is less often noted that the years between about 1910 and 1935 marked another explosive era for new movements and sects, some of which were communal and authoritarian. Though some scholars dismiss the decade after 1925 as the "American religious depression," that was only true from the point of view of mainline Christian churches, and certainly not for the mystical and apocalyptic groups.[6] By the late 1920s, the country was "overrun with messiahs. . . . Each of these has seriously made himself the center of a new theophany, has surrounded himself with a band of zealous apostles, has hired a hall for a shrine, and has set about busily to rescue Truth from the scaffold, and put it on the throne." Or as one of Sinclair Lewis's characters phrased it in

1935, there were, "Certainly a lot of messiahs pottin' at you from the bushes these days."[7]

The most celebrated new movements were concentrated in California, which had already staked its irrevocable claim to an image of eccentricity, but no region of the country was immune from sensational groups. By the 1920s, swamis and occult temples could be found in most major cities. New Orleans had its old established voodoo practices, and related religious forms were found in many northern areas. Detroit had a substantial Black Muslim presence, while Muslim and black Jewish sects were found in most major African-American communities. The most influential of the new trends were Christian Science and New Thought, which acquired mass national followings but were still denounced as cults. It is surprising to find Martin E. Marty writing of American religion between 1919 and 1941, "It was not a fertile period of new eruptions of intense religious groups of the sort later called cults."[8] I would argue that it was such a fertile period, and the word "cult" had been used in this precise sense since the turn of the century.

Eccentric-seeming religious ideas became part of the common intellectual currency during the 1920s, which possessed what later scholars have termed a "cult milieu." This phrase was coined in the 1970s during the boom in marginal religions; a time when the act of joining a fringe religion became something that was in the air, was part of the culture, when ideas and influences freely circulated between movements of very different ideological colors. The concept of a cult milieu can be applied to the 1840s and also to the 1920s. In this last period, a Protestant evangelist like Aimee Semple McPherson imitated the rhetoric and pageantry of a Theosophist commune, while notionally Muslim sects like the Moorish Science Temple and the Nation of Islam both borrowed from New Age and Theosophical ideas. Meanwhile, a number of enterprising individuals concocted whole new synthetic religions out of the detritus of a dozen esoteric movements: Guy and Edna Ballard created their hugely successful I AM movement by plundering the various occult and New Age traditions of the day, while William Dudley Pelley's Silver Shirts tried to turn a cult movement into a national political party. Repeatedly, marginal movements have formed the basis of popular culture treatments, which in turn inspired authentic new sects, so that the line separating fiction and reality is never too clear.

Upsurges of activism on the religious fringe—what we might call "cult booms" or "cult waves"—have been so frequent in American religious history that they are intrinsic to it. As Charles W. Ferguson remarked in 1928, "The truth is of course that the land is simply teeming with faith—that marked credulity that accompanies periods of great religious awakening, and seems to be with us a permanent state of mind."[9]

## Degrees of Commitment

It would be very useful to give hard numbers for this kind of activity at any particular historical moment—to say, for example, that X million people were members of apocalyptic or esoteric movements in 1900 or 1940. Sadly, this precision is impossible. The problem is that such ideas can be widely shared without formal participation in an organized community, and individuals have varying degrees of active involvement in such groups. Sociologists often distinguish between degrees of involvement in cult activity.[10] At the lowest level of participation, we find the *audience cults*, which have little formal structure and may not even have actual meetings; instead, they service consumers through books, magazines, mail-order courses, or videos. An individual can have connections with dozens or even hundreds of such movements, grazing among the various ideas and picking and choosing those that appeal, even if they are drawn from quite distinct subcultures. Rather more commitment is involved in *client cults*, in which consumers interact with the cult rather as a patient does with a therapist. The highest degree of involvement is found in *cult movements*, which have formal membership and meetings. In this last case, followers might even relocate to distinct, cult-owned properties.

Unorthodox ideas can be very widespread through audience cults, though without much measurable participation or affiliation. To illustrate this, we might consider the parcel of New Age ideas, which includes belief in astrology, channeling, reincarnation, neopaganism, and goddess spirituality. A general impression based on the mass media suggests that New Age believers are very numerous, and someone is presumably buying the vast numbers of books, magazines, and videotapes produced each year. Nevertheless, this community is barely visible, even to sophisticated survey techniques. One of the best analyses recorded only fifty thousand New Age believers in the whole nation in the early 1990s, and this startlingly low number was reached only by including followers of the movements Wicca and ECKANKAR in addition to respondents explicitly describing themselves as "New Age."[11] While this low figure seems counterintuitive, it is readily explained. The vast majority of people holding New Age beliefs do not identify themselves as representing a distinct denomination, but describe themselves as Unitarians or Jews, Methodists or Catholics. This is a classic audience cult. If contemporary New Agers are so difficult to locate with certainty, it is even harder to quantify the influence, as opposed to the formal membership, of spiritualism in the 1860s or Theosophy in the 1920s. Though the U.S. Census in 1926 found fewer than seven thousand declared Theosophists in the entire nation, that movement had already succeeded in making its views a familiar component of religious thought.

The fact that fringe religious ideas are not expressed in formal organizations or churches does not necessarily mean that they are unimportant. If, for instance, we find that the proportion of Americans believing in reincarnation grew enormously over the course of the twentieth century, that would be an immensely significant statement about the national religious consciousness, whether or not the change has been reflected in the membership rolls of reincarnationist sects. Over the past century, many ideas originally associated with fringe or occult sects have enjoyed such a wide dissemination, most dramatically in the 1920s and 1970s.

## The Anticult Heritage

Just as no era lacks its controversial fringe groups, so no era fails to produce opponents to denounce them: anticult movements are also a long-established historical phenomenon. Anticult rhetoric is strikingly constant, or is at least built upon a common core of allegations and complaints. When an emerging group today is denounced as a cult, its critics are employing, consciously or not, a prefabricated script some centuries in the making, incorporating charges that might originally have been developed long ago against a wide variety of movements. Allegations can even originate in popular culture or as urban legend, yet are soberly incorporated into the anticult indictment as matters of fact.

The concept of the deviant cult—authoritarian, deceptive, exploitative, violent—can be traced deep into the past. Few groups have epitomized the cult image better than the Christians of the first two centuries. Christians held self-evidently extreme and nonsensical views, which had been imported into the Roman world from the fanatical Orient. The sect broke up existing families, it was dominated by charismatic religious leaders, and its ritual practices were believed to include incest, orgies, child murder, and cannibalism. How else would one explain their "love feasts" for brothers and sisters who ate the flesh of the Son of God? Since that time, countless other groups have attracted a similarly florid range of accusations, usually exaggerated and sometimes wholly fictitious. None of the charges levied against the cults of the 1970s would have been unfamiliar to critics of the Methodists in the eighteenth century or of the Freemasons, Roman Catholics, and Latter-Day Saints in the nineteenth. At any given point over the last century, some peripheral religions were being denounced for driving their adherents to bankruptcy or insanity, and prophetic leaders were attacked as molesters or confidence tricksters. In each era, a few well-authenticated cases appeared to substantiate the wider validity of such charges.

In some periods, the convergence of separate scandals led to a general denunciation of cults as a distinctive social problem or threat, very much as in the 1970s. A wave of scandals in the late 1920s led to an intensification of the volume and vigor of anticult writings. This was the time of Sinclair Lewis's novel *Elmer Gantry* and Dashiell Hammett's *The Dain Curse*, of exposés of mediums and cults by Houdini and his followers, and of Morris Fishbein's denunciation of cult quackery in *The New Medical Follies*. There were also sober surveys like Charles W. Ferguson's *The Confusion of Tongues* and Hugo Hume's sardonic overview of *The Superior American Religions*. Shortly afterwards, we hear of southern California as the "proving ground" for the nationwide "cult racket." In 1933, Louis Binder's *Modern Religious Cults and Society* affected to be an objective scholarly analysis, but began from the standpoint that "at best, the cults are a dreadful reality in modern religious life." In 1936, sociologist Read Bain offered a comprehensive definition of pathological "religious cults" that sounds remarkably modern: "[A cult] has a revered, almost sacred, leader-symbol; it contains mystical elements which provide escape-mechanisms for many of its followers; its proponents and adherents often show delusions of persecution and grandeur; its opponents indulge in heresy-hunting and vitriolic condemnation; there are numerous bitter feuds and fanatic factions within the fold; symbolism, ritualism and logical confusion abound; it flourishes upon dogmatic denial of the ordinary postulates and methods of natural science."[12]

A renewed assault on "crackpot religions" followed in the 1940s: in 1944, as in 1929, cults were a major topic of media concern, and the issue now entered the political arena, creating a situation with many parallels to the modern era. The main problem cults were those suspected for their Far Right or antiwar sentiments, including I AM and Mankind United, the Jehovah's Witnesses, and the Nation of Islam. Other movements providing steady media copy included the snake-handling Holiness sects concentrated in Appalachia, the surviving sects of Mormon polygamists, and some dubious groups offering the wisdom of the ancients through the mail. The established churches debated how they could respond to the pressing problem, and this decade was marked by intense legal activism to control the religious fringe. The cult controversies of the 1940s did much to define the constitutional limits of religious freedom and toleration, with implications reaching far beyond the immediate limits of sects like I AM and the Witnesses.

## Cult and Anticult: The Cycle

The resemblances between the successive waves of anticult reaction are sufficiently similar to suggest that they follow broadly similar internal dynamics. We can chart in the form of a table some of the obvious parallels between two successive eras (Table 1.1).

This model should not be pressed too far because the most intense phase of official concern and intervention occurred at a different stage of the cycle in the earlier wave than it did in the later. Still, the similarities are suggestive, notably in what I call the phase of *Speculation*, in which fairly well-grounded criticisms of marginal religions escalate into wild fantasies: recall the nightmarish events of the 1980s, when so many innocent people had their lives ruined by absurd charges that they were clandestine Satanists who abused and murdered children. What is less well-known is that similar rumors about bloodthirsty devil cults had also run rampant fifty years previously, and in many ways this first panic served as a foundation for the more recent one. We find in this earlier era the beginnings of the modern mythology about homicidal satanic networks being embedded in American neighborhoods, schools, and churches.

## Defining Cults

The long and often troubled history of America's marginal religions raises important implications for the vexed question of defining cults.

Table 1.1
Cults and Anticult Reactions: A Cycle

| Emergence | 1910–1935<br>Surging interest in fringe re-ligions and occult; creation of many new marginal groups and sects. | 1960–1980<br>Surging interest in fringe re-ligions and occult; creation of many new marginal groups and sects. |
|---|---|---|
| Reaction | 1925–1930<br>Wave of scandals involving fringe religions and leaders. Popular recognition of cult phenomenon; framing of "cult problem" in exposés and in popular culture. | 1976–1981<br>Wave of scandals involving fringe religions and leaders. Popular recognition of cult phenomenon; framing of "cult problem" in exposés and in popular culture.<br>Intense activism by law en-forcement agencies and pres-sures for restrictive legisla-tion. |
| Speculation | 1932–1940<br>Sensational media-led specu-lations about supposed outer reaches of cult problem: voo-doo, witchcraft, human sacri-fice. | 1984–1992<br>Sensational media-led specula-tions about supposed outer reaches of cult problem: Sa-tanism, ritual abuse, human sacrifice. |
| Second Peak | early 1940s<br>New wave of cult-related scandals; activism by law en-forcement agencies and pres-sures for restrictive legislation. | mid-1990s<br>New wave of cult-related scandals leads to resurgence of popular concern. |

When public opinion is aroused by a particularly disturbing scandal or a mass suicide, legislatures sometimes attempt to regulate cult activi-ties, hoping to control unpopular groups like the Unification Church (the "Moonies"), the Hare Krishna movement, the followers of Bhag-wan Shree Rajneesh, or the International Churches of Christ. Any such measures are bound to fail, however, and not just on the obvious con-stitutional grounds of freedom of religion. It is all but impossible to define cults in a way that does not describe a large share of American religious bodies, including some of the most respectable. The distinction between cults and religions or denominations is not self-evident, nor

is it obvious which groups can be graced with the title "mainstream."
(Frank Zappa once observed that the only difference between a church
and a cult is the amount of real estate each owns.) Sporadic efforts to
pass anticult legislation therefore provoke resistance from across the
religious spectrum, even from groups that have a powerful vested interest in fighting what they see as cult seduction of young people.[13] As
definitions vary so widely, it is not surprising to find enormous vari-
ations in the estimates offered for the number of cult groups at any
given time. Are there a few dozen? Five hundred? Or five thousand?

The word "cult" has acquired over the last century or so such horrible connotations that it can scarcely be used as an objective social
scientific description. It is now a pejorative word only used by enemies
or critics of the movement concerned: did anyone ever announce,
straight-faced, that he or she had joined a cult? Some writers try to
avoid this problem by offering what seem to be objective or nonjudg-
mental definitions, but they face an insuperable task. One major study
notes that "[c]ults tend to be totalistic or all-encompassing in controlling their members' behavior and also ideologically totalistic, exhibiting
zealotry and extremism in their world-view."[14] But few movements are
as totalistic as the Amish, who are respected and idealized by the wider
society; they would never be described as cultlike, nor would Hasidic
Jews. Furthermore, the difference between zeal (laudable) and zealotry
(undesirable) is entirely subjective. If we argue that cults hold extreme
or eccentric beliefs diverging radically from those of the mainstream,
we must then ask, which mainstream? Some opinion polls suggest that
about half of Americans accept Creationism, a belief system that effectively rejects most of the bases of modern science, while many millions
expect the imminent Second Coming of Christ. These beliefs could be
described as eccentric or extreme from some points of view, but no
belief held by so large a proportion of the people can properly be rel-
egated to a religious margin. What is normal?

Nor can cults be identified purely in terms of behavior, in the sense
that there are some types of conduct (exploitative and psychologically
dangerous) that demarcate cults from churches, sects, or denominations. One difficulty is that it is far too easy to gather information
about the disreputable groups, making it tempting to overemphasize
their importance in the overall picture of the religious fringe. Movements marked by scandals, fraud, and violence are and always have
been much in the news, and their doings can be easily traced in official

documents. But although overt swindlers and megalomaniacs do operate within the marginal groups, they represent only the most conspicuous aspect of a far larger phenomenon. It is all too easy to visualize
a "cult problem" in terms of demonized individuals like Ben Purnell,
Charles Manson, and David Koresh. Anticult accounts rarely mention
the many small sects, esoteric or otherwise, that continue for decades
under responsible leaders and are quite successful, insofar as the success
of any religious movement can be evaluated in any objective terms. At
least they provide their members with new spiritual insights, help them
cope with their lives, and teach them to live in greater harmony with
their society and surroundings.

Differences of power and size go far towards explaining what we
know, or think we know, about differences in the conduct of small and
large religious groups. If we observe that small groups are likely to
have scandals involving sexual misconduct, particularly involving children, we might suggest that this type of misbehavior is a cult characteristic, and that would lead us to propose theories about the pernicious
nature of leadership in these settings. But numerous recent scandals
have taught us that sexual abuse is a common difficulty in all religious
groups and denominations, including the largest and most respected,
and some of the most outrageous instances of abuse by mainstream
clergy occurred in the 1970s and early 1980s, when the cults were
drawing such intense fire.[15]

As always, the media reacted very differently to the churches and
the cults. Stories of sexual deviance meshed precisely with public expectations of cult leaders. But they seemed improbable and atypical for
established clergy, so that rumors would be much more likely to be
investigated and published in the context of the small groups than the
large. Also, while nothing was to be lost by offending the members
of a quirky local commune, it took a brave editor to run a story attacking a mainstream denomination, which could respond with an advertising boycott or a venomous letter-writing campaign. Hence, the
"pedophile priest" scandals in the mainstream churches were largely
kept from public view for decades, until the explosion of public concern
in the mid-1980s. And though financial manipulation and tax evasion
have attracted less notoriety than sexual issues, the same principles
apply to reporting ecclesiastical misdeeds in these other areas: larger
and more powerful groups are let off more easily than the small and
unpopular.

## Cult, Sect, and Church

What is the difference between a church and a cult? Sociologists traditionally classified religious bodies as either churches or sects. According to this model, churches are larger bodies, more formally structured
in terms of hierarchy and liturgy, which appeal to better-off members
of society; sects, in contrast, are smaller, less structured, and more
spontaneous and draw their members from working-class or lower-class
people. Members of churches are born into them; sects find their membership by recruitment and conversion. While churches place minimal
demands on their members, sects are "greedy" groups, demanding that
adherents follow practices that can pose major difficulties for them in
everyday life, even to the point of earning social ostracism. Model
churches in contemporary America might include the Episcopalians or
Methodists, while the Jehovah's Witnesses or Seventh Day Adventists
would typify sects. Over time, sects tend to become churches, and then
the cycle of sect formation begins anew.[16]

Initially, cults did not feature in this scheme, but they were incorporated in the 1960s. According to the new view, cults are like sects in
being at odds with the wider society, but they are also more innovative,
more conspicuously deviant. Churches are thus defined as "religious
bodies in a relatively low state of tension with their environment;"
sects are in a high state of tension, but remain within the conventional
religious traditions of a society; cults, likewise, exist in a state of tension, but they "represent faiths that are new and unconventional in a
society" or have no prior ties to any established body in the wider
society. Cults "do not evolve or break away from other religions as do
religious sects, but rather offer something new and different." Whether
as the result of invention or innovation, cults are unconventional. This
definition initially seems reasonable when we think of a group like the
Hare Krishnas (properly, the International Society for Krishna Consciousness, ISKCON), who deviate radically from the religious and cultural practices of the vast majority of Americans; they certainly seem
unconventional.[17]

But what is conventional in American religion? To speak of established traditions suggests that the United States was conceived with an
approved range of faiths and religious practices, from which no devi-
ation was to be tolerated. By this standard, there are no cults since
virtually all bodies so described have grown directly out of quite long-
standing traditions in the society. The Branch Davidian group, which

was at the center of the Waco disaster, was formed in the 1920s as an offshoot of the Seventh-Day Adventists, who in turn trace their ancestry to the 1840s: the Davidians themselves had been based at Waco since 1935. Jim Jones's People's Temple grew out of an active evangelical church, which in its early days was unconventional only in its commitment to interracial cooperation. Jones himself was ordained in a well-established and fairly conservative denomination, the Christian Church, Disciples of Christ. His more eccentric ideas derived from Father Divine, who was preaching his own godhood as early as 1915. Another notorious cult figure was Jeffrey Lundgren, whose group undertook several ritualistic slayings in the late 1980s: Lundgren's origins lay in the Reorganized Church of Latter-Day Saints, a reputable and conservative branch of the Mormon tradition.[18]

A historical perspective shows that other so-called cults have equally respectable lineages, and even the most unconventional-seeming religions can be traced far back into the American past. If we take the more conspicuously foreign Asian religions, both Buddhism and Hinduism have had some presence among white Americans since the late nineteenth century, and swamis of various kinds were already a familiar part of the spiritual landscape before 1900. Though the Hare Krishna movement itself was only imported in the 1960s, it represents an authentic face of the Hindu tradition. The United States had Buddhists before it had Pentecostals, just as American Rosicrucians and alchemists predate its Methodists. At the other extreme, the conservative churches that have denounced the cults began their own histories as controversial movements attacked for their fanaticism and divisiveness. The torrent of abuse directed against Scientology or the Unification Church in the 1970s is very much like that suffered by the Baptists in the seventeenth century and Methodists in the eighteenth. Even if cults do not have roots in a society, they can develop them quite securely within only a few decades and give the impression that they have been there since time immemorial.

If we exclude the unconventionality theme, then all that remains to distinguish between cults and mainstream bodies is the issue of tension, which means how each is regarded by society at large, not necessarily on any objective or rational grounds. To take an unusual example, it is difficult to think of a religious body more at odds with its society than the Confessing Church founded in Germany in the 1930s in protest against Nazi racial laws. A tiny body utterly convinced of the justice of its position, the church plotted against the government, and some of its leaders conspired to assassinate the Nazi leadership. In consequence, the group was brutally suppressed, and its leader, Dietrich Bonhoeffer, was executed in 1945. Far from being regarded as a violent cult leader, however, Bonhoeffer is venerated as a towering figure in the history of twentieth-century Christianity. In the judgment of history, churches can on occasion be terribly wrong, and cults right.

## Explaining Cult Scares

Cults differ from churches in no particular aspect of behavior or belief, and the very term "cult" is a strictly subjective one; it tells us as much about the people applying that label as it does about the group that is so described. Briefly, cults are small, unpopular religious bodies, the implication being that much of their cultish quality comes not from any inherent qualities of the groups themselves, but from the public reaction to them. We might draw a parallel between cults and weeds, the latter being a much-used term that has no botanical meaning, which refers only to plants which have no obvious use for humanity. To speak of acute tension between a religious group and the wider society implies a two-way street: we need to understand both what the cult does to attract disapproval and why mainstream bodies feel the need to apply this damning label to it. It is just this relative quality that makes concern about cults such an important gauge for the state of American religion. Because cults are unpopular and unorthodox, by studying changing perceptions of these movements we can discover what the public thinks religious orthodoxy is, or ought to be: we cannot discuss deviancy without a standard of normality, and normality is a fluid concept.

While the changing shape of the cults themselves tells us much about religious enthusiasms in a particular period, equally informative are the responses of those who choose to denounce the small movements—and who, thereby, lay claim to a mainstream position in American life. This insight raises questions about eras like the 1940s or the 1970s when concern about cults became so intense and generalized as to justify the term "moral panic," when anticult themes permeated popular culture, and stirred legislators to contemplate draconian measures of repression.[19] In these years individual horror stories were viewed as part of a larger social threat, and it became commonplace to speak of a "cult problem" or "cult crisis." This notion escalated the severity of the religious challenge and demanded a public response.

Cult scares might just reflect a period of unusual activity among fringe religious groups. As we have seen, however, no period of American history entirely lacks these movements: in a sense, cults are always with us. The size or vigor of a given movement is not necessarily proportionate to the number of column inches it receives in the press or the number of segments on television news. Intense public interest or fear may be aroused by a tiny sect with a handful of members, as illustrated by the vast alarm stirred by relatively tiny groups like the Hare Krishna movement. Conversely, highly deviant marginal groups can operate for many years without attracting much public attention. Even if some groups are scandal prone, their misdeeds are not necessarily contextualized as part of a general problem or social issue. Much depends on the attitudes of the news media, and the audiences they seek to serve.

Several factors explain the changing construction of the cult menace over time. Visibility is one issue, namely that small movements are now more exposed to the public gaze. Over the last century, the range of potential conflicts between isolated groups and the wider society has grown enormously because of developments like compulsory education, military conscription, social security taxes, and the growth of bureaucracies to investigate child abuse. The Amish, for example, attracted little official notice prior to the First World War; since then, their distinctive practices have repeatedly led to legal confrontations, some of which have been taken as far as the U.S. Supreme Court. Even in what had been the American wilderness, there are no hiding places left. To escape persecution, Mormon polygamists in the 1930s chose to establish a settlement in one of the most remote corners of the nation, on the northern frontier of Arizona, where any police or officials wishing to visit would have to drive the arduous route around the Grand Canyon. Even so, state and federal authorities launched raids in 1944, and again in 1953, in an attempt to stamp out what was sensationally portrayed as a "sex-cult" that exploited children.

Society has become more nationalized and so has the mass media. Stories that a century ago would have been purely local or regional are increasingly brought before a national audience. Presenting issues as of national concern can lead people to believe, incorrectly, that conditions typical of, say, California are spreading to all parts of the country. The growing nationalization of the cult problem during the twentieth century owed much to the changing media technologies that permitted both cult groups and their detractors to transmit their views. In 1959, for instance, a television exposé on the hitherto obscure Black Muslim movement aroused alarm among white viewers nationwide, while giving an enormous boost to the group's black membership: a national phenomenon was born. Since the end of the nineteenth century, too, standards of media coverage have evolved in ever more sensationalistic directions, so that exposé stories about extreme religious or sexual deviance can appeal to a mass market. Indeed, the development of public concern about cults is in large measure a history of changes in the mass media.

## Age, Race, and Gender

The cult issue, like any social problem, is socially constructed. This does not mean that negative stories are false or even exaggerated, and some cult groups may indeed be committing criminal and dangerous acts: multiple murders and mass suicides genuinely were committed by Jim Jones's followers and, more recently, by the Heaven's Gate group. However, the level of public concern about cults at any given time is not necessarily based on a rational or objective assessment of the threat posed by these groups, but rather reflects a diverse range of tensions, prejudices, and fears.

Demographic changes play a role here and help explain the long cycles of concern that we noted above (Table 1.1). Each period of cult proliferation (what I call the phase of *Emergence*) occurred during the latter stages of a baby boom, a period of steep population growth and very high birthrates. In the first two decades of the twentieth century, American birthrates stood at a remarkable 30 or so per 1,000, almost double the modern figure; the national population grew at a faster rate between 1890 and 1915 than in any subsequent era, including the post–Second World War baby boom. In such an environment, new religions can successfully appeal to an unusually young community, who are more open to cultural innovation. Conversely, the dark fantasies of the Speculation phase years, the mid-1930s and mid-1980s, coincide with deep troughs in the national birthrate: at such times, an aging population with smaller families provides a natural audience for frantic warnings about the threat posed to the vulnerable young by homicidal cults.

Though predicting the future is foolhardy, precedent suggests that a renewed upsurge of cults might well occur in another decade or so, beginning around 2010, when the proportion of adolescents in the population will be higher than at any time since the 1970s. Moreover, the baby boomers will be entering their sixties then and should provide a rich market for movements offering miraculous cures for the ills of mind or body, or extensions of the lifespan. Will the cycles of cult formation described here replay themselves once more? It is intriguing to think that the prophets and magi of the next New Age are already among us, preparing for their careers.

Racial factors are also significant in sculpting cult fears. Cults serve as a symbolic focus for ethnic tensions, which are more acute in some periods than others. These resentments surface in attacks on religious groups accused of transgressing racial boundaries, usually by importing into the white community behaviors and beliefs associated with outsiders, with Africans or Asians. Even early Mormonism was interpreted according to lurid contemporary stereotypes of Islam. At least since the end of the nineteenth century, the delineation and defense of "whiteness" has been a theme in most waves of concern about cult activity.

The very word "cult" acquired its present connotations around 1900, under the influence of malignant stereotypes about non-Western religions that had been encountered during imperial adventures. This development also reflected technological change, as the new Victorian world of railroads and steamships permitted an unprecedented degree of contact between the spiritual traditions of East and West, an interaction in which Eastern traditions made real advances. The early twentieth century marked the high point of American scientific racism, when many feared racial decline or atavism and were unnerved to see white Americans being seduced by what was portrayed as Asian fanaticism or African primitivism. In the 1970s and 1980s again, cults were blamed for converting young Americans to "Asian" modes of superstition and slavish devotion. Throughout the century, racial concerns have permeated the ostensibly religious rhetoric about the subversion of Western Christianity by alien creeds. Nativist and xenophobic prejudice have always been implicit in anticult rhetoric, usually in the form of a kind of sinister Orientalism.

Similarly, concerns about cults are influenced by changing views of gender roles and sexual conduct. New religions flourish by providing believers with what they cannot obtain in the mainstream organizations of the day: sects and cults live on the unpaid bills of the churches. This has often meant catering to the needs of women who feel excluded from established belief-systems. Women have repeatedly played important roles as founders, leaders, and members of fringe religions that have explored "enthusiastic" styles of worship—often denounced as feminine and emotional, and considered inferior to the masculine habits of the rational, cerebral churches.[20] Such new religions have been particularly successful in times when ideas about gender and sexuality have been in rapid flux, such as the 1920s and the 1970s. In the early twentieth century, new religious traditions like Adventism, Pentecostalism, and Christian Science all owed much to female prophets and preachers, respectively Ellen G. White, Aimee Semple McPherson, and Mary Baker Eddy.

The centrality of gender factors in shaping new religions helps us understand why such movements are so often depicted as the fads and affectations of silly women. Likewise, men who join cults must be giving way to effeminacy. The conspicuous role of women also explains the prominence of sexual themes in anticult rhetoric over the centuries. Critics imagine the worst sexual excesses for women transgressing traditional religious boundaries, and the sexual nightmares of anticult propaganda depict gullible female converts exposed to the lusts of their male leaders and colleagues. According to this stereotype, separation from the world, whether in convents or compounds, merely gives the false prophet and his minions all the more opportunity to carry out their debaucheries.

## Activists

Concern about cults is usually generated by activism on the part of groups or individuals dedicated to exposing the evils of the marginal religions; a cult scare requires both cults and anticult activists. In various periods, cult opponents have included journalists, law enforcement officers, clergy and religious writers, medical and professional organizations, psychiatrists and therapists, political leaders, and the friends and families of cult members. These different elements sometimes cooperate to form a coalition or even, as in the 1970s and 1980s, a well-organized national movement. As we are dealing here with social movements, we must apply the methods social scientists have developed to understand why such public campaigns succeed or fail. We must find who is making the claims about particular religious groups, as well as the means by which each side projects its arguments and the changing tastes of the audiences to whom they are seeking to appeal.

To use a commercial analogy, we need to know the competing retailers, the purchasers, and the means of packaging and distributing claims, and a change in any one of these can make an item either more or less saleable. For example, one striking feature of the anticult literature during the last century is a fundamental shift of definition as to what constitutes a cult. Prior to 1940, any list of cults would certainly begin with various Christian denominations—albeit ones with unusual theologies or practices, like Christian Science, Mormonism, Seventh Day Adventism, Pentecostalism, and the Jehovah's Witnesses—whereas these movements would rarely appear in any modern catalog of deviant groups. The groups in question may have moved more towards the social mainstream, but the shift in attitudes might also mean that society as a whole is less agitated by charges of theological unorthodoxy and reserves the term "cult" for movements posing a clearly secular threat. Heresy is no longer alarming; fraud and child abuse are. As the market for claims about cults has changed, anticult groups have tailored their arguments accordingly.

Any or all the diverse factors affecting the making and marketing of claims can change over time. Anticult groups can become more or less vigilant, or the anticult cause can be strengthened by the adherence of some new and powerful interest group. Marginal sects themselves might become more militant, more prepared to fight their opponents with public relations campaigns or libel suits. Moreover, social and demographic changes can condition the wider public to accept claims made about cult menaces, and a series of scandalous incidents creates new opportunities for rhetoric and for making claims. As in the case of small businesses, the success or failure of religious denominations is closely attuned to the changing legal environment and the likelihood that official agencies will intervene against heterodox movements. A change in any of these factors can produce a more or less hostile attitude towards cults in particular eras, regardless of the activities of the fringe groups themselves.

The modern American encounter with cults is by no means as one-sided an affair as it sometimes appears. However we define them, cults have had an impact on American society and religious thought far beyond what might be suggested by their actual membership. Apart from their Constitutional and legal significance, they have provided effective laboratories for new ideas and practices which in some cases have entered the social and religious mainstream. Some good has come from the religious fringe, and the anticult movements have on occasion done real harm, not least by creating a mythology that stigmatizes religious innovation. Though many anticult assumptions have now acquired the status of orthodoxy for both media and policymakers, tracing the development of these ideas shows how dubious and ill founded their origins often were. The cult problem as we observe it today is the product of decades of cultural and political work, which has succeeded remarkably in defining popular attitudes towards the outer reaches of American spiritual life.

# TWO

# False Prophets and Deluded Subjects
## *The Nineteenth Century*

In what civilized country do evidences of religious fanaticism more abound?
Frederick M. Davenport, *Primitive Traits in Religious Revivals*

Modern opposition to cults and cultlike behavior has deep historical roots. The modern cult stereotype is a complex construction, drawing on concepts originally developed to confront several quite distinct religious groups that would over time merge into one barely differentiated attack. When a modern critic attacks a deviant religious group as a cult, the images evoked are ultimately a mélange of rumors and allegations variously made against Catholics, Masons, Mormons, Shakers, radical evangelicals, and others. Anticult rhetoric encapsulates the whole history of American religious polemic. In the 1870s and 1880s, attacks on deviant religions developed something very like their modern form, owing in large part to the emergence of the mass circulation press in those years and the rise of exposé journalism.[1]

At every point, the stereotypes applied to modern "Moonies" and "Hare Krishnas" find parallels dating back many centuries. Perhaps the persistence of these charges just means that the deviant behaviors in question have always existed, that small religious groups have always engaged in the familiar sorts of violent and exploitative behavior. However, the continuity of rhetoric does have a consistent internal logic. Given that claims to perfection or superior sanctity automatically arouse suspicions of hypocrisy, it is not surprising that we so regularly find the same stereotype of religious fanaticism. Basically, anyone claiming mystical or charismatic authority is likely to be viewed as a rogue or a maniac, and his or her followers are portrayed as unstable dupes ready to perform any action, however degraded or criminal. As America has been so richly productive of prophets and visionaries, it is only to be expected that so many would be denounced as dangerous charlatans.

## Prophets and Fanatics

The contemporary image of the cult leader who seduces his fanatical followers into destructive conflict with the established authorities is centuries old; it is even mentioned in the New Testament. In the European Middle Ages, a recurrent nightmare figure was the *prophetas*, the charismatic leader who decided that he (it was usually a man) had a special revelation from God to uproot the current political and ecclesiastical order and initiate a new order of righteousness, commonly by force of arms. Prophets were also accused of sexual unorthodoxy, of orgies or plural marriage. These deviant practices were sometimes justified by antinomian ideas, the view that moral laws had been repealed by the new revelation.[2] The sexually promiscuous messiah leading his armed devotees to a fortress in the wilderness was a stereotypical figure in Europe centuries before the image reappeared in Utah or Texas.

Such military millenarians arose sporadically throughout the medieval centuries, culminating in the great Anabaptist risings of the sixteenth century. In 1534, the prophet Jan of Leyden introduced communism and polygamy in the German city of Münster, in a Utopian regime enforced by the ruthless violence of the "saints," the Children of God. The experiment was destroyed with utmost ferocity by the established order of lords, bishops, and patricians. The Anabaptist sects became over time a far gentler breed, whose modern heirs are found among the Amish and Mennonites, but Jan of Leyden and his like were cited for centuries afterwards as the logical outcome of religious excess. The names of the Münster prophets had the same resonance in the seventeenth or eighteenth centuries that Jim Jones and David Koresh have for modern ears.

The equation seemed obvious: claims of personal revelation led to violent subversion and unrestrained sexuality, which if unchecked would destroy the social order. Lacking a central mechanism to regulate religious belief and practice, society would be at the mercy of fanatics, prophets, and impostors. The full consequences of unregulated religious debate emerged during the English Civil Wars of the 1640s, when the government lost control of public preaching and printing. The result was an upsurge of every kind of extreme and heretical belief. The crisis reached its blasphemous climax in 1656 when Quaker James Nayler staged a messianic entry into the city of Bristol with himself as Christ, mounted on a donkey, while faithful women followers strewed his path with branches and cried, "Hosanna to the son of David."

Though the word "cult" would have meant little to Nayler's contemporaries, this generation was in fact creating the first anticult literature in English. In 1646, orthodox Protestant writer Thomas Edwards published his encyclopedic *Gangraena* ("gangrene"), which provided "[a] catalogue . . . of many of the errors, heresies, blasphemies and pernicious practices of the sectaries of this time." In the process, he offered a list of almost every extreme and esoteric belief that would resurface in America over the next two centuries. Already Edwards was attacking Ranters and antinomians, pantheists and nudists, communists and perfectionists, self-anointed prophets and disorderly women.[3] Like their counterparts in later centuries, conservatives were reluctant to credit that such extravagant beliefs could have been held seriously, or spread without deceit, so Edwards and his like borrowed from the contemporary true crime literature to depict sect leaders as confidence tricksters, thieves, and sexual exploiters.

In understanding these outbreaks, critics like Edwards turned to the writings of the Church Fathers, who had confronted so many heresies in the early Christian centuries—to authors like Irenaeus, Eusebius, and Augustine. They found there the vocabulary required to combat the newly labeled "fanatics" and "enthusiasts." These epithets had a long history. The fanatic exemplified the sort of mindless devotion expected of the adherent of the temple, or *fana* (as in Samuel Butler's reference to "our lunatic, fanatic sects"), while the enthusiast literally claimed to be filled with the power of God, or of a god. Both words, "fanatic" and "enthusiast," have become debased in later speech ("fanatic" is the origin of "fan"), but at the time, they conveyed an all-too-serious threat. Well into the eighteenth century, "fanatic" was the normal word for describing those Protestant sects and preachers who lay outside the established Anglican Church, including Presbyterians, Baptists, and Congregationalists.

From earliest times, the English colonies in America likewise saw themselves as imperiled by subversive religious doctrines and sects of dubious sanity. The most alarming was the Quaker, or Friends, movement of the 1650s, the spiritual kin of James Nayler: the Friends argued that Christ was found in the Inner Light that guided each believer. Outsiders observing their enthusiastic worship style dubbed them "Quakers," which was an insulting epithet, rather like later smear words such as Shaker, Methodist, Mormon, and Moonie. As radical democrats, the Quakers rejected tokens of social hierarchy and challenged the power of clergy by vocally disrupting the formal services of the "steeple houses." Equally shocking, their most active preachers were often women. Between 1659 and 1661, four members of the sect were hanged on Boston Common.

Subversive images recurred during the Great Awakening of the 1730s and 1740s, when the ordained clergy were challenged by revivalists asserting that only those properly filled with the Spirit could lead the churches. The stress on direct revelation opened the way to the emergence of charismatic leaders, some of whom created scandal by their wild excesses, and revived shades of Münster. And when some evangelical leaders created their own communes and religious settlements, rumors about orgiastic celebrations and polygamy soon followed. In Pennsylvania, the Moravian leader Count Zinzendorf, who held daring ideas about sex and spirituality, was a special target for charges that he exploited his female disciples: his enemies christened him the *Herzens Papa*, or "Hearts' Daddy."[4] Like its successor revivals over the next two centuries, the Great Awakening was also criticized for encouraging bizarre and enthusiastic behavior. In the second great revival, which reached its height in 1799 and 1800, we hear of believers driven into ecstatic trances, convulsions, and jerks—wild frenzies that supposedly endangered their sanity. Conservatives charged that abandoning restraints in this way opened female believers to wild sexual excesses, so that the legendary camp meetings were criticized as orgies of debauchery.

### Awful Disclosures: America, 1830–1870

American suspicions of fringe religious movements escalated rapidly during the 1830s and 1840s, as simultaneous campaigns against Catholics, Freemasons, and Mormons provided rich new materials for conceptualizing religious exploitation. The anti-Papist image had colonial roots, but was amplified by the presence of significant numbers of Catholic immigrants from the 1830s onwards. Virulent anti-Papist propaganda in American newspapers and pamphlets depicted lay Catholics as ignorant puppets, whose priests were sexually exploitative and conspiratorial. All the later anticult images were present here: Catholics exemplified mindless obedience to a deceitful religious leader, and authority was founded upon bloodthirsty enforcement. These ideas were long-lived. A Sinclair Lewis character noted in 1927 that the Church "requires you to give up your honesty, your reason, your heart and soul," while some years later the *Harvard Journal* described the Legion of Decency as a "Catholic organization, with its regimental draft of blindly obedient underlings on the one hand, and its Machiavellian pontiff on the other."[5]

This alien religion proselytized vigorously, drew naive young people into its web, and lured them to renounce their careers and prospects in order to enter celibate and totalistic religious communities. Convents and religious houses, which were found in all major American cities by the Civil War era, seemed as glaring an offense to personal freedom and intellectual liberty as the cult houses and headquarters of the 1970s. The notion of "escaping" from a religious community first appeared in the context of Catholic convents. Some of the bloodiest urban riots of the antebellum period erupted when citizens tried to liberate nuns from their supposed captivity or else to seek evidence of their crimes. Particularly sought after were the secret tunnels said to link the dwellings of priests and nuns, and the hidden cemeteries in which were buried the murdered babies resulting from these liaisons.

Also foreshadowing modern trends, the anti-Catholic movement paraded defectors from this evil organization, purported former nuns and priests whose firsthand accounts confirmed the worst charges about the sexual exploitation said to be rampant behind the walls of convents and rectories. These ideas surfaced in the sensational *Awful Disclosures of Maria Monk* (1836), which told of life in a Quebec convent and is the prototype for all subsequent defector memoirs. The book portrayed nuns as sex slaves, and its lurid depictions of flagellation added to its strong sadomasochistic appeal. Later bestsellers in this prurient tradition included *The Priest, the Woman and the Confessional* (1875), by the apostate priest Charles Chiniquy, who described the sexual exploitation of women parishioners by lustful priests. It was in the early 1890s that the American Protective Association propaganda campaign reached its height, with its tales of convent life as "grotesque ceremonies, orgies of sex and sadism" at the hands of "licentious and lecherous priests . . . seeking to lure young and innocent girls into sin."[6] Even in the mid-twentieth century, every issue of the *Converted*

*Catholic Magazine* recounted horror stories of Catholic misdeeds, which included sinister associations with every dictatorship and massacre in modern history. Through the 1940s, there was a substantial industry in lecture tours by purported former nuns recounting pornographic fantasies to entranced Protestant audiences.

Anti-Catholicism can be seen as the largest and most potent anticult movement in American history. Several mass political movements aimed to destroy Catholic power, from the Nativists and Know-Nothings of the mid-nineteenth century to the American Protective Association (APA) of the 1890s and the Ku Klux Klan of the 1920s, and each crusade had a sizable impact on the national politics of its day. Each had its scurrilous press, which rehearsed stories of the Inquisition, the seditious secret oaths taken by the Knights of Columbus, the conspiratorial nature of the Jesuit order, and always, of course, the promiscuous nuns and lecherous priests. Reading the lurid charges presented in propaganda sheets like *The Menace* was enough "to make any boy wonder if the priest kept beautiful young girls tied up in the confessional booths, and if there was really an arsenal in the church basement."[7] The most damaging feature of APA propaganda was the publication of bogus statements and documents allegedly derived from Catholic sources, which warned that Catholics planned to exterminate all American Protestants as heretics.

In the mid-nineteenth century, anti-Catholic rhetoric and folklore merged with the polemic against other scapegoat groups, namely Freemasons and Latter-Day Saints. As David Brion Davis has shown, the movements against these three menaces drew on very similar images: "If Masons, Catholics, and Mormons bore little resemblance to one another in actuality, as imagined enemies they merged into a nearly common stereotype."[8] According to their enemies, Masons and Mormons, like Catholics, belonged to a sinister false religion with clandestine methods and secret goals of secular power. Each was a closed secretive organization that maintained order and discipline through the threat of violence. The anti-Masonic movement erupted in 1826 because the group had supposedly kidnapped and murdered William Morgan, a defector who had threatened to reveal their secret rituals, with all their threats of bloody vengeance. The condemnation of the movement reached its height in the next decade, when an Anti-Masonic political party became a national political force.[9]

Anti-Mormon literature integrated the anti-Catholic charges with the older image of the *prophetas*, who claimed to be motivated by

special direct revelations from God and who replaced the Christian
Scriptures with his own invented texts. These attacks drew on the popular Orientalism of the day, framing Joseph Smith in terms of the
Prophet Muhammad, whom contemporary Christians saw as the prototypical religious impostor.[10] Muhammad was viewed as a self-
proclaimed prophet or messiah who attracted a blindly obedient following prepared to die or kill for the new cause. His divine messages
opened a new age of sexual excess, allowing the leader and his key
followers sexual access to any woman follower. Finally, this new movement was transformed into a worldly kingdom, as followers carved out
a secular realm. Joseph Smith himself drew the Muslim analogy, warning in 1838 that he "will be to this generation a second Mohammed,
whose motto for treating for peace was 'The Alcoran or the sword.' "
His movement became "the Islam of America."[11] Muslim analogies
became more pronounced in 1852 when the new sect overtly declared
its doctrine of polygamy. Polygamy became a prominent element in
the anti-Mormon critique, both because it represented the most flagrant
violation of conventional morality and because polygamy, like Catholic
nunneries, offered such scope for prurient imaginations.

### Flawed Utopias

Every element of the modern anticult polemic was a familiar component of American culture by about 1840, and the critique was power-
fully reinforced from the upsurge of outré religious groups between
about 1830 and 1860. Apocalyptic notions gave rise to the new Adventist churches, and millenarian ideas reached new intensity nationwide with the great revival of 1857. Mesmerist and Swedenborgian
mystical notions were well-established by the 1830s: these contributed
to the new spiritualist movement, which emerged following the accounts of supernatural visitations at Hydesville, in New York state, in
1848.[12]

Common in the religious thought of the time was a sense of uto-
pianism, the idea that humanity could achieve perfection in this life,
without postponing that prospect to heaven or the Day of Judgment.
Perfectionist ideas were implemented in utopian communes, which
tried to reform the human condition through new patterns of property
ownership, sexual relationships, and changes in diet and healing methods. One celebrated colony was established by John Humphrey Noyes
on the principle that the Second Coming had already occurred. His

group practiced community of property and experimented with ideas of complex marriage, dismissing monogamy as "idolatrous love." In 1847, the commune took up residence at Oneida, in New York state, where it flourished into the 1880s; at its height, the membership reached almost three hundred.

Alongside the noble experiments of these exciting years, there were more worrying developments on the religious fringe. Scandal followed Robert Matthews, the Prophet Matthias, who declared himself the incarnated Spirit of Truth, and who gathered a band of dedicated followers in the New York City of the 1830s. Partly on the strength of his similar name, Matthias consciously identified himself with the sixteenth-century Anabaptist Jan Mathys, one of the leaders of the revolutionary commune in Münster. The New York affair ended in disaster, when Matthias was charged with swindling and murdering one of his followers.[13] Together with the sensational publicity about the Mormons, the case of Matthias revived ancient ideas of the prophet as exploiter and false teacher.

Still more enduring, and more widespread, were the charges against the Shaker movement. Established in the United States since the late eighteenth century, the communal and celibate Shakers enjoyed their greatest period of expansion during the religious fervor of the 1840s. By 1860, perhaps six thousand members were scattered among nineteen settlements. The more converts there were, however, the more grounds for controversy. Shakers attracted popular hatred for much the same reasons as modern-day cult groups. Their religious system was believed to be anti-Christian, with its extreme veneration of prophetic founder Mother Ann Lee, whom critics painted as a drunkard and lecher. And Shaker rituals were dismissed as unorthodox and blasphemous, with services that involved ritual dancing, and enemies charged that secret ceremonies were carried out in the nude.

Most damaging (said critics) were the effects of membership on individuals and families. Families joined the Shaker communities en masse, but individuals resisted losing control of their children to the elders, who inflicted extreme physical punishments on them. When a member of a family tried to defect, the issue arose of his or her access to the children who remained within the sect; property signed over to the Shakers was another tender issue. Defectors fought to regain access to their children and, in so doing, aroused public sympathy for their cause by publishing harrowing accounts of Shaker misdeeds: obviously, these documents made no attempt at objectivity and painted the worst possible picture. During the first half of the century, these sensational conflicts regularly appeared in local newspapers across the country, but mainly in the Shaker heartland in the northeast.

The Shakers' most determined enemy was Mary Dyer, who was with her husband a member of the community from 1799 to 1815, and who left ("escaped") after the collapse of her marriage, and the deaths of two of her children. Her printed revelations of Shaker atrocities went into several editions, the most comprehensive of which appeared in 1847. She placed Ann Lee in the long succession of religious impostors that began with the serpent in the garden of Eden, and progressed through Simon Magus and Muhammad. Despite the sect's affected piety and egalitarianism, Dyer claimed that Shaker communities were slave societies, in which the leaders and elders lived richly, and violated rules against drunkenness and sexual vice, while ordinary believers became serfs once they had signed over their property. Families were divided, so that spouse was not able to talk to spouse or parent to child. The elite enforced their rule through physical violence, backed with sweeping threats of hellfire for any who should leave. Throughout, Dyer's story is substantiated by affidavits from former Shakers who had lost their families and goods to the sect, and who testified that youngsters were savagely beaten. Dyer also described the secret sexual practices of the Shaker leadership, who purportedly enhanced their pleasure by means of electric charges. Shakers were accused of employing both electricity and mesmeric spiritual powers for their secret ends, and Mesmerism was cited as the means by which they recruited converts and broke their wills. In summary, "this Shaker system is a combination of paganism, atheism and a spurious gospel, by means of which every member of the community is made a lanced spy upon the rest. . . . The subordinate members are taught that it is a duty to keep within the bounds of those revelations which their leaders blasphemously pretend to receive from the Deity."[14]

## Fighting the Sects, 1870–1890

Though controversy had always surrounded marginal religious groups, it was during the 1870s and 1880s that an accumulation of scandals and exposés led to a public reaction against fringe religions and a demand for official restrictions. The assault was sufficiently intense and widespread to permit us to speak of a cult scare, or at least a national anticult reaction. No one book offers the kind of generic denunciation of fringe religions that would become so commonplace in the 1920s or 1970s, but the concatenation of scandals produced an impression of a broad social threat. Between 1875 and 1887, public attacks on religious deviance were intense enough to foreshadow the outbreaks of the "cult wars" that would occur in the 1920s, the 1940s, and the late 1970s (see Table 2.1).[15]

The new hostility to marginal groups partly reflected real evidence about fraud and criminal practice in these quarters, but political leaders were also more prepared than hitherto to enforce a degree of Christian religious orthodoxy. Both Evangelicalism and revivalism were riding high, and the Protestant ethos of this time saw few difficulties in using the law to enforce public morality. Between 1864 and 1874, evangelicals sponsored a lively campaign to pass a constitutional amendment that would have formally declared the United States a Christian nation.[16] Despite the rhetoric of religious freedom, toleration was extended only grudgingly to groups outside the Judaeo-Christian tradition. Toleration did not comprehend Native American religious upsurges like the Ghost Dance movement, which was brutally suppressed in 1890. As late as the 1920s, the federal Bureau of Indian Affairs was actively seeking the suppression of Native American religion and fighting manifestations of "paganism."[17]

### The Mormon Crisis

One major target among the new religions was the Church of Jesus Christ of Latter-Day Saints. Although their settlement in Utah would soon be seeking statehood, the religion was bedeviled by attacks on its bloodthirsty record. Between 1856 and 1858, the U.S. government had fought a literal war against the sect, a conflict marked by guerrilla operations and punitive raids. The most notorious event was the Mountain Meadows massacre of 1857, in which 120 emigrants on a wagon train, both men and women, were killed by Mormon paramilitaries. The incident was eclipsed by the worse horrors of the struggle between abolitionist and slaveholding supporters in Bleeding Kansas and then the Civil War itself, but the massacre cast a long shadow. In 1872, Mark Twain's popular book, *Roughing It*, reminded readers of the crime, when "the whole United States rang with its horrors." Twain also told of the Mormons' Destroying Angels, the Danites, who were "set apart by the Church to conduct permanent disappearances of obnoxious citizens": generally, Utah was "a luscious country for thrilling evening stories about assassinations of intractable Gentiles."[18] The

Table 2.1
Cults and Cult Scandals, 1875–1888

1875    Theosophical Society founded.
Charles Nordhoff publishes *The Communistic Societies of the United States.*
Ann Eliza Young, *Wife No. 19, or The Story of a Life in Bondage.*
Charles Chiniquy, *The Priest, the Women and the Confessional.*
Mary Baker Eddy, *Science and Health.*

1877    Execution of Mormon bishop John Lee for his part in the Mountain Meadows massacre.
Fanny Stenhouse, *Tell it All: The Story of a Life's Experience in Mormonism.*
Publication of *Mormonism Unveiled.*
H. P. Blavatsky, *Isis Unveiled.*

1878    Formation of the Anti-Polygamy Society.

1879    U.S. Supreme Court decides case of *Reynolds v. U.S.*
J. H. Noyes flees the Oneida colony.
Alleged human sacrifice in Pocasset, Massachusetts.
First Church of Christ, Scientist, founded.
First publication of *The Watch Tower.*

1881    Assassination of President Garfield by Charles Guiteau.

1882    Federal Edmunds Act criminalizes polygamy.
Fanny Stenhouse, *An Englishwoman in Utah.*
Jennie Anderson Froiseth edits *The Women of Mormonism.*
Society of Psychical Research formed.

1883    Joseph Pulitzer acquires the *New York World.*

1884    Madame Blavatsky's associates accuse her of faking mediumistic phenomena.

1885    Society of Psychical Research condemns Blavatsky in its "Hodgson Report."

1887    Arthur Conan Doyle publishes *A Study in Scarlet.*
Federal Edmunds-Tucker Act introduces more intrusive procedures to detect and suppress polygamy.
*Preliminary Report* of the Seybert Commission published.

1888    Margaret Fox describes deception in origins of Spiritualist movement.
Reuben Briggs Davenport, *The Death-Blow to Spiritualism.*
H. P. Blavatsky, *The Secret Doctrine.*

Mountain Meadows slaughter was again in the headlines in the mid-1870s, when Bishop John Lee went on trial for ordering the attack; Lee was eventually executed in 1877. One explosive element of the case was the charge that real guilt should be assigned to Brigham Young, for whom Lee was serving as a scapegoat, "an official assassin of the Mormon church under the late Brigham Young." One 1904 account of Young's rule in Utah highlighted "the Mountain Meadow massacre—the reign of terror in Utah—the doctrine of human sacrifice . . . the facts of polygamy."[19]

Anti-Mormon tracts appeared at an accelerating rate from the early 1870s, with sensational books on polygamy like *Wife No. 19: A Complete Exposé of Mormonism*, by "Brigham Young's Apostate Wife." A later edition of this book bore the elaborate title *Life in Mormon Bondage*, and promised "a complete exposé of its false prophets, murderous Danites, despotic rulers and hypnotized deluded subjects," which is a fair epitome of the whole tradition of anticult polemic. Drawing from anti-Catholic stereotypes, a Massachusetts paper described Mormonism as founded upon "the ambition of an ecclesiastical hierarchy to wield sovereignty, to rule the souls and lives of its subjects with absolute authority, unrestrained by any civil power."[20]

Charges that Mormon death squads and Danites wrought bloody vengeance upon the movement's enemies were sufficiently well-known to provide the basis of the first Sherlock Holmes story, *A Study in Scarlet*, which appeared in 1887 and is perhaps the first example of the use of a cult setting in a mystery story. Conan Doyle's story relies on the anti-Mormon tracts that publishers had poured out over the previous two decades, especially the autobiographical memoir published by Fanny Stenhouse.[21] *A Study in Scarlet* depicts a region living under a reign of religious terror: "To express an unorthodox opinion was a dangerous matter in those days in the Land of the Saints." The Church's secret enforcement arm "appeared to be omniscient and omnipotent, and yet was neither seen nor heard. The man who held out against the Church vanished away, and none knew whither he had gone or what had befallen him. . . . To this day in the lonely ranches of the West, the name of the Danite Band or the Avenging Angels is a sinister and ill-omened one." Conan Doyle added another twist to the mythology of polygamy when he charged that Church leaders kidnapped women for their harems.

The polygamy question now led to one of the most sweeping episodes of religious persecution in American history. From 1862, federal antipolygamy laws threatened the whole legal basis of the religion and invalidated Utah laws sanctioning multiple marriage. After the Civil War, the federal government had even less tolerance for regions claiming the right to defend local traditions that violated national law. Appealing to this centralizing principle, critics of polygamy cited the practice as Utah's "peculiar institution," a phrase that recalled southern slavery. In 1878, Protestant women formed an Anti-Polygamy Society, explicitly modeled on the old Anti-Slavery Society. The traditional religious critique of polygamy was now reinforced by a feminist assault on the male subjugation of women.[22]

The religious freedom issue found its way to the U.S. Supreme Court, which had recently ruled in 1871 that "[t]he law knows no heresy, and is committed to the support of no dogma, the establishment of no sect." However, that case, *Watson v. Jones*, had concerned a theological squabble within an established denomination, namely the Presbyterians; the laissez-faire principle was not extended to new sects. In 1879, the Court overruled objections that antipolygamy statutes violated the constitutional freedom of religion, affirming in the case of *Reynolds v. U.S.* the principle that religious freedom extended only to belief, not to action. "Congress was deprived of all legislative power over mere opinion, but was left free to reach actions which were in violation of social duties or subversive of good order."

New federal measures fought polygamy with draconian policies that made serious inroads into traditional constitutional and legal protections, and that brought the federal government deep into the business of enforcing religious orthodoxy. The Edmunds Act of 1882 declared polygamy a felony and made polygamous "unlawful cohabitation" a misdemeanor. The law disfranchised polygamists, excluded them from public office or jury service, and banned most Mormons from participating in the government of a territory in which they made up 85 percent of the population. Polygamist exclusion was enforced by test oaths, and in 1887, a new law demanded that wives testify against their husbands. Mormon leaders were arrested or forced to flee, and some 1,300 men were convicted under the Edmunds law. The Church of the Latter-Day Saints was disincorporated and its property escheated to the United States. The crisis ended only in 1890, when Mormon President Wilford Woodruff declared that he had received a revelation ending polygamy at least as earthly practice (Mormon men could still enjoy plural wives in the afterlife). This change of doctrine paved the way for Utah's admission as a state in 1896,

though the traditional anti-Mormon polemic would often resurface in
the new century.

### Attacking the Communes

The communes were also attracting critical interest in these years. Since
the 1840s, various communes had been rent by accusations that they
were being usurped by dictatorial and authoritarian self-appointed spiritual elites. Even in the liberated Transcendentalist group at Fruitlands,
women members charged that overweening male leaders trampled their
rights. In 1875, Charles Nordhoff, in *The Communistic Societies of the
United States*, published sympathetic accounts of groups as diverse as
the Zoarites, Icarians, and Shakers. Nordhoff nevertheless raised troubling questions about the fate of the individual will and personality in
such settings and about the lack of privacy. He also described one of
the harrowing group criticism meetings by means of which the Oneida
group maintained internal order.[23] Though still a long way from the
charges of brainwashing that would be directed against the cults of the
1970s, critics of the communes cited Nordhoff's account to show that
group pressure could produce disturbing changes in personality—and
possibly mental instability.

Of much more concern to the critics was the liberated sexual ambience at Oneida, which encouraged the idea that "commune" was simply a code word for group sex. By 1870, the press was denouncing the
commune for its depravity: surveying press reports about themselves,
the Oneida community's news sheet reported, "The word filth, with
its derivatives filthy, filthiness, etc, occurs nine times; abomination,
abominable, etc, six times; depravity, depraved, etc, six times; lust four
times; blasphemy three times; licentiousness three times; bestial, foul,
and horrible, each twice." Pubescent youngsters were encouraged to
enter freely into the communal sex life, and community head J. H.
Noyes was often the one to offer sexual initiation to girls of twelve or
thirteen. Given the contemporary age-of-consent laws, this was not
necessarily criminal in itself, but there was always the danger of other
sex-related charges, like fornication. By 1879, the clergy and media
were pressing for prosecution: using an ominous analogy, a Syracuse
newspaper saw "the Oneida Community as far worse in their practices
than the polygamists of Utah."[24] In response, Noyes suddenly abdicated
from Oneida and fled to Canada.

Two years later, the commune received more scandalous publicity
when one of its alumni assassinated President Garfield. The culprit,

Charles Guiteau, had been a member of the Oneida group from 1860 to 1866, leaving in part because of the impossibility of finding sexual partners. In 1867 he launched a moralistic campaign against Oneida and its alleged vices. Adding to the "cult" element of the assassination, Guiteau was a profound believer in spiritualism, and he blamed the spirits for motivating him to undertake the key decisions of his life, including the attack on Garfield. In the ensuing trial, Guiteau's religious fanaticism was cited as a textbook example of the conditions likely to drive a person to violent insanity.[25]

Other commune leaders were haunted by sexual allegations. One such was Thomas Lake Harris, whose career on the religious fringe spanned the second half of the nineteenth century. Originally a spiritualist and a Swedenborgian minister, he operated a series of communes from 1850 onwards and led a sect known as the Brotherhood of the New Life, which he ruled autocratically as "Man, Seer, Adept, and Avatar." Harris preached a complex sexual mysticism that presumed the existence of both masculine and feminine divine spirits: believers were urged to find their spiritual "counterparts" with whom they would beget spiritual offspring. Though commune members apparently lived in strict chastity, tales of orgies, wife swapping, ritual nudity, and child molestation followed the Brotherhood from the late 1860s onwards. Also criticized was the practice of breaking up earthly families and removing children from their parents. Perhaps to escape the scrutiny of the New York newspapers, Harris's group migrated to northern California in 1875, but through the 1880s, the sect was riven by personal feuds, in which each faction publicly denounced its rivals as fanatics. A delighted press picked up the ensuing scandals, reporting on orgies in the Santa Rosa commune and charging that Harris used his hypnotic powers to control his followers and victims. In 1892, the San Francisco *Wave* stated that "his religion is just a trifle worse than Mormonism . . . the place is an idealized house of sin, a den of iniquitous debauchees, whose only religion is the satisfaction of the passions, where there are no ties of affection, and where both sexes of one family bed together like dogs in a kennel."[26]

### The Crisis of Spiritualism

Another new religious system that now found itself under attack was spiritualism, which predictably boomed following the Civil War, as thousands of grieving families sought to contact their lost loved ones. Religious critics had long attacked the movement as criminal necromancy, charging that spirit manifestations were the work of deceptive demons. The new critique was strictly secular and practical, branding spiritualism as a blatant confidence trick. The movement was discredited by copious evidence of fraudulent mediums, particularly the racket in spirit photography, in which photographic images were crudely retouched to suggest the presence of a ghost. The pioneer of this process went on trial in 1869. In 1882, the Society for Psychical Research was formed, and it publicized the extensive evidence of trickery and deception it found among the vast majority of the mediums it examined. Deriding mediums became a literary cliché: in 1883, Twain's *Life on the Mississippi* offered a transcript of a seance in which the medium characteristically spoke in utter generalities, omitting any concrete fact that might have proved the truth of communication from the beyond. By the 1880s, spiritualism had to a large extent lost its niche in high society, and a Henry James character could scoff at the progressive subculture of Boston's "witches and wizards, mediums and spirit rappers, and roaring radicals."[27]

The reaction against spiritualism culminated with several developments from 1887 to 1888. The most damaging involved Margaret Fox, one of the two girls who had been at the center of the original visitation at Hydesville forty years previously. On joining the Catholic Church, Fox published a full confession of "this horrible deception" perpetrated by her sister and herself. The mysterious knocks and clicks had been quite material things, which the girls had done by rapping with their feet, or manipulating the joints in their toes and fingers. Margaret demonstrated the whole technique to a journalist for Pulitzer's *New York World*, for whom she was able to summon forth answers from the great beyond. Among other things, she produced the spirits of Napoleon Bonaparte and Abraham Lincoln, and Napoleon obligingly stated, through rapping, that he had known the journalist well, eighty years before. Although she would later recant her recantation, the whole affair was ruinous. In 1888, a sensational New York trial resulted in the imprisonment of medium Ann O'Delia Diss Debar, for attempting to defraud a client.[28]

About the same time, the University of Pennsylvania published the results of an investigative commission that had been established with funds left by Henry Seybert, who had wished to see the truth of spiritualist claims established for the public record. The Seybert commission was made up of ten open-minded scholars, who worked for three years witnessing some of the best-known mediums of the day. Even under these optimum conditions, spiritualism could not be verified: "In every case with but one exception the result was either a blank seance, a positive failure, or a deliberate cheat." Margaret Fox easily convinced the commission that she had been faking her claims, and shortly afterwards the Fox story was reported in a book with the optimistic title *The Death-Blow to Spiritualism*. It was no such thing, and a new Nationalist Spiritualist Alliance of Churches was formally organized in 1893, but the movement's popularity reached a low ebb at the turn of the century.[29] In 1898, an Episcopalian critic claimed to "see in spiritualism nothing but useless and profitless imposition, deceit and trickery, accompanied by most mercenary motives. Moreover, even if these mediums are influenced by spiritualistic powers, they are the forces of darkness, not of the light."[30]

## Theosophy

A similar scepticism extended to sects with practices akin to spiritualism, like Theosophy. The Theosophical Society was formed in New York City in 1875 by Helena P. Blavatsky and Henry Olcott, both of whom had a long-standing interest in seances and mediumship: the two leaders met when both came to the defense of two allegedly bogus mediums. As outlined in Blavatsky's influential books *Isis Unveiled* (1877) and *The Secret Doctrine* (1888), the Theosophical movement integrated spiritualist ideas with a great deal of Hindu and Buddhist thought, including the theories of karma and reincarnation. The movement also offered an extensive history of human civilizations dating back millions of years through the time of Atlantis, incorporating the stories of many lost races and civilizations. Blavatsky claimed to have obtained her wisdom in hidden lamaseries in Tibet and central Asia, where she had found secret texts like the (imaginary) *Stanzas of Dzyan*. She also relied on material channeled from great supernatural Masters, members of the Great White Brotherhood, a select club that included Jesus, the Buddha, Confucius, Mesmer, and Cagliostro, as well as real-life occultists she had consulted over the years.

Theosophy was enjoying a global boom by the early 1880s and its ideas would have a profound influence on all subsequent occultism, but the movement entered a period of crisis in 1884 with a series of scandals. There were the usual mediumistic tricks and equally embarrassing was the leadership's use of letters supposedly channeled from higher spiritual realms. The contents of these letters provided all-too-convenient ammunition for internal factional squabbles. Blavatsky's other difficulties involved the living Masters, whom she had exalted into mythological supernatural beings: "Mahatmas, who . . . could hold the Mount Meru on the tip of their finger, and fly to and fro in their bodies at their will, and who were . . . more gods on earth than a God in Heaven could be." The discovery that these individuals were all too human led to general disappointment among the group's followers, but critics were delighted.[31]

Theosophy also suffered from troubling charges of literary fraud and plagiarism, of the sort that were continually directed against the Mormon scriptures. Reviewers pointed out that if in fact ascended Masters or Mahatmas had assisted Blavatsky in writing her great spiritual texts, then they had a nasty tendency to plagiarism. One scholar claimed to demonstrate that everything in the pioneering Theosophical text *Isis Unveiled* was derived from a corpus of about a hundred books, all available to the supposed channeller, Madame Blavatsky. The Masters also demonstrated a remarkable ignorance of Indian culture and tended to rely on modern popularizations. In 1898, the magazine *Contemporary Literature* attacked the founder of Theosophy in a biting article entitled "Madame Blavatsky and Her Dupes."[32]

## The Media and the Cults

During the latter years of the nineteenth century, the climate for the new sects became chillier as the news media became more sensational in tone, finding rich material in the religious fringe. When, for instance, a murder case could be linked to religious extremism, it was interpreted as the outcome of cult fanaticism rather than simple insanity. In 1879, a brutal child murder in Pocasset, Massachusetts, was reported in a contemporary pamphlet, *The Victim of a Father's Fanaticism!* According to this account of "the Pocasset fanatics . . . Charles Freeman, the 'second Adventist,' imagining himself another Abraham, slays his little daughter, offering up his darling child as a human sacrifice!"[33]

American journalism experienced a revolution in the 1880s, inaugurated by Joseph Pulitzer's acquisition of the *New York World* in 1883. The Pulitzer press pioneered the modern era of crusading exposés, the "new journalism," also known less flatteringly as "yellow journalism." The tradition was pushed to even greater lengths after William Randolph Hearst bought the *New York Journal* in 1895. The phenomenal success of the *World* and the *Journal* inspired other press lords across the nation: the number of daily newspapers in the United States rose from 574 in 1870 to 2,600 by 1909, their combined circulation from 2.6 million to 24.2 million. Both Hearst and Pulitzer chains made campaigns against cults and bogus religions a staple of their coverage, so that any new claims to divine inspiration could expect to be greeted with the debunking zeal that had been directed against Theosophy and spiritualism. Happy was the newspaper that had within its market area an eccentric commune ready to be investigated and exposed during slow news periods. Some papers developed a minor specialization in cult debunking, above all the *New York World*, but also the *Los Angeles Times* and the *San Francisco Examiner* (the *Examiner* was another Hearst organ). In the first decade of the new century, the *Brooklyn Daily Eagle* successively declared war upon Christian Science, the Emmanuel Movement, and the Watch Tower Society.[34]

The media found a continuing stream of ludicrous and scandalous material in various sects, some of which recalled the great days of communal expansion.[35] One controversial figure was John Alexander Dowie, who practiced spiritual healing until in 1895, when he was denounced by the *Chicago Tribune* for unlicensed practice of medicine. By 1901, he had founded a theocratic commune at Zion City, Illinois, and declared himself Elijah the Restorer; he believed that the earth was flat and was described as a "paranoiac swindler." The affairs of Zion City offered lively scandal to the press until the settlement was finally burned to the ground in 1937.[36]

Just as eccentric as Dowie was Dr. Cyrus R. Teed, who adopted a range of quasi-Hindu and reincarnationist beliefs. He also preached that the world was hollow and that we are living within it. Teed developed a colony of true believers at the Church Triumphant in Florida, where he took the messianic name Koresh, recalling the Hebrew title of the biblical king Cyrus. He survived until 1906, becoming something of a tourist attraction in the Fort Myers area, where his sect survived into the 1940s. After his death, his disciples kept watch over his body in expectation of his resurrection, giving up only when he showed unmistakable signs of decomposition. The same story about followers expecting a deceased messiah to arise is told of several other groups in this era, suggesting that the motif had become a media cliché: it had been applied to Ann Lee and also appears in the context of Thomas Lake Harris and Benjamin Purnell.[37]

Apart from depicting cult leaders as cranks, news stories also reinforced images of sexual excess and immorality. Even the new sect of

Christian Science was blamed for dividing families and encouraging vice, and by 1890, "the odium of increasing divorce and domestic alienation the land over was often attributed to Christian Science."[38] The lurid publicity surrounding the Mormon polygamists was reinforced by other instances of "love cults" and "sex cults," often involving underage girls. One such affair in Oregon culminated in 1906 when the outraged relatives of a young victim murdered a self-proclaimed Elijah the Prophet, after he had drawn dozens of local girls and women into his messianic cult.[39]

Much more substantial was the House of David group, which provided a remarkable link with the most extreme sectarian movements of the eighteenth century. The movement traced its spiritual ancestry to the revelations of Joanna Southcott, the English prophetess of the 1790s, who claimed to be the first in a sequence of Divine Messengers who would usher in the End Times. By the 1890s, the Flying Rollers (or Israelites) had formed a communal settlement headed by Michael Mills of Detroit. At the turn of the century, however, Mills went the way of many other messiahs and was convicted of the statutory rape of a young colony member during a religious rite. The publicity ignited a scandal that forced the colony out of Detroit amidst threats of lynching, and newspaper headlines about "A Bestial Religion" and the "Long-Haired Prince of Darkness."[40] Not for the last time, the Detroit and Chicago newspapers could rejoice at the presence of the House of David in their readership area.

At just the same time as the Mills affair, the *Los Angeles Times* determined on a crusade against its own local cultists, namely the Theosophical commune Katherine Tingley had founded at Point Loma, near San Diego. In 1901, accusing the Theosophists of conducting "weird orgies," the paper offered headlines like "Outrages at Point Loma Exposed by an Escape" and "Women and Children Starved and Treated Like Convicts. Thrilling Rescue." The *Times* reported how at midnight the pilgrims, "in their nightrobes, each holding a torch," went to a sacred spot on the Point Loma peninsular where "gross immoralities were practised by the disciples of spookism."[41] Tingley successfully sued the paper for libel and used the threat of legal sanctions repeatedly against later challenges from other powerful papers, including the *New York World*. Even so, the affair illustrates the emergence of what had come to be a potent cliché of cults and communes, which in the public mind already evoked "gross immoralities" and "thrilling rescues."

The intensity of the criticism directed against fringe religions did not necessarily impede their growth or discourage the emergence of ever newer ones. As we will see, the 1880s were an exciting time of growth for the new movements promising spiritual healing, which coalesced into the church of Christian Science and the various schools of New Thought, while occult and Theosophical groups also prospered. But all the emerging movements faced deep hostility from the media and other critics, who now lumped the new creeds together under the suspicious title of "cult."

# THREE

# Anti-Christian Cults?
## *The Christian Sects, 1890–1930*

There is no separation between your soul and the soul of the universe. In the deepest sense, you are the great universal soul. . . . Man is God incarnate.
Ralph Waldo Trine

The first literature to attack cults under that particular name was primarily aimed at fighting heresy, rather than suppressing any secular damage wrought by the fringe movements. In most books on cults published from the turn of the century into the 1960s, the largest share of space is devoted to movements that generally viewed themselves as Christian and eventually would be recognized as respectable denominations: Christian Science and New Thought groups, the Latter-Day Saints, apocalyptic sects like the Jehovah's Witnesses and Seventh Day Adventists, and Pentecostal churches. Much of the writing on cults was undertaken by Christian writers attacking other Christians (although the critics were usually challenging the credentials of the newer sects to bear the label "Christian"). The small sects were attacked because they were theologically wrong, not because they were subversive "sex cults," still less because of any violent associations.

With so many more eccentric groups around, it is surprising to find such continued dedication to fighting the supposed sectarian menace. But in the context of the time, the sects were espousing quite radical ideas, and some were arguably venturing into the realm of the occult. Some influential movements were making troubling claims about the divinization of humanity, contradicting the fundamental beliefs of Western monotheism. In the Judaeo-Christian scheme, the rank of deity is uniquely exalted: since God is the absolute and eternal force that created the world and sustains it, any human claim to such a rank is *ipso facto* evidence of delusion or megalomania. Terms like "messiah" and "son of God" are regarded as unique ranks beyond the aspiration of any mere mortal. In other religious traditions, however, godhood can be more accessible. In Chinese religions, in Hinduism, or in the religions of Classical Greece or Rome, an individual might attain divine status in life or be elevated to it after death, while for pantheists, every living thing shares a portion of divinity. Partly under Asian influence, a number of American sects in the late nineteenth century were crossing that perilous boundary between the human and the divine.

Concern about the Christian sects must also be explained in terms of the scale of the respective movements: while a typical occult school of the 1920s might at best have attracted a few hundred adherents, groups like Christian Science and the Latter Day Saints already had memberships in the hundreds of thousands. The new movements were showing impressive signs of growth, which became evident during each religious census. According to one cult critic comparing 1926 to 1916, "the Christian Scientists show an increase of 67 percent, the Spiritualists 74 percent, the Mormons 21 percent, the Theosophists 27 percent, the Pillar of Fire group 116 percent." Conversely, many mainstream churches were relatively static in their membership or actually declined.[1] If the sects were indeed outside true Christianity, if they were "anti-Christian cults," then this was an alarming example of a dechristianizing trend.

Attacking the supposed cults was a useful exercise for mainstream critics because the polemic reinforced the position of orthodoxy within the major denominations. Attacking the excesses of Jehovah's Witnesses or Pentecostals helped channel and contain premillenarian impulses within evangelical groups. Similarly, exposing the heterodox concepts of God and Christ held by Christian Science served to restrain overliberal theorizing within the regular churches. Once a position could be defined as cultlike, it became difficult to hold it within an established denomination: nobody wanted to be seen as espousing an "-ism" named for a particular leader and wanted even less to be viewed as a Holy Roller. By saying that these groups were non-Christian cults, the orthodox were declaring definitively what Christianity was, marking where the limits of that religion lay, and restricting the scope of possible theological exploration. Depicting cults as an external Other reasserted doctrinal boundaries in a time of religious ferment.

## Imagining Cults

At the end of the nineteenth century, the emerging sects were increasingly treated as a united social phenomenon, even as a distinguishing sign of the age (though it is an open question whether the number of new sects was any greater than in earlier eras). For Christians, the rise of such movements had apocalyptic overtones, as Jesus had listed among the signs warning of the end of the world the coming of "false Christs and false prophets [who] will show signs and wonders." Apocalyptic hopes and fears were intense as the world entered a new century, which witnessed a wave of exposé literature directed at Christian Science, Theosophy, and other movements. In 1889, a book on *Modern Messiahs and Wonder Workers* discussed, among others, Ann Lee, Joseph Smith, Thomas Lake Harris, and Madame Blavatsky. J. V. Coombs offered a similar survey of the "false faiths of to-day" in his *Religious Delusions*, with its sections on "Mormonism," "Spiritualism," "Adventism," "New Thought," and "Christian Science." In 1917, the comprehensive *Timely Warnings* provided "[a] brief critical examination in the light of the Holy Scriptures of some of the prevailing heresies and false teachings of today."[2]

Around 1900, too, the term "cult" replaced the older polemical language of delusions, fanatics, enthusiasts, and impostors. The word has several distinct meanings. In its original Latin sense, *cultus* simply implied a religion or a type of religious practice, and this sense was adopted into English to signify a religious denomination or a particular tradition of worship. Scholars still speak of the cult of relics, the cult of the Virgin, and the cult of saints, while modern archaeologists might describe a temple site as cultic in nature, and in none of these phrases is there any suggestion of savagery, fanaticism, or charismatic leadership.

The new and more hostile meaning of the word derived from growing Western contact with non-Christian and polytheist religions in Asia and Africa, which were presented in the West in terms of primitive idolatry and ritual violence. This theme was exemplified by the Indian Thugs, a ritual murder sect suppressed by British forces in the 1830s and 1840s: the stereotype of thuggish fanaticism is neatly captured in the famous 1939 film *Gunga Din*. A pioneering account of Tibetan Buddhism, published in 1895, told of *Lamaism with Its Mystic Cults*.[3] The term "voodoo cult," well-established at the turn of the century, suggested what contemporaries saw as the primitive pagan superstition preserved by people of African descent in the Caribbean and the American South, with all the attendant implications of orgies and blood rituals.[4] In both Asian and African cases, a racist subtext implied that such practices and superstitions were typical of the various lesser breeds without the law, and unfitting for advanced, rational Europeans, who could only be drawn to such primitive beliefs through a kind of atavism. Cults implied extravagant personal devotion to a leader or spiritual teacher, and it was in this sense that late-nineteenth-century Americans extended the concept semiseriously to literary fanaticism, in phrases like "the cult of Poe" or "the cult of Shakespeare."

These exotic connotations were now attached to innovative domestic sects, implying that these too were bizarre, exotic, and non-Christian and were unfit for intelligent (white) believers. An academic study published in 1905 noted that practices like spiritualism and faith healing, which naive whites believed to be so progressive, had in fact been pioneered among Native American movements like the Ghost Dance and the so-called Indian Shakers, dismissively termed "cults." Apparently the first book title to use the word in its modern sense was the 1898 study of *Anti-Christian Cults* by A. H. Barrington, an Episcopal minister in Wisconsin. His work was "[a]n attempt to show that Spiritualism, Theosophy, and Christian Science are devoid of supernatural powers and are contrary to the Christian religion."[5]

The date 1898 is doubly suggestive. During this year, the climax of the British wars in the Sudan meant that the news was full of the messianic figure of the Mahdi, together with his fanatical dervish followers. For Americans, the year also marked the acquisition of an Asian colonial empire, and the churches were excited at the new opportunities for making converts to evangelical Christianity, which had long been seen as a primary component of American national destiny. Orthodox believers had been horrified, however, to witness throughout the 1890s not the subjection of non-Christian creeds, but the importation into the United States of Asian-derived and mystical ideas. Hindu ideas and Vedanta mysticism both enjoyed a huge vogue in the United States following the World Parliament of Religions held in Chicago in 1893. It was in these years that swamis and Hindu teachers became the familiar feature of the religious fringe that they would remain throughout the coming century. Theosophy and New Thought were at their height exactly in the mid-1890s. When Theosophists founded their

Point Loma settlement in 1899, the Protestant clergy of nearby San Diego were horrified to find "a defunct Hinduism landed at our very doors."[6]

The formulation of the cult problem owed much to anti-Asian sentiment, which was running high in the United States at the turn of the century and drew little distinction between the peoples of East and South Asia. Asian immigration into the United States was restricted by the discriminatory Oriental Exclusion Acts, passed in the 1880s and made permanent in 1902. The term "yellow peril" dates from 1895, when a notorious cartoon of that name depicted the white nations gazing in alarm at the sinister figure of a monstrous Buddha arising from the Orient. In 1900, U.S. forces were at war in two separate Asian theaters, in combat against the Boxer rebels in China and the native revolutionaries in the Philippines. After the Russo-Japanese war of 1905, Americans began to perceive a significant military threat from Japan.[7] In popular culture, the character of the evil Chinese genius Fu Manchu first appeared in a novel published in 1913. These noxious stereotypes pervade early American discussions of emerging religions and cults.

### Cults Versus Christianity

Against this troubling background, anticult books became a flourishing genre in the new century. They usually targeted the same range of movements. In 1906, a Denver minister published his sermon on *Christian Science Examined . . . The New Cult*, and a 1908 pamphlet discussed *The Emmanuel Movement: A Brief History of the New Cult* (this movement was an Episcopalian attempt to provide medical healing within the framework of the church as a counterweight to Christian Science). In 1918, a tract on the "cult phenomenon" bore the title *In the Cult Kingdom: Mormonism, Eddyism and Russellism*. Using terms like "Eddyism" for Christian Science suggested irrational personal devotion to the movement's charismatic founder, Mary Baker Eddy, the sort of loyalty that an African or Asian might show for a spiritual leader. Other Western movements were likewise defined in terms of personalities and their "-isms": the Watch Tower movement (the later Jehovah's Witnesses) became "Russellism" after its founder, while the new Oxford Group would be called "Buchmanism."[8]

For critics, a sect's dependence on a human leader was associated with the claim to possess new inspired scriptures intended to be set aside the Bible, or even to replace it. This was one of the worst atrocities charged against any cult, from Christian Science through the Children of God, and any boast of new inspiration was a sure sign that a new group was heretical and cultish. The enterprise of disproving divine inspiration often focused on debunking such new scriptures and seeking to show that these texts were in fact drawn from preexisting materials. Much ink was spilled trying to prove that Christian Science derived its sacred writings through plagiarism, that Mormons acquired their texts through the inventions of one man, that Jehovah's Witnesses altered the Bible text at will to fit their tortured theology, and that Theosophical scriptures had only fraudulent claims to inspiration. Mary Baker Eddy, Ellen G. White, Joseph Smith, and Madame Blavatsky were all dismissed as plagiarists on a vast scale. The underlying assumption was that a text that drew heavily on literary predecessors must be merely a human invention; this represents a distinctly modern and Western attitude to the process of literary construction. Christians contrasted the supposed forgeries of the new sects with their own claim to the one immaculate, inspired text of their Bible, which had withstood the test of the centuries. Conservative critics thus asserted the absolute truth and reliability of the Christian Scriptures, conveniently ignoring contemporary scholarly attacks on those same writings.

At least until the 1960s, the majority of books concerning cults followed this same pattern, comprising Christian, and usually evangelical, attacks on other Christian and Christian-derived movements. Standard books on cults included J. K. Van Baalen's much imitated *The Chaos of Cults: A Study in Present-Day 'Isms* (1938) and Anthony A. Hoekema's 1963 work, *The Four Major Cults*, which studies Christian Science, the Jehovah's Witnesses, Mormonism, and Seventh-Day Adventism.[9] In 1965, the longest chapter of Walter Martin's classic *Kingdom of the Cults* still concerned the Jehovah's Witnesses, while a hundred-page appendix was devoted to debating whether Adventism could legitimately be ascribed cult status. Martin thought not, but many disagreed, one point of controversy being whether the works of founder Ellen G. White were exalted by the Adventists to the scriptural level of a Third Testament.

Among the many sins of the new sects was their deceptive claim to orthodoxy. While no potential recruit was likely to confuse Theosophy or an occult group for a Christian denomination, other sects explicitly presented themselves as Christian. This aroused the fury of orthodox commentators, who pointed out exactly how sects deviated from traditional norms. Cults were to be feared because they sailed under false colors, and their misrepresentations threatened to mislead the unwary. The very name of *Christian* Science asserted its claim to the inheritance of Jesus, as did that of the Church of Jesus Christ of Latter-Day Saints. Explicit anti-Christian polemic or violence could be dealt with overtly, but the cults were threatening subversion from within. For Walter Martin, the doyen of evangelical anticult critics, all the cult leaders had one thing in common: "they take Biblical Christianity and change it into a clever counterfeit of the real thing." Cultism meant "the adherence to doctrines which are pointedly contradictory to orthodox Christianity and which yet claim the distinction of either tracing their origin to orthodox sources, or of being in essential harmony with those sources."[10] As Van Baalen complained in 1938, "When Seventh Day Adventists and Russellites lecture against evolution, when Mormons condemn the evil of divorce, and Buchmanites stress the need for a religious experience in a time of much dead orthodoxy, much error may be slipped in with much truth."[11]

For their Christian critics, the cults fell short of full or authentic Christianity. In 1928, Charles Ferguson tried to convey the scope of the cult problem when he noted that of 140 newspaper advertisements for religious services in Manhattan, "fully half had to do with cults and sects of cults bearing no relation to any form of orthodox Christianity."[12] The loaded word here is "orthodox," which for Ferguson, as for many contemporaries, excluded Christian Science, the Watch Tower, and the Mormons. The evangelical magazine *Christianity Today* lamented in a 1960 editorial, "The cults know no Triune God, no incarnate Word, no vicarious sacrifice, and no risen Savior in the sense of historical Biblical theology."[13]

The critics thus took a narrow view of the limits of "true" Christianity, and specified that anything outside this was un-Christian and cultish. This enabled them not only to attack the cults, but to score rhetorical points in internal struggles between conservatives and liberals within the major churches. Many of the distinctive ideas held by the cults were also espoused by a wide range of Christians within the mainstream denominations, as theological modernists tried to reconcile Christianity with the insights of Bible criticism and of recent scientific discoveries, especially evolution. By the early twentieth century, modernists within the churches had serious doubts about the Trinity, the Incarnation, the Resurrection, and the doctrine of Atonement, and much of what evangelicals considered "historical Biblical theology."

Between 1890 and 1930, modernists made rapid advances in key seminaries and denominational hierarchies, and wars between modernists
and fundamentalists were raging in many churches. Conservatives responded by publishing the series of tracts known as the *Fundamentals*
(1910–15), and the first congress of the newly christened "fundamentalists" occurred in 1920.[14] These events help us to understand both
the vigor and the chronology of the anticult reaction, and particularly
the focus on visible new sects like Christian Science and the Watch
Tower.

Ostensibly attacking cults, conservative polemicists were also con-
fronting their liberal rivals. In a classic example of guilt by association,
Van Baalen concluded his attack on the customary range of cult targets
(Mormons, Adventists, Jehovah's Witnesses) with a chapter on Unitarianism and Modernism, implying that modernist thinkers like Harry
Emerson Fosdick and the liberal *Christian Century* were cultish rebels
against orthodox Christianity quite as much as the better-known
heresiarchs. For evangelicals like Reuben Torrey, speaking in 1918, the
anti-Christian and diabolical forces at work in the contemporary world
included not just the cults, like Christian Science, occultism, and Theosophy, but also modernist German theology.[15] Conservatives were arguing that liberal Christianity had betrayed the religion's vital doctrines, leaving only a vague ecumenism, and thereby had opened the
door to seductive superstitions, whether Asian or occult. As so often
before and since, cults were such attractive targets because they were
so rhetorically useful.

### Mind-Cure

Throughout the first half of the century, the primary target of cult
critics was Christian Science, together with the associated mind-cure
movements generally known as New Thought. These are the original
cults in the modern sense of the word. When Glenn G. Atkins published a survey of *Modern Religious Cults and Movements* in 1923,
over half the book was devoted to Christian Science and New Thought.
In the *Reader's Guide to Periodical Literature*, the topic heading "Cult"
made its debut that same year, with a citation to an article in the *Nation*
on the same two movements.[16]

Christian Science and New Thought both emerged from a common
intellectual background in mid-nineteenth-century New England, and
they shared many influences from an older mystical and magical fringe,
including Swedenborgian teachings, Mesmerism, and Transcendental-

ism. The central figure and prophet of the emerging synthesis was
Phineas P. Quimby, "the John the Baptist of Christian Science," whose
faith-healing work began in 1838. Quimby and his followers taught
the overwhelming importance of thought in shaping reality, a message
that was crucial for healing. If disease existed only as thought, then
only by curing the mind could the body be set right: disease was a
matter of wrong belief.[17]

The most important of the sects preaching these principles was
Christian Science, founded by Mary Baker Eddy, whose text *Science
and Health* (1875) acquired scriptural status. She was deeply influenced
by Quimby, to the extent that she would face continuing controversy
over her alleged plagiarisms, but she may also have drawn on even
older heterodox traditions, notably Shakerism. There had been a Shaker
colony near her childhood home, and like Eddy, the Shakers venerated
their "Father and Mother in Heaven." Shakers also held that "sickness
is called devil—we must fight and overcome it."[18] In 1879, Eddy
founded the First Church of Christ, Scientist, in Boston, and the movement grew rapidly. From only 27 Christian Scientists in 1880, there
were 8,724 a decade later, 66,000 by 1906, and 200,000 by 1926. The
rate of growth slowed at that point, but by 1936 the church had 269,000
members. Throughout the first half of the century, the largest concentration of churches would always be in California, but the movement
had an impressive national distribution, with pockets of strength across
the Midwest and West. Mark Twain resorted to the familiar Muslim
analogy when in 1899 he suggested that Eddy's movement might make
"the most formidable show that any new religion has made in the
world since the birth and spread of Mohammedanism, and that within
a century from now it may stand second to Rome only, in numbers
and power in Christendom."[19]

### New Thought

Other healing movements grew up alongside Eddy's church. These
were formed by dissident Christian Scientists, by some former pupils
of Quimby, and by other thinkers exploring the same range of ideas,
which collectively flourished as the "Boston craze" of the 1880s. Former Eddy student Emma Curtis Hopkins founded the movement that
would later be known as New Thought. The various emerging groups
held national gatherings through the 1890s, culminating in a national
convention in 1899. An International New Thought Alliance was
formed in 1914, and by the 1940s, some eighteen distinct New Thought

sects and churches were operating, bearing names like the Institute of Religious Science, Metaphysical School of Health, and Church of Advanced Thought.

A few of these movements went on to success in their own right. Among the more influential were Divine Science and the Unity School, both of which date from 1889.[20] Under the leadership of Charles and Myrtle Fillmore, Unity flourished through its exploitation of modern techniques of marketing and advertising. It was by the 1920s "an enormous mail order concern dispensing health and happiness on the large scale of modern business enterprise. It is mass production in religion and its work is carried on shrewdly and systematically."[21] Through the twentieth century, Unity provided emergency spiritual assistance for anyone seeking aid by telephone or through the mails. A splendid headquarters complex near Kansas City was formally opened in 1927.

Though they agreed on many basic principles, the various therapeutic schools differed as to the relationship of mind and matter: New Thought groups believed in the paramount role of mind in controlling matter, while Christian Science preached an absolute idealism, altogether denying the existence of matter. For Eddy, "Mortal existence is a dream; mortal existence has no real entity, but saith, 'It is I.' " Still, the schools were at one on fundamentals, in their optimism, and the belief in the divinization of humanity. A healthy mind and body were to be achieved by recognizing the oneness of our human lives with the life of God, a point suggested by the title of Ralph Waldo Trine's bestselling *In Tune with the Infinite* (1897).[22] If men and women all partook of the divine, could they not in a sense claim to be God? Similar ideas underlay most of the subsequent occult and New Age movements that were so pervasively influenced by New Thought, from the assertion of godhood by leaders like Father Divine and Wallace Fard to the glorification of the "Mighty I AM" presence by the sect of that name.

New Thought was syncretistic and drew on religious and philosophical traditions well outside Christian orthodoxy. From its foundation in 1889, Charles Fillmore's magazine, *Modern Thought*, offered articles on "spiritualism, Unitarianism, rosicrucianism, transcendentalism, Christian Science and New Thought," and his theological system included reincarnation. Among the influences on mind-cure, William James listed "the four Gospels; another is Emersonianism or New England Transcendentalism; another is Berkeleyan idealism; another is spiritism, with its messages of 'law' and 'progress' and 'development'; another the optimistic popular science evolutionism . . . and finally,

Hinduism has contributed a strain." Though New Thought prefigured modern-day therapy movements, it was also rooted in older ideas: "with its constant thought of prosperity, its opulent-consciousness, its belief in the limitless possibilities of the individual, [it] is simply American psychology on dress parade." As a rationalist critic dryly remarked, "Their doctrine is 'Be your own savior; don't ask someone else to do it for you.' Isn't this American independence?"[23]

This combination of the familiar and the exotic proved irresistible, so that by the 1920s Christian Science and New Thought ideas became a national presence. Among the unorthodox religious services advertised weekly in Manhattan, "the most outstanding of them were perhaps Russellism, New Thought, Theosophy, Spiritualism, Christian Science, Unity, the Four Square Gospel, and the various lectures of the swamis."[24] Nor was this phenomenon confined to New York. On a typical Sunday in 1923, Detroit newspapers carried advertisements for "Vedanta, Spiritist and Spiritualist groups (the Spiritist group calls itself the Spirit Temple of Light and Truth), the Ultimate Thought Society, the First Universal Spiritual Church, the Church of Psychic Research, the Philosophical Church of Natural Law, Unity Center, The Culture of Isolan, Theosophy, Divine Science Center, and lectures on Divine Metaphysics."[25] The sects had arrived on Main Street, or at least appeared suggestively in Sinclair Lewis's 1920 novel of that name. Even in a community as remote as his small Minnesota town, the author could plausibly portray a character, Mrs. Dyer, as "devoted to experiments in religious cults, illnesses and scandal-bearing." This is about 1914. Though the main cult in question is Christian Science, Mrs. Dyer has an interest in "every doggone kind of New Thought and Bahai and Swami and Hooptedoodle meeting you can find."[26]

### "Eddyism"

Both Christian Science and New Thought attracted fierce criticism, and it has been fairly said of Christian Science, "Against no modern religious movement has so bitter an attack been made, unless it be Mormonism."[27] In *Main Street*, a character aspiring towards Protestant unity hopes that a new coalition might confront the twin chief perils of the age, namely Catholicism and Christian Science, and Lewis is accurately reflecting the views of the contemporary evangelical press. At this point, of course, Catholicism counted its American followers in the tens of millions and Christian Science, in the low hundred thousands.

At the simplest level, Christian Science was dismissed as a profitable confidence game. Already in the 1880s, Mrs. Eddy was charging pupils $300 for her courses in the new approach to mind and health, a significant sum in that day. Her disciples also made substantial incomes, amounting to several thousand dollars a year. In other money-making schemes the faithful were pressured to buy books, photographs, and approved memorabilia, perhaps the most outrageous of which was a souvenir spoon depicting Eddy's birthplace. The spoon was recommended for "grace and healing" and retailed for an impressive $5 in the 1890s.[28] For modern readers, Eddy's profitable practice recalls the therapy movements of the 1970s, in which trainers were said to grow rich by peddling mysticism to a gullible public.

Eddy maintained tight control over her organization and her franchise, attracting criticism for her authoritarian personality: she was aggressively litigious. Her attacks on rivals and insubordinate followers were given a supernatural basis in the form of Malicious Animal Magnetism, MAM, by which one individual could inflict occult harm on another at a distance: Eddy accused her enemies of constantly mounting MAM attacks upon her, to the point that she was aptly accused of "demonophobia." The ensuing conflicts gave rise to predictable press reports of "modern witchcraft" and witch trials, while critics saw the church's attempts to control or excommunicate dissidents as heresy hunts.[29]

The church repeatedly demonstrated its rigid intolerance of dissent or criticism and fought to prevent the publication of any coverage it considered hostile. This led to repeated controversies between 1906 and 1909, when a torrent of exposés threatened to destroy the founder's reputation altogether. A furor developed over a series of articles about Mrs. Eddy published in *McClure's Magazine*, coauthored by Willa Cather and Georgine Milmine, which were collected for publication in 1909 as a book-length biography. Cather and Milmine richly documented every piece of chicanery and foolishness in the movement's history, so effectively that the church strove to suppress the book. Eddy loyalists bought up all available copies and ensured that any library volumes remained constantly on loan to the faithful. As a result, the book vanished from sight for decades.[30]

Eddy's attempt to control any information about herself and her movement was so critical because she frequently tried to rewrite history, to conceal or disguise past claims that might be taken as arrogant or worse. The worst sin of Cather and Milmine was to uncover such past embarrassments, including some disturbing episodes when Eddy had claimed divine or supernatural status and exalted her own scriptures above those of the Bible. Extremist views came to light through the activities of Eddy's close friends and aides, who publicly exposed opinions they claimed to have received from her secret teachings. One scandal involved Josephine Woodbury, who in 1890 boasted that she had given birth to a son conceived immaculately (he was christened "Prince of Peace"): although hitherto a member of Eddy's inner circle, she was now excommunicated from the fold. In the 1920s, devoted disciples advertised in the press that Mrs. Eddy had not died but would soon reappear upon earth as "the ever-present Christ, the Son-Daughter of God," while some declared that she had already been reincarnated. To her intimates, Eddy claimed to have found herself prophesied in the Book of Revelation as "the woman clothed with the sun." These disputes have modern echoes: in the 1990s, Christian Science would face internal turmoil over the official publication of a book that presented Eddy as equal to Christ, a divine figure who fulfilled biblical prophecy.[31]

The opening years of the century witnessed increasing public attacks on the movement, especially after Josephine Woodbury went public in 1899 with media revelations about her former mentor's divine pretensions. Woodbury found a ready-made platform in the progressive magazine *Arena*, which was linked to those New Thought leaders who venerated Quimby and regarded Eddy as a usurper. Under the banner headline of "Eddyism Exposed," Woodbury charged that Eddy had discovered nothing more than "ways and means of perverting and prostituting the science of healing to her own ecclesiastical aggrandizement, and to the moral and physical depravity of her dupes" (the term "ecclesiastical" invoked Catholic-like arrogance). In 1906, Pulitzer's *World* reinforced its role as the scourge of all cults by charging that Eddy was senile or perhaps dead and that an inner clique was running the church. The *McClure's* series followed shortly afterwards.[32]

Eddy's reputation suffered further in 1907 when Mark Twain's book, *Christian Science*, attacked her spiritual dictatorship. Twain presented Eddy as a megalomaniac with divine pretensions and "a hunger for power such as has never been seen in the world before." He too drew on the worst anti-Papist stereotypes to condemn the movement: the "countless vassals" of Christian Science owed their allegiance to "the other papacy," with its "new infallibility." The church's internal disciplinary proceedings demonstrated "Satanic considerations of irresponsible power." In the 1920s, H. L. Mencken bracketed Eddy with Madame Blavatsky: "both were copious and shameless plagiarists . . . both loved money and knew how to get it, both suspected their immediate followers of evil designs, and both have been purged *post mortem* of their plentiful blunders and rascalities, and elevated to what amounts substantially to sainthood."[33]

Ironically, Twain tended to accept the movement's claims to healing powers, and his book was denounced by the medical profession for its excessively positive portrait of Christian Science. Contra Twain, most enemies of the new church saw the healing claims as the movement's most dangerous feature: "Christian Science is a menace to society because ignorant quacks under the garb of religion are permitted to trifle with life."[34] Mencken agreed with this view of the effects of the "quack healing cults," though he said that the movements might serve a sound eugenic purpose, in that anyone stupid enough to resort to them should be encouraged to die before they could pass on their genes. If Christian Science and New Thought were prohibited, he argued, mainstream medicine would keep many of these individuals alive, with the result that the average intelligence level of the nation might fall to the abysmal levels currently prevailing in Tennessee or Mississippi.[35]

### Defending Orthodoxy

The main thrust of the attack on "Eddyism" faded rapidly after the founder died in 1910, and by 1923 *The Nation* could note that Christian Science was "popular, powerful, and almost conservative now." For most ordinary citizens in recent years, the movement's name has usually been associated with its sober and well-respected publication, the *Christian Science Monitor*. Even so, religious critics would long continue to denounce Christian Science as a cult, and as late as 1992 the church still merited a starring role in the latest edition of Walter Martin's *Kingdom of the Cults*.[36]

Mind-cure continued to attract a powerful and lasting religious polemic because it seemed to be importing into Christianity ideas with strong occult and Asian connotations, misleadingly labeled a rediscovery of an authentic Christian tradition. At the same time, this new Christianity was excluding or rationalizing away most of the familiar landmarks of orthodoxy. For orthodox Christian writers, New Thought and Christian Science represented heresies so gross and fundamental that they had scarcely been encountered since the earliest days of the Church. Its willingness to trample over every aspect of traditional

Christian orthodoxy also permitted conservatives to present Christian Science as a symbol of the worst excesses of ecclesiastical modernism.

In this polemic, Christian Science and New Thought were commonly bracketed with Theosophy. The linkage was natural enough: the Theosophical Society was founded in 1875, the same year *Science and Health* was published. The movements seemed like parallel alien intrusions into Christian America, a conduit for the importation of Asian ideas. In his 1898 attack, Barrington treated the three movements together, claiming that all denied the proper Christian conceptions of the universe and eliminated essential distinctions between the human and the divine. In 1899, a coalition of San Diego clergy denounced Theosophy as "the antithesis of Christianity. It is a system of pantheism— the denial of personality. . . . Its foundation principles leave room logically for neither religion nor ethics. Its doctrine of fatalism is destructive alike of aspiration and hope." This was a cousin of Hinduism, the religion that had "left India a moral and spiritual desert." Similar perceived flaws inspired the "severe onslaught . . . based upon Bible grounds" that the evangelical clergy of San Francisco had launched against Christian Science in 1886.[37]

Most pernicious, the new sects denied original sin and believed that humanity could progress to a higher spirituality or even perfection unassisted by Christ or grace. If there were no sin, there was no need for redemption and no salvation, so Christ had died in vain. Mrs. Eddy denied the Virgin Birth, the miracles of Christ, the Atonement, and the Resurrection or at least so allegorized these concepts that they seemed to vanish: Jesus' death was as much an illusion as any other form of sickness or misfortune. For Theosophists, similarly, Jesus was merely a highly evolved spiritual being, an enormously admirable figure, but in no sense unique and no more the Son of God than any other sentient being. Christ was merely "a title given to all triumphant initiates who have passed the symbolical crucifixion and have become the anointed masters of all nature." Theosophist leader Annie Besant spoke of many Christs, of whom Jesus was only one: "when a new era in human evolution begins, a world teacher comes in a voluntary incarnation and founds a religion that is suited to the requirements of the new age."[38]

New Thought and Christian Science both viewed themselves as representing the apex of modern thinking, and it was precisely this ideology of progress and perfectionism that angered conservative critics.

Counterblasts to the liberal trend came in the writings of G. K. Chesterton who had an enormous (mainly Catholic) readership in North America. In 1911, Chesterton's fictional detective Father Brown encountered a cult embodying both occult and New Thought ideas in the story "The Eye of Apollo." The sect is led by Kalon ("the Good"), the New Priest of Apollo, who has founded "a new religion. One of those new religions that forgives your sins by saying you never had any," it is explicitly compared to Christian Science. The Nietzschean "blond beast" Kalon offers complete healing of all physical ailments by preaching the total command of the mind over the body, which among other things permits believers to gaze worshipfully at the sun. The cult uses this device to blind a gullible rich follower, who then falls to her death in a murder designed to look like an accident. Chesterton's point was straightforward: though denied by New Thought, original sin is a basic human reality that religion ignores at its peril.

Chesterton's argument was that the rhetoric of science and modernity inexorably led not to progress but to a revival of the worst kinds of superstition. In 1923, *The Nation* drew comparisons between present-day conditions and the decadence of the Roman Empire, when "[o]ccult Eastern rites were brought to Rome; people were healed by magic of all sorts" and "the disillusioned matrons of the outworn aristocracy" clamored for cures "of their largely fancied ills." For the *Nation*, this situation was now recreated in New York in the form of Christian Science, New Thought, Theosophy, and their countless variants.[39] An equally cynical picture emerges from Sinclair Lewis's 1927 novel *Elmer Gantry*, the story of a corrupt evangelist. After being discredited as a Baptist preacher around 1910, Elmer gravitates to the emerging New Thought racket, with its "pure and uncontaminated bunk." He attaches himself to "the proprietor of the Victory Thought-Power Headquarters, New York, and not even in Los Angeles was there a more important center of predigested philosophy and pansy-painted ethics. . . . She taught, or farmed out, classes in Concentration, Prosperity, Love, Metaphysics, Oriental Mysticism, and the Fourth Dimension. She instructed Select Circles how to keep one's husband, how to understand Sanskrit philosophy without understanding either Sanskrit or philosophy, and how to become slim without giving up pastry."[40] The "paying customers" were dignified with the title *chelas*, a Hindu word the proprietor had learned from Kipling's recent novel, *Kim*.

### Millions Now Living Will Never Die

Christian Science was by no means the only ostensibly Christian movement to be labeled as a cult and thereby placed outside the scope of
acknowledged Christianity. Though differing vastly from Christian Science in their ideas and appeal, these other sects were excluded on
broadly similar grounds, namely possessing invented scriptures and
heretical ideas of divinity or the Christian salvation-history.

Another much denounced sect was the Watch Tower Bible Society,
which emerged from the evangelical background of the 1870s. The
movement was started by Charles Taze Russell (hence "Russellites"):
he was a hugely prolific writer and an experienced preacher, who fell
under Adventist influence. Believing in the imminent end of the world,
in 1879 Russell founded a newspaper, *The Watch Tower*. Though he
was an exact contemporary of the founders of Theosophy and Christian
Science, his ideas are so radically different that he seems to belong to
a different century. Russell's group grew rapidly, and the international
crises of 1914 seemed initially to bear out his claim that this year would
indeed mark the end of the present ungodly age. Explanations for the
world's subsequent failure to end as predicted were easily found, and
following Russell's death in 1916 he was succeeded by another able
leader, Judge J. F. Rutherford, who in 1931 would introduce the "Jehovah's Witness" name. By the 1920s, the movement was gaining public visibility, as the slogan "Millions now living will never die" literally
became part of the American landscape, so widely was it painted on
telephone poles, rocks or mountainsides. In 1925 alone, some two million copies of Russell's works were distributed.[41]

At first sight, the *Watch Tower* movement seems like no more than
an enthusiastic evangelical sect, which scarcely explains the attacks it
drew from Christian writers throughout the century. It was by no
means as innovative or syncretistic as New Thought. The hostility can
be understood in terms of the group's theological peculiarities. Charles
Russell was an idiosyncratic thinker, who rejected such traditional
foundations of Christian belief as the Trinity and the existence of hell.
In his account, one all-powerful God, Jehovah, begot two sons, Logos
("the word") and Lucifer, and the former became Christ. Russell was
also a mortalist, believing that the souls of the dead remained dead
until resurrected at the Last Judgment. These ideas, which have many
precedents among Christian sects throughout the centuries, were justified in terms of a "corrected" translation of the Bible peculiar to
the movement. For orthodox Christian writers, the anti-Trinitarianism

and the modification of the Bible were both enough to prove that the sect had moved beyond authentic Christianity into the realms of sub-Christian heresy. Orthodox believers were impelled to convince potential converts that the group's ostensible Christianity was a smokescreen.

The Jehovah's Witnesses also attracted secular critics, who viewed Russell as a confidence trickster or a holy hypocrite. In 1908, he was involved in a well-publicized divorce, and subsequent scandals concerned his financial malpractice and personal authoritarianism. The Watch Tower Society was constructed so that Russell had complete financial control of the organization, without responsibility to anyone. Between 1908 and 1916, he was a frequent target of the *Brooklyn Eagle*, which argued that "Pastor Russell's religious cult is nothing more than a money-making scheme."[42] One embarrassing story involved Russell's scheme to sell overpriced wheat seed to believers on the grounds that it was "Miracle Wheat" and thus far more productive than its profane rivals. In 1913, Russell unsuccessfully sued the *Eagle* for libel over its coverage of this affair. Other critics showed that Russell had throughout his life made fraudulent claims with respect to credentials and experiences and had none of the scholarly background that might permit him to undertake his radical reinterpretation of the Bible.

Neither the theological oddities nor the charges of corruption, however, can explain the severity of the anti-Witness activity that erupted at various points during the century. Apart from their religious opponents, the Russellites provoked official critics by their stance on secular issues; the group opposed participation in the First World War as part of the continuing diabolical work of earthly governments. At a time of hyperpatriotism and spy fever, this stance invited persecution, and law enforcement authorities throughout the United States began investigating the Russellites as deadly enemies of the state. When the sect disseminated its antiwar views, it ran the risk of charges of sedition or treason. In 1918, the FBI and state authorities targeted the book *The Finished Mystery*, a continuation of Russell's writings, which included a fierce denunciation of war. It was alleged that the German government had financed publication, enabling the book to be distributed free in large quantities, and some 850,000 copies appeared between 1917 and 1920. Police infiltrated religious meetings in small towns and industrial communities, and tracked the distribution of Russellite literature. Possessing *The Finished Mystery* for sale was enough to earn prosecution under the draconian Espionage Act, and Rutherford and several associates received long prison terms.[43]

The Russellites were by no means the only religious group to suffer thus. Some minor Pentecostal sects also faced sedition charges for resisting the war, and pacifist sects like the Amish and Mennonites suffered badly for their draft resistance. Suspicious eyes also turned towards Point Loma, which was strategically located near a major naval base.[44] Nevertheless, the Witnesses were by far the most visible and nationally active group. Their fate contrasted sharply with that of the Mormons, who won public favor by their loyal support of the war effort and their high enlistment rates, proving themselves good Americans.[45] By the 1920s, Russellism had the dubious distinction of being perhaps the most unpopular of the fringe religions, and took the brunt of both theological and popular opposition. Matters would become even worse during the 1930s, as the sect attracted both official suppression and mob violence on a scale not seen since the earlier Mormon crises.

### The Latter Rain

Yet another contemporary tradition to be dismissed as cultish was Pentecostalism, which would ultimately dwarf both Christian Science and the Jehovah's Witnesses in numbers and importance. The Pentecostal revival is conveniently dated from the first days of the new century, when the gift of tongues was received by Bible student Agnes Ozman in Topeka, Kansas (though the phenomenon had also been reported elsewhere in the recent past). In their first decades, Holy Rollers, or Pentecostals, were consistently viewed as another classic cult, though they were usually deemed so outrageous and even ludicrous as not to need the detailed refutation offered by scholars like Martin and Van Baalen. In fact, some Pentecostals did accept heretical and anti-Trinitarian views, but we rarely find their opinions denounced by the theologians who were in these same years dissecting Pastor Russell's Christology in such detail. As a movement associated with the poor, rural dwellers, and racial minorities, Pentecostalism was beneath contempt and chiefly featured in the mainstream media as a source of humor or shock value. If New Thought was a modernist fad of the leisured, Pentecostalism seemed a bizarre irruption of pre-Christian primitivism into the twentieth century. (They were the "Noisyrenes".)

The Pentecostal movement grew out of the nineteenth-century Holiness revival, which sought to restore the church of the New Testament era. By the 1890s, there was great interest in the phenomenon of speaking in tongues, first described in the second chapter of the Book of Acts. This visitation from the Holy Spirit, the Latter Rain, was believed to presage the coming of Christ and the End Times. Glossolalia occurred during the Welsh revival of 1904, and it spread in America during the revival that began at an Azusa Street church in Los Angeles in 1906, when apocalyptic fears were acute following the recent earthquake in San Francisco. Pentecostal sects flourished over the coming decade, a period characterized by enormous millennial hopes, which culminated during the international crises of 1914. A number of Pentecostal denominations were founded during this time, most important of which were the Assemblies of God, the major white grouping, and the Church of God in Christ, which attracted black support.[46]

The movement did not lack critics, who used very much the same arsenal of taunts that had been employed against the Methodists 150 years previously and would be revived once more for use against the cults of the 1970s. The most savage attacks came from evangelicals, unsurprisingly given the close relationship between the two movements and the sense that Pentecostals were leading believers away from the revealed truth: this was a vicious intrafamily feud. Evangelicals stressed the faddery of the new movement, all the more so given its origins in the cult wonderland of Los Angeles, "the home of almost numberless creeds." British critics scorned a movement born in America, "the land of wonder-meetings and freak religions."[47] This was no Christian development, but a snare of Satan.

Enemies of Pentecostal fervor charged that the movement enticed the faithful to desert reason for a dangerous emotionalism. In their crazed fanaticism, believers risked their life and health, and flirted with commitment to insane asylums. Some charged that converts were stirred up to murder their enemies.[48] Pentecostalism was mindless enthusiasm in the old sense of that word. The *Los Angeles Times* initially reported the 1906 revival with headlines such as "Weird Babel of Tongues—New Sect of Fanatics is Breaking Loose—Wild Scene Last Night on Azusa Street—Gurgle of Wordless Talk by a Sister." Those present were "breathing strange utterances and mouthing a creed which it would seem no sane mortal could understand . . . devotees of the weird doctrine practice the most fanatical rites, preach the wildest theories and work themselves into a state of mad excitement in their peculiar zeal . . . pandemonium breaks loose, and the bounds of reason are passed by those who are 'filled with the spirit,' whatever that may be."[49] The *Times* kept up its assault over the coming months, following

its familiar habit of denigrating fringe religious movements that threatened the reputation of southern California at a time when the region
needed sober and substantial migrants from the east.

The media caricatured the racial element of the incipient Holy Roller
movement. In its initial 1906 report, the *Times* reported, " 'You-oo-oo
gou-loo-loo come under the bloo-oo-oo boo-loo;' shouts an old colored
'mammy;' in a frenzy of religious zeal. Swinging her arms wildly about
her, she continues with the strangest harangue ever uttered." The fact
that congregations like Azusa Street were racially mixed raised a desperately sensitive issue at a time of intense segregationist feeling. Critics argued that white believers were being tainted by the primitive
"jungle" religion of the African Americans, which expressed itself in
dance and ecstatic states. Even Charles Fox Parham, one of the first of
the Pentecostal evangelists, attacked the Azusa Street movement as
"Southern Darkey camp meetings."[50]

The presence of "excitable females" among the Pentecostal leadership was only marginally less horrifying than the racial mingling.
Apart from defying Scripture, the presence of so many women confirmed the neurotic origins of the supposed "signs and wonders." And
once again, sexual fantasies ran rampant: when a woman abandoned
social restraints, her sexual modesty would soon follow. Evangelical
critics feared "a pit of moral and spiritual pollution in which free-
loveism was a dominant feature" and from which gullible women
might be led into debauchery, adultery, or white slavery. Women for-
sook their family duties, arousing fears about the special danger posed
to children. In 1915, the city of Topeka tried to ban children from
attending a fiery revival, and we hear of families forcibly removing
their offspring or spouses from Pentecostal gatherings.[51] The elders of
the new sects were portrayed as corrupt exploiters of their uneducated
congregations, mendacious showmen who faked their healing miracles.
Sexual charges against some early leaders were widely publicized, notably the case of Charles Fox Parham, who was arrested in 1907 for a
homosexual contact.[52]

### Sister Aimee

A like contempt extended to religious celebrities who drew on the Pentecostal tradition, especially evangelist Aimee Semple McPherson, who
was attacked as a cynical would-be messiah, as much pagan as Christian. She arrived in southern California in 1918 and soon built up an
astonishingly successful evangelistic enterprise. By 1925 she had

amassed a million-dollar fortune, and her Angelus Temple had a 5,000-seat auditorium and a complete broadcasting studio. Her station KFSG broadcast the Foursquare Gospel, and 240 lighthouses or local churches were affiliated with the temple. By 1929, she was said to have twelve thousand followers in Los Angeles, thirty thousand elsewhere—though the official religious census conducted in 1936 found only sixteen thousand adherents. She also made the transition from her Pentecostal origins to a more mainstream Baptist affiliation and did her best to preserve good relations with moderate evangelicals. Still, she never lost the label of cult leader, partly because of the powerful sexuality and "animal magnetism" that she was accused of deploying in her public appearances. It was difficult for male writers to imagine a woman religious leader succeeding quite so spectacularly without deploying sexual weapons. Carey McWilliams described McPherson's group as "the outstanding cult movement in southern California in the twenties," and she is regularly catalogued alongside the other swamis and occult leaders of the era.[53]

This occult association was not completely outrageous as Sister Aimee seems to have borrowed her distinctive style of presentation from the contemporary New Age and mystical groups that were so prevalent in southern California at this time. Though she had been preaching in the East since 1915, her services became much more ornate following her arrival in the West, where she at first made her home in San Diego. She apparently adopted for her own religious movement the "uniforms, pageantry and showmanship" that were associated with Katherine Tingley's Point Loma settlement, and Aimee's Foursquare Gospel logo recalls New Age and Rosicrucian symbols. Sinclair Lewis may have been referring to this linkage when in *Elmer Gantry*, he made his thinly disguised Aimee character "Sharon Falconer" a covert pagan, who worships Ishtar, Isis, and Astarte in a clandestine chapel dedicated to the Mother Goddess. Sister Sharon "saw herself another Mary Baker Eddy, an Annie Besant, a Katherine Tingley . . . she hinted that, who knows, the next Messiah might be a woman, and that woman might now be on earth, just realizing her divinity."[54]

In southern California, the dividing line between the Pentecostals and the New Age sects was never as hard and fast as one might expect. While Pentecostal and millenarian believers had high hopes that the present age would perish in or shortly after 1914, many of the occult and Theosophical believers had similarly messianic hopes about an imminent New Age, an Aquarian era of miracles and prophecies, which would be marked by a new spiritual consciousness. At Azusa Street, evangelist William Seymour was repeatedly troubled by mediums and occultists who used Pentecostal services as a setting for seances, and a visiting preacher was shocked to see "the manifestations of the flesh, spiritualistic controls, [and] saw people practicing hypnotism at the altar over candidates seeking the baptism."[55] Charles Fox Parham was a firm believer in British-Israel doctrines, according to which white northern Europeans were the descendants of the Ten Lost Tribes of Israel, and these mystical ideas were now imported into the Californian Pentecostal movement.[56] The two seemingly incompatible strands of belief, Pentecostal and New Age, were also united by their belief in spiritual healing and alternate forms of medicine. Sinclair Lewis remarked that although spiritual healings like Sister Aimee's would soon become a feature of evangelistic services, they were in the early days more closely associated with Christian Scientists and New Thoughters.[57] Pentecostal sects, like the New Age groups, also had strong female components in their leadership. However little it superficially resembles New Thought, Pentecostalism was similarly denounced as a vehicle for Oriental and occult influences.

Aimee McPherson's image as a cult leader was sealed when a scandal suggested that she was a hypocrite who used religion to make a good living, perhaps committing the very sexual sins that she so often denounced. In May 1926, reports that Aimee had drowned while swimming caused enormous grief among her followers. Several days later, however, she reappeared in Mexico, claiming that she had been kidnapped. Her story fell apart, and the mysterious incident seems instead to have involved a romantic escapade with her lover, a married engineer at station KFSG. She faced trial for conspiracy to produce false testimony, though her popularity was still sufficient to save her from jail. The case once more confirmed the worst stereotypes of the new generation of religious entrepreneurs.

The concept and language of cult emerged in the context of marginal new Christian groups and their leaders and was chiefly formulated by orthodox religious rivals. While it is possible still today to find books attacking these sects in the standard anticult language, this literature has become more scarce and is usually confined to the shelves of fundamentalist Christian bookstores. In fact, any writer today describing Mormons or Christian Scientists as cultists would immediately be marked as an unreconstructed fundamentalist. Since the 1960s, the upsurge of far more alien religious traditions has made the old "estab-lished cults" look quite respectable in comparison. Also since the 1960s, most of the older fringe religions have seen quite startling surges in membership, to the point where they challenge or actually outnumber many of the respectable denominations. There comes a stage when even the deadliest enemies of a so-called cult have to grace it with the name of "church."

Although the Christian sects initially attracted most of the furor about cults, by the 1920s this term expanded to take account of other movements even less integrally connected to the Christian mainstream, namely occult and esoteric groups that often drew inspiration from Asian religions. For the popular media, if not for the Christian polem-icists, the cult concept largely shifted its meaning to comprise these still more outré movements, which were proliferating so impressively. Already by the 1920s, the word "cult" had acquired virtually all its modern freight: it described small religious groups with highly unor-thodox ideas, unshakably loyal to a teacher or prophet, who might well bear some Oriental title like "guru" or "swami." And at least in some instances, cults and gurus were associated with corruption, fraud, and sexual license.

# FOUR

# The First New Age

Be Lemurian, and rank yourself with the race that aspires to be royal.
Slogan of the Temple of the Jeweled Cross, Los Angeles.

Observers of the 1960s and 1970s believed that the United States was experiencing a sudden growth in occult and mystical ideas, in new religious practices and beliefs that often found their source in the great religions of Asia. While Aquarian and Asian ideas increased in popularity during these decades, they were in fact anything but new. As J. Gordon Melton has pointed out, virtually every aspect of the "new religious consciousness" was in place before 1900, as were most components of what would come to be known as the New Age.[1] Most of these ideas had deep historical roots—not, as enthusiasts sometimes claimed, back as far as Atlantis or ancient Egypt, but traceable at least to the last third of the nineteenth century. In what I have called the period of Emergence, between 1910 and 1935, eccentric religious and mystical ideas became commonplace, providing rich opportunities for religious entrepreneurs. The result was an upsurge of small groups with innovative religious practices. Some of these groups would certainly count as cults according to both contemporary and modern definitions.

As in the hippie era, this earlier cult milieu had its greatest strength in the western states, particularly California, but fringe groups were able to popularize themselves nationwide through a vastly expanded mass media and by novel forms of marketing and advertising. By the 1930s, the concepts of this first New Age were being sold in packaged form through new religions claiming to offer the wisdom of the ancients. The period between the two world wars produced a model cult explosion, which in turn set the scene for a major social reaction against cults and the threat they were believed to pose.

### Light from the East

In the history of religious thought, beginnings are very difficult to pinpoint. Most of the ideas of the American religious fringe of the 1920s could be traced directly to the occult and Theosophical world of the late nineteenth century; that in turn grew from a mid-Victorian boom in Mesmerism and spiritualism. The chain could be traced back still further, to the Hermetic and Neoplatonic thinkers of the Renaissance. Though less visible in some periods than others, the occult vision never entirely vanished in either Europe or North America. Even so, we can legitimately point to the last third of the nineteenth century as an era of ferment for the esoteric tradition, in that old, established ideas were vastly enriched by new insights and discoveries, many of which derived from an idealized Orient.[2]

Though spiritualism never entirely vanished after its slump in the 1880s, it was increasingly modified and even supplanted by Asian mystical traditions, Hindu and Buddhist, which were transmitted through both Theosophy and New Thought. The importation of Hindu influences owed much to the Transcendentalists. While at Walden Pond in the mid-1840s, Thoreau recorded how he would "bathe my intellect in the stupendous and cosmogonal philosophy of the *Bhagvat-Geeta* [sic], since whose composition years of the gods have elapsed, and in comparison with which our modern world and its literature seem puny and trivial." Emerson was influenced by the Upanishads, and in 1883, Emerson's widow hosted a lecture by a visiting Hindu teacher. In 1879, American critics reacted enthusiastically to Sir Edwin Arnold's *The Light of Asia*, which retold the story of the Buddha in the form of an English epic poem; in 1885, Arnold published his translation of the *Bhagavad Gita*.[3]

Asian influences got a boost from the World Parliament of Religions held in Chicago in 1893, which introduced many Americans to Hindu and Buddhist belief. Among other things, this event marked the American debut of Zen Buddhism. Indian traditions found a charismatic and attractive face in the holy man Vivekananda, "the first heathen we had seen face to face." He was lionized, becoming the subject of a Broadway play, and in 1895, he led the first yoga class ever held on American soil. Within a few years, American Vedanta societies had been established, with members drawn from New Thought, Theosophical, and Unitarian congregations.[4] In 1900, the New Thought national convention heard a lecture by Swami Abhedananda, who was, like Vivekananda, a pupil of the great Hindu reformer, Ramakrishna. Showing just how fashionable swamis had become, Abhedananda was introduced to President McKinley. Vivekananda's example created an enduring vogue for real or supposed Indian swamis.[5]

Vivekananda popularized ideas already introduced by the Theosophists in the 1870s: his beloved *Gita* preached reincarnation and taught how successive ages were enlightened by the avatars, or wise masters, who were manifestations of divine beings. This had an obvious resonance for Theosophists who venerated the Ascended Masters, great spiritual teachers who shared their wisdom with selected human pupils. The Ascended Master idea also owed much to the Buddhist belief in the *bodhisattva*, a perfect being of vast compassion, who had earned the right to slip into the bliss of nirvana, but rather chose to remain accessible to the world until all sentient beings had achieved salvation.

## The Victorian Heritage

But Theosophy was more than a simple adaptation of the religions of South Asia; it combined these inextricably with Western esoteric traditions. The concept of the Ascended Master was drawn from the novels of Bulwer Lytton, which were enormously influential in the English-speaking world as well as Europe. Though Lytton is today remembered for what is commonly regarded as the worst opening line of any novel ever written ("It was a dark and stormy night . . ."), for contemporaries, his work excited interest as the manifesto of a learned occultist.

Lytton's best-known works include *Zanoni* (1842), about a potentially immortal alchemist and adept during the French Revolution. The character of the magus is based on the historical Count of Saint-Germain, a figure at the eighteenth-century French court. Saint-Germain attracted many stories suggesting that he was at least centuries old and had gained access to the mystic knowledge of the East. He had supposedly passed on his knowledge to various successors, including Franz Mesmer. Not surprisingly, Saint-Germain featured among Blavatsky's Great White Lodge of Masters, and he became a hero for later occult theorists. Lytton again created a sensation with his 1871 novel, *The Coming Race*. This featured a secret underground race of superbeings possessing the overwhelming psychic powers known as *Vril*, an idea that owes much to Mesmerism: Lytton's book warned that some day, unless human beings developed their own *Vril* capacity, this hidden race would emerge and conquer the planet. Despite their origins in fiction, characters like Zanoni and concepts like *Vril* exercised a powerful spell on the esoteric subculture on both sides of the Atlantic.[6]

Another potent idea of these years concerned the promise of ancient wisdom, a treasure long associated with ancient Egypt. Charles Piazzi Smyth's 1864 tract, *Our Inheritance in the Great Pyramid*, inspired a whole pseudoscience of pyramidology.[7] According to taste, the lessons of the Great Pyramid could confirm the truth of the Bible, the Jewish Qabala, or the teachings of ancient mystery schools. Meanwhile, the modern mythology of Egyptian mummy's curses and haunted pyramids dates from a story published by Louisa May Alcott in 1869, and the theme was developed by novelists Bram Stoker and H. Rider Haggard. Egyptian fads reached new heights following the sensational discovery of the tomb of Pharaoh Tutankhamun in 1922, which among other things ignited a national vogue for Egyptian themes in design and graphics.

The timescale for ancient wisdom was pushed into the remote human past when in 1882 Ignatius Donnelly published *Atlantis: The Antediluvian World*, which argued that the lost continent described by Plato had been an advanced civilization of huge accomplishments. Donnelly's ideas were taken up enthusiastically by Theosophists and others, who claimed that the remnants of Atlantean wisdom could be traced in various parts of the world, including Egypt and Tibet: once again, we see how Western and Asian mystery traditions were integrated in the new synthesis. Theosophists offered a detailed history of Atlantis over hundreds of thousands of years, describing how it was destroyed after its rulers turned to black magic and claiming that its fall was the historical basis of most mythologies worldwide. The Hebrew myth of the Fall, for instance, reflected human memories of this lost golden age. For the lay audience, the Atlantis idea gained plausibility from the well-publicized success of mainstream archaeologists throughout the nineteenth century in uncovering the remains of lost civilizations like Assyria and in translating the scripts of long-dead languages. If the myth of Troy could be validated by contemporary science, why should not that of Atlantis?[8]

Like Theosophy and pyramidology, the Atlantis myth implied that great spiritual wisdom was to be found in alien cultures and that these secrets had been passed on through the traditions of occult movements or secret societies, perhaps in coded form. It was in the late Victorian era that tarot cards came to be seen as a veiled textbook of initiatory practices, something far more valuable than a mere fortune-telling device. The 22 greater trumps, or major arcana, were prized as a richly symbolic series of guideposts on the path of the adept. Though opinions differed about its origin, the tarot was said to epitomize the mysteries of ancient Egypt.[9]

Also in the 1880s, the tradition of ritual magic was revived in London by a group of Masonic adepts, who formed the Order of the Golden Dawn, which would prove an incalculable influence on the whole subsequent history of occultism. The Golden Dawn drew on Hermetic, Masonic, and alchemical currents and used the tarot as a form of spiritual instruction. The London society also explored the legends of the Holy Grail, seeing in the medieval Arthurian legends yet another coded account of occult initiation, with the Grail as the ultimate spiritual perfection. Like many groups before and since, the society venerated the seventeenth-century texts of the rosicrucians, the Brothers of the Rose Cross, an imaginary order said to have preserved the mystical secrets of the ancient world. The rosicrucians were "revealed" to the world in a fictional text published in 1614, and over the next three centuries, many were inspired by the dream that the sect's mysteries and powers might be achieved in the real world. Golden Dawn members like A. E. Waite, Aleister Crowley, and S. L. MacGregor Mathers translated and published many works previously unavailable except to specialists with access to the best libraries in London and Paris. These included medieval textbooks of ritual magic, as well as Qabalistic texts and the works of nineteenth-century scholars like Eliphas Lévi, Lytton's pupil. The texts and commentaries of individual society members like Crowley and Dion Fortune retain a substantial following today. Together with the Theosophists, the Golden Dawn gave the would-be adepts of the new century the vocabulary and the intellectual tools they needed to construct an alternative mystical universe. Appropriately, it was in the early 1880s that the words "occultism" and "occultist" acquired their present-day meaning.[10]

## The Esoteric Vision

By the 1890s, occult, mystical, and esoteric schools were flourishing, and it is useful here to summarize the spectrum of beliefs that were now taken up by American enthusiasts. Most of the developing movements drew indiscriminately on the various available traditions, making it difficult for us to distinguish clearly between different ideologies or schools of thought. Though we are dealing with many distinct and even contradictory strands of thought, some core themes can be identified. These common factors can help us understand just why some of the new groups developed the cultlike tendencies that they did and why esoteric circles occasionally provided rich pickings for confidence tricksters.

The word "occult" means simply "hidden," implying that the subject deals with truths not accessible to the masses, but only to selected followers with the will and the determination to investigate such matters. Occultism refers both to a body of knowledge and assumptions and to the secret or mysterious means by which this information must be conveyed: ideally, such truths are acquired through private teaching and initiation, through a school or teacher claiming special access to a higher reality. This instruction was arduous, taking the pupil gradually through successive stages of initiation (the Golden Dawn model had ten grades, ascending from the basic Neophyte to the godlike Ipsissimus). As American occultist Manly P. Hall wrote in 1926, "Realizing that nothing is more dangerous than the indiscriminate circulation of occult secrets, the Mysteries established their Schools for the purpose of concealing rather than revealing the knowledge."[11] The ideas discussed were not intended for public circulation—though, of course, some entrepreneurs did seek a mass market. This emphasis on secret transmission justified the existence of the many small circles and study groups, as well as their authoritarian structures: the guru, magus, or hierophant was indispensable to the belief-system.

Generally, the esoteric schools offered a profound statement about the nature of the universe, which they believed was a far more complex structure than that proposed by conventional Christian or Jewish belief. Though there might not be a personal God, there was an ultimate reality. Supernatural realities were inscribed in Nature, so that everything was a symbol or reflection of the divine, to be observed and decoded by the informed mind: the world below, the microcosm, reflected the larger universe, the macrocosm. Mystic truths could therefore be studied through the occult properties of numbers and geometric forms, of birds, plants, and animals, while Manly Hall expressed the common view that "the oldest, the most profound, the most universal of all symbols is the human body." These ideas were influenced by Qabalistic texts like the *Sefer Yezirah*, which explored the mystical connotations of the Hebrew letters, each of which was connected with particular planets, constellations, elements, parts of the body, and days or months. The belief in symbolic correspondences found its most popular expression in astrology.[12]

The occult vision was hierarchical in nature, reflecting the influence of Qabalistic and Neoplatonic thought as well as Hinduism. The universe contained countless beings at different levels of spiritual development, including what past cultures have called gods, demons, and angels, and these beings or forces could be induced to serve the human adept possessing the appropriate techniques. In 1888, a text on rosicrucianism claimed that members of the group "say that if our spiritual powers of perception were fully developed, we should see the universe peopled with other beings than ourselves, and of whose existence we know nothing at present. They say that we should then see this universe filled with things of life," including the famous elemental spirits of Renaissance magic: nymphs, salamanders, gnomes, undines, and fairies.[13] Far more exalted were the planetary spirits, former human beings who had attained near-divine powers.

Humans were an integral part of this celestial hierarchy. As the spiritualists had supposedly shown, sentient existence did not cease with death, so the soul existed as an eternal spiritual presence. Many went still further in their belief in human survival, as both reincarnation and karma became tenets of most mystical movements. The process of rebirth was part of the soul's evolution towards perfection and union with the Divine, the ultimate goal of all mystical enterprise: in this vision, alchemy was a material symbol for the inner transformation of the baser elements of the individual soul into heavenly fire. The idea that humans could progress towards divinity meshed well with the optimism of New Thought and with the popular evolutionary ideas so prevalent at this time. Most occult authors were fascinated by evolution, seeing it, however, in terms far broader than materialistic Darwinism.

Great mystics or prophets might represent souls in a very advanced state of spiritual progress, who should be regarded as the rightful teachers of humanity, Masters or Secret Chiefs. This idea explains the ambiguous attitude towards established world religions: the Buddha, Jesus, and other leaders were seen as highly evolved souls who offered authentic wisdom, however much their words had been twisted by their followers. Many Western occultists saw their own belief-system as a return to an authentic Christianity, which preached a message that was identical to Buddhism, as well as to Mesmerism, alchemy, and rosicrucianism. Whereas conventional Christians saw only the external truths, esoteric believers heard the real Jesus. To quote Manly Hall again, "So wisdom drapes her truth with symbolism, and covers her insight with allegory. Creeds, rituals, poems are parables and symbols. The ignorant take them literally and build for themselves prison-houses of words. ... Through the shadow shines ever the Perfect Light."[14]

In addition to the overall belief-system, believers were offered a vision of a vastly expanded human potential. Then as now, one of these fundamental truths was that human beings contained within themselves immense forces presently unknown to science and that these powers could be mobilized by an individual with the proper insight, training, and initiation. Though some of the methods advocated to this end were purely magical (such as the recitation of spells or names of power), much occult training consisted of attempts to master one's own body and mind through breath control, the regulation of sexual desire, and the development of skills like meditation and visualization. This shared many points of contact with the New Thought belief in the power of the will to control the ailments of mind and body, though occultists went still further, suggesting that a trained adept would be able to exercise skills such as precognition, psychokinesis, telepathy, miraculous healing, astral travel, and other traditional magic arts.

That such powers could be unleashed seemed confirmed by accounts of Saint-Germain or Lytton's Zanoni, and the spiritual masters whom many sects claimed as founders. In 1888, the legendary rosicrucians were described as "a secret society of men possessing superhuman—if not supernatural—powers; they were said to be able to prophesy future events, to penetrate into the deepest mysteries of nature, to transform iron, copper, lead or mercury into gold, to prepare an Elixir of Life or Universal Panacea by the use of which they could preserve their youth and manhood, and moreover it was believed that they could command the elemental spirits of nature, and knew the secrets of the Philosopher's Stone, a substance which rendered him who possessed it all-powerful, immortal and supremely wise."[15] Whether these forces were more accurately categorized as scientific or supernatural was of little interest to practitioners, though many Victorian and early twentieth-century occultists saw themselves as in the vanguard of scientific research: as Arthur C. Clarke remarked, famously, any sufficiently advanced technology is indistinguishable from magic. The obsession with the superbeing helps account for the messianic and autocratic tendency among some occult groups, which were all too willing to acclaim particular individuals as incarnate masters who would usher in a glorious new age.

It was further believed that this esoteric worldview, with the associated powers, had been well-known to past civilizations, which had bequeathed their immense knowledge in the form of legends, secret rituals, or mystery schools. Much of the writing on the occult therefore explores matters of archaeology, ancient history, mythology, and comparative religion, and authors were eclectic in using the materials they found, whether these derived from Babylonia or medieval France, from Aztec Mexico or Egypt, from Druids or Brahmins. Theorists also drew freely from historical groups who were believed to have possessed ancient secrets, especially the Freemasons, and more shadowy entities like the rosicrucians and Knights Templar. The goal of the adept was to find the one universal spiritual truth, which different societies perceived under various cultural forms. Western seekers for truth now had access to a bewildering range of traditions and beliefs through which they could search for the scattered traces of the lost wisdom.

### The American Esoteric Boom, 1910–1935

In the early twentieth century, these various strands of thought became acclimatized in the United States and were popularized through a number of evanescent churches, secret societies, and mystical orders. The main activists came from the generation born between 1874 and 1886. They entered early adulthood around the turn of the century, sharing the general excitement of these years about occultism, New Thought, and Asian religion (see Table 4.1). These leaders were still young enough to found and lead their own movements in the 1920s. This was the generation of rosicrucian revivalists R. S. Clymer and H. Spencer Lewis, I AM leaders Guy and Edna Ballard, Psychiana founder Frank B. Robinson, occult writers Lewis Spence and Paul Foster Case, and Silver Shirt chief William Dudley Pelley. Other contemporaries included Aleister Crowley, the magician; Edgar Cayce, the prophet; Ed-

Table 4.1
Birthdates of Major Religious and
Mystical Figures, 1874–1890

| | |
|---|---|
| Lewis Spence | 1874 |
| Harry Houdini | 1874 |
| Charles Fort | 1874 |
| Aleister Crowley | 1875 |
| Edgar Cayce | 1876 |
| R. Swinburne Clymer | 1878 |
| Frank Buchman | 1878 |
| Guy Ballard | 1878 |
| Edward A. Wilson | 1878 |
| George Baker (Father Divine) | 1878* |
| Alice Bailey | 1880 |
| H. Spencer Lewis | 1883 |
| Paul Foster Case | 1884 |
| William Dudley Pelley | 1885* |
| Frank B. Robinson | 1886 |
| Noble Drew Ali | 1886 |
| Edna Wheeler Ballard | 1886 |
| William Seabrook | 1887 |
| Aimee Semple McPherson | 1890 |
| H. P. Lovecraft | 1890 |

*In some cases, like Father Divine and William Dudley Pelley, precise dates of birth are controversial.

ward Wilson, the new messiah; and African-American mystagogues like Father Divine and Noble Drew Ali.

Though the new groups were building on older traditions, some developments of the early twentieth century helped stimulate growth. One factor was the First World War; the passionate hopes and fears aroused by the conflict were expressed in countless tales of visions, prophecies, and miracles on a scale not witnessed since the Thirty Years War.[16] The war revived spiritualism, as newly bereaved families sought contact with their dead: unlike the Vietnam era, families could not take refuge in the comforting myth that lost soldiers were somehow alive, either imprisoned or missing in action. Between 1906 and 1916, membership in spiritualist churches had fallen from 35,000 to 23,000, but the 1926 figure rebounded to over 50,000, and these figures represent only formal membership in organized churches, not unaffiliated believers.[17]

Postwar social developments enhanced the vogue for esoteric movements. The 1920s marked the height of popularity of secret societies like the Freemasons. Though American Masons did not necessarily have any psychic or occult interests, Masonic ideas and rituals provided a widely available fund of commonplaces from which other groups could draw. Moreover, any serious investigation of the Masonic tradition would soon lead the curious to the extensive and often-reprinted works of Albert Pike from the 1870s, with his esoteric and Gnostic interpretations of Freemasonry. It might also bring the seeker to Hargrave Jennings's book *The Rosicrucians*, and thence to the corpus of literature that had originally inspired the Theosophists. Freemasonry opened an enticing doorway to the wider occult world.[18]

Masonic precedents also assisted the growth of other traditions, such as the Ku Klux Klan, whose resurgence became a national phenomenon between 1921 and 1926. In order to appeal to Masons and other fraternal organizations, the Klan adopted a rich mythology and heraldry, with all the mystique implied by its hierarchy of "Hydras, Great Titans, Furies, Giants, Exalted Cyclops, Terrors," its distinctive secret language, and an elaborate system of signs and countersigns. The Klan briefly had five to eight million members nationwide, and it became a hugely profitable operation through its sales of memberships, robes, and regalia. The early 1920s were, in addition a golden age for American conspiracy theory, with the publication of the *Protocols of the Elders of Zion* and Henry Ford's revelations about the plotting of *The International Jew*. Others speculated about the plots of secret societies like the Bavarian Illuminati over the centuries. According to taste, either Zionists or Illuminati could be blamed for the recent Bolshevik Revolution.[19] If true, such charges showed that history was indeed a plaything of covert secret societies, of Secret Masters of Good or Evil, just as Theosophists claimed.

Another social development of these years was the changing role and improving status of women. The suffragette years before 1920 show many parallels to the organized feminist movement that emerged during the late 1960s. In both eras, women enjoyed a higher degree of economic independence and a new social and political power, which was symbolized by important legal victories. For the generation of the 1920s, this meant the suffrage and prohibition; in the 1970s, it would involve sharply increased public awareness of issues of sexual violence. Both decades were also marked by the surging popularity of women-oriented religious ideas and sects, in the early part of the century, the groups founded by leaders like Madame Blavatsky, Aimee Semple McPherson, Myrtle Fillmore, Ellen White, and Mary Baker Eddy.

## Theosophists and Rosicrucians

The mystical ideas formulated in earlier decades spread rapidly in the early twentieth century. Theosophy, which possessed a widespread network of lodges in North America, deserves much of the credit for popularizing yoga and associated Hindu ideas, as well as terms like "karma," "mahatma," "guru," and "chela." The Theosophical tradition also disseminated ideas like the Ascended Masters and reincarnation, which diffused throughout the California sects of the next half century. In 1898, the American Theosophical Society fell apart amidst vicious internal squabbles, but several new groups sprouted from the wreckage. Some of these factions were short-lived but others thrived, such as Rudolf Steiner's Anthroposophy.

One American strand of Theosophy was dominated by Katherine Tingley, who in 1899 established her headquarters at Point Loma, her "White City in a Land of Gold beside a Sunset Sea." This became a Xanadu dreamworld, in which forty buildings represented a spectrum of architectural styles, with "Muslim domes, Hindu temples, Egyptian gates, and Greek theaters." Point Loma gave Tingley a base for her educational and archaeological projects, which included a theosophical university and a raja yoga college. At its height, the colony supported three hundred residents under the autocratic rule of the Purple Mother, and some 2,500 children were educated there between 1897 and 1942. The community became an established part of the southern California social landscape, and it survived for several years after Tingley's death in 1935.[20]

The experiment had enduring results. Carey McWilliams suggested that "[i]t was through Point Loma that the yogi influence reached Southern California. . . . After Mrs. Tingley's appearance in Southern California, the region acquired a reputation as an occult land and Theosophists began to converge upon it from the four corners of the earth." The location fitted well with the Theosophical worldview, in which a series of great races are said to have dominated the planet at various times since the primeval Lemurians and Atlanteans. Soon, a sixth race was expected to arise and replace the European Aryans; some writers prophesied that this new group would appear in the Pacific regions of the United States. By the 1920s, other Theosophical visitors to California included Annie Besant, a bitter rival of Tingley, and Krishnamurti, whom Mrs. Besant proclaimed to be a messianic figure. Krishnamurti was presented as the long-sought world teacher, successor to Christ and the Buddha. He was lionized on several American visits in the late 1920s, until in 1929 he repudiated both Besant and the messianic claims: later, he would warn listeners against all would-be messiahs and prophets. Another Theosophical immigrant was Alice Bailey, a prolific British writer on all manner of occult topics, who claimed to be channeling a spirit known as "The Tibetan." Bailey later relocated to New York, where her Arcane School (founded in 1923) dispensed correspondence courses in mysticism.[21]

Besides Theosophy, the main vehicle for esoteric theories was rosicrucianism, which had an authentic American history beginning from the time of the seventeenth century German settlers in Pennsylvania. A new group, the Rosicrucian Fraternity, emerged on American soil in the 1860s through the many-sided work of the remarkable pioneer Paschal B. Randolph, who was originally a spiritualist medium. After extensive travels in Europe, Randolph developed a complex occult system that incorporated sexual magic and used hashish to alter consciousness. Randolph made direct contact with European mystical societies, so that the new American rosicrucianism was linked to the ancient roots of occultism: these impressive activities predated the work of both Blavatsky and the Golden Dawn.[22]

Despite these older connections, the modern rosicrucian movement is largely an artificial creation, with its origins in academic histories of the occult. In 1902, R. Swinburne Clymer of Quakertown, Pennsylvania, published his history of the rosicrucian movement. Shortly afterwards, he founded his own Rosicrucian Fraternity, complete with a hierarchy of Masonic-sounding titles: below the Imperialistic Council and Venerable Order of the Magi were the degrees of the Priests of Melchizedek, and the Knights of Chivalry and Order of the Holy Grail. A new wave of interest followed in 1914 during the tercentenary of the original rosicrucian manifesto. In 1915, H. Spencer Lewis founded the Ancient and Mystical Order Rosae Crucis (AMORC), which borrowed extensively from both Theosophy and the Golden Dawn. Originally based in New York, he soon joined the general westward migration of the esoteric sects: in 1918 he relocated to San Francisco, and in 1927 he created a world headquarters for his movement in San Jose. Also in California, in 1915 Max Heindel formed his own Rosicrucian

Fellowship in Oceanside.[23] Heindel had also been a Theosophical lecturer and was influenced by Annie Besant and Rudolf Steiner.

## Prophets of the New Age

The enormous output of the occult publishing industry between about 1910 and 1940 shows how firmly American esoteric thought was rooted in late Victorian speculations about Atlantis, the Great Pyramid, and the rosicrucians. Both Lewis and Heindel were prolific authors in their own right, and their organizations published numerous tracts over the next three or four decades. Heindel's *Rosicrucian Christianity* included the sections "Astronomical Allegories of the Bible," "The Mystery of the Holy Grail," "The Coming Force, *Vril* or What?" and "The Angels as Factors in Evolution."[24] Other writers were equally active. During the 1920s, Evangeline Adams of Boston became "America's first astrological superstar." Paul Foster Case published on rosicrucianism and the tarot, among other subjects, and in 1920 he founded his mystical order, the Builders of the Adytum. Some authors made their living by popularizing the mysteries of the East. Between 1924 and 1935, Baird T. Spalding published his five-volume account of the *Life and Teachings of the Masters of the Far East*, and Paul Brunton made a literary career from romantic books like *A Search in Secret India* (1934) or *A Search in Secret Egypt* (1936).[25] Occult ideas were also disseminated by novels: in 1933, James Hilton's *Lost Horizon* created a Himalayan dreamworld populated by immortal mystics, in a vision derived ultimately from Blavatsky.

Though esoteric ideas were often presented by specialized presses and offbeat magazines, they also made their impact upon the mainstream. In the scholarly text *From Ritual to Romance* (1920), Jessie L. Weston traced the medieval Holy Grail myth back to ancient fertility rites. According to Weston, these primeval customs were preserved through secret initiatory groups, who among other things used the tarot, which was precisely the historical view held by occult groups like the Golden Dawn and the rosicrucians: Weston drew her information about the tarot from Golden Dawn members A. E. Waite and W. B. Yeats. Weston's theories and the associated tarot imagery were popularized in T. S. Eliot's *The Waste Land*, perhaps the best-known English poem of the twentieth century.[26]

Meanwhile, tales of lost continents not only flourished, they proliferated. Throughout the twentieth century, believers would claim access to a whole alternate history and archaeology of the human civilization, venturing many thousands of years before the meager period marked out by staid academics. The ancient civilization of Atlantis was soon joined by the lost land of Lemuria, said to lie under the Indian Ocean and to have left traces throughout the Pacific world, making it of great interest to West Coast occultists. Historical accounts of this lost society were mainly derived from mediumship and channeling. The most-cited source for the Lemurian idea was Rudolf Steiner's *The Submerged Continents of Atlantis and Lemuria,* which was translated from the German into English in 1911. By the 1920s, James Churchward was claiming to have discovered secret records from yet another sunken continent, that of Mu, the "Motherland of Man," which had left its remnants in Polynesia. In his view, "[t]he Garden of Eden was not in Asia, but in a now sunken continent in the Pacific Ocean," and memories of Mu were found scattered across the world, in Mayan, Indian and Egyptian records, on Easter Island, and in the rituals of Freemasonry. Churchward claimed that Mu had foreshadowed and even excelled all modern science, "We are probably now treading the same road which our forefathers trod over 100,000 years ago." Contemporary groups hoped to gain access to these ancient secrets: in 1936, a Lemurian Fellowship was founded in Wisconsin; it relocated to Los Angeles in 1942.[27]

The breadth of esoteric interests and concerns at this time is exemplified by the work of Manly Hall, the hypnotist who in 1936 founded the Philosophical Research Society in Los Angeles, a long-lasting occult study group. In 1928, he published his *Encyclopedic Outline of Masonic, Hermetic, Qabalistic and Rosicrucian Symbolical Philosophy*: the frontispiece was, not surprisingly, a portrait of the Count of Saint-Germain. The book proceeded through subjects as diverse as the ancient mystery schools, Mithraism, Gnosticism, the works of Hermes Trismegistus, the continent of Atlantis, the significance of the Great Pyramid, and Pythagoras's work on mathematics, color, and music. The *Outline* goes on to explain the occult significance of stars and stones, fish and birds, trees and plants; the meaning of the zodiac; and the insights of Qabalism, rosicrucianism, and esoteric Christianity.[28]

These varied themes were synthesized in many works of popularization, which tried to make contemporary speculations available to a mass audience. Among the most enduring were the writings of F. Homer Curtiss and Harriette Augusta Curtiss. Homer Curtiss began the series in 1909 with his *Letters from the Teacher,* a book that purported to be channeled, or more precisely, "Transmitted by Rahmea, Priestess of the Flame." This proclaimed the formation of a new mystic order, the Order of the Fifteen, later the Order of Christian Mystics, "a great Cosmic Order which has always existed and through which all souls who have reached Mastery have passed on some plane, at a certain stage of their evolution." The order claimed to have been founded in Egypt in 4700 B.C. with its mystic symbol a sphinx, "and today, as this great Aquarian age begins its cycle, those souls must once more gather together their reincarnated students and followers that that which was symbolized in stone may be manifested in the world today."[29] In 1912, the couple published *The Voice of Isis*, beginning a joint publishing career that stretched into the 1930s.

The Curtiss books were highly eclectic, dabbling in "Masonic symbols, the Trinity, the Elohim, angels, mythology, evolution, cycles, initiations, etc." The books claimed to offer "the philosophy of Christian psychology and mysticism in plain, comprehensible terms and applied to the daily life. Not mere theory and metaphysical speculation, but a definite and comprehensible philosophy of life and Soul-growth. . . . which includes a rational explanation of all forms of mysticism and Biblical Occultism, as well as the vital and complex problems of modern life and all after-death conditions." The emphasis on a distinctively Christian and biblical esoteric tradition was characteristic of the age, as was the assertion of a plurality of divine teachers: Jesus was "[a] great Avatar, the Son of God. All such come into the world at stated times and give to the World their blessing and their teachings." The goal of occult inquiry was to arouse the Christ-Consciousness in each individual.[30] *Realms of the Living Dead* recalled the spiritualist tradition, with its mythology of spirit guides, earthbound spirits, astral helpers, and elemental spirits. *Coming World Changes* examined "the philosophy of planetary changes such as sank Atlantis," and explored prophecies concerning "[t]he king of the world and the predicted Asiatic invasion of Europe." In *The Key to the Universe* and *The Key of Destiny*, the Curtisses explained themes like reincarnation and alchemical transmutation.

We can take *The Key of Destiny* as typical of the allusive methodology and broad scope that characterized the writing of the Curtisses, as well as Manly P. Hall and the Curtisses' many New Age colleagues: it also indicates the remarkably self-contained world of occult thought, with its own distinctive logic. The book presents a system of number mysticism that draws on correspondences between numbers, Hebrew letters, zodiac signs, and the greater trumps of the tarot deck, and they cite such diverse sources as the apocryphal *Book of Enoch* and Lytton's *Zanoni*. For example, some fifty pages are devoted to discussing the significance of the number fifteen "a very powerful number and one that is very little understood."[31] Their investigation drew on Qabalistic methods, noting that the number fifteen corresponds to the Hebrew letter *Samekh*, which in turn is connected to the zodiacal sign Sagittarius, and the greater trump known as The Devil. After a lengthy meditation, the Curtisses conclude that the number has a profound message for the believer, that "the pure Christ-light is beginning to shine within him like the Sun rising on a new day." All that from just the number fifteen.

## The Aquarian Age

The upsurge of occult speculation was well fitted to the Aquarian Age, a phrase used much in the early twentieth century, and one that would become very familiar in the 1960s. The term requires explanation. During different historical eras, the sun is located in different houses of the zodiac, each of which is believed by astrologers to determine the character of those centuries under its influence. When the dominant sign was Taurus, around 1500 B.C., this constellation controlled the ancient era of bull cults and bull sacrifice. Near the birth of Jesus, the sun entered the sign of Pisces, and the next two thousand years were dominated by the religion of Christianity, whose earliest symbol was a fish. During the twentieth century, the sun would enter a new house, that of Aquarius, and according to occult belief this event would be marked by a profound new spirituality, a time of mystical enlightenment and enhanced intuition, possibly symbolized by the appearance of a new messianic figure—hence the stir over Krishnamurti. Aquarian terminology was popularized by Levi H. Dowling's book *The Aquarian Gospel of Jesus the Christ*, an esoteric account of Jesus' life. The book first appeared in 1907, and its numerous reprintings indicate its continued popularity in the Theosophical and mystical subculture up to the present day. In 1918, an Aquarian Ministry, practicing New Thought principles, was founded at Santa Barbara. In 1921, the Curtisses proclaimed *The Message of Aquaria*.

The Aquarian era would also be a New Age. This phrase appeared in the 1880s, when John Ballou Newbrough claimed to channel a text published as *OAHSPE: A New Age Bible*, and the usage spread with the dawn of the twentieth century: this was also the era of the new woman, the new state, and of New Thought itself.[32] Aleister Crowley dated his New Aeon from the channeling of his new scripture the "Book of the Law" in 1904. Writers of the 1920s and 1930s presented themselves as advocates of a New Age of occult enlightenment, and Alice Bailey did much to popularize the dual terms "New Age" and "Aquarian." In 1935, Paul Foster Case published a study of the Great Seal of the United States, studying "its history, symbolism, and message for the New Age." Southern California-based Corinne Heline wrote on themes like *Color and Music in the New Age* and *The New Age Bible Interpretation*, the latter from her own New Age Press.[33]

### The American Audience

The popularity of occult, Asian, and New Thought ideas laid the foundation for a new wave of fringe religions, attracting a sizable audience of spiritual seekers. As early as 1896, we hear grumbling about a wave of new prophets "sent from some great hierophant of the 'Brotherhood of the Motherhood of the Golden Candelabra' and similar and unknowable Gobi and Himalaya dwellers to start some new sect for the salvation of the world, and pocket from $25 to $100 initiation fee from fools ready to pay it."[34] Such complaints would become commonplace in the new century.

Journalists remarked how ostensibly secular and modern people fell instantly for supernatural claims if they were proclaimed in suitably exotic style. A 1927 account in *The Nation* noted how a normally skeptical young woman was enchanted by the Washington presentation of an orange-robed swami, who talked of "happiness, diseaselessness, material success, scientific law, God, Jesus, and the great cosmic source of energy. There was never once anything concrete, specific, detailed. But it was intimated that such marvels would be revealed to an inner circle with $25 each to enable them to meet for twelve intimate personal contacts with the Swami in the Rose Room of the most expensive hotel in the city." Cult leaders were a migratory species who became scarce in eastern cities during the winter, "for it is then that the swamis and yogis leave their haunts in Gotham and go to Florida or to the Middle West, where they give courses in astrology to devout governors, or prey upon fat ladies in the dimly lighted shrines of opulent hotels."[35]

Most of the resulting movements were transient, but a few found deeper roots, particularly in the West. In the late nineteenth century, Boston had been host to many of the fringe groups, but after 1900, the new religions found their main home in California, in the wake of Katherine Tingley. California's occult sects of the early twentieth century have been described as "the sick survivors of New England transcendentalism," and there are obvious resemblances between the religious ambience of Boston in 1870 and that of Los Angeles in 1920.[36]

Though contemporary comments leave no doubt about the prevalence of New Age ideas in the West, the distinctiveness of California may be exaggerated by the diligent work of libraries and universities in that part of world in preserving books and ephemera with local imprints. In consequence, we overstate the strength of occult ideas in California to the detriment of other western states like Washington and New Mexico, to say nothing of Michigan or Pennsylvania. There was a lot more to the cult boom than merely Los Angeles. As a tract on "mystic cults" warned in 1913, "In Seattle, in San Francisco and in Los Angeles, are temples to Buddha and Krishna . . . Lowell, Massachusetts, is another center for the propagation of obscure faith, and as for Chicago, that place is the breeding-place apparently of all the erratic, erotic, ridiculous and sacrilegious rites under heaven."[37] Nevertheless, much of our available evidence concerns California.

New Thought was vital in transmitting metaphysical ideas and in promoting new sects in the West. The movement began in New England, but it was imported to Los Angeles about 1904, and from about 1915 most of the New Thought leaders established institutions on the Pacific coast. George Wharton James accurately spoke of California as "the natural home of New Thought." To quote Carey McWilliams, "these two imported movements—Theosophy and New Thought—constitute the stuff from which most of the later creeds and cults have been evolved . . . the mystical ingredients came from Point Loma; the practical money-mindedness from the New Thought leaders."[38] For both strands of the emerging tradition, the year 1915 proved a crucial turning point. This marked the twin great expositions in San Francisco and San Diego, which attracted an unparalleled number of visitors to California, with the San Francisco Exposition actively promoting New Thought as the religious vanguard of the new century. These events occurred during a period of amazing population expansion in the far West: Los Angeles grew from 50,000 residents in 1890 to 577,000 by 1920; Seattle's population expanded in the same period from 43,000 to 315,000.

The new sects benefited from the distinctive nature of migration to the West, which advertised itself as a haven of wellness. In California, as in Arizona and New Mexico, many new migrants were sick people constantly in search of miraculous cures, especially from tubercular conditions. Patients cared little whether solutions came from Christian and Pentecostal sects or from occult temples claiming to dispense the wisdom of Lemuria. The West and Southwest had also become the voguish destination for bohemians wishing to establish artistic and cultural colonies, and the eastern discovery of Taos and Santa Fe was at its height in the second decade of the century.[39] On a practical level, California law made it very easy to establish a new religious body. The process was basically open to anyone who could lay their hands on a small filing fee and produce a couple of witnesses. Finally, Californian real estate was very cheap by eastern standards, so that a modest investment could produce an imposing temple or sanctuary with substantial grounds. Religious entrepreneurs found in the West the means, motive, and opportunity to form new sects.

Furthermore, new groups faced little opposition from established churches, which throughout the twentieth century were weaker in the western states than anywhere in the nation. Scholars like Rodney Stark and William S. Bainbridge have shown that the far West has always been a largely unchurched territory, with rates of church attendance, church membership, and orthodox religious belief well below the national average. Conversely, census records from the early part of the century always show far higher western rates of adherence to fringe religious groups. As we have already seen, it is very difficult to assess the impact of cults using data that track individuals who declare themselves to be adherents of a particular movement, because that misses the large floating population who are under the influence of fringe ideas. In the 1926 religious census, only a tiny number of fringe believers identified themselves nationwide: apart from 200,000 Christian Scientists and 50,000 members of spiritualist churches, we find only some 14,000 combined for the Theosophists, Liberal Catholic Church, Divine Science, Vedanta Society, and Bahais. Even in guru-rich Los Angeles, the 1926 census recorded that only 1.7 percent of religious adherents, some 5,500 people, belonged to fringe movements like Christian Science, Theosophy, and spiritualism. Obviously, we are missing a very large number of small temples and esoteric centers, to say nothing of the whole Foursquare Gospel, which was too new to be recorded. Nor are major African American sects like the Moorish Science Temple included.

Still, the available figures are suggestive. Whatever the problems with the data, there is no doubt of the western predominance in fringe belief and practice, as membership rates for the metaphysical groups are generally far higher in the Pacific coast states than elsewhere. Westerners were far more likely to record their official occupation in terms of esoteric practice or mystical healing, what Stark and Bainbridge call "client cult occupations," like naturopaths, homeopaths, faith healers, and chiropractors. In 1930, the number of such "healers" per hundred thousand employed persons was by far the highest in the West, in the states of New Mexico (123), California (116), Arizona (102), Oregon (89), and Washington (74). By the same measure, chiropractors were most numerous in California and Colorado.[40] In Canada likewise, the western province of British Columbia has always shown the weakest adherence to established churches, and the greatest appetite for fringe movements.

### California Cults

Even before the jazz age was under way, southern California was legendary both for cults and for the occult. In 1913, an observer remarked on Los Angeles's tendency to quackery, to "faddists and mountebanks—Spiritualists, mediums, astrologists, phrenologists, palmists, and all other breeds of esoteric windjammers . . . whole buildings are devoted to occult and outlandish orders—Mazdaznan clubs, yogi sects, homes of truth, cults of cosmic fluidists, astral planers, Emmanuel movers, rosicrucians and other boozy transcendentalists." (The Zoroastrian-derived Mazdaznan movement combined veneration for the sun with breathing exercises and diet reforms and was said to count fourteen thousand American followers by 1913.)[41] When in 1926, H. L. Mencken tried to explain the popularity of Aimee Semple McPherson, he suggested dismissively that "there were more morons collected in Los Angeles than in any other place on earth. . . . The osteopaths, chiropractors and other such quacks had long marked and occupied it. It swarmed with swamis, spiritualists, Christian Scientists, crystal-gazers, and the allied necromancers."[42]

Some of the new movements contributed to the cultural and economic development of the growing city of Los Angeles: in a sense, Hollywood is built on occult foundations. One pioneer was the Krotona

Theosophical settlement founded in Hollywood by Albert P. Warring-
ton in 1911 and named for the ancient mystical school of Pythagoras.
An autobiographical novel set in these years recalls "the hills of Krotona where the temple was, and the lotus pond and the vegetarian
cafeteria. There were several smaller tabernacles as well, a metaphysical
library, a Greek theater where *The Light of Asia* was being played, and
numerous dwellings cut into the hillside above and below the winding
road . . . Krotona was one of the most beautiful spots on the planet and
a highly magnetized spiritual center as well." "Courses were given in
Esperanto, the Esoteric interpretations of music and drama, and the
human Aura."[43] In 1920, Krotona relocated to the Ojai valley, between
Los Angeles and Santa Barbara, in an area that had become famous as
an international occult center, but Hollywood retained its esoteric slant.
When Aleister Crowley visited Los Angeles in 1918, he was appalled
at the clamor he encountered from occult amateurs, the "cinema crowd
of cocaine-crazed, sexual lunatics, and the swarming maggots of near-
occultists." Crowley's popularity in decadent circles received odd confirmation shortly afterwards. During the investigation of the 1922 murder of director William Desmond Taylor, perhaps the biggest scandal
to hit Hollywood during the silent era, a love letter providing key
evidence in the case was found in Taylor's copy of Crowley's scandalous book *White Stains*.[44]

The fringe religions varied in seriousness, and some spectators apparently attended chiefly for spectacle and entertainment value, but
even the most dubious events demonstrate how domesticated the occult
elements had become. We have the following recollection of a service
held in San Francisco about 1920: "We went to a fake ——— church,
and there was a lot of chicanery. The priest and priestess sitting in two
gold chairs with the twelve vestal virgins as the choir. Behind them
was a great illuminated cross with flashing lights. During the service,
the very lightly-clad vestal virgins threw flowers among the audience.
It was a scream. Afterwards came the Love Feast. A virgin held a basket
of bread and the audience were asked to join the holy order, which was
non-sectarian. Another virgin held a loving cup of wine. Talk of hyp-
nosis, would you believe it, over one hundred and fifty people went
forward and partook of that sacrilegious feast."[45] The incident was recorded not because it was considered at all unusual in the area at this
time, but because of its possible later consequences: among the con-
gregants were Guy and Edna Ballard, later founders of the I AM sect,
who would borrow from these services in their own rituals.

New sects grew rapidly. By 1930, there were said to be three or four hundred cults in southern California, appealing to a total audience of a hundred thousand or so.[46] When Carey McWilliams surveyed the small sects of southern California in 1946, he listed among others the Agabeg Occult Church, the Ancient Mystical Order of Melchizidek, and the Great White Brotherhood, while at the Agasha Temple of Wisdom, Richard Zenor channeled an ancient Egyptian priest for the benefit of his five hundred followers. In the 1930s, Nathanael West's *Day of the Locust* portrayed the odd undergrowth of Hollywood sects, which preached "a crazy jumble of dietary rules, economics and Biblical threats." Fictional (but plausible) groups listed included "the Tabernacle of the Third Coming, where a woman in male clothing preached the Crusade Against Salt, and the Temple Moderne, under whose glass and chromium roof 'Brain-breathing, the Secret of the Aztecs' was taught."[47]

One particularly successful group was the Self-Realization Fellowship, founded in India in 1921, and representing a fairly orthodox Hinduism. The fellowship established its American operation in the early 1920s under Paramhansa Yogananda, who commanded large audiences during a national speaking tour in 1925. Several thousand enthusiastic hearers turned out to hear him in Los Angeles, and this city became the group's American base. The fellowship prospered: by the 1950s, it was credited with ten thousand local followers, although such round numbers are questionable at best and usually reflect a media preference for a large and impressive-sounding statistic. At any rate, the fellowship had enough support to make it an economic powerhouse through the 1950s, with its twenty-acre Golden World Colony, a Lake Shrine with a golden temple, and a golden-domed India Center. Other Hindu movements also flourished in the West: by 1930, the Ramakrishna movement operated ten Vedanta Centers in the United States, of which four were based in Southern California, in addition to one each in San Francisco and in Portland, Oregon.[48]

One of the oddest Californian movements in an odd era was the Perfect Christian Divine Way, which was founded as a commune by William E. Riker in San Francisco in 1916. Riker's beliefs were an amazing mish-mash of doctrines, all geared to establish the World's Perfect Government and to secure the racial superiority of whites and Jews. In 1919, he established Holy City, in the Santa Cruz mountains, where a commune of about thirty members lived sexually segregated lives. They turned over their property to Father Riker, whose own lifestyle was lavish. Holy City became legendary for its garish displays, which included multiple Santa Claus statues, and the site attracted aficionados of eccentricity until its destruction by fire in 1959.[49]

Stories about California's religious oddness became almost a genre in their own right. Through the 1950s, most travel writers describing Los Angeles in particular felt the need to explain its reputation for crackpots, for "swamis, svengalis, and just plain oddballs." Already in 1938, *Time* described the state as a "hothouse of cockeyed sectarianism." Walter Duranty provided an explanation in terms of the culture shock experienced by the mainly midwestern immigrants: "Iowa comes here and goes crazy." When Upton Sinclair mounted his quixotic California gubernatorial campaign in 1934, even a sympathizer noted the crank elements making up his support: "quack astronomers . . . mind readers, members of the powerful Utopian Society . . . Theosophists from Ojai, rosicrucians from San Jose."[50] In 1947, journalist John Gunther commented, "Pick up any copy of a Los Angeles newspaper and read the religious advertisements. They are unique; this is theology in extremis." Such accounts usually concentrated on the ludicrous aspects of the fringe movements. Hidden between the lines is the fact that the cults often commanded wide followings and represented a well-rooted religious tradition. "Crackpot" is a strictly relative term. Gunther rightly added that "the fabulous economic power of the chief crackpot groups is not always appreciated. The size of their congregations, the amount of real estate they accumulate, the number of contributors on whom they call, can become staggering."[51]

## The Cults Go National

Though in the 1920s the New Age sects were firmly concentrated on the Pacific coast, a few groups would use mass-marketing to project their ideas onto the national stage, bringing the word of mystic revelation to millions. Earlier Californian precedents faded into insignificance beside three national movements that now emerged: the Psychiana movement of Frank B. Robinson the Silver Legion of William Dudley Pelley, and the I AM sect founded by Guy and Edna Ballard.

### Psychiana

The fact that Psychiana was created as a purely commercial operation did not prevent it enjoying phenomenal success, demonstrating the vast hunger of the seekers fascinated by the occult. Its creator, Frank B.

Robinson, was an expatriate British pharmacist whose checkered career included being thrown out of both the Royal Canadian Mounted Police and the U.S. Navy for drunkenness. Taking up residence in Moscow, Idaho, he edited a small newspaper, and in 1928, "a time of great psychic ferment in America," he began placing magazine advertisements declaring that "I TALKED WITH GOD. Yes I did—actually and literally!"[52] Curious readers were invited to subscribe to a correspondence course in spiritual truth. The ideas presented were skeptical of Christianity and other established religions; instead, Robinson's religion venerated the Life-Spirit, which was largely identified with the natural forces then being revealed by scientific explorations of the subatomic world. Psychiana, the New Scientific Religion, taught readers to follow the inner God-Law, in order to find "health, wealth, and happiness," a phrase repeated so often in the lessons as to become a mantra. Prayer consisted of visualizing those things the believer sought, in such a way that they would actually come true. Psychiana obviously drew on New Thought, and it foreshadowed *The Power of Positive Thinking*. In later years, Robinson drew more heavily on Theosophy and described himself as an adept.[53]

Psychiana was a gold mine. The basic twenty-lesson course cost $28 ($8 off for cash), and three advanced courses went for $10, $40, and $100, respectively, with a money-back-if-not-entirely-satisfied guarantee, of the sort not offered by competing religions. The adherent could also buy extra books, emblems, and records. Robinson pursued a clever marketing strategy from his base in Idaho, advertising in magazines whose audiences might be interested in his readily accessible form of popular mysticism: at the height of his business, he was advertising in two hundred publications. As he boasted, the orthodox might dismiss their rivals as lunatics, crackpots, and racketeers, but "we lunatics have more than we can do. I don't print application blanks by the tens of thousands, I print them by the 500,000. I buy envelopes by the five million lot." In the first nine months of 1933, Psychiana took in revenues of over $130,000, with expenses at $80,000, and Robinson lived in luxury.[54] At its height in the Depression, Psychiana reached hundreds of thousands of Americans, perhaps millions. Robinson also boasted highly placed followers, including Idaho's U.S. Senator William Borah, who was able to save him from deportation (Mussolini was also said to admire the movement). However, Psychiana was in decline by the Second World War, with large debts from unpaid bills for correspondence courses, and the movement staggered on for only a few years after Robinson's death in 1948. Predictably, Psychiana's critics presented the "Moscow Jesus" as peddling "lunatic," "crackpot" ideas to the gullible masses.[55]

Robinson could have drawn his commercial approach from any one of a number of contemporary models. He had surely noted how the Ku Klux Klan had persuaded millions of Americans to join a pseudo-mystical order, and in these same years Aimee Semple McPherson was triumphantly developing her Foursquare Gospel mission. Other striking parallels are found in Unity, the first religion to apply modern mass-advertising techniques, and Alice Bailey's booming Arcane School, which at its height employed 130 secretaries to serve the scattered faithful. Psychiana was an attempt to cash in on a separate but equally large potential public. In turn, Psychiana inspired other mail-order esoteric schools, including the Mayan Temple, which flourished from the mid-1930s into the early 1960s. Despite its name, this San Antonio-based group offered a hodgepodge of Qabalism, Buddhism, reincarnation, and esoteric Christianity, and it allowed the home-based student to rise through successive grades of adeptship by means of correspondence courses and examinations. Initiates received the most arcane secrets of "Mayanry" by means of a simple cipher, which was intended to guard against profane inquiry.

### The Silver Shirts

Besides Frank Robinson, another religious leader who communed directly with God about this time was William Dudley Pelley (c. 1885/ 1890–1965). Pelley was a publisher, magazine writer, and minor novelist who by the 1920s had explored most of the available fringe religions, including British Israelitism, Atlantis theories, and pyramidology. He had also lived in Hollywood at the height of its occult boom. In 1928, while in the mountains near Pasadena, he had an alleged near-death experience, during which he was granted visions of the afterlife and the Ascended Masters. He told the world of the truths he had learned during his "seven minutes in eternity," which was also the title of an article he published in the *American Magazine*. As advertised in his many books and tracts, Pelley, like Christ, was a leader of the cosmic forces of Light.[56]

Pelley was typical of the New Age sects in attempting to draw on contemporary scientific and psychological advances. Presenting mystical teachings in pseudoscientific guise was scarcely novel: Mesmerism had claimed to be using a new form of magnetism, while spirit rapping

was presented as a kind of spiritual telegraphy. Twentieth-century occult groups likewise drew on the new scientific findings of their era, at
least as far as they understood them, and this apparent ultramodernity
was part of their appeal. These sects not only accepted the concept of
evolution, they imported it into the spiritual realm. They also adopted
ideas like multiple dimensions, and Psychiana borrowed from subatomic theory. Pelley similarly dressed spiritualism in the language of
science, or at least science fiction. He communicated to his followers
the messages received from his "hyper-dimensional instructor" and the
other Great Souls, which he heard via the Psychic Radio. Others at the
time incorporated words from the newest technology: Upton Sinclair
undertook telepathic experiments via what he called the "mental radio," and Father Divine employed his "spirit wireless."[57]

Unlike Robinson, Pelley was not content merely to found a mail-
order audience cult, and in 1933 he formed a new political-religious
movement, the fascist and anti-Semitic Silver Legion of America, the
Silver Shirts. This was "a great Christian Army fortified by the invi-
olable principles of the Christ."[58] Pelley was the "beloved Chief," a
term that could equally well refer to his role as American Führer, or
as the living Secret Chief, a not-yet-ascended Master: he was aspiring
to be Zanoni as much as Hitler. The Silver Shirts were explicitly modeled on the German Nazi Party, and Pelley claimed that he was inspired
to form his movement on January 30, 1933, the day Hitler became
German chancellor. He may have drawn some of his images from the
popular media, as this day also marked the first broadcast of the radio
western series, *The Lone Ranger*, with its heroic rangers and the recurrent silver themes: Pelley's followers were also called "Silver Rangers," and that was the title of one of his newspapers. Whatever the
origins of the idea, Pelley now focused on the Jews as the source of
most evils and problems in the world, and he offered a solution based
on the formation of a Christian Commonwealth, a Christ-Democracy.
Through the 1930s, the legion continued to circulate its anti-Semitic
views in books like *No More Hunger*, *The World Hoax*, and *The Protocols of the Elders of Zion*. Pelley became the nation's best-known
figure on the paramilitary Far Right, and he inspired Sinclair Lewis's
imaginary American dictator Buzz Windrip in the 1935 novel *It Can't
Happen Here*.

The Silver Shirts boomed in the mid-1930s, and the movement may
have had as many as twenty-five thousand members nationwide at its
height from 1933 to 1934. Support was heavily concentrated in Cali-

fornia, Oregon, and Washington, though other centers of strength were scattered across the Midwest in Chicago, Cleveland, and in the Ohio steel districts. Within California, the group found most adherents in the southern parts of the state, in Los Angeles and San Diego.[59] Though the movement looks like a classic fascist sect, it never lost its strong occult motivation, and some adherents claimed to be less interested in the anti-Semitic rhetoric than in Pelley's mystic revelations. After the movement was suppressed during the war years, adherents abandoned their overt political ambitions and drifted back to their Theosophical roots.

### Mighty I AM

The third of these movements was the most successful in terms of its national impact. In 1930 former medium, hypnotist, and gold prospector Guy Ballard claimed to have had a personal encounter on California's Mount Shasta with none other than the Count of Saint-Germain, the figure who had fascinated Lytton and the original Theosophists. Though now thousands of years old, Saint-Germain lived on as an Ascended Master, who chose Ballard as his earthly vehicle and the channel of the forces of light: Guy and his wife, Edna, now became Accredited Messengers of the Masters. Ballard founded the movement of I AM, which claimed to show adherents how to achieve perfect unity with the higher self, the God within. Publishing under the pseudonym of Godfre Ray King, Ballard promulgated his beliefs in a number of books, including *Unveiled Mysteries* (1934), the title of which recalls Blavatsky's *Isis Unveiled*.[60] In 1932 the movement set up headquarters in Los Angeles, and it used profits from the books to advertise heavily on radio.

Critics attacked I AM for its flagrant exploitation of public gullibility, especially in cult-prone California. In 1938, the *Christian Century* described the new movement under the weary headline "Another One in Los Angeles."[61] One of the deadliest enemies of the group was Gerald Bryan, who produced a series of embarrassing revelations about its origins through the late 1930s. Among other things, Bryan showed that Ballard had plagiarized much of his written material from Theosophical works written over the previous forty years or so, which described meetings with ascended masters in words almost identical to Ballard's, specifically naming the Count of Saint-Germain.[62] Visual portrayals of the Ascended Masters were also borrowed, uncredited, from standard Theosophical works.

Bryan shows once again how commonplace such esoteric ideas had become in popular culture by the 1920s and how easily a whole religious system could be concocted from materials lying readily at hand. He claimed that the Ballards "imbibed a little of Christian Science, read a bit of the Walter Method C. S. [Christian Science], branched over to the Unity School at Kansas City, linked up with the Ancient and Mystical Order Rosae Crucis (AMORC), joined the Order of Christian Mystics [the Curtiss group], studied under Pelley the Silver Shirter, sat at the feet of some of the Swamis, read a little of Theosophy, looked into the magic of Yogi philosophy and Oriental mysticism, [and] interested themselves in Baird T. Spalding and his *Masters of the Far East.*"[63] Ballard also consulted with Frank Robinson, who "just warned him to keep off my [Robinson's] stuff."[64] Pelley had also had his vision of the Masters on a California mountain, and like Pelley, the Ballards drew from the pulps and popular science magazines. I AM claimed access to "great and mighty Ascended Masters speaking audibly over a dazzling LIGHT AND SOUND RAY [*sic*]," which manifested in the Ballard headquarters in Chicago. This could easily have been borrowed from a contemporary science fiction magazine like *Astounding*, if not from a *Flash Gordon* movie serial.[65]

Whatever its origins, I AM developed its own style of meetings and ceremonials, emphasizing the roles of both Jesus and Saint-Germain. To attract the curious, large public meetings were held in elaborately decorated public auditoria, while permanent I AM temples were developed to serve the fully committed initiates, the Hundred Percenters. Five I AM centers appeared in California, two in Florida, others in Philadelphia, Seattle, and Chicago. Members' services were reminiscent of traditional seances. Also recalling spiritualism, the Ballard system involved exorcising the countless psychic entities that threatened the human race, with the believer invoking Saint-Germain or some other higher presence: on one occasion in 1939, some four hundred thousand troublesome entities were removed from greater Philadelphia. As well as raiding the ranks of spiritualism, "they have taken followers from Christian Science, Unity, the various metaphysical cults and even from the older religions; many persons of education and refinement are included in their number."[66]

I AM played to enthusiastic audiences across the nation, with a series of ten-day classes or crusades focusing on particular cities and regions. The movement's claim to have a million followers is doubtful, but there were at least tens of thousands prepared to support a sizable merchandising operation, which included books, records, pins, rings, posters, and portraits of the Masters, including Saint-Germain and Guy Ballard himself. I AM rings sold for $12, photographs of Ballard for $2.50, a chart of the Magic Presence for $12, and $1.25 bought a special binder in which to store the flood of continuing I AM edicts. New Age Cold Cream was also available.[67] By such means I AM allegedly took in $3 million during its first decade of existence.

As with Psychiana and the Pelley crusade, the success of the Ballard movement pointed to the existence of a widespread hunger for esoteric spirituality. At the same time, the sects were bound to draw criticism, not least for their flagrant commercialism and their political implications. In addition to reaching a wider audience, the success of the three national movements alerted potential opponents to the scale, and often the radicalism, of new religious developments. As we will see, this laid the foundation for intensified anticult activism during the 1930s and afterwards.

# FIVE

# Black Gods

My name is *Mahdi*: I am God.
  Wallace Fard, quoted in Claude Andrew Clegg, *An Original Man*

Africa Americans were subject to the same forces that fostered so many new religious groups among whites, so it is not surprising to find a comparable upsurge of new black religious movements in the early twentieth century. Although scholars tend to treat black and white movements as separate phenomena, the two grew from exactly the same cultural roots and bore far more mutual resemblance than either might have cared to admit. For both races, the first quarter of the century was a time of effervescent religious creativity, and both were exposed to the enticing "doctrine of 'the God within,' a mixture of Christian Science, New Thought, Theosophy, Spiritualism, and plain foolishness."[1] This phrase originally referred to the New York religious milieu that produced Father Divine, but it could with equal justice be used for many of his contemporaries. By the 1930s, these ideas were influencing national movements, I AM and the Silver Shirts for whites, the Nation of Islam and Father Divine's Peace Mission among blacks.

Just as predictable as the upsurge of new groups was the unsympathetic public attitude towards what the press termed "the Negro cults": for blacks as well as whites, a period of Reaction soon followed the period of Emergence. However, the whole concept of cult was applied more generously to black movements, which at every stage were depicted as far more extreme, ludicrous, and dangerous than their white counterparts. Most of the different kinds of new African-American movement swiftly earned the title of cult, including the followers of

Father Divine and the Muslim sects, and essentially all movements outside established churches like the Baptists and Methodists. One scholarly 1944 account of black "cults" includes not only the Muslims but also the Holiness, Pentecostal, and faith-healing traditions.[2]

According to the common racist stereotype of the time, blacks were vulnerable to cult-like behavior: a gullible, superstitious, primitive, and exotic people, they were subject to unrestrained sexuality and violence. When not restrained by white control, it seemed only natural that blacks would revert to these so-called jungle, or African, characteristics. These black-derived images would be crucial for the public attitude to all cults, as these stereotypes were increasingly applied to white movements. This influence was largely responsible for the idea that cults tended to be bloodthirsty or homicidal, an image drawn partly from sensationalist coverage of voodoo practices in Haiti. In the worst age of segregation and prejudice, any association with supposed black characteristics added to the existing condemnation of all fringe religions, regardless of their racial makeup.

## The World of Father Divine

For both black and white Americans, the first quarter of the twentieth century was a time of rapid social change. African-American migration to northern and midwestern cities accelerated during the First World War in response to acute labor shortages, and the thriving urban cultures of the 1920s were fertile ground for all manner of religious and political innovation. A new racial consciousness was reflected in the emergence of organizations like the NAACP, founded in 1909, and in the rise of independent black newspapers and media outlets. Militancy and racial pride were strengthened in response to the savage black-white conflicts and rioting that occurred between 1919 and 1921, and to the revival of lynching. Black nationalism during the 1920s was expressed in mass support for Marcus Garvey and his Universal Negro Improvement Association, which taught black Americans that they had a true spiritual and national home in the land of Ethiopia. Garvey's messianic movement also developed its own African-derived religious arm, and his followers freely compared him to Jesus and Buddha.[3]

Black religious movements proliferated in these years. In 1935, novelist Claude McKay remarked that "the most African characteristic of Harlem, after the color of its people, is the multitude of amazing cults. . . . To say there is a cult on every block would be no exaggeration. . . .

It is through religion, more than any other channel, that primitive African emotions find expression in our modern civilization." Ira Reid scoffed at the whole ramshackle culture of "[b]ishops without a diocese, those who heal with divine inspiration, praying circles that charge for their services, American Negroes turned Jews overnight, theological seminaries conducted in the rear of railroad apartments."[4]

Some of the new sects attracted media attention precisely because they seemed so outrageous, so vulnerable to racial parody. "Primitive emotions" were exemplified by George Baker, Father Divine, whose followers believed that he was, literally, God. If, as seems probable, he was born in 1878 or 1879, then "the Father" was a contemporary of rosicrucian and Theosophical figures like Guy Ballard, R. S. Clymer, and Edward A. Wilson, as well as of Frank Buchman. By the age of twenty, the Father had already associated with several messianic figures, one of whom, Father Jehovah, was influenced by New Thought. Following his move to Harlem, Baker was exposed to the intoxicating fringe ideas of the day, which in various ways taught that all human beings were ultimately divine. By 1915, he was preaching that "God ... [was] repersonified and rematerialized" in himself.[5]

During the 1920s, the newly proclaimed Father Divine led "a holy-rolling kind of black and white cult" based in a "heaven" at Sayville, Long Island. When this mixed-race establishment aroused resentment among neighbors, Divine was prosecuted for maintaining a public nuisance, and in 1932, he was jailed pending psychiatric evaluation. Soon afterwards, the judge who had issued this order died suddenly, giving rise to claims that Father Divine had struck him down for blasphemy. This moral victory created tumultuous excitement, as the Father was hailed in the streets with slogans like "God! There goes Father! Father Divine is God! The true and living God." Over the coming years, the Father's followers promoted a steady flow of similar tales of miraculous punishments of the faithless and disrespectful. For the media, he replaced Sister Aimee as the stereotypical American cult leader, as the flamboyant "God in a Rolls-Royce."[6]

Father Divine established a national Peace Mission, dedicated to peace and universal racial equality. Its newspaper, *New Day*, enjoyed scriptural status, and issues were dated A.D.F.D., or *anno domini* Father Divine. A network of headquarters or divine kingdoms spread across the nation, with centers in New York, Philadelphia, Newark, Seattle, and Los Angeles: the number of separate groups peaked in 1941 at 178. Services mainly consisted of hymns of adoration for the Father and gratitude for all he had given his adherents through material prosperity and healing. The number of followers was uncertain: "Father Divine has anywhere from five thousand to five million, depending on his statistical mood."[7] Though support was mainly black, there was a sprinkling of white and Latino followers: a substantial majority were women. Many followers had long records of activity in other marginal movements, "people, many of them whites, who have been Baptists, Holy Rollers, Christian Scientists and Theosophists before coming to Father."[8]

The movement gained credibility by its social action programs, which included free food for the homeless. As a white character opined in Sinclair Lewis's novel *It Can't Happen Here*, the best of the current wave of messiahs "is this darky, Father Divine. He doesn't just promise he's going to feed the underprivileged ten years from now—he hands out the fried drumsticks and gizzard right along with the salvation."[9] The source of the money for these operations was as mysterious as the overall membership figures, but disciples gave generously. By the 1950s, the organization owned "thirty apartment houses . . . a dozen city hotels, fourteen residence clubs, twenty properties in foreign countries, some twenty luxurious country estates, several schools, churches, and business establishments too numerous to mention." Even the largest real estate purchases were always made in cash.[10]

However benevolent in many ways, Father Divine ran his group in a manner reminiscent of the most authoritarian cults of modern times. As an observer commented in 1944, within the group, "Father Divine is the organization. . . . Father Divine is God. He is everywhere, knows everything, sees and hears all things. Even though he dwells in New York City or Philadelphia, a decision made by a follower in California could not have materialized independently, but must have been the result of spirit wireless directly from Father Divine." There were two categories of members: the brothers and sisters, who accepted the group's doctrine; and the higher category of absolute devotees, or angels. An angel "has renounced the things of this world completely. He no longer plans his own life, but lives it completely in accordance with the instructions of Father Divine. If he is the possessor of worldly goods, he disposes of them in a manner agreed upon between him and the leader. . . . Such members are the true angels of the cult."[11] These absolute members were required to seek permission from Father Divine to change their routine in any way, to relocate or make any other significant decision in life, and carried on no business or job except as ordered by the Father. Having said this, commentators found little evidence of hardship in the movement, which was praised for offering followers stability and decent living conditions in a time of economic collapse.[12]

But Father Divine was by no means the only prophet of this era. Only marginally less exalted in his claims was Sweet Daddy Grace, who began his preaching in 1919, and who became absolute head of the United House of Prayer for All People. The group soon possessed twenty churches along the eastern seaboard.[13] In many ways, this was "a Christian sect of the Holiness type, believing in conversion, sanctification and the intervention of the Holy Spirit," but Daddy Grace was the centre of a cult of personality and veneration far above what was found in most such groups. He boasted of taking on earthly form specifically to help elevate the humbled black race, and he pursued his task through divinely granted powers of healing. Daddy proved his bona fides by applying to himself all New Testament passages concerning Grace, such as "Salvation is by Grace only. . . . God and Grace are one. God is invisible and Grace is visible."[14] In return for his blessings, all members were to give very generously to Daddy, ideally to the extent of all their worldly goods. Like I AM, Psychiana, and other fringe groups, Daddy Grace developed merchandising to a high art, offering a special range of products bearing his name, everything from cosmetics to cookies, as well as uniforms, buttons, badges, and banners, and his *Grace Magazine*. His services used radio for advertising, and the services were broadcast live. When Grace died in 1960, he left a House of Prayer some 25,000 strong and an estate valued at $25 million. In the 1990s, the church still commanded a real estate empire worth hundreds of millions of dollars.[15]

## Black Jews

For all their theological quirks, movements like these remained recognizably Christian, at least in their worship style. Other groups departed still more radically from traditional modes. An early example was the black Jews, who gained a solid foothold in African-American communities in the 1920s. Under the influence of insurgent racial nationalism, these new movements reinterpreted biblical history through an African lens, claiming that the story of the Hebrew people and the early Christians was in reality the story of oppressed blacks, who had struggled against white oppressors. In this account, Jesus, David, Abraham, and all other biblical heroes were black Africans. Then in later years, "We were chased out of Palestine by the Romans (Italian) into the west coast of Africa where we were captured and sold into this great USA."[16]

Several sects claimed primacy as the original black Jewish movement, but the first was probably the Church of God and Saints in Christ, which was organized by William S. Crowdy, a former cook on the Santa Fe railroad. Following a visionary experience in 1896, Crowdy formed a church in Kansas City, which he headed as bishop. Crowdy's Church adopted Jewish customs and feast days, and its clergy gradually adopted the title of "rabbi." It also foreshadowed other African American sects by drawing on Masonic ritual and symbolism. Among other movements influenced by Crowdy's ideas was the Church of the Living God, which was originally formed in 1889 by William Christian of Arkansas, who also claimed a special divine revelation. One wing of this church was founded in Philadelphia in 1915 by F. S. Cherry, who remained its inspired prophet and absolute leader.[17] The group venerated the Hebrew scriptures, as Hebrew was the authentic ancient language of the black race who subsequently became African Americans: the so-called Jews were impostors. The group kept Saturday as the Sabbath and began the year from Passover. Yet another group emerged about 1900 when Warren Robertson founded a communal settlement in Virginia on black Jewish principles, under the title of the Temple of the Gospel of the Kingdom. The movement developed several settlements or "kingdoms" across the country, but the sect collapsed following Robertson's conviction on sex charges in 1926. Finally, the Black Jews of Harlem were founded by a former officer of the Garvey movement.[18]

The racial appropriation of biblical history and ancestry was scarcely new or daring, as African Americans were explicitly doing what every white church did unconsciously when it posted pictures of a blond and blue-eyed Jesus standing proud before the swarthy Levantine Pharisees. The claim to be the "real" Jews was exactly the same as that made by white followers of the contemporary British Israel movement, which was spreading in North America in these same years. When blacks made similar declarations, however, white observers saw the matter as merely ludicrous, and the existence of black Jewish groups may have contributed to the comic vision of black Old Testament prophets in the 1936 film *Green Pastures*, with its parade of racist clichés. But this black trend was of far-reaching religious importance, and we can see many resemblances between such nationalist-oriented black groups and the contemporary white Theosophical movements. Both trends claimed religious roots far deeper than would be accepted by contemporary scholarship, and both boasted access to secret racial histories, thousands of years for the black Hebrews, perhaps millions for believers in Atlantean and Lemurian theories.

The search for ancient and authentic roots was naturally at its most intense among relatively new and displaced migrant communities, respectively, urban blacks recently arrived from the countryside and white midwesterners relocated to California. Following the collapse during the Depression of their newly aroused expectations, both communities were likewise vulnerable to prophets or messiahs who boasted direct access to divine wisdom. Though the first beneficiaries were black Jews and individual messiahs like Father Divine, the quest for racial authenticity led some African Americans altogether outside the Judaeo-Christian tradition, to create an Americanized Islam.

### Black Muslims

The pioneer of the American Muslim movement was Timothy Drew, or Noble Drew Ali, who preached a heterodox Islam with himself as the last prophet, a figure on a par with Jesus, Buddha, Confucius, and Zoroaster. Drew had no qualms about creating his own scriptures, creating a Holy Koran that attached his own statements and parts of contemporary New Age works to the established holy writ of the Arabic *Quran*. Large sections of his Holy Koran were appropriated from Levi H. Dowling's esoteric *The Aquarian Gospel of Jesus the Christ*, which reported the career of "Jesus in India, Europe and Africa, in the land of Egypt."[19] This first American Islam owed as much to the contemporary New Age sects as to any authentic Islam. The decision to cast the new religion as a form of Islam reflected Drew's ostentatious rejection of white Western culture and history, in the very years that fanatical stereotypes of non-Western religions were most pervasive.

Like Bishop Crowdy, Drew was also indebted to Freemasonry. This package of mystical ideas held a particular appeal for black Americans, who by the early twentieth century were largely excluded from the regular Masonic lodges in which whites satisfied their own curiosity about esoteric religion. Though there were thousands of black Masons, pressure from southern segregationists meant that nonwhites were confined to what were technically clandestine lodges. By the turn of the century, a whole parallel structure of Negro Masonry was using pseudo-Arabic language drawn from the white Shriners, the Ancient Egyptian Arabic Order of the Mystic Shrine, which erected temples and dated events in terms of Ramadan and the Hegira. These exotic precedents certainly influenced the thinking of Drew and later Muslim sects.[20]

In 1913, Drew founded his Moorish Science Temple, MST, in Newark, New Jersey. The name was auspicious: though "Moor" was the archaic name for Muslims of North Africa (to which Drew promised to return his disciples), the word was derived from the Greek word for dark-skinned, so the concepts of black and Muslim were neatly combined. However, Drew believed that Moors had Asian rather than African origins and should properly be termed Asiatics: Islam was the distinctive religion of Asiatics, just as Christianity was the religion of white Euro-Americans. Like the sects of black Jews, the Muslims claimed to be restoring the authentic religious and racial character of African Americans, who were cast in a messianic role. Incidentally, there had been a Moorish Zionist Temple in Brooklyn as early as 1899, the name perhaps echoing the World Zionist Congress held only two years before.[21]

The new MST movement spread quickly, appealing particularly to Garveyites, and temples developed in most major northern cities, as well as across the South. By the late 1920s, membership peaked around fifteen or twenty thousand, and sect members became a visible presence on the streets through their red fezzes, which derive from Shriner precedent.[22] Believers adopted Muslim names incorporating the elements -Bey or -El, foreshadowing the practice made famous by the later Nation of Islam. Because the movement was firmly focused on Drew's own personality, it was irretrievably weakened when he disappeared in 1929, while awaiting trial for the murder of a rival, and the group split into several competing factions. Violence resulting from this schism resulted in a near riot in Chicago in 1929, an event that alerted white Americans to the existence of the new Muslim sects.[23]

Still, Islam retained its appeal. By the 1940s, some fifty Moorish Science Temples spread over eighteen states: over half were located in Ohio, Indiana, Illinois, and Michigan. This was in addition to local clubs and sects, such as a Hamitic Mohammedan Club in Rochester, New York, the Addeynue Allahe Universal Arabic Association of Buffalo, or the Pittsburgh-based African Moslem Welfare Society of America. There was also an immigrant Muslim presence: during the 1920s,

Syrian and Lebanese merchants were building the nation's first-known mosques. About the same time, the United States was visited by missionaries from the Indian-based Ahmadiyya, a messianic sect of Islam whose leader claimed to be the *Mahdi*, the Expected One: Ahmadiyya groups were found in Chicago, Detroit, and other cities. Every black community of any scale had at least a vestigial Muslim group, which laid the foundation for the Black Muslim expansion in later decades.[24]

## The Nation of Islam

By far the most important of the Muslim movements originated in Detroit about 1930 under the auspices of a mysterious peddler. The man, Wallace Fard (or Wali Farad or Wallace Ford Muhammad), developed a reputation as a prophet, using the Bible as a means of introducing his new religious teachings, until disciples could be brought to full knowledge of the true word of God, the *Quran*. Fard claimed charismatic skills and declared himself an envoy from the city of Mecca, who would one day be seen in royal robes. He taught that the Muslim religion was intended to help free black peoples from oppression by whites, the blue-eyed devils, and their deceitful religion of Christianity. "The black men in North America are not Negroes but members of the lost tribe of Shebazz, stolen by traders from the Holy City of Mecca 379 years ago. The prophet came to America to find and to bring back to life his long lost brethren, from whom the Caucasians have taken away their language, their nation and their religion."[25] Just as Garvey promised a return to Ethiopia and Drew to Morocco, so Fard offered the prospect of a regathering in Mecca. As we can see from the precedents of the black Jews and the MST, Fard was not introducing any radical new doctrine but was rather returning to a well-tilled field.

This radical antiwhite doctrine had a particular appeal during the depths of the Depression. Soon a Temple of Islam opened in Detroit, and the new Nation of Islam movement was consolidating the vestiges of other sects, including MST followers in Chicago and elsewhere. Converts were given true, original names to replace the slave names that had been imposed upon them. Fard charged ten dollars for each individual naming, and must have made a substantial sum from the estimated five to eight thousand Detroit residents who became Black Muslims in these years. Considering that the black population of Detroit at this time was around 120,000, the Muslims represented a significant religious minority. When Fard left the city in 1934, he was succeeded as leader by a convert who had taken the name Elijah Muhammad. Elijah Muhammad dominated the group until his death in 1975, and under his leadership, the sect peaked at between seventy and a hundred thousand members.

The new American Islams differed substantially from mainstream Muslim tradition. The Ahmadiyyas were attacked as heretical for their messianism. Noble Drew Ali violated two basic principles of the religion, namely, the centrality of the revelation to the Prophet Muhammad and the unchangeable validity of the *Quran*, and the MST even adopted reincarnationist ideas. Wallace Fard went further, allegedly claiming the role of Supreme Ruler of the Universe. In Black Muslim writings, Fard becomes the "Supreme Being among all black Men," and the movement celebrates his birthday as that of the Savior. The doctrine of incarnation would horrify most Muslims around the world, for whom the act of associating any creature with Allah is an ultimate blasphemy, *shirk*. And while mainstream Islam prides itself on being blind to distinctions of race or ethnicity, the Black Muslims were ferociously antiwhite, recognizing no salvation for any whites, even if they were loyal Muslims. Equally alien to democratic Islam is the authoritarian leader-cult centered around Fard and his successors.

In addition, Black Muslims claim a variety of special revelations beyond those in the original Quran. Fard passed on his secret teachings through an orally transmitted *Secret Ritual*, available only to initiates. According to Elijah Muhammad, God taught his people the mysteries of "science and astronomy, the civilizations on other planets, and the knowledge of self."[26] Already in these pioneer days, we find the number mysticism that would so often recur in the movement up to the present day: when Louis Farrakhan spoke at the Million Man March in Washington D.C., in 1995, he invoked numerical oddities and parallels that often mystified his audience, but which had deep roots in Nation of Islam thought. The Nation taught the complex history of a universe said to be seventy-six trillion years old, in which there were said to be many inhabited worlds, and the movement recounted the secret histories of otherworldly civilizations on Mars and elsewhere.[27] Blacks, the Original People, dominated the planet for trillions of years, achieving astonishing feats of science, until the calamitous rise of the white race. Whites were the result of a genetic experiment gone horribly wrong, the work of Yacub, "a black scientist in rebellion against Allah." These monstrous creations were permitted to oppress other races for six thousand years until God became incarnate in the man

Wallace Fard, an event signaling the beginning of the end of white supremacy. Imminent Armageddon would be initiated by the Mother Plane, a colossal UFO that would annihilate America and the white powers.

### The Roots of Black Islam

Early writers assumed that the Black Muslims were simply misunderstanding Islam, or adapting it for their own ideological purposes, while perhaps trying to compete with the claims of Father Divine, but the new movement must be placed in the context of the contemporary religious fringe. Although Fard himself claimed little formal education, he was an eclectic thinker who borrowed from Freemasonry, Jehovah's Witness doctrines, and Baptist apocalyptic, among other sources. The Witness connection probably explains the key importance of the year 1914 in Nation of Islam thinking, as the year in which the white race is judged, even though Divine mercy permits its unjust rule to stagger on for a few additional decades. Both Fard and Elijah Muhammad professed great respect for Noble Drew Ali, and like the founder of the MST, Fard had drunk deeply from the springs of New Age teaching. Fard lived in Los Angeles from 1918 through 1929, the period of the messianic hopes surrounding Krishnamurti, and coincidentally or not, the Nation of Islam was founded in the same year as I AM. As we have seen, New Age ideas in southern California already had several points of contact with the Pentecostal and Christian apocalyptic tradition. As a spokesman for the Ascended Master Wallace Fard, Elijah Muhammad had much in common with his white Theosophical contemporaries, serving as earthly interpreter much as Guy Ballard did for his own Count of Saint-Germain.

Literary sources may also have influenced Nation of Islam thought. In 1927, journalist William Seabrook published his popular *Adventures in Arabia*, which described secretive Muslim sects like the Druze. The Druze give scriptural authority to their distinctive Book of Wisdom, parts of which are available only to initiates: "[the Druze,] like Freemasons and rosicrucians, have secret formulas and passwords."[28] Another conceivable influence was Olaf Stapledon's 1931 science fiction novel, *Last and First Men*, an account of the evolution of the human race as it migrates through the solar system over the coming two billion years: this reads like the elaborate multitrillion year interplanetary history depicted in NOI mythology. The Nation may have drawn on Theosophical speculations about the rise and fall of successive Root Races, as the account of Yacub's creation of the white race echoes contemporary writings about the emergence of a new race in the Pacific West.

Many of Fard's religious idiosyncrasies find parallels in the sectarian Islam of Syria and Lebanon. Even the incarnationism has echoes here: some Shi'ite sects believe that God has successively manifested himself in several earthly figures, including Muhammad and Ali, while the Druze accept the divinity of the tenth century Caliph Hakim. Furthermore, Shi'ites have a high regard for the charismatic and clerical authority of their spiritual leaders, the imams. Particularly Shi'ite is the idea of occultation, or *ghaib*, the notion that great leaders and imams do not die but remain concealed from the world until the time is right for their reappearance.[29] This may provide a context for Fard's role after 1934, when his departure from Detroit gave rise to so many legends, speculating that he had perhaps become a human sacrifice or been killed by rivals: a Shi'ite would have spoken in terms of an imam retreating into holy obscurity. The presence of these ideas would be easier to explain if we knew more about the origins of the mysterious Fard. Police thought he was Polynesian or Hawaiian, while his Detroit followers believed he was a Syrian or Lebanese peddler. The latter view is easier to reconcile with the prophet's facial features, which look more Levantine than Polynesian: perhaps Fard invented his Polynesian/Hawaiian origins in order to avoid deportation. If he was in fact a Lebanese follower of one of the esoteric Shi'ite sects, then his American pupils were indeed receiving ancient and authentic Islamic beliefs, albeit in a form that most Muslims would regard as heretical.

### Sacrifice

As an autonomous separatist movement, the Black Muslims attracted profound suspicion from the authorities, as well as from African-American Christian leaders. The group attracted many stories concerning its violent tendencies, and it developed an armed paramilitary organization, the Fruit of Islam. There were even accounts of human sacrifices, and the group's oral *Secret Ritual* was reported to have taught "that it was the duty of every Moslem to offer as sacrifice four Caucasian devils in order that he might return to his home in Mecca." Police and court records of the early 1930s suggest that sacrificial incidents did occur, though it is controversial whether these involved the following of secret doctrine or just outbreaks by deranged individuals; the Detroit police believed the former. One notorious offender was the "fanatical" Robert Harris, or Robert Karriem, who threatened two women welfare workers for sacrifice, as each was a "no-good Christian." In November 1932, Harris induced his roommate to volunteer to be stabbed to death as a ritual sacrifice. Though Harris claimed membership in a splinter group, the Order of Islam, his crime was blamed on African-American Muslims in general, and the media claimed that politicians were targeted for assassination. In early 1937, another man "was arrested as he prepared for the ceremonial slaying and cooking of his wife and daughter," in order to cleanse himself from sin.[30]

The Harris murder provoked a major anti-Muslim movement between 1932 and 1934. Detroit's black clergy launched a fierce attack on on the "fanatical teachings and barbarous practices" of the Muslim cult and urged police to combat "the sinister influences of Voodooism." The *Detroit Free Press* used the term "voodoo" in virtually all its stories about the movement in these years, with headlines like "Negro Leaders Open Fight to Break Voodooism's Grip" and that referred to the "Voodoo Altar Slaying." Police intervention drove Black Muslim activities underground, which resulted in Fard's arrest and departure from Detroit. Supposedly, he even confessed to police interrogators that his whole scheme was from the very start a money-making racket. By 1933, the *Detroit Free Press* could declare that "Voodoo's Reign Here is Broken." Fard's successor, Elijah Muhammad, often had occasion to move his activities to Chicago, Milwaukee, or Washington, D.C., as the pressure became too great in Detroit. Legal assaults continued through the decade, including efforts by Michigan's Board of Education to close Islamic schools, and there were armed confrontations with police. In 1934, Elijah Muhammad himself was arrested for "contributing to the delinquency of a child, and Voodooism."[31]

## Voodoo

In seeking to understand the religious upsurge among African Americans, whites relied on long-established racist caricature, but with a pernicious new element, namely the notion of voodoo. Reference to "voodooism" pervaded official reaction to the new black Islams. When in 1937 the prestigious *American Journal of Sociology* published a scholarly account of Black Muslim origins in Detroit, it did so under the bizarre title of "The Voodoo Cult Among Negro Migrants in Detroit," discussing "[t]he Nation of Islam, usually known as the Voodoo cult."[32] A less suitable parallel could scarcely be imagined, given that voodoo and Islam are located at opposite ends of the religious spectrum in terms of their attitude to divinity and the nature of religious practice. Still, in the thought-world of the time, any autonomous black religion was assumed to be voodoo-related, with all that implied about primitive violence and orgiastic sexuality. (Nor did the author feel the need to discuss the word "cult," which seemed self-explanatory.) The insistence on seeing black religions as forms of voodoo extended beyond the Muslims. When a group of white Columbia University students attended one of Father Divine's services, they anticipated "an evening's entertainment consonant with popular ideas of African fetish or Haitian Voodoo worship."[33]

Voodoo certainly existed, in the sense of African-derived rituals and folk-beliefs that were strong in the Caribbean and the American Deep South, but a sharp line has to be drawn between the real religious practice, now conventionally referred to as "*Vodun*" or "*Vodoun*," and the farrago of myths and legends called "voodoo" that became a media commonplace.[34] This voodoo myth provided a frame through which all the new African-American religions were interpreted—and distorted. If it did not exist, a homicidal American voodoo cult would have to be invented, and so, under media influence, it was. This largely imaginary movement in turn became one of the most frequent targets of cult exposés for some decades. Much like the anti-Satanism crusades of the 1980s, the attack on voodoo in the mid-1930s mobilized anticult sentiment against an illusory target, and as later with Satanism, there were just enough grains of truth to provide some plausibility to the harrowing picture.

Americans had a long familiarity with voodoo through travelers' tales of the Caribbean and especially Haiti, a territory with which the United States had a long and mixed relationship. In 1884, one study, *Hayti; or, The Black Republic*, portrayed the voodoo religion in terms of human sacrifice and rampant cannibalism. This image seemed amply confirmed when two years later the *New York World* reported a well-documented case of the sacrificial killing and eating of two children. In 1908, the *Metropolitan Magazine* reminded American readers of the Haitian horrors, especially the idea of the ritual sacrifice of a young child, known as the "goat without horns."[35] In 1915, the U.S. military occupation of Haiti increased the likelihood of direct contact with voodoo belief. The existence of voodoo aggravated relations between the occupiers and the local people, as Americans believed that missing or killed Marines had been mutilated, sacrificed, or eaten in pagan rituals, and such legends occasionally provoked massacres of civilians. The initial legend held that three Marines had been ritually killed, but the story escalated to claim that many victims were kidnapped and murdered "solely for the sake of the ritual cooking-pot."[36] Following nationalist risings in 1929, the U.S. government deliberated for several years how best to return the nation to local control, making Haiti a newsworthy topic in the American media until the end of the occupation in 1934. Voodoo was a natural angle for reporters to pursue, especially after the appearance of William Seabrook's account of voodoo, also in the pivotal year of 1929.

### The Magic Island

Seabrook's book, *The Magic Island,* set the tone for all later writings on voodoo. This was a follow-up to his Arabian travelogue, which we have already mentioned as a possible influence on the emerging Nation of Islam. The author, a former features writer for the Hearst syndicate, was by far the most important occult popularizer of the interwar years and did much to shape American perceptions of witchcraft, Satanism, and parapsychology, as well as voodoo. He introduced the mass American audience to such technical terms as the *papaloi* and *mamaloi* (the priests, that is, *Papa Roi* and *Mama Roi*) and the *houmfort* (mystery house, or temple), and his book introduced the word "zombie" to the English language.

Seabrook quoted extensively from voodoo rituals, describing ceremonies that are not only bloody, but also involve a powerful sexuality, with elements of perversion and bestiality: Haitians were presented as a "blood-maddened, sex-maddened, god-maddened" people. These accounts of voodoo ritual are laden with pornographic themes that could scarcely have appeared in any mainstream book of these years if the author had not had the excuse of describing primitive rituals. Though Seabrook distinguished between normal voodoo practice and evil ritual magic, a large portion of his book concerns the specialized *culte des morts,* with its themes of fear, death, and bloodshed, of death curses, zombies, and animal sacrifice: this is suggested by chapter headings like "Black Sorcery," "The Altar of Skulls," "Dead Men Working in the Canefields." It remains open to debate whether he was accurately describing Haitian realities or if he was projecting his own admittedly Gothic obsessions. Seabrook's autobiography is frank about his long-standing fascination with "the foulest, most absurd and darkest phases of the so-called occult," and a scandal followed when in his 1931 book *Jungle Ways,* he admitted having experimented personally with can-

nibalism. As so often in the history of anticult exposés, the more outrageous charges may tell us more about the observers than the conditions on which they are supposedly reporting.[37]

Though Seabrook's version of Haitian voodoo was much criticized,
it nevertheless provided a template for most of the voodoo-related fiction and reportage proliferating between 1932 and 1936. Most of the
travelogues belonged to what might be called the "white man in darkest
Africa" genre, describing how the writer or journalist had penetrated
the inner secrets of a cult that held its midnight meetings in a jungle
clearing. Seemingly taken direct from the *Heart of Darkness* were the
accounts of Faustin Wirkus, a white Marine serving as an officer in the
Haitian *gendarmerie*, who became legendary in the American media as
"the white king of La Gonave." He portrayed voodoo in terms of all-
powerful high priests and priestesses, presiding over an orgiastic religion in a society endemically terrified of curses and witchcraft. Wirkus
even reported the existence of "a secret high priest, a kind of Pope,
who is supreme over all the *bocors* ['magicians'] and *hougans* and *pa-
palois* of that religion." Remarkably, Wirkus discovers this international voodoo empire from information received not in Haiti, but in
Harlem.[38]

The view of an evil religion founded upon human sacrifice and cannibalism was extended to other African-derived movements throughout
the Caribbean and, by extension, to parallel movements in the United
States.[39] In 1937, the *Literary Digest* reported on the struggle of Cuban
authorities to eradicate a "cult practicing kidnapping and human
sacrifice": though apparently the practices described are Santería, the
rituals are identified totally with Haitian voodoo. The article claimed
that Haitians practiced snake worship "with dancing and sexual
orgies. But for generations, rites centered around the sacrifice of a
white child known in the ceremonies as the Goat Without Horns.
Stupefied with drugs, the sacrificial victim was killed and parts of its
dismembered body given to worshipers who believe its virtue purified
them."[40] The notion that the sacrificed child should be white was a
recent embellishment.

Similar images dominated Richard Loederer's 1935 account of Haitian religion. Loederer claimed, "Only at dead of night could they
gather together in the secret places of the forest and celebrate their
ancient rituals. On these occasions, the primitive instincts of the blacks
were given free rein, and the monotonous rumble of the tom-toms
inspired demoniacal dances, mad drinking orgies, and sexual frenzies.

. . . With the massacre of the whites and the establishment of the black empire, Voodoo attained its zenith. . . . From out of these sexual orgies grew the atavistic impulse towards cannibalism. Definite feasts were instituted at which there was a ritual slaughter of children and even grown men, followed by a meal of roast flesh."

Loederer also wrote of the zombie, the figure raised from the dead by a voodoo priest to do his bidding, making the religion "stronger even than death."[41] Zombies became a recurring element in popular culture depictions of voodoo, in horror films like *White Zombie* (1932) and its many imitators, all of which drew ultimately from Seabrook. The decade after 1936 brought B-movies like *Revolt of the Zombies* (1936), *King of the Zombies* (1941), *Revenge of the Zombies* (1943), *Voodoo Devil Drums* (1944), and *Voodoo Man* (1944). There was also the more serious treatment in Val Lewton's brooding and atmospheric 1943 film *I Walked with a Zombie* with its knowledgeable depictions of voodoo rituals.

Most such accounts rarely lost an opportunity to stress the quintessentially African character of the devotees, how in fact the worshipers are reverting to their ancient tribal selves, freeing themselves of the veneer of Christian and Western civilization; this is, we are told, the real African character. As racist theorist Lothrop Stoddard wrote in 1921, "The Negro when left to himself, as in Haiti and Liberia, rapidly reverts to his ancestral ways." Loederer further claimed, "Voodoo is the sublimated expression of the African mentality . . . under a thin veneer, the ancient African nature forces its way out like a volcano from beneath the crusts of the earth." Not until the 1950s did more serious and critical accounts appear, which treated voodoo as an authentic religion rooted in Africa.[42]

### Hoodoo and Voodoo

However diabolical the stereotype of Haitian voodoo, at least it took place on foreign shores. During the 1920s and 1930s, however, the voodoo stereotype was increasingly imported into the United States. This was partly a matter of loose definition, as "voodoo" came to be a generic term for all African-based folk-beliefs and practices in the Americas, including the diverse Afro-Caribbean traditions more properly known as Macumba, Candomblé, and Santería. Within the United States, the demonized term "voodoo" gradually came to incorporate African-American beliefs that were far less organized and did not constitute an alternative religion in the Haitian sense.

Through the nineteenth century, it was commonly acknowledged that rural blacks, like their white neighbors, had well-developed magical traditions, together with a body of supernatural folklore. These ideas were known by various names, including "hoodoo," but in 1893, a classic study of black Missouri folktales reminiscent of Uncle Remus used the title *Voodoo Tales*, although there was no suggestion of any pagan worship or ritual magic.[43] The distinction was neatly drawn by a 1908 exposé of the "voodoo cult," which quoted all the familiar Haitian images, but stressed that these horrors were not generally found among black Americans, "superstitious and childish types" though they were. The author, Marvin Dana, offers a classic account of "[a] mad band of dark-skinned savages," who practice "nameless debaucheries. . . . And sometimes, the devout seek the pleasuring of their god by offering up to him a human sacrifice. Thereafter, they feast upon the victim's flesh. But such phases of Voodoo worship are far from the experience of most of the colored folk in our country."[44] In contrast to Haitian conditions, Dana describes the flourishing American subculture of spells and witchcraft, together with the ubiquitous voodoo doctors who could cure a disease or raise a hex. Though part of the allegedly global cult, these were only weak manifestations of the problem.

The closest American parallel to Haitian voodoo was found in Louisiana, and especially New Orleans, where through the nineteenth century there were reports of organized rituals and ceremonies, of dances and animal sacrifices, attended by perhaps thousands of devotees: this was the age of legendary witches and voodoo queens like Marie Laveau. From the 1850s onwards, there were also sporadic rumors and panics concerning the kidnapping and murder of children and the sacrifice of the "goat without horns." This does not mean that the charges were objectively true, any more than allegations in northern cities about atrocities committed by Catholic priests or Freemasons, but the existence of the legends illustrates the lively folklore surrounding voodoo belief. By the end of the century, stories of rituals and orgies were collected and elaborated by Romantics and antiquarians, whose accounts were still being quoted verbatim decades later. The imaginative process was assisted by an increasingly sensationalistic media, for which tales of dancing by scores of naked women, black and white, were always good copy. When in 1911 and 1912, Texas and Louisiana suffered one of the several waves of serial murder then under way across the United States, the newspapers blamed the fifty or so killings and mutilations upon an obscure black religious sect, the Church of Sacrifice, which was said to be linked to voodoo. Though police did investigate these cult ties, no connections were ever substantiated.[45]

Over the next three decades, accounts of voodoo in New Orleans produced little evidence of any organized blood cult. A 1926 study of *Folk Beliefs of the Southern Negro* included major sections on what was called voodooism, but virtually all the sources the author found for ritual dances, snake-worship ceremonies, animal sacrifice, and blood drinking came from the romantic/decadent books and articles published at the turn of the century, referring to events long ago, usually before the Civil War. Posing as a conjure doctor about 1925, N. N. Puckett found that "remnants of Voodooism, in the form of spells, tricks, conjurations and witchcraft of all kinds still persist, but the closest search fails to reveal any underlying organization; and real Hoodoo men, who inspire the fear and patronage of countless superstitious clients, have confided to me that they have long wished to join the Voodoo society, but years of residence in New Orleans have failed to bring to light the existence of any such. With the death of Marie Laveau [about 1890], Voudouism all but disappeared from New Orleans." This was the conclusion reached by Robert Tallant's critical 1946 study of *Voodoo in New Orleans*. Most of the contemporary voodoo described by Tallant involved the spells and divinations of individual magicians, the two-headed doctors, who were heavily influenced by white spiritualist thought and rhetoric.[46]

One firsthand account of twentieth-century ritual came from Zora Neale Hurston, who describes her elaborate initiation at the hands of several New Orleans hoodoo doctors, in ceremonies that involved the sacrifice of sheep and chickens. At times, she seems to confirm the reality of the organized Voodoo myth, speaking of "rites that vie with those of Haiti . . . deeds that keep alive the powers of Africa." In *Mules and Men*, published in 1935 at the height of the demonization of voodoo, she declares that hoodoo "or Voodoo, as pronounced by the whites, is burning with a flame in America, with all the intensity of a suppressed religion. It has its thousands of secret adherents. . . . It is not the accepted theology of the Nation, and so believers conceal their faith." On the other hand, she stresses the individual work of spells and conjures, and mocks the "Voodoo ritualistic orgies of Broadway and popular fiction . . . drum-beating and dancing."[47] Her ambiguity reflects the mixed feelings felt by educated black Americans towards the voodoo tales. While hoodoo might have a romantic appeal for intellectuals, folk traditions and hoodoo witchcraft were viewed very differently by the aspiring urban middle classes, whose views are represented in black newspapers like the *Pittsburgh Courier* or the *Chicago Defender*. In these circles, such superstitions were at best irrelevant, at worst an embarrassment that could threaten a hard-won respectability.

### Voodoo in America?

Traditional African-American customs and folklore were brought to northern cities during the great migration between 1910 and 1930, and popular fascination with Haitian magic led to these domestic traditions being reinterpreted as voodoo. In 1927, the *American Mercury* published an article identifying the witchcraft and hoodoo customs of black Americans with Haitian *vaudoux*. However, the Washington, D.C., "mulatto" informant who makes this identification is chiefly indebted to popular culture: " 'Haven't you never seen it in the movies?' she asked. . . . One film in particular which had impressed her had gone back to the very roots of the cult, and laid bare the rites of its priesthood in a far-away jungle." The confusion between (domestic) hoodoo and (foreign) voodoo was reinforced by Zora Neale Hurston's 1938 book, *Tell My Horse*, her study of African-derived beliefs in Haiti and Jamaica. Though intended as a celebration of African culture, the book encouraged the idea that black Americans were likely to be involved in savage rites.[48]

American voodoo now became a staple of the American media. In 1932, a voodoo king was said to be based in a Florida jungle.[49] The following year, a book on *Voodoos and Obeahs* juxtaposed two recent news stories, implying that they were describing related phenomena. One, from the *New York Times*, was headed "Seize Price Lists of Voodoo Doctor" and described how police seized the advertising circulars of a Brooklyn man who sold "all sorts of love powders, wishing dust, lucky charms and incantations." Though there is no element here of an organized cult or religion, the story immediately following is headlined "Save Child from Torture" and tells how Cuban "Voodoo worshippers" kidnapped and almost sacrificed a white toddler.[50]

The press concluded that black Americans must be engaged in secret blood rituals. In 1937, the *Literary Digest* agreed that most American voodooism consisted in "hocus-pocus charms and fetishes," but still, "in the turpentine camps of Georgia, the cotton fields of Texas, and the cypress swamps of Louisiana, good old fashioned snake-worship with all its half-crazed rites is known to exist. Chickens, goats and cows are offered up at rough jungle altars." To the music of the "tom-toms" played by faithful "darkies," the rituals culminate when "a huge black steps into the circle under the moonlight with a cane-knife, slits the throat of the sacrificial victim." American cities even had colonies of Caribbean sacrificial cults. In 1940, the *New York Herald Tribune* reported that a California woman who had killed her five-year-old daughter belonged to a voodoo cult that practiced ritual murder.[51]

Such domestic stories were a gift for the authors of pulp fiction. In 1935, a New Orleans-based cult provided the foundation for Cornell Woolrich's short story, "Music from the Big Dark" (Woolrich was a highly regarded noir suspense writer, from the same tradition as Dashiell Hammett). The story concerns a bandleader who enjoys huge success by appropriating voodoo music and rhythms for his nightclub act, which indicates the contemporary white interest in this exotic culture. However, Woolrich's description of the rituals recalls the bloodiest Haitian accounts. Animals are sacrificed, and an orgy ensues as dancers are "lashing themselves to a frenzy, tearing at their own and each other's clothes, drawing blood with knives and fingernails, eyes rolling in ecstasy that colder races cannot know."[52] A voodoo magician wears a death's head *juju* mask throughout the rituals: this is the all-powerful *papaloi*, a term imported from the Haitian tales. One potent theme throughout the story is that of racial subversion, as white characters are drawn into the voodoo movement. The terror of miscegenation is manipulated by the cult, who use drugs to induce subtle skin changes in their white dupes, convincing them that they are reverting to primitive type, racially as much as spiritually.

The chronology of the voodoo scare does much to explain the contemporary interpretation of the Nation of Islam as a voodoo cult, as the authentic Muslim movement was emerging in exactly the years of the media frenzy. Popular accounts of American voodoo may well have influenced the police in Detroit, Chicago, and elsewhere in determining that the Nation of Islam was launching a homicidal race war against whites under the guise of religion. And if sober academics could not discriminate between voodoo and Islam, why should law enforcement agencies be any more perceptive?

# SIX

# The Cult Racket
## Anticult Campaigns, 1920–1940

Under the guise of religion, these cults are growing in America and the
number of their victims increasing with each succeeding year.
  Frederick S. Miller, *Fighting Modern Evils That Destroy Our Homes*

If the nation was indeed overrun with messiahs, whether white or
black, then it is scarcely surprising to find there was a counterblast
from alarmed groups and individuals. By the mid-1920s, there
emerged a powerful secular critique of the unorthodox religious movements, variously charging that cults were authoritarian, exploitative,
sexually predatory, antifamily, and downright fraudulent, as well as
personally destructive to the health and sanity of cult members.

Cult opponents in the early twentieth century represented an impressively broad coalition. Between the 1920s and the 1940s, exposés
were normally initiated by individual activists or entrepreneurs genuinely outraged at religious exploitation; we also find the familiar figure
of the cult defector or apostate, an individual who abandons the movement in order to expose it to a wider world. Some of the most active
and venomous critics were drawn from interest groups that saw themselves as actual or potential competitors of the new movements. Most
conspicuously, this meant the Christian clergy, who feared the growth
of powerful rival denominations outside the orthodox fold, but the
medical profession was similarly alarmed at the rise of heterodox healing techniques. Other competitor groups included professional magicians, who were appalled to see their stagecraft hijacked for purposes
of fraud and thereby discredited. Meanwhile, reputable esoteric believers feared, plausibly, that the disgraceful stunts of some of the new

sects could lead to a general public reaction against all religious innovation. Debunking work found institutional bases within groups like the American Medical Association and the Society of American Magicians, and the latter launched the most knowledgeable and systematic assaults on fraudulent religions.[1] In addition to these interest groups, the psychiatric profession provided the scientific rhetoric that seemed to confirm that both cult leaders and followers were suffering from varying degrees of mental disorder or defect. It was a professional commonplace that religious enthusiasm and cult involvement led the emotionally vulnerable to the brink of insanity—and beyond.

Anticult critics easily found an audience for their message through the media, which used cult misdeeds as the basis for prurient exposés. Most leading metropolitan papers involved themselves in at least one long-running crusade against small sects in the first half of the century, and anticult ideas made inroads into popular culture and in films, novels, and pulp magazines. In one respect, cult opponents in the earlier period had advantages over counterparts during the 1970s and 1980s in that the legal environment made it easier to invoke official sanctions against religious groups, who could be attacked on grounds of fraud or sexual deviance. Small religions were harassed by police bunco squads, and social welfare agencies had few qualms about intervening to rescue children from immoral environments, for example, settings in which polygamy was practiced.

Forceful action against cults was made easier by the growing popular belief that fringe religious groups were involved in violent activities, including human sacrifice. This was partly a consequence of the torrent of vilification directed against black movements through the 1930s, which associated cults with voodoo and ritual murder. Though charges of cult violence were very poorly substantiated in the context of any racial group, the popular media made up for this by an active process of literary invention, which proceeded apace through the Depression years. By the late 1930s, as in the 1980s, the popular indictment of cults included rumors of violence and sacrificial murder, and the stereotype of sex cults segued into that of blood cults and death cults.[2] A period of anticult *Reaction* in the 1920s thus evolved into what I have termed the period of Speculation—and indeed, of panic.

But the notion of sacrificial violence posed some difficulties. With blacks, the argument of the day went, a reversion to primitive savagery might be easily explained, but what sort of creed could produce such aberrant behavior among whites? An answer was found in romanticized and reconstructed images of witchcraft and Satanism, which vastly enriched the snowballing anticult mythology. Just as bucolic hoodoo was reconceived as bloodthirsty voodoo, so rural witch-traditions were integrated into a new system of imagined devil-worship.

## The Medium Racket

Much of the anticult rhetoric of the 1920s originated with the older attack on spiritualism, and indeed, indicting cults as mere covers for fraud and crime harked back to the exposure of deceptive mediums in the mid-nineteenth century. This critique intensified after the First World War, when mediums preyed upon the emotionally vulnerable and exposing the "medium racket" became a crusade for some in the 1920s. A sequence of scandals and criminal cases during the mid-1920s reinforced public doubts about the spiritualist movement. In his 1929 crime novel, *The Dain Curse*, Dashiell Hammett refers to the well-known tricks of the "spook racket": his private detective had recently been "digging down in a chain of fake mediums who had taken a coal-and-ice dealer's widow for a hundred thousand dollars."[3]

The best-known antifraud activist was the escape artist Harry Houdini, whose own knowledge of the tricks of showmanship allowed him to unravel even the most cunning spiritualist performances. Houdini comprehensively exposed the medium's craft, all the technical skills required to shake a table, produce writing on a blank slate, manifest ectoplasm, or levitate. He even had to debunk overenthusiastic observers who cited his own escape tricks as proofs of the reality of psychic power, as triumphs of dematerialization and psychokinesis. Knowing the methods of vaudeville mind readers, Houdini described the many ways in which swindlers could find confidential information about a subject, making it seem as if they could only have obtained these facts by supernatural means. His 1924 memoir *A Magician Among the Spirits* described the techniques of all the great mediums and recounted harrowing stories of brazen confidence tricksters. One telling exhibit in his gallery of spiritualist crime concerned Ann O'Delia Diss Debar, a New York swindler with a record of homicidal violence, who in the 1880s used her seances to fleece rich clients. She later formed Theocratic Unity, "an exceptionally immoral cult" in London, which lasted until her husband raped a devotee during a ceremony. She disappeared about 1909.[4]

Houdini's crusade was carried on by the Society of American

magicians, SAM. The Society's press committee was chaired by Julian Proskauer, whose 1932 book, *Spook Crooks!*, exposed "the secrets of the prophet-eers [*sic*] who conduct our wickedest industry." The danger was all the greater after the stock market crash of 1929 left so many desperate people seeking supernatural aid to save or restore their fortunes. Proskauer claimed that the occult racket duped perhaps thirty million people each year, making a profit of $125 million. "In return for their comfortable livelihood, they ruin many of their victims, cause the suicide of others, even drive some of them insane."[5] The SAM campaigned against permitting astrologers and fortune-tellers access to radio, and between 1931 and 1932, the number of radio astrologers was reduced from 147 to 4. By the late 1920s, this debunking work had made the society the most prominent campaigner against religious fraud, and its magazine, *The Sphinx*, regularly excoriated fortune-tellers and mediums. The society published illustrated accounts of how even the most impressive stunts could be performed. The SAM press office responded to queries with form letters demonstrating, for instance, just how easily anyone could obtain credentials as a "recognized medium." The mechanisms were very simple: in 1931, two dollars bought a "medium's certificate" from the National Spiritualist Alliance, and five dollars would purchase a church charter. A minister's certificate followed with little difficulty, which allowed the individual to obtain donations without risking prosecution as a fortune-teller.[6]

The society's targets included not just fraudulent mediums but also various types of shady fortune-tellers, astrologers, and cult tricksters, which indicates just how far spiritualism had fallen since its Victorian heyday. At least some fraudulent cults were drawing directly on the age-old tradition of traveling fairground or carnival culture and its associated confidence tricks. Proskauer related one impressive "spook fraud": A group approached a recently bereaved college professor, claiming to be part of "The Cult," which received messages through their guide, Lucarius the Sun-Worshiper. Cult members showed their supernatural powers by producing ectoplasm and withstanding extreme heat, a power inherited from Lucarius's earthly career as an Aztec fire-priest. After several months, the spirit messages from his wife began suggesting that the widower turn over all his earthly belongings to the Cult. Luckily, though, just as he was about to deliver the money, the professor found police officers in the process of raiding the Cult's premises. Proskauer remarks that "the entire fraud was the work of a clique which has been working the Sun Worshipers' Racket for more than forty years, and handing it down through the generations." The gang's trade secrets involved the chemicals necessary to allow the requisite effects of mysterious flames and apparent immunity from fire.[7]

### Cults as Confidence Tricks

Doubts about the bona fides of mediums extended to the new wave of cult leaders, especially those offering miraculous medical cures. In a 1927 book, Morris Fishbein lamented the extensive range of "cults and quackeries" that Americans turned to in lieu of seeking proper medical attention and complained, "Of all the nations of the world, the United States is most afflicted by its healers." Fishbein was a visible national figure, a syndicated columnist who also edited the *Journal of the American Medical Association* and *Hygeia*. His book listed and denounced many pseudoscientific fads derived from chiropractic and homeopathy, but there were also spiritual healing techniques like New Thought, Christian Science, and Divine Science, and mystical doctrines like astral healing, Dowieism, Zodiac Therapy, and several orders of "blood-washers," like the Christos cult. Though snake-oil salesmen were by no means a new feature of American life, many in the early twentieth century had learned the value of adopting a religious guise for their ideas in order to evade regulation by professional bodies, in addition to winning tax advantages; chirothesianism was "a method of mixing religion and fake healing to get around the medical practice laws." Typical of Fishbein's examples was the Christian Philosophical Institute of Oakland, California, founded by Wilbert LeRoy Casper, who used "the Sixth Sense method of mental discernment in locating the patient's ailments." Casper played "the cult game clear across the board," selling paper diplomas and degrees.[8]

Hostility to cults escalated thanks to the popular distaste for religious fanaticism following the 1925 Scopes trial in Tennessee and the scandal that befell Aimee Semple McPherson the following year (see Table 6.1). Deceptive cult leaders now became a staple of popular fiction. In 1927, Sinclair Lewis's controversial novel *Elmer Gantry* depicted the evangelical world as the realm of cynical tricksters on the make, spiritual leaders for whom revival meetings were a money-making device little different from a traveling show and whose sexual morality fell far short of the standards they demanded of their listeners. The McPherson case was the major source for Frank Capra's study of a phony healer named Florence "Faith" Fallon in the 1931 film *Miracle*

Table 6.1
Cults and Cult Scandals, 1926–1929

1926   Mysterious disappearance of Aimee Semple McPherson.
Conviction of Warien Robertson, founder of the Temple of the
   Gospel of the Kingdom.

1927   Trial of Benjamin Purnell, leader of House of David.
Morris Fishbein, *The New Medical Follies*.
Herbert S. Gorman, *The Place Called Dagon*.
Sinclair Lewis, *Elmer Gantry*.

1928   Frank B. Robinson founds Psychiana.
William Dudley Pelley experiences his "Seven Minutes in Eter-
   nity."
Collapse of Theosophical colony led by Brother XII.
Charles W. Ferguson, *The Confusion of Tongues*.
Hugo Hume, *The Superior American Religions*.
H. P. Lovecraft, "The Call of Cthulhu," published in *Weird Tales*.

1929   Witchcraft trial in York County, Pennsylvania.
Krishnamurti repudiates messianic claims.
Violence and mob activity surround breakup of Moorish Science
   Temple movement; disappearance of Noble Drew Ali
*San Francisco Examiner* exposé of Riker's Holy City.
E. F. Dakin, *Mrs. Eddy—Biography of a Virginal Mind*.
Dashiell Hammett, *The Dain Curse*.
William Seabrook, *The Magic Island*.
Aleister Crowley, *Moonchild*.

*Woman.* This work even goes beyond *Elmer Gantry* in its depiction of
the corruption surrounding show-tent religion: the healer's managers
are shown bribing politicians for the right to operate and commit murder to prevent exposure of their racket. Aggravating the McPherson
scandal were the recent memories of the Ku Klux Klan boom of the
early 1920s: although this was ostensibly a political and racial movement, Klan leaders were superbly successful in peddling what amounted
to a synthetic quasi-religious cult. In the 1936 film *Black Legion*, the
leaders of a Klan-like organization boast how much more easily money
could be made through a pseudoreligion than through traditional pur-
suits like selling Florida swampland.

   Through the interwar years, scandals surrounding spurious cults did
immeasurable harm to the image of legitimate small and nontraditional
religions. One perennial media favorite was Edwin J. Dingle, who

claimed to have encountered in China "the last of an age-old chain of wise men" from whom he learned great spiritual wisdom and mental secrets. In the 1920s, under the name of Ding Lei Mei, he established his Institute of Mentalphysics [sic] in Los Angeles and sold religious secrets guaranteed to attract prosperity for any user. As late as the 1950s, he still had a local following of a thousand or so, in addition to another ten thousand mail-order adherents.[9]

Images of deception and hypocrisy were reinforced by the stories surrounding Father William Riker's Holy City. Through the early 1920s, he was facing periodic criminal investigations for false pretenses and conspiracy to corrupt public morals. In 1929, he was plotting a huge expansion that would include an amphitheater seating seventeen thousand people, who would witness "bodies lifted up to heaven by wires and mirrors; men from the colony to masquerade as crippled, blind and deaf, then to be magically cured by the Father."[10] Unfortunately, he confided his plans to an undercover reporter for the *San Francisco Examiner*, which printed a disastrous exposé. In the same year, Los Angeles police investigated "The Divine Order of the Royal Arm of the Great Eleven," the prophet of which was awaiting angelic inspiration before revealing the location of rich deposits of gold and oil; a failed healing ritual allegedly caused the death of one follower.[11] In 1945, the leader of the Los Angeles-based Temple of Yahweh was jailed on theft charges. This eccentric movement claimed direct contact with Yahweh, a resident of the star system Orion; the group also held British Israelite views.[12]

Just as unsavory was the story of Mankind United. The movement was founded by Arthur L. Bell in San Francisco in 1934, and it appealed to an audience much less sophisticated than that which normally responded to esoteric movements. Bell, "The Voice," freely plagiarized existing movements: like Theosophy, he claimed, his own group had also been founded in 1875 under the instruction of ultraintelligent beings, though his were "Sponsors" rather than "Masters." The Sponsors aimed to assist humanity to free itself from the tyranny of its "hidden rulers," who were seeking to establish a worldwide slave state. Followers were promised a world of minimal toil and enormous material wealth, under the auspices of its omnipotent leader. Among other powers, Bell claimed possession of secret ray weapons, which could knock the eyeballs out of people hundreds of miles away, and he could allegedly transport himself to any location instantly through his own will. Between 1934 and 1941, fourteen thousand Californians joined the group, mainly "elderly persons or individuals who had suffered severe economic losses."[13] The movement reached its peak in 1939, partly because it seemed to offer a miraculous solution to the impending war crisis. Though Mankind United collapsed in the early 1940s, Bell promptly organized a new Church of the Golden Rule, to which followers would donate all their worldly goods. He commanded $3.4 million in assets in various parts of California and Oregon, including "two laundries, six hotels, business buildings, five restaurants, two canneries, two lumber mills, Santa Monica's lush Sorrento Beach Club, a thousand head of cattle, a cheese factory, and ten thousand acres."[14] As employees were church members, they received low wages for long hours, and Bell paid no taxes.

## Love Cults

Cult horror stories often involved titillating sex scandals: indeed, the press frequently reported on love cults and sex cults, generally referring to forms of polygamy or free love. Other usages were more insidious and suggested sexual perversion. When American social investigators uncovered homosexual and transvestite underworlds in major cities, with their distinctive slang and customs, these subcultures were likewise discussed in terms of cults. By about 1911, the metaphor of a homosexual cult became standard in the American media. In 1925, raids on a pioneering gay rights organization in Chicago led to newspaper headlines on the lines of "strange sex cult exposed." Through the 1940s, antigay writers charged that homosexuals, male or female, converted the child victims they molested to become perverts themselves, in a process described as "proselytizing." Victims learned "all the practices and ceremonials of homosexualism."[15] In what became a cause célèbre, in 1918, a British newspaper attacked a performance of Wilde's *Salome* on the grounds that its performers and audience were mainly lesbian or homosexual. As neither word was acceptable in print, the paper resorted to what was then an obscure medical term in its headline, claiming that the deviants belonged to "The Cult of the Clitoris."[16]

The newspapers also applied their "sex-cult" coverage to religious and mystical groups, particularly those that imported Asian beliefs. In the first quarter of the century, religious cults were one of the very few areas of life in which whites, especially white women, would regularly defer to the authority of Asian leaders. Racist concerns about this authority were expressed in sexual terms. American women were said to be particularly vulnerable to the exotic enticements of Asian mysticism. Gullible women were thus reopening the gates to paganism, and a 1912 article on contemporary swamis claimed that "Eve is eating the apple again." As anticult critic Fred S. Miller argued in 1913, "The dull and pampered natures of such women crave the mysterious and the sensual. . . . What has come over our women?"[17]

Sexual and racial dangers both featured in Miller's 1913 tract on menaces to the Christian family, among which were "the wiles and trickery of mystic cults." This was illustrated by the tale of "how lovely Mrs. Prince was fascinated, then fell—a victim to the sad voice, the unctious [sic] personality and the seductive smile of a pagan priest lover from a tropic land where heathen lust-gods rule." Mrs. Prince fell victim to one of "these swarthy, black-eyed, magnetic and persuasive priests from the far East."[18] Miller warned of these "unclean abominations" and exposed "licentious tendencies and unchaste practices of foreign religious cults whose leaders come from heathen countries, finding a rich harvest of dollars in America; and for our gold establish here their indecent doings and damnable enticements—How some of our fairest women listen to the voice of the fire-eyed Oriental and lose honor's precious jewel." Cult leaders used religion to seduce their followers: "Gently it is intimated to her that she may become (who knows?) the mother of the new messiah, whose coming is confidently expected."[19] Miller's tract was one of the first to speak of cult "victims," a usage that enjoyed wide currency later in the century.

During the mid-1920s, the whole culture of small religions was disgraced by a series of scandals involving more or less blatant confidence tricks and often sexual misdeeds. One media mainstay was Oom the Omnipotent, otherwise Pierre Bernard, who became a bugbear of the Hearst press.[20] In 1910, Bernard opened his Sanskrit College in New York City, and he later served as guru and charismatic leader for a Tantric-based movement with its headquarters at Nyack, New York. The group attracted a number of wealthy devotees, including representatives of elite families like the Vanderbilts, Rutherfords, and Dukes. Over the next three decades, the press reported his ceremonies in the most lurid and ludicrous terms, suggesting (probably correctly) that Oom practiced sexual rites with his female followers in an orgiastic "love cult." Though the guru faced difficulties with police on a number of occasions, the Nyack cult survived into the 1940s.

## The Scandals of the 1920s

Such scandals were becoming commonplace by the mid-twenties. Even Point Loma had its scandal in the 1920s when Katherine Tingley was sued for alienation of affections. This was in no sense a matter of weird orgies or perverse sexuality, but rather a personal romantic triangle: Tingley herself was then in her seventies. Still, the scandal was damaging for one of the most reputable of the fringe groups. In 1926, one of the black Jewish sects was uprooted following the imprisonment of its prophetic leader for immorality charges, specifically for violating the federal Mann Act of 1910, which forbade transporting women across state lines for immoral purposes. In this case, the head of the Temple of the Gospel of the Kingdom was arrested in connection with a New Jersey-based "baby farm," where devotees would bear his offspring.[21]

Even more lethal was the case of the itinerant British messiah Edward A. Wilson, the Brother XII.[22] Between 1924 and 1926, Wilson claimed a series of visions that declared the onset of a new world age, which would be ushered in following disasters and travails on a scale unparalleled since the destruction of Atlantis. Through automatic writing, he received communications from the Masters known as the Great White Lodge, long venerated by Theosophists. Wilson was now elevated to the position of the twelfth member of that lodge. As the Brother XII, he formed his Aquarian Foundation and gathered disciples whom he led to his settlement on Vancouver Island, which would be the nucleus of a new race that would dominate the world, the Knights of the Grail. In Canada, Britain, and the United States, he found a ready audience in preexisting occult and especially Theosophical lodges; he more or less co-opted the membership of Canadian Theosophy. Not surprisingly, Wilson also gained many followers in California, where Theosophists were already thrilled by the hopes surrounding Krishnamurti. By late 1927, Wilson's Foundation had 125 groups in North America, each comprising ten members; at its height, the island colony had hundreds of members.

Wilson exploited his occult role in order to attract the wealthy and gullible, while using sexual ritual magic to seduce female followers. When the Aquarian Foundation collapsed among internecine disputes and legal conflicts, Wilson formed a new communal center for his remaining hard core of loyal followers. The disciples turned over their possessions to him in exchange for the privilege of being subjected to prolonged forced labor in conditions that may have been deliberately intended to hasten the members' deaths. Discipline was maintained by the Brother's supposed mastery of curses and black magic. Wilson apparently died in 1934, having made perhaps half a million dollars from his religious racket.

The case added to the publicity woes of the new sects. When the Brother XII story broke in 1928, the original Canadian news coverage exposed the operation as "a free-love colony, and the resort of weak-minded money-mad Americans who have been resorting there by the hundreds"; it was proclaimed: "Weird Occultism Exemplified." Recalling recent spiritualist scandals, the newspapers suggested that if the colony was not suppressed, its members would all run the risk of insanity. When the affair was reported in the U.S. papers that same year, it was under misleading headlines such as "Free Love Cult Laid to Californians" and "Californian Called Head of Love Cult," on the grounds that only a Californian would be likely to head such a dubious operation.[23] The Wilson case followed shortly after the House of David trial, which had occurred in 1927. That affair focused on Benjamin Purnell, "King Ben," who had succeeded his disgraced predecessor Michael Mills in 1900 and over the years had faced sporadic scandals and press denunciations. These peaked with Purnell's trial for sex crimes, which confirmed a widespread public stereotype about lascivious prophets. The cliché was enduring. When modern American nudism emerged in southern California during the early 1940s, the press applied the familiar "love cult" script, again claiming that "unspeakable orgies" took place in the closed compounds.[24]

Popular images of the cults are summarized in Hammett's The Dain Curse, which could have been inspired by any of the numerous scandals of the mid-1920s. The book involves a fringe group called the Temple of the Holy Grail, founded by a theatrical couple, the Haldorns, who were looking for a money-making angle. "Thinking in that direction meant pretty soon thinking about Aimee, [Frank] Buchman, Jeddu what's-his-name [Krishnamurti], and the other headliners. And in the end, their thinking came to, why not us? They rigged up a cult that pretended to be the revival of an old Gaelic church, dating from King Arthur's time. . . . They brought their cult to California because everybody does, and picked San Francisco because it held less competition than Los Angeles."[25] The detective cynically comments that the mystical order dated not from the time of King Arthur but of Arthur Machen, the turn-of-the-century occult novelist: this is a shrewd remark both in terms of the modernity of the ideas represented and their artificial literary quality. Enlisting an assistant who is expert in the tricks of stage magic, the Haldorns use lights, smoke, and perfumes to create illusions during their rituals, even to the point of inducing a gullible believer to carry out a sacrificial murder on their behalf. Hammett's descriptions probably draw from Houdini's technical exposés.

Apart from the account of the Holy Grail sect itself, *The Dain Curse* is fascinating evidence for just how commonplace such groups and ideas had become at all levels of society. The Haldorns' Holy Grail was "the fashionable one just now. You know how they come and go in California," so this was not just "the Holy Roller or House of David sort of thing."[26] In terms of the contemporary view of cults, all that was really lacking from the Haldorn operation is the suggestion of perverse sex. That element was supplied in abundance by William Seabrook's book on Haitian Voodoo, *The Magic Island*, which also appeared in 1929.

## Cults and Insanity

If indeed the cults were so deviant, irrational, and criminal, then their followers must themselves be of questionable sanity, and psychiatric experts of this era indeed claimed that the fringe religions attracted the mentally unbalanced, much as their present-day successors argue that cults appeal to the maladjusted. This attitude was in keeping with the early-twentieth-century tendency to medicalize types of deviance and to seek psychodynamic explanations for all forms of criminality. In turn, cult activity was thought likely to cause mental instability and outright insanity, and psychiatrists regarded the marginal religions as strictly within their area of expertise. Throughout this literature, we find a persistent reluctance to acknowledge that experimental religious activity might reflect any honest intellectual endeavor or genuine spirituality, even where the specific traditions involved were of long historical standing.

The supposed link between cults and insanity dated back at least to the nineteenth century and the trial of the presidential assassin, Charles Guiteau. The belief was promoted by contemporary assumptions about the peculiar female tendency to neurosis since women were so active in many fringe movements. As Fred Miller claimed in 1913, "In Chicago not long ago, a beautiful young maiden of culture and refinement was taken screaming from one of these foreign religious

temples—praying and tossing her light white raiment to the winds—
and was incarcerated, a maniac, in the Illinois asylum for such unfor-
tunates." In 1911, the courts overturned the will of an American
woman who bequeathed her wealth to the Ramakrishna Order on the
grounds that her practice of Hindu spirituality was *ipso facto* evidence
of insanity.[27]

In the same years, religious revivalism was variously analyzed in
terms of mass hysteria, atavism, and degeneracy. One academic observer of the Pentecostal revival wrote in 1905 that "the most important purely pathological phenomenon of superemotional revivals is
insanity," and in 1925, psychologist W. T. Root argued that "neuras-
thenics" and degenerates "constitute the emotional core of successful
Holy-Roller or gift-of-tongue orgies." Such low mental types were
dangerously vulnerable to hypnotism, which was said to be the secret
weapon of every successful revivalist and cult leader. From this point
of view, it was no coincidence that revivalism enjoyed its largest followings in the rural South, where eugenic theorists claimed to
find so many depressing examples of hereditary crime, insanity, and
alcoholism, in legendary families like the Jukes and the Kallikaks. It
seemed that degenerate white trash composed the natural audience for
revivalism.[28]

The insanity theme reemerged forcefully during the post–First
World War antispiritualist movement. In 1919 and 1920, the new popularity of mediums and seances led to a media panic over clients supposedly driven mad by occult involvement. Reporting a wave of incidents in the northern California community of El Cerrito in March
1920, the *San Francisco Chronicle* included front-page headlines like
"Ouija Board Seance Drives Seven Insane" and "Question of Abolish-
ing Seances is Discussed by Experts," while the *San Francisco Examiner* offered "Ouija Board Drives Policeman to Street Naked: Mystic
Word Sends Man to Seek Enemy." The same issue of the *Examiner*
included a story under the heading "Ouija Said to Hasten Insanity—
Contributing Cause of Lunacy—Mental Experts Discuss Effects."[29]
State legislators proposed the formal abolition of the seance and the
ouija board. Seances were blamed for other violent or irrational acts,
though usually we can presume that the disasters would have occurred
without the occult stimulus, and the media were merely latching on to
a then popular villain. In 1922, newspapers reported that a San Francisco man who killed two of his small sons did so under instructions
from his dead wife, with whom he had been in communication. The

following year, New York state legislators proposed to ban seances following the suicide of a Barnard College student, who killed herself in order to join a spirit with whom she had fallen in love.[30]

As Houdini noted, the "by-products of spiritualism" could be devastating, and similar charges followed each new movement. In the 1930s, critics of the Ballards' I AM sect charged that followers were forced to concentrate on its doctrines "with such intensity and emotionalism that a number of them have had nervous breakdowns, or have been confined to psychopathic wards and insane asylums. . . . It has produced untold mental suffering from fears of cataclysms, entities, black magicians, destructive decrees, and other fear-inspiring bogeys."[31]

The psychiatric approach reached new heights in the 1930s, reflecting the growing dominance of Freudian theories. In 1933, Louis Binder's pioneering sociological analysis of cult leaders and members fully accepted a psychopathological interpretation of the movements' appeal, relying on pop psychoanalysis: throughout the work, terms like "pathological," "complex" and "hysterical" recur. The following year, the *American Journal of Psychiatry* published a paper on the millenarian Adventist movement, which had swept through the United States in 1843 and 1944, under the revealing title of "The Miller Delusion: A Comparative Study of Mass Psychology." Sociologist Read Bain argued in 1936 that "much flight to structural psychotic groups, gangs, homosexual colonies, bizarre cults and so on, is merely an attempt, sometimes successful, to escape individual psychopathy." Locating cults alongside other such antisocial groups was not uncommon: in 1938 a study of "The Kingdom of Father Divine" appeared in *The Journal of Abnormal Psychology*. Following a surge of media interest in snake handling sects in 1940, *Science News Letter* offered a report, "Snake Handling Cultists Resemble Other Groups," pointing out that one might theorize about the cult member as a specific type of deviant individual. [32]

Meanwhile, studies of religious leaders like Mary Baker Eddy emphasized the personal mental disorders and neuroses that had given rise to their ideas. Binder blamed a "sex neurosis" for many of Eddy's ideas and actions, due to her "repressing the natural sex urges which she had failed to sublimate."[33] When Nation of Islam leader Elijah Muhammad was placed in a federal prison in 1943, his psychiatric evaluation claimed that he had the IQ-level of an eleven-year-old child, that he was suffering from "dementia praecox, paranoid type," and his schizophrenia was demonstrated by his bizarre belief that Allah had communicated with him "in visual and auditory form." Surely, only a severely disturbed individual could believe that God had taken human form and spoken directly to his followers and, moreover, that God incarnate might not be white.[34] Cultists, whether leaders or followers, must be sick.

## To What Green Altar?

The question of just how aberrant cult behavior could be was raised in acute form at the end of the 1920s by allegations that fringe religious groups might be involved in ritualistic violence and murder. Fundamental to the notion of cult violence was a radical reshaping of older notions of witchcraft, a change that reflected the speculations of academic anthropologists. According to the most extreme interpretation, witchcraft was not merely folk magic, but a complete alternate religion, a secret domestic paganism that practiced human sacrifice. These revised concepts of witchcraft were forged during a period of intense cultural work in the decade after 1925, and they gradually merged with the gruesome stereotypes derived from the voodoo panic. Though literary and artificial in nature, tales of American blood cults were soon being treated seriously by journalists and police. Charges that some cults might be involved in murder affected perceptions of all eccentric religious groups, particularly those living in isolated enclaves, removed from the public gaze.

The first tales of clandestine alternate religions in the heartland date from an era of rapid change in the American countryside and in the relationship between urban and rural societies. The 1920 census was the first to show a majority of Americans living in cities rather than the countryside, while the popularity of the private automobile vastly increased the opportunities for city dwellers to explore those rural landscapes that now seemed so exotic. As tourism boomed, entrepreneurs made all they could of the exoticism of the countryside, selling as commodities the authentic folk-traditions of regions like New Mexico, the Ozarks, or the Louisiana bayou. A serious scholarship of folklore flourished alongside this popular hucksterism, and ethnographic observations of backward rural communities flourished in the interwar years. Though their goals were more exalted than the marketers, ethnographers, too, exaggerated the primitive and sensational elements they encountered. Interest in rural folk-traditions received a boost in the

1930s when the Federal Writers Project encouraged the collection of oral history accounts to preserve a vanishing popular heritage.

Because of its proximity to major East Coast cities and newspapers, German Pennsylvania was a particular target for such romantic investigations. The popular discovery of the Amish dates from the publication of the 1905 novel *Sabina*, which launched a whole subgenre of fiction set among quaint sectarian groups, and already by 1915, Pennsylvania possessed a whole industry of Amish postcards and souvenirs. Also at the turn of the century, the urban media began reporting on the thriving witch traditions of the Pennsylvania Germans. Removed from their decorative origins, hex signs were marketed as symbols of a society terrified of witches and the occult.[35] Images of witches and pagan-sounding folk-beliefs were welcomed by a new popular media in search of sensational stories, during a great era for newspaper stunts and tabloid exposés.

The extent of popular interest in the "pagan countryside" became obvious during 1928 and 1929 when an incident in Pennsylvania's York County attracted worldwide attention. In November 1928, three young men murdered the reputed witch Nelson Rehmeyer, whom they accused of hexing them. One of the killers, a witch in his own right, also wanted to seize Rehmeyer's pow-wow book, or manual of spells. The media frenzy over the ensuing trial was led by the *New York World*, but major stories followed in all the major magazines, including *Fortune*, the *North American*, the *Nation*, *Colliers*, *Mentor*, and the *Literary Digest*.[36]

The York story was reported across the globe, partly because the depiction of such primitive conditions exactly fitted international stereotypes of American country bumpkins in the aftermath of the Scopes trial. Typical reporting in the papers from New York City and Philadelphia portrayed rural Pennsylvania as a medieval community living under the constant shadow of spells and superstition, where "the ignorance and fear of the savages have not been uprooted by our boasted civilization." Media investigations brought to light the numerous other magicians, "brauchers," or pow-wowers scattered across the state, and the *hexerei* they employed. The main occultism expert conscripted to comment on the York case was William Seabrook, whose expertise lay in the quite dissimilar world of Haiti, but for the media, Pennsylvania witchcraft was an equally mysterious subculture. In this area, observed the *Literary Digest*, "Witchcraft rears its head and flourishes as it did in the Medieval Ages, and does now along the Kongo." As evidence that the York crime was no isolated event, another similar murder was reported in Virginia about the same time, in which a Lunenburg County man killed his supposed occult tormentor.[37]

For years afterwards, the media sought hungrily for any hint of a new "witch murder" in Pennsylvania and exaggerated the slightest hints of the occult in the most mundane crimes. The closest parallel to the York County sensation was the 1934 murder of a Pottsville woman by a man who believed she had bewitched him and who duly claimed self-defense at his trial.[38] Other stories concerned small children who had died while being treated by pow-wowers instead of being taken to doctors employing modern remedies. As in the York County case, the element of witchcraft here did not imply any kind of organized cult, nor did the violence have any sacrificial purpose, but these cases encouraged journalists and urban readers to imagine pagan secrets smoldering beneath the tranquil surface of an otherwise modern farming landscape.

Witchcraft was a hot topic in the American media in the 1920s and 1930s, usually in the context of distinctive ethnic communities like the Pennsylvania Germans or of those urban Slavic and Italian immigrants who retained a powerful belief in folk magic.[39] When Seabrook published *Witchcraft: Its Power in the World Today* in 1940, he noted that "[C]urrent American witchcraft cases occur with steady frequency, and in pleasing variety, at the rate of several dozens a year." A handful of the most extreme instances involved the murder of supposed witches, usually by people who believed that this was the only way of removing a curse.[40] Native American traditions also made headlines, and in 1930 the New York City papers exposed witchcraft practices on reservations near Buffalo. In southwestern states like New Mexico, where witches had been lynched at least up to the end of the nineteenth century, stories and incidents recorded in the 1930s demonstrate the continuing vigor of Native American and Hispanic occult traditions.[41]

### The Witch Cult

That American witchcraft still existed was beyond question, but in these same years, a diverse group of anthropologists and sensationalist writers reinterpreted these vestigial practices to construct an enticing mythology of a powerful organized movement. The ultimate influence was Sir James Frazer, whose book *The Golden Bough* first appeared in 1890. Frazer claimed that fertility cults represented a universal primal religion, which practiced regular human sacrifices, and these ideas had an enduring impact on both elite and popular culture. The concept of rural nature spirits being appeased by blood sacrifice was given an American setting in John Steinbeck's 1933 novel, *To a God Unknown,* while D. H. Lawrence's "The Woman Who Rode Away" (1924) explored the human sacrifice theme. Lawrence's story imagines a cult among Indians in northern Mexico, who inherit a clandestine tradition from the ancient Aztecs.

Also saturated in Frazer's theories was Margaret Murray, whose 1921 book, *The Witch Cult in Western Europe,* formulated the concept of widespread secret religions. Murray argued that the witch hunters of the sixteenth and seventeenth centuries had exposed an authentic underground religion, which was the lineal descendant of an ancient European paganism dating back to the time of the Palaeolithic cave paintings.[42] In her view, the so-called witches of early modern France or England had been adherents of this goddess-worshipping Old Religion, and the witch-hunters were reporting no more than the sober truth when they told of cells ("covens"), each comprising thirteen members. Each coven was headed by a disguised leader bearing some title, such as The Devil or The Black Man, and the groups met in periodic assemblies known as "esbats" and "sabbats." Also accurate, according to Murray, were accounts of the witches' calendar, which preserved ancient agricultural cycles, with key dates like Halloween and May Eve (Walpurgis Night, or April 30). When early modern Christians denounced so-called witchcraft, they were actually describing the European manifestation of Frazer's primal religion, in which the orgiastic rituals of the Sabbat were really fertility rites.

Murray's influential account is the grandparent of all modern pagan and Wiccan belief and practice, though as a historical picture, it is worthless. No modern scholar of witchcraft accepts the notion of an underlying Old Religion, at least in the sense of an organized movement, and few would acknowledge that the witch-hunts were responding to any authentic pagan survivals. Among other flaws, Murray paid no attention to the brutal judicial means by which the witch-hunters obtained their stories, and to say the least, she massaged the evidence to produce the "witches' calendar," which she found so infallibly in whatever account she examined. Even so, her ideas inspired a thorough revision of conventional views of witches and witchcraft.

Murray's prominent use of the word "cult" as a description of covert occult or satanic groups helped popularize the idea of a secret religion in North America as well as Europe. She argued that the Salem trials genuinely had exposed at least one pagan coven, with Puritan minister George Burroughs as Black Man, the literal Devil of Salem, and other thirteen-member covens could be found in the history of seventeenth-century New England. This view ran contrary to the accepted commonplaces of the nineteenth century, when Salem had become a symbol for Puritan intolerance, greed, and wild superstition. Standard historical authorities like Charles W. Upham referred simply to the great "witchcraft delusion," the "fanaticism," when "it was in the power of every man to bring down terrible vengeance upon his enemies by pretending to be bewitched by them." This was also the image proposed in works like Hawthorne's *House of the Seven Gables*.[43] The witch-hunts long continued to be powerful metaphors for unreasoning intolerance, as in the 1937 film *Maid of Salem*, which brought the story before a mass public once again. As for the alleged orgies and sexual rites, the liberal view saw them as no more than fantasies arising from Puritan repression.[44] But Murray's work raised the question whether America's numerous witches were part of some secret cult. The *Literary Digest* concluded its 1930 investigation of witchcraft among New York's Native Americans with the remark that "no organized cult . . . seems to exist," a note which would have been superfluous only a decade previously.[45]

### Pulp Fiction

The speculations of Murray and Frazer would have remained an academic curiosity if they had not been taken up so avidly by a new generation of sensational writers, for whom they offered wonderful new material. During the 1920s, the world of popular fiction was revolutionized by mass marketing and the pulp magazines. By 1934, about 150 pulps were being published in New York alone, and a few famous names redefined whole genres. The most prominent titles included *Black Mask* (detective stories) and *Astounding* (science fiction), while the key name in the horror genre was *Weird Tales*, the legendary magazine that published all the major American horror authors from 1923 until its demise in 1954. As exemplified by writers like H. P. Lovecraft, the *Weird Tales* type of horror story often used the American backwoods as a setting for secret horrors, depicting cults, witches, and sacrificial religions. Although *Weird Tales* did not reach a mass national audience, it is representative of a large area of popular culture, and similar themes now pervaded not just the pulps but cheap novels, and they appeared in radio serials and films.

The notion of an American witch cult proved extraordinarily attractive for Lovecraft and the *Weird Tales* generation, many of whom were immersed in antiquarian scholarship. Fantasy writers began treating Salem as if the witchcraft genuinely had represented a serious occult movement, and the village had been the scene of evil rituals by an organized movement. The pioneering fictional work was Herbert S. Gorman's novel *The Place Called Dagon* (1927), which portrays a secret cult in a western Massachusetts town populated by descendants of refugees from Salem who were still practicing "the morbid and degenerate horrors of the Black Sabbat."[46] In light of Murray's work, the name Dagon evoked some bitter controversies of Puritan New England, which suggested that this Puritan society really had had its covert pagan side. The case in question was the notorious incident in 1627 in which dissidents erected a maypole of the type familiar from the English countryside and held a festive gathering under the auspices of the Lord and Lady of the May (the story is recounted in Hawthorne's "Maypole of Merry Mount"). Aware of its pagan connotations, outraged Puritan leaders denounced the maypole as a Dagon, after the Philistine idol mentioned in the Bible. Both Gorman and Lovecraft appropriated the name, implying that the maypole incident had been part of an American section of the witch cult.

The Dagon theme appeared in Lovecraft's "The Shadow Over Innsmouth," (1931), one of his best-known stories. This portrays a forbidding New England town, dominated by an evil race whose secret rituals are carried out under the cover of The Esoteric Order of Dagon, "a debased, quasi-pagan thing imported from the east," "a degraded cult" linked to devil worship: the order had its special holy days on Halloween and May Eve. In "The Haunter of the Dark" (published in *Weird Tales* in 1936), the secret cult is the Church of the Starry Wisdom, which is said to have flourished in Providence until eradicated by neighbors outraged at the disappearance of local children. Though entirely Lovecraft's concoction, the portrait of this cult draws heavily on actual esoteric movements of his own day, with elements taken both from the Golden Dawn magical tradition and from ancient Egyptian elements. Lovecraft explicitly cites the work of both Murray and Frazer, in addition to creating his own battery of spurious occult texts that sound so convincing that many readers then and since have thought them genuine. The main difference between him and equally creative contemporaries like Guy Ballard and Wallace Fard was that Lovecraft never pretended that his invented scriptures were to be taken seriously.

Lovecraft portrayed secret cults as the conduits by which evil humans commune with malign alien intelligences, by means of the mass sacrifice of animals and, often, humans. This theme first appears in the 1926 story "The Call of Cthulhu," which shows how an evil "Cthulhu cult" has operated in various parts of the world over the centuries.[47] The movement is related to other manifestations on the religious fringe, including "Voodoo orgies" in Haiti and "the wooded swamps south of New Orleans," and "ominous mutterings" in parts of Africa, while in California, "a Theosophist colony" dons "white robes *en masse* for some glorious fulfillment which never arrives" (Lovecraft could be thinking of either Point Loma or Ojai). The word "cult" is repeatedly used throughout to describe the real-life world of voodoo as well as the imaginary followers of Cthulhu, and cultists are responsible for abducting and sacrificing women and children.

Lovecraft often used this idea of subterranean colonial cults. In *The Case of Charles Dexter Ward* (1927), Lovecraft depicts Salem's Rev. Burroughs as the leader of a group of evil sorcerers, some of whom escape to carry on the cult into the present day. In "The Dreams in the Witch-House," reincarnated Salem witches in a modern city wait to celebrate Walpurgis Night, when "there would be bad doings, and a child or two would probably be missing."[48] Other *Weird Tales* writers concurred with his view: in 1936, Henry Kuttner referred to Salem's "old days, when Cotton Mather had hunted down the evil cults that worshiped Hecabe and the Magna Mater in frightful orgies."[49] America not only had real witches surviving into the twentieth century—the York case proved that—but they might be part of an ancient historical tradition, a deeply rooted homicidal cult. The presence of the Caribbean slave-woman Tituba in the original Salem tale allowed twentieth-century writers to link the episode with voodoo.[50]

### The Black Mass

During the 1930s, the concept of rural paganism increasingly merged with that of religious Satanism, another notion constructed from imported literary materials. This would be important in shaping media perceptions of American occultism and in creating stereotypes that would be projected on authentic movements of the religious fringe. Ultimately, the fictional synthesis would also contribute to the evolution of a real-life American Satanism.

Quite separately from the fantasies of the witch-hunters, an authentic religious worship of Satan can be found in western Europe of

the seventeenth and eighteenth centuries, where it found its most notorious expression in the the Black Mass. This parody of the Catholic
ritual was celebrated by a defrocked priest, who used a naked woman
for his altar and who sacrificed living creatures, including children. The
Black Mass achieved a literary revival in the decadent literature of late-
nineteenth-century France, and an extensive account appeared in J.-K.
Huysmans's novel *Là-bas (Down There.)*[51] Shortly after the English
translation of *Là-bas* was published in 1924, elaborate stories of the
Black Mass began appearing in the American pulps, familiarizing
American readers with the concepts of satanic worship. In 1925, this
ritual was the basis of an E. Hoffmann Price story in *Weird Tales*, and
in 1931, the same magazine offered a lengthy description in Seabury
Quinn's "Satan's Stepson." Quinn's Satanists desecrate a Catholic
church, replacing the consecrated host with the putrefying carcass of a
cat. Their Black Mass involved the sacrifice of "a little baby, most usually a boy, who has not been baptized": at the climax of the ritual, the
priest "cuts the helpless infant's throat and drains the gushing lifeblood
into the chalice." The story thus offered a white counterpart for the
Haitian goat without horns.[52]

   Tales of Satanism had an obvious appeal for sensational writers, but
the problem was that the Black Mass was initially too exotic to be
relevant to American circumstances. The ceremony only acquired its
blasphemous meaning in the context of a Catholic society, and it had
no precedents in the English-speaking world. Both the *Weird Tales*
stories employed a foreign setting, Price's in an Oriental never-never-
land, while Quinn located his ritual in Huysmans's Paris. Still, it would
not be long before the Black Mass idea was imported onto American
or British soil, both as fiction and as an alleged reality. The central
figure in this development was Aleister Crowley, the publicity-loving
English occultist whose followers indulged freely in magic based on
sexual rituals and drugs: Crowley also sacrificed animals. There were
even rumors of child sacrifice, though these accounts were fictions,
spawned by Crowley's lust for notoriety.[53]

   Crowley's appalling reputation in the British media was reflected in
the United States, which he visited on several occasions, traveling
widely across the continent. From 1914 to 1919, he lived in Greenwich
Village, and his arrival in the United States was greeted by a *New York
World* exposé of what were described as London's Satanists. Journalist
Harry Kemp affected to be appalled by Crowley's quarters, which were
"decidedly uncanny," "queer," "decidedly sepulchral;" the article in-

cludes a text from a Crowley ritual, with its "slow, monotonous chant of the high priest: 'There is no good. Evil is good. Blessed be the principle of evil. All hail, Prince of the World, to whom even God himself has given dominion.' A sound as of evil bleating filled the pauses of these blasphemous utterances. . . . In the third and largest room stood a tall perpendicular canopy under which the high priest stood during the celebration of black mass."[54]

Though Crowley described the story as "balderdash," this may be the first account by the American media about the actual existence in the English-speaking world of bona fide practitioners of black magic or Satanism. Shortly afterwards, the leader of this group stood on American soil. Crowley's occult group, the OTO, or *Ordo Templi Orientis*, already had a lodge in Vancouver, and he developed a following in southern California. Agape Lodge #2 was founded in Los Angeles in the 1930s, and the heavily Californian composition of Crowley's following led him to refer punningly to the headship of the American OTO as "the Caliphate."[55] His American friends included William Seabrook, who used Crowley as a source for his influential accounts of modern-day black magic, while American-born Leah Hirsig was Crowley's mistress, disciple, and chosen "Scarlet Woman." Another devout Californian follower, Jack Parsons, was obsessed with the darkest corners of magic and in 1945 was said to be "enamored with witchcraft, the *houmfort*, Voodoo." Parsons tried to undertake the rituals necessary to incarnate the Moonchild, an Antichrist figure who would be born to a woman, as described in Crowley's novel *Moonchild*.[56]

These American connections ensured that Crowley's activities would fascinate papers like the *New York Journal*, which in the 1920s reported on the sexual and occult doings at his magical commune, the Abbey of Thelema, at Cefalù in Sicily. Such accounts helped establish the genre of the cult headquarters where the rich and gullible were maltreated by a leader until their money and patience ran out. A particularly violent media attack ensued in 1923 when one of the Cefalù disciples died: although the death was natural, Crowley was, of course, accused of foul play. In 1928, Leah Hirsig's sister published an account of "life in a love cult" as "a warning to all young girls."[57] In 1934, Boris Karloff used Crowley as the model for his role as a satanic cult leader in the horror film *The Black Cat*, which features a Black Mass.

Despite public perceptions, Crowley's particular kind of magic had nothing to do with either Satanism or the Black Mass, but was rather a bookish combination of Hermetic and Gnostic traditions. As he pointed out, he could scarcely perform a true Black Mass, as he was not an apostate Catholic priest. Nor did his occultism have any points of contact with any kind of backwoods paganism. Nevertheless, Crowley's bizarre world became the subject of fictional writings in which all these diverse elements were mingled together, so that witchcraft, Satanism, and black magic became indistinguishable in the popular mind, contextualized with sexual orgies and ritual violence.

The merger of these divergent traditions owed something to romantic scholarship in the work of authors like Seabrook. In 1939, Jules Michelet's celebrated history of French witchcraft, *La Sorcière*, was translated under the evocative title of *Satanism and Witchcraft*, while in 1945, Montague Summers published his credulous study of *Witchcraft and Black Magic*. American readers were also fascinated by the discovery of the Middle Eastern sect of the Yezidis, who were misleadingly presented as authentic ancient diabolists who had preserved their rituals over the millennia and are cited thus by Lovecraft. In 1927, Seabrook's *Adventures in Arabia* inevitably included a description of his encounter with the "Yezidee Devil Worshipers."[58]

Novelists shared much of the responsibility for mingling Satanism and witchcraft. One culprit was Dennis Wheatley, British author of numerous black magic novels, in which Crowley generally served as the model for successive archvillains.[59] *The Devil Rides Out* (1934) is important as the first attempt to synthesize the hitherto unrelated worlds of ceremonial magic (authentic) with the accounts of the medieval witch trials (fictitious). Thus the evil magicians do not work alone, as in tradition, but have followers who gather in covens at the great seasonal meetings, the orgiastic Sabbats, the accounts of which borrow extensively from the Black Mass. Though fictional, books like this played an indispensable part in shaping the new occult groups from the 1960s onwards, including real-life Satanists. *The Devil Rides Out* was also pivotal for anticult critics, as the Sabbat scene contains virtually all the charges that would be so popular in the literature of anti-Satanism in the 1980s, including the notion of child sacrifice. Though Wheatley's writings were not initially well-known in America, the originally discrete worlds of witchcraft and Satanism did become fused in this country as well as Britain. Crowley himself became the prototype for most fictional evil magi over the coming decades.

Partly through such literary influences, some self-described Satanists were practicing in the United States by the late 1930s. By 1940, Seabrook was reporting the existence of networks of genuine Satanists in Great Britain and the United States, some of which practiced the Black Mass. He claimed to have attended Black Masses in Paris and Lyons, and at least one celebrated "within less than a mile of the Washington Arch, in New York." In 1948, Toledo, Ohio, became home to Our Lady of Endor Coven of the Ophite Cultus Satanas. By 1956, on no known evidence, *Newsweek* declared that some forty groups in southern California alone "devote themselves to the celebration of the Satanic Mass."[60]

### Ritual Murder

By 1930, tales of ritual human sacrifice in the United States had become a familiar theme in popular literature, but the idea of sacrificial cults soon moved out of the realm of sensational fiction. Both newspapers and pulp magazines charged that "cult" motives might be involved in some of the real-life serial murder stories that were so commonplace in media reporting of the time: these instances appeared to confirm the existence of secretive human sacrifice cults. In assessing these tales, much depends on the definition of ritual murder. We can scarcely apply this term to an individual who merely cites religious motives for a crime, for example, to a man who believes that he is entrusted with a divine mission to kill prostitutes. Nor should we include murders that feature some occult-related motive, like the revenge killings of witches, though this distinction was often lost on the media. Strictly, the ritual murder concept should only apply to a killing carried out by an organized group, with the specific intent of fulfilling the prescribed demands of a given religious ritual. By this strict standard, the last killing carried out in the United States unequivocally recognizable as ritual in nature would be the often-described human sacrifice of a young girl by the Pawnee tribe in what is now Nebraska in 1838, though other later acts of this kind might have escaped the attention of observers.[61]

Despite the lack of genuine incidents, a vigorous ritual murder mythology has flourished over the last century. In addition to crimes attributed to real or alleged occult sects, other rumored culprits included the Jews, whom anti-Semites accused of undertaking acts of human sacrifice. The blood libel story that Jews ritually killed Christian children for festivals like Passover is at least a thousand years old, and it does have a subterranean history in the English-speaking world. In the American context, stories can usually be traced back to the mythologies of some Christian immigrant group derived from an area where such stories were strong, particularly in eastern Europe.[62] The American media discovered the phrase "ritual murder" in 1913, while reporting anti-Semitic trials in tsarist Russia, and over the next decade or so, the term exclusively implied a Jewish context. In just this year, and reflecting eastern European influences, we find domestic blood libel rumors in New York City and in Pennsylvania. In 1919, the stories reemerged in Fall River and Pittsfield (both in Massachusetts) and in Chicago. In Pittsfield, a young Polish boy claimed to have been dragged to the basement of a synagogue where he was to be drained of blood. In 1928, a rumored case developed in Massena, New York. Human sacrifice tales revived in the early 1930s during an upsurge of popular anti-Semitism, at a time when Americans feared the renewal of mass Jewish immigration. For the fascist right wing, the Lindbergh baby murder of 1932 was certainly a Jewish ritual murder, supposedly carried out at the Feast of Purim. Two more child murders were reported in San Diego between 1930 and 1933, both marked by the draining of blood, which supposedly proved the Jewish ritual element in the crime. San Diego was a center for the Silver Shirt movement, which trumpeted the various human sacrifice charges in its newspapers, *Liberation* and *The Silver Ranger*.[63]

### The Media and Human Sacrifice

Whether under the influence of anti-Jewish legends or Haitian fantasies, the media discovered human sacrifice as a popular theme from the early 1930s. In 1932 Detroit police claimed that they had uncovered a real-life ritual murder linked to the city's so-called voodoo cult, that is, the Nation of Islam, which may be the first time "ritual murder" was extended beyond anti-Jewish accusations. Soon afterwards, the concept was extended to other religious cults. One of the first such stories to gain national attention occurred in Inez, Kentucky, in February 1933, when an old woman was killed by believers from a Holiness or Pentecostal sect. According to the *New York Times*, she was "choked to death in a religious frenzy to prove their power over death" during a ritual to celebrate "the death of sin," which had involved a week of dancing, fasting, and speaking in tongues. Supposedly, the woman in question agreed to be killed by her son, and several other women stood ready to face the same fate. The *Times* headlined a "cult slaying" and (a striking novelty) a "human sacrifice."[64]

The ritual murder theme reemerged during the still-unsolved Cleveland torso slayings of the late 1930s, when seventeen victims were killed and mutilated in poor areas of that city and some other victims recorded in western Pennsylvania. As public frustration and panic reached new height in 1938, both police and media began investigating possible ritualistic elements, finding in the process some remarkable aspects of Cleveland's religious underworld. Police encountered "a wide range of unorthodox sects—blacks practicing Haitian Voodoo, covens of self-proclaimed witches and warlocks, and even a Hispanic group observing some obscure, ancient Aztec religion." Though none of these leads proved relevant to the case, the national public was further sensitized to the idea of authentic human sacrifice.[65]

Just as notorious as the torso killings was the sensational "poison-for-profit" ring discovered in Philadelphia in 1939, an insurance fraud operation that may well have claimed fifty lives. A mixed Italian and Jewish gang operated a criminal racket in which families took out insurance policies on the lives of relatives, who were then poisoned. The ring found its victims through a network of folk healers, exorcists, and popular magicians in the unassimilated ethnic communities, and the case offers an unparalleled glimpse into the plebeian occult underworld of the 1930s. The chief villain of the case was Morris Bolber, reported to be the greatest faith healer and witch doctor in the city, who claimed to have treated some twenty thousand patients. Bolber and his circle drew on very varied traditions, including Jewish popular Qabalism, German *Hexerei*, and Italian folk magic, or *Fatura*, while his colleague, Paul Petrillo, had sold his soul to the devil for the power of raising demons. Bolber reported attending a "midnight assembly [in Philadelphia] where weird rites were practiced and black and white magic created strange illusions" and where "witches and magicians could assemble, in the dark of night, in a dimly lighted room" in what earlier generations would have labeled a witches' Sabbat. Despite Petrillo's confessed diabolism, the magic revealed was more populist and peasant in nature, rather than resembling a Black Mass: the normal spell or cure involved carrying blessed eggs or summoning spirits with a special knife, and Bolber's chief talent involved his evil eye. Though the crimes were not sacrificial in nature, tales of violent murder were juxtaposed once more with words such as "witchcraft" and "cult," and naturally the media dwelled on the occult components of the case. The cases were generally known as the "Mass Witchcraft Murders."[66]

Media coverage of these cases could not fail to attract horror authors, who in turn cultivated the developing mythology. The main activist was Lovecraft's young protegé Robert Bloch, who through the 1930s and 1940s repeatedly explored concepts of cults and human sacrifice.

Bloch was fascinated by the idea that apparent serial murders might be disguised ritual sacrifices. In 1943, *Weird Tales* published his widely anthologized story "Yours Truly, Jack the Ripper," which imagines that the original London Ripper carried out his murders as part of an obscure ritual—a spurious theory that Crowley had done much to promulgate.[67] In Bloch's story, the Ripper was magically seeking eternal life and youth, and the same individual was in fact responsible for countless murders in successive decades, up to and including the Cleveland torso killings. Bloch retained a lively interest in the relationship between popular culture and the mythology of cults. In his 1947 novel, *The Scarf*, he depicts a sensationalistic California journalist urging a colleague to write a book on the Cleveland murders: "People like to read about it. Look at the way those true detective magazines sell. Sex crimes. Blood. Everybody wants to know. . . . Ever hear about the ritual murders we had out here? The devil worshipers? They cut up a kid." The notion that authentic American "devil worshipers" might "cut up a kid" would have been astonishing to the thought-world of 1920, but a generation later, it had become a cliché.[68]

In any given period over the last hundred and fifty years, we can find a similar array of charges mobilized against small religious groups, though the actual balance of charges might shift in individual cases. In the late 1930s, attacks on Psychiana or Mankind United were framed in terms of gangsterism and deception, while African American movements were stereotyped in the language of voodoo, but the rhetorical arsenal from which allegations were chosen remained relatively constant. About this time, however, the critique of cult activities was vastly aggravated by two largely novel kinds of allegation, which combined to make cults appear much more insidious than hitherto. One, obviously, was the ritual murder idea, which came to fruition with the cases in Cleveland and Philadelphia. The other was the charge that marginal religious groups were fronts for sedition or subversion. Security concerns created an atmosphere that made it easier for authorities to take official measures against sectarians who might earlier have been tolerated or ignored, making the early 1940s a bleak era for the right of religious expression.

# SEVEN

# The Purge of the Forties

I would . . . have done with this business of judicially examining other
people's faiths.
Justice Robert Jackson

By 1940, war threats had made American authorities particularly
sensitive to possible threats from any movements seen as active
or tacit supporters of enemy powers. Prominent among these
potential subversives were some major organizations on the religious
periphery, which naturally included the Silver Shirts, with all their
overt fascist trappings, but also some other conspicuous groups.
Charges of disloyalty raised the stakes in the struggle against cult excesses, and serious official sanctions were imposed in the early 1940s.
Because the courts were initially less supportive of minority religious
rights than they would be later on, they permitted a broad purge of
various unorthodox movements: by 1943/44, a newspaper headline
about "Cult Arrests" or "Cult Leaders Held" might refer to any one
of a dozen groups, in any part of the country. The chillier climate for
religious tolerance was reflected in an outpouring of books and articles
that attacked the fringe religions as part of a sinister cult phenomenon.
This alarmist message was carried to the general public through films,
magazines, and other popular culture outlets.

## Subversives

One major target of cult critics was "Ballardism," which had already
been attacked in newspapers across the nation in the late 1930s. Carey
McWilliams described it as "a witch's cauldron of the inconceivable,

the incredible and the fantastic . . . a hideous phantasm."[1] The movement was attacked by occultists no less than skeptics, because of I AM's
bastardized version of esoteric teachings and its vast appeal to New Age
believers. Theosophical magazines rejected Ballardism as a perversion
of occult inquiry, and in 1937, rosicrucian H. Spencer Lewis denounced
these "mystical racketeers": he ruefully confessed that his own writings on Lemuria had provided Ballard with some of his sources.[2] The
most powerful condemnations are found in the pamphlets produced
from 1936 onwards by the occultist, and former Ballard student, Gerald
Bryan. The I AM leaders instructed movement followers to buy and
burn Bryan's work, which they did "with all the fanaticism of a witch-
burning rite, reminiscent of a former age of bigotry and superstition,"
but Bryan's attacks continued to flow.[3] His work culminated in the 1940
book, *Psychic Dictatorship in America*, which has such striking parallels to modern anticult works.

Bryan comprehensively attacked the dubious origins of the movement, its plagiarized scriptures, and the mercenary motives of the founders. He also charged that I AM devastated the lives of its members.
Bryan argued that "probably in no other movement has there ever
been such widespread interference with the personal lives of its members as in this cult of the Mighty I AM." Members were told to sever
all contact with anyone who rejected I AM teaching, even family members, and the strain on family life was enhanced by the Ballards preaching against sexual desire, which was an enemy to be suppressed. I AM
prohibited sex except for procreation, and recommended against bringing children into a world so close to its end. "Husband, wife, mother,
or some other relative living in a fanatical Mighty I AM family has
actually been kept in another part of the house and denied former
privileges because he or she would not embrace the Ballard doctrines."[4]
Intolerance was demanded of "hundred percent students." Also bizarre
was the Ballard view that animal life was the creation of black magicians and that spirits in animals should be freed, in other words, that
members should "release" their animals by having them killed.

Even if we grant the literal truth of all the allegations made against
I AM, members were subjected to no form of distress to which they
did not consent, so that official intervention was unlikely. Matters were
however changed utterly by the movement's powerful political dimensions, which led to it being condemned as a cryptofascist sect. This idea
is invoked by the title of Bryan's *Psychic Dictatorship*, which also suggests the totalitarian lifestyle inflicted upon followers. The Ballards in-

vited these fascist comparisons by their growing use of superpatriotic rhetoric and symbolism. I AM boasted of being "not a religion but a patriotic movement," aimed at purging the United States of "vicious forces" within its borders, variously identified as black magicians, communism, the war menace, and so on. The group spawned an inner circle of Minute Men of Saint-Germain, along with Daughters of Liberty and an Inner Secret Service.[5] This language was worryingly reminiscent of the Silver Shirts, and critics of I AM stressed the parallels with William Dudley Pelley, whose ideas Ballard had plundered. The Ballards also sought to co-opt the Silver Shirts. In 1934, they channeled a vision in which Saint-Germain recalled nostalgically how some of Pelley's leading followers had been associated with him in previous lives, many millennia past, and he urged them to ally with the present-day I AM movement.

Carey McWilliams believed that I AM had "Hitlerian overtones," and other groups attracted similar suspicions. As John Gunther claimed, "most of the extreme cultists have, or had, strong fascist leanings, since they believe in salvation through energy and power," and perhaps because the leaders were attracted by the fascist cult of personality.[6] When Arthur L. Bell of Mankind United proclaimed in 1934 his opposition to the hidden rulers of the world, his ideas had an obvious overlap with the theories of contemporary anti-Semitism, not to mention the conspiracy ideas of the *Protocols of the Elders of Zion*, which was a favorite text of both Pelley and the Brother XII. British Israel doctrines contributed a religious justification to anti-Semitism by pillorying the Jews as impostors.

Also controversial was Frank Buchman, the former Lutheran minister whose Oxford Group (founded in 1909) tried to convert influential followers during high-pressure gatherings that culminated in intense outpourings of communal confession. These intrusive tactics foreshadowed the psychological methods for which cults and therapy sects would become notorious in the 1970s. As most of the material confessed tended to be sexual in nature, critics were horrified at the image of the young and well-to-do women publicly parading their most intimate secrets and fantasies. The Oxford Group had often been denounced as cultish, and in 1924 it was banned from operating at Princeton University after Buchman declared that 85 percent of the students there were sexual perverts. In the 1930s, Buchman aroused political alarm by his advocacy of "a God-controlled fascist dictatorship." He would long be haunted by his cry that "I thank heaven for a man like

Adolf Hitler who built a first line of defense against the Antichrist of Communism! . . . Think what it would mean to the world if he surrendered to the control of God. Or Mussolini. Or any dictator. Through such a man God could control a nation overnight and solve every last bewildering problem."[7] Throughout 1938 and 1939, Buchman conducted an international revival campaign demanding "Moral Rearmament" amidst rallies and pageantry of a kind that had acquired extremist political connotations. Though Buchman was not in the same flagrantly political category as Bell or the Ballards, his high-profile activities did tend to attach a political label to the cults.

## Suppressing the Cults

In the late 1930s, I AM and other sects fell victim to a broad federal action against the extreme Right. This campaign found public expression in the House Committee on Un-American Activities (the Dies committee), while the administration inspired media leaks that portrayed domestic fascist groups as a dangerous fifth column. Concern grew after war broke out in Europe. The summer of 1940 was a uniquely tense time, with the British Empire standing alone against Hitler and the likelihood that the United States might soon have to confront a German-dominated Europe. The concentration of "fascistic" cults on the West Coast was alarming, given the abundance of defense-related industries and military bases and the possibility of Japanese invasion. In early 1940, Pelley faced a grueling interview before the Dies committee, and shortly after Pearl Harbor, he and several key lieutenants faced federal sedition charges.[8] Silver Legion leaders were banned from residing in the western states for the duration of the war for fear that they might assist Axis invaders. The Ku Klux Klan, which had staged a minor revival in the late 1930s, was so harried by federal and state authorities in the early 1940s that it formally ceased to exist by 1944.

Other sects were treated equally harshly. Also accused of sedition was Arthur L. Bell, who had claimed that American planes had bombed Pearl Harbor under orders from the "hidden rulers of the world." He was summoned before the Tenney committee, which the California legislature had appointed to investigate subversive activities, and in December 1942, Bell and sixteen followers were arrested by the FBI for disseminating false information about the U.S. war effort. Though his conviction was eventually overturned in 1947, the prolonged appeal process broke the group's momentum.[9] Father William Riker faced sedition charges for publishing pamphlets praising Hitler and urging peace with the Axis, though he was not remotely as significant as some other leaders, and he was acquitted.[10] Psychiana also encountered difficulties in the late 1930s, with investigations of its activities by the Treasury Department, Post Office, and the FBI, as well as the American Medical Association, and Frank Robinson briefly faced the threat of deportation.[11] In this case, however, the movement remained unmolested, presumably because the British-born Robinson was a vociferous supporter of the war effort, to which he claimed to be devoting all his spiritual energies.

The Black Muslims faced a dreadful time of trial during the Second World War. Though the remaining followers of Noble Drew Ali were patriotic, the Nation of Islam and some other sects rejected the war as a contest between whites and refused to serve in the military. Some actively supported the Japanese as a fellow colored race and attacked the Jews for their persecution of Palestinian Arabs. Some American Muslims had also been impressed by the role of Moorish regiments on the pro-Fascist side in the Spanish Civil War. After Pearl Harbor, an alarmed FBI investigated accounts of the spread of pro-Axis sentiment among black Americans and undertook a national survey of black racial consciousness and dissent, RACON, the findings of which attested to the spread of Muslim belief. Though little active disloyalty was found, Nation of Islam temples were raided in Chicago and elsewhere, and federal sedition charges were pressed against leaders in Chicago, Milwaukee, and Washington, D.C. Dozens of Muslims were prosecuted for draft evasion, including Elijah Muhammad himself, who remained in prison from 1942 through 1946. Illustrating the official attitude to the religion, the warden of the Cook County jail refused his request for a Quran, telling him that "that is what we put them in prison for" and urging him to read the Bible instead.[12]

### The Ballard Prosecution

I AM was a prominent victim of the purge. In July 1940, a federal grand jury in Los Angeles indicted twenty-four leaders of the group for mail fraud on the grounds that the Ballards were falsely claiming to heal the sick and communicate with the spirit world and that they "well knew" these claims were bogus. The group's final provocation had been to use the mails to sell paintings of Jesus and Saint-Germain, supposedly taken from life. A trial judge, nervous about constitutional issues, ruled that the jury could not assess the literal truth of the claims "but could inquire whether the defendants knew them to be untrue," and the defendants were convicted. The indictment threatened to penalize I AM for distributing false religious teachings, in turn raising the knotty question of what was "true" religious doctrine. Even if Ballard's claims to revelation were suspect, they were not necessarily more so than those of any other prophet through the ages. No religious claim, scripture, or doctrine is demonstrably and verifiably true in the same sense as the statements of an engineering textbook. Guy Ballard's revelations were no more questionable than those of Joseph Smith, whom he resembles in so many ways.

The *Ballard* case was appealed to the Supreme Court, which upheld the exclusion of any testimony concerning the truthfulness of the Ballards' claims, but with two important dissents. Chief Justice Harlan F. Stone could not agree "that freedom of thought and worship includes freedom to procure money by making knowingly false statements about one's religious experiences." On the other side, Justice Robert Jackson went considerably further in a memorable dissent. He "could see in [the Ballards'] teachings nothing but humbug, untainted by any trace of truth. But that does not dispose of the constitutional question whether misrepresentation of religious experience or belief is prosecutable; it rather emphasizes the danger of such prosecutions." Cults could do financial harm to "overcredulous people," who sometimes received "mental and spiritual poison" in consequence, but even so, "the price of freedom of religion or of speech or of the press is that we must put up with, and even pay for, a good deal of rubbish." If religious motives were to be examined, "such inquiries may discomfort orthodox as well as unconventional religious teachers, for even the most regular of them are sometimes accused of taking their orthodoxy with a pinch of salt."[13] Jackson's words are rightly quoted as a milestone in the defense of religious freedom, but the affair was not an unqualified victory for I AM since other convictions were restored by the lower courts, and the movement was forbidden the use of the U.S. mails until 1954.

The official decision to go after I AM must be seen in the context of general concerns about fascist sects and "shirt" movements, but another more subtle agenda may have been present. By far the best known of the media religious tycoons was Catholic priest Charles Coughlin, a populist demagogue whose financial enterprises were quite as suspicious as those of the Ballards. Listeners were sending him large sums, ostensibly for the support of his Michigan-based Shrine of the Little Flower, which one exposé suggested renaming the Shrine of the Silver Dollar.[14] From 1938 onwards, Coughlin's broadcasts became anti-Semitic and pro-German, and the Roosevelt administration faced the dilemma of how to silence the priest without alienating the Catholic hierarchy and creating a martyr. The timing of the I AM case raises the possibility that this affair might have been a shot across the bows of other Far Right religious broadcasters with shady accounting procedures. Coughlin himself was finally silenced in 1942 when growing federal pressure cut him off from his twin pulpits on the radio and in the press.

### The Fate of the Witnesses

Demands for political conformity affected other groups, notably the Jehovah's Witnesses, who had had such dreadful experiences during the previous world war. Their position had if anything deteriorated in the intervening years; by the 1930s, Watch Tower believers held a deeply hostile view of government that would become a self-fulfilling prophecy. While the sect did not exactly invite persecution, it made no compromises in order to prevent it, and repression reinforced the apocalyptic rejection of all earthly powers. The Witnesses sounded revolutionary in their appeal to the lower classes and the disinherited, who were offered a vision of a world in which the mighty were overthrown, the unbelievers exterminated, and the righteous poor entered into their habitations. Witnesses saw the Christian churches as utterly corrupt, "religionist" rackets designed to deceive the people. While other groups might have held such dualistic opinions, most kept their opinions to themselves or lived in remote enclaves, and so impinged little on public opinion. Witnesses, in contrast, were difficult to avoid. The group's "publishers" felt an absolute need to evangelize, to spread their message not just about their own beliefs, but about the evils of rival churches. This was certain to cause offense among other denominations, especially among Catholics, who by this time had become a powerful political bloc. Preaching the abrasive gospel of the Witnesses in a Catholic neighborhood was to invite mobbing or worse. In 1940, the *Reader's Digest* claimed, starkly, that "Jehovah's Witnesses hate everybody and try to make it mutual. . . . Jehovah's Witnesses make hate a religion."[15]

Witnesses taught that since governments were of the devil, their legitimacy should be rejected, and this attitude extended to refusing public expressions of patriotism, like saluting the flag. This was a dangerous position in many working-class communities where the flag served as a cherished symbol of Americanism and national unity, overriding ethnic particularisms and Old World sentiments. By 1940, such public assertions of loyalty became still more sensitive at a time of renewed fears about domestic spies and saboteurs. Witnesses, however, refused any act they considered obeisance to pagan idols and prepared themselves to face the consequences. As in 1917, the group opposed the war, and its members became conscientious objectors. Some five thousand believers were jailed during the war years.

The sect faced sanctions from the police and courts, as well as vigilantes. In 1937, Newark police jailed a hundred Witnesses because they were "considered dangerous." In response to aggressive Witness preaching, many local communities tried to regulate public speech, setting off a series of actions that produced key decisions by the U.S. Supreme Court. Some conflicts resulted in straightforward Witness victories: when a Georgia town prohibited the distribution of literature without prior official approval, the Court upheld the challenge of a Witness who felt that this restricted her rights to free speech, and in 1940, the *Cantwell* case invalidated a rule in Connecticut that prevented Witnesses from presenting their incendiary views through phonograph records played in the street, even in a highly Catholic area. Nevertheless, in 1940 the Supreme Court overrode Witness objections when it upheld a local Pennsylvania ordinance requiring children to salute the flag as a means of inculcating political loyalty in a decision that confirmed the expulsion of two Witness children who had refused to bow down before what they saw as Dagon.[16]

The next three years were bitter ones for the Witnesses, who faced what has been termed "the greatest outbreak of religious intolerance in twentieth century America."[17] Much of the worst violence occurred in 1940: a Witness meeting in Little Rock was stormed by a mob, resulting in two Witnesses being shot and several others being hospitalized. Witnesses were tarred and feathered in Wyoming and a Nebraska believer was castrated, while other mob violence occurred sporadically through the war years. Elsewhere in North America, the sect was banned in Canada, with adults placed in work camps and some children removed from their families.[18] In 1941, a critic of American cults marveled at the success of Witness leader Judge Rutherford, who "offers his disciples . . . nothing but misunderstanding and trouble, the lockup and fractured skulls. They love it. They go happily here and there getting cracked heads and being thrown into jail for the cause, having their children mobbed in school for refusing to salute the flag and their houses painted a sickly yellow for refusing to paint them themselves."[19] The following year, the Supreme Court's *Chaplinsky* case held that free-speech protections did not cover the Witnesses' intemperate denunciations of church and state, so that an evangelist could be punished for calling a police officer "a god-damned racketeer" and "a damned fascist."

The legal tide did not turn for the sect until 1943, when a new Supreme Court case reversed the flag-salute decision, and a series of cases struck down local ordinances designed to curb Witness street preaching. In 1948, a divided Court even agreed that police could not prevent the Witnesses from using loudspeakers to spread their controversial views. *Cantwell* and other pro-Witness decisions were of far-reaching legal significance, marking the first time that the Supreme Court asserted the need for the states to defend first amendment protections. As Martin Marty remarks, "ironically, it was the antinational Jehovah's Witnesses who did most to nationalize religious freedom cases."[20]

## Polygamists

Though not directly concerned with war fears, other anticult campaigns in the 1940s show a reduced willingness simply to leave alone groups who sought seclusion from the world. This may have reflected the growth of the federal role in government and law enforcement in the New Deal years and the attempt by state agencies to compete with the publicity reaped by Hoover's G-Men. Among the main victims were the Mormon fundamentalists, who had resisted the church's abandonment of polygamy and maintained separate colonies in remote areas. The major sect was the United Effort Order, which had its communal headquarters in Short Creek, on the Arizona-Utah border; it claimed some twenty-five hundred members. Though these "cultists" were usually ignored, there were sporadic investigations and prosecutions, beginning in 1935 when welfare claims from the area exposed a system of highly unusual family structures. The legal situation was sensitive because community girls generally married at ages much younger than had become the American norm, so sect activities were portrayed in terms of a sexual threat to children. The authorities leveled criminal charges that misleadingly made the polygamists sound like a vicious sex cult engaged in child rape and abduction.

A series of arrests in 1943 and 1944 demonstrated the new severity. In late 1943, one family was arrested after they had transported a fifteen-year-old girl across the Utah-Nevada state line to become a plural wife. This action was held to violate the Mann Act, a law normally applied in cases of commercial prostitution and white slaving. More general federal and state action followed in March 1944 with the arrest of fifty people in Utah, Arizona, and Idaho; the incident dominated national headlines for several days. The charges included Mann Act violations and conspiracy, and even invoked the Lindbergh kidnapping law. According to the charges, sect members misused the mails to distribute obscene materials when they circulated literature advocating their religious position as authentic Mormonism. The courts were skeptical of the more extreme charges, but nine members were eventually sentenced. Their cases wended their way through the appeals process until in 1946 they reached the U.S. Supreme Court, which held that plural marriages could in fact constitute immoral purposes under the terms of the Mann Act. This decision gave federal authorities all the warrant they required to suppress the practice of polygamy, or even its advocacy. The antipolygamy campaign had the enthusiastic support of Latter-Day Saints authorities, who were anxious to disassociate themselves from the practice. Church leaders disparaged what they called the "cultists," whom they claimed (dubiously) were mainly drawn from the ranks of Protestant eccentrics rather than from misguided followers of Joseph Smith.[21]

Though on a smaller scale than the purges of the 1880s, the new pursuit of polygamists reached significant proportions. The movement culminated in 1953 when Arizona authorities undertook a massive sweep aimed at eliminating the main traditionalist center of Short Creek. This action was justified by the claim that the community was in a state of insurrection, and Arizona responded with an operation involving a hundred state police officers, forty county deputies, and dozens of other state and local officials. A raid on this scale made national headlines and even made the front page of major papers like the *New York Times* on the very day the armistice was signed ending the

Korean War. The Short Creek assault resulted in the arrest of 36 men and 86 women, while the state took into its custody 263 children, who would be placed in foster homes: 40 more accused believers fled. In an attempt to eradicate the sect, 200 remaining women and children were later evacuated from the settlement, leaving Short Creek a ghost town. The news media paraded the now classic charges of cult abuses, stressing "child brides" and "white slavery," and promising to save "the numerous women who . . . were forced into the cult's bizarre system against their will." *Time* headlined the "Great Love-Nest Raid." The governor declared, "Arizona has mobilized and used its total police power to protect the lives and future of 263 children. They are the product and the victims of the foulest conspiracy you could possibly imagine."[22] Ultimately, over a hundred defendants stood trial in a mass prosecution that was billed as an epic cult trial.

Still, the purge failed to eliminate the practice of polygamy, and the harrowing images of children being dragged from caring if unorthodox families created a backlash. The *Arizona Republic* published a cartoon depicting a heartless judge bullying a mother by threatening to take away her children: she is told, "Sign away your rights as a citizen and the custody of your faith, or else you'll never see them again." These events ensured that future administrations would pursue a policy when dealing with plural marriage of what would later be called "don't ask, don't tell." Though exact figures are shaky, the number of Mormon polygamists in the United States grew steadily in coming decades, from perhaps four thousand in 1950 to forty or fifty thousand today.[23]

### Serpent Handlers

The Pentecostal/Holiness tradition also produced its share of sensational cult scandals, in the form of snake handling. The idea that believers could safely handle serpents and drink poisons has excellent scriptural warrant in the form of Jesus' words in Mark 16:18, and from about 1910, evangelist George W. Hensley developed both practices as a regular sign of faith. Because the churches that adopted snake handling were concentrated in remote areas of southern and Appalachian states, adherents came to the attention of the media infrequently, but by the late 1930s, scandals became more common as hill dwellers migrated far afield during the Depression era.[24] In 1936, moreover, Hensley made snake handling a regular part of his Holiness Faith Healing sect. By 1940, a press headline featuring the word "cult" was more likely than not to feature a rural Holiness or Pentecostal church, usually in the context of snakes. For urban and middle-class readers, the movement was almost too good to be true: confirming the most offensive stereotypes of evangelical religion that had emerged during the Scopes trial and reinforcing the voodoo-derived image of a backwoods serpent-worshipping cult. Over the next quarter century, the dual caricatures of snake handlers and Holy Rollers went far to defining the elites' stereotype of fundamentalism.

Images of "rattlesnake religion" and "snake-handling cults" gained their greatest notoriety in the early 1940s, at just the same time as the more general reaction against subversive or fascist sects. Two key incidents occurred within a few days of each other in the summer of 1940. In one, a five-year-old girl was bitten during services in Georgia; in the other, several "cultists" suffered snakebite in services at Cincinnati. The twin incidents gained national coverage over the succeeding days, with continuing bulletins about the health of the child and the possible legal proceedings against the churches and families involved, who refused to seek medical aid for the child.[25] After several deaths, states responded forcefully: Kentucky banned snake handling in 1940, Georgia, the following year.

Media reports stressed the primitive and benighted state of the rural sects. When the child was bitten in the Georgia case, the *New York Times* quoted evangelist Hensley as saying that "faith'll make it well ag'in." While Hensley might indeed have pronounced the word "ag'in," the media only provided such a phonetic spelling in order to emphasize local color or to show that the speaker was ignorant and ill-educated. To take a parallel from about the same time, it would have been unthinkable for the *Times* to have reported that during his first inaugural speech, President Roosevelt had declared that the only thing the nation had to fear was *"feah* itself." Primitivist themes reappeared during the renewed wave of official investigations and persecutions between 1944 and 1947, when Virginia churches were raided by police, who killed the snakes kept by the believers. *Life* magazine offered a harrowing photo spread of snake-handling services, with captions describing "cultists" and "hysterical saints" led by their "self-appointed, unordained parson." When these "illiterate" believers spoke in tongues, the magazine reported this as "a frenetic gibberish to which the cultists resort." *Newsweek* similarly portrayed a "weird cult" of "fanatical, jerking, cultists."[26]

## Defining the Cult Problem

Though sensational coverage of fringe religions was far from new in the mass media, the tone of reporting changes noticeably during the late 1930s with the rise of conspicuous profit-oriented groups like I AM and Psychiana. Such religions were painted in the worst possible colors by association with criminal or subversive sects. The media illustrated their suspicion of the cults through the selection of the groups they covered. In the 1940s, this often meant the most aberrant of the religious fringe, especially the snake handlers. Other bizarre groups who attracted headlines in this decade included the flat-earther Koreshans and that perennial favorite, voodoo.[27] Focusing on these eccentric traditions gave the impression that all cults were involved in dubious and dangerous activities.

Although perceptions of a general cult phenomenon dated back to the 1920s, from around 1940 we find a new spate of books and articles surveying what seemed to be a rising problem of cults, some of which, like the Jehovah's Witnesses, were growing explosively. As a Baptist critic claimed in 1940, there were "many hundreds of religious cults that flood this land of the free and home of the brave, that lends itself readily to religious novelties and new messiahs, most of which are founded on half-baked religious ideas."[28] Among the harshest of the new wave of articles was F. S. Mead's 1941 piece in the *American Mercury*, "Lunatic Definition of Religion: Rapid Expansion of Crackpot Religions," which concentrated on the most bizarre and dubious groups. Meanwhile, the mainstream churches expressed concern about their potential rivals, and periodicals like the *Christian Century* struggled to find what could be learned from the apparent success of the new movements.[29]

Not all studies were so confrontational, and several important books published between 1937 and 1949 treated the small sects sympathetically as a familiar and even necessary part of religious life. These now-classic works included Elmer T. Clark's *The Small Sects in America*, Marcus Bach's *They Have Found a Faith*, Arthur Fauset's *Black Gods of the Metropolis*, and Charles S. Braden's *These Also Believe*. Bach spoke happily of the "culting hobby" that had led him to observe the lives of so many apparent crackpots, and all four writers made heroic efforts to permit cult leaders and members to represent their own positions as fairly and fully as possible. These books supplied a solid foundation for the scholarly study of the marginal groups, but the very fact that so much cult material was becoming available itself raised public awareness of the issue. When Braden gave an objective conference presentation, an audience member urgently slipped him an envelope promising "God's truth concerning the cults," which included a dozen pamphlets, each of which painted a particular movement as diabolically inspired. The depth of public suspicion and hostility was illustrated by the uproar which occurred in 1948 when it was revealed that third-party presidential candidate Henry Wallace had been associated in the mid-1930s with occultist Nicholas Roerich, whom Wallace had addressed as his "guru". The media paraded the now-familiar range of anti-occult stereotypes, as when a Chicago newspaper mockingly declared that "If only Wallace the Master Guru becomes president, we shall get in tune with the Infinite, vibrate in the correct plane, outstare the Evil Eye, reform the witches, overcome all malicious spells, and ascend the high road to health and happiness."[30]

For a few years, the scope and seriousness of the "cult problem" appeared too obvious to be questioned, and perceptions were reinforced by popular culture treatments. In the war years especially, the most sensational depictions of cults and the occult were disseminated to a mass audience. By this point, ideas of evil cults, witches, and devil worship were such familiar components of popular culture that they could be introduced without the labored explanations needed before. Even Satanism and human sacrifice could now be depicted in a modern American context, rather than being transposed to seventeenth-century New England or *fin-de-siècle* Paris.

The popularity of witchcraft themes during the Second World War presumably reflects the changing demographics of the audience. When millions of men were absent in the armed forces, the cinema made an unprecedented effort to cater to a predominantly female audience, which responded to tales of powerful, female, supernatural characters. In 1943, the suspense film *The Seventh Victim* showed a clandestine satanic cult operating in contemporary New York City and carrying out sporadic human sacrifices: the film was directed by Val Lewton, who in the same year made the voodoo-oriented *I Walked With a Zombie*. Popular novels of the war years included Abraham Merritt's *Burn, Witch Burn* (1942), depicting a real witch killing victims through devil dolls, and Fritz Leiber's *Conjure Wife* (1943), which described a battle between good and bad witches for influence within a university community; Leiber's book was pirated for the 1944 film *Weird Woman*.[31] The 1942 comedy film *I Married a Witch* involved a Salem witch returning to the present day to take revenge on the descendants of the Puritans who had caused her death.

The human sacrifice motif also flourished, particularly among the friends and literary disciples of H. P. Lovecraft, who had died in 1937. We have already seen the continuing activity by the various *Weird Tales* writers, who explored possible ritualistic elements in serial murder cases. In 1948, the magazine published August Derleth's "Night Train to Lost Valley," about secret devil worship in rural New Hampshire. In the story, the entire population of a small town heads into the woods for a Sabbat, the communal worship of the diabolical Ahriman: This culminates in a human sacrifice when a baby's head is smashed against a stone altar. Subsequently, the community conspires to disguise the death as resulting from natural causes.[32] Though the image of the secret village cult was almost a cliché in the pulp magazines, it could still create a sensation when brought before a mainstream public. In 1949, Shirley Jackson published "The Lottery," which became one of the best-known of American short stories. Much of its impact comes from the shocking incongruity of finding human sacrifice rituals in what initially seems like a pure middle American setting, from the vision of a bloodthirsty paganism on American soil (her scapegoating theme is, of course, taken from *The Golden Bough*).[33]

Witchcraft, black magic, and the whole cult underworld had become sufficiently familiar to be parodied. In 1942, Anthony Boucher's comic novella, *The Compleat Werewolf*, used as villains the members of a cult called the Temple of the Dark Truth, worshipers of Beelzebub who gather on Walpurgis Night. The leaders cynically manipulate their gullible followers, who do not know that the exotic words of power used in the rituals are in fact no more than the Sanskrit numerals. Also drawing on contemporary stereotypes, Boucher depicts the group as a cover for a Nazi spy ring.[34]

Another tongue-in-cheek work was Robert Heinlein's *Magic Incorporated* (1940). Heinlein imagines an America in which magic and witchcraft have become everyday realities, with practitioners duly licensed by the state. However, an organized crime ring uses violence and intimidation to dragoon all magicians into a mob-controlled cartel: the story's title recalls the Murder Incorporated gang that had become notorious around this time. The story's hero defeats the gangsters with superior occult expertise, as well as the assistance of a demon, who proves to be an undercover FBI agent from the agency's antimonopoly division. *Magic Incorporated* demonstrates Heinlein's thorough acquaintance with the language of the occult, with elemental spirits, gnomes and undines, mandrakes, occult scripts, qabalistic symbols, the technical terminology of African witch finding, and the names of the chief demons of hell. Characters even use arthames, or ritual knives, long before that very rare term was popularized (as *athame*) in the witchcraft revival of the 1950s.[35]

Even when they were intended to be funny, such portrayals of witches and devil worshipers had troubling implications. Not only did they associate cults with satanic worship, as the most stringent evangelicals had always charged, but they assumed that small religious groups were mere fronts for criminal activity. Far from being seen as inquisitive free spirits, cultists in the 1940s were portrayed in very unflattering terms and were variously depicted as fifth columnists, ritual killers, snake handlers, sex maniacs, child molesters, flat earthers, and at the very least, confidence tricksters. As so often, popular culture portrayals were reflecting a much more hostile public mood, which the media and the pulp magazines themselves had done much to foster in the interwar years.

# EIGHT

# The New Boom
## 1960–1980

Millions of people are searching desperately for a true Father-Magician, especially at a time when the clergy and the psychiatrists are making rather a poor show, and do not seem to have the courage of their convictions, or of their fantasies.

Alan Watts, "The Trickster Guru," in *The Essential Alan Watts*

Though acknowledged as a menace during the 1940s, popular concern about cults faded during the next decade, to the point of near invisibility in the media. The hiatus of public interest during the 1950s had important implications for later perceptions of cults, as many once-thriving occult and sectarian traditions were consigned to historical oblivion. With few acknowledged precedents, scholars and journalists assumed, wrongly, that the new spirituality of the 1960s and 1970s was an entirely new phenomenon. Observers scarcely knew how to explain this apparently unprecedented situation in which young people were drawn into odd or alien movements, seduced by fashionable gurus, and proclaiming a new mystical Age of Aquarius. Controversial cults like the Hare Krishna movement seemed only the most visible face of a general social and spiritual transformation: in Harvey Cox's phrase, American religion seemed irrefutably to be "turning East."[1]

Of course, these trends were far from new. They neatly reproduced the conditions of forty years previously, or even earlier: America had been at least tilting to the East spiritually since the 1890s (a book entitled *Hinduism Invades America* appeared as far back as 1930). Also, although the religious fringe was not as much in evidence in the 1950s as in earlier decades, this does not mean that experimentation and innovation had ceased: the midcentury years should rather be seen as a seedtime, in which later developments were germinating unobserved. Many of the movements perceived as new during the hippie era were in reality old, established groups that only now received their share of media attention. Very little of the New Age was terribly novel to the 1960s or 1970s, and a great deal of it was based on movements and writings firmly rooted in the age of Guy Ballard and Aleister Crowley, and of that remarkable cohort of leaders born between 1874 and 1886.[2] Though we do find some apparently new influences on the modern New Age (for example, UFOs and psychedelic drugs) a remarkable number of these elements had parallels before 1940. A new generation was thus rediscovering and building upon that great era of experimentation in the early part of the century: one period of Emergence echoed another.

While new spiritual ideas may have achieved a much wider audience in the 1960s than hitherto, we can scarcely speak of a revolutionary new consciousness. The exact scale of the new spiritual upheaval is also open to debate. In retrospect, we can scarcely see a major trend in the direction of occult and oriental religions, and none of the new so-called cults enjoyed anything like the explosive growth that was implied by media reporting. Finke and Stark write of the supposed boom in New Age and Asian movements as a "recent religious eruption that failed to happen."[3] Though American religion did undergo major changes in this era, the main beneficiaries were not the conspicuous new sects like the Hare Krishnas or the Unification Church, still less the Church of Satan, but theologically conservative Protestant churches, which were fundamentalist, evangelical, and often Pentecostal in their belief and practice.

## Continuities

Contemporary media coverage suggests that cult and occult activity reached a low ebb in the 1950s. In the *Reader's Guide to Periodical Literature*, there is a steady stream of titles under headings like "cult," "occult," "witchcraft," and "voodoo" from about 1920 until 1950, but it dries to a trickle until a revival of interest in the mid-1960s. The only exception to this statement comes with the Black Muslim scare of the late 1950s, but this was clearly a different and more explicitly political phenomenon, catalogued under the special heading of "Negro cults," rather than simply the general "cults."

Yet cult stories never wholly vanished. Some scandals of the 1950s presaged events like Jonestown as much as they recalled the glory days of the 1920s. One figure from these transitional years was Krishna Venta, born Francis Pencovic, who in 1948 formed the WKFL Foundation of the World, which taught "wisdom, knowledge, faith and love." Krishna Venta formed a colony in California's Ventura County and decided that he was Christ, dressing accordingly in beard, flowing robes, and a large cross medallion. He also declared that he had arrived on earth in a spaceship two hundred forty thousand years ago. Krishna Venta traveled widely as his disciples spread his gospel; in Seattle in 1952, he attracted audiences several hundred strong. In 1958, however, Krishna Venta and several disciples were assassinated in a bombing attack by disenchanted followers who resented his dallying with their wives. The affair provoked renewed press coverage of what one story referred to as "California cults and crackpots."[4]

Such sensational stories apart, the religious fringe survived and even prospered: Los Angeles was home still to a hundred so-called cults, with much overlap of membership. In his 1958 book *California Cult*, H. T. Dohrman depicts a thought-world that would have been familiar thirty years previously: "In the overall cult world, a person might simultaneously belong to the Technocrats and the Rosicrucians, he might attend flying saucer conventions in Hollywood hotels, in the meantime he might maintain his membership in the Mother Church of Christian Science, while becoming familiar with stellar healing, induced emotion, and extrasensory perception at the Religion of the Stars services." The typical believer "prides himself in his freedom from bigotry. His aim, he will tell you, is to obtain the truth. . . . [H]e knows something about the Lemurians, the Rosicrucians, the Technocratic, the Mormons, the Anglo-Israelites, I AM, New Thought, Unity, Theosophy, Yoga, Hermetics, Metaphysics, pyramidology, spiritualism, the OAHSPE Bible, faith-healing, flying saucers and the latest metaphysical innovations. . . . selecting what seem to him to be pertinent tidbits of knowledge, he adds them to his stock of cultic convictions."[5] Although a few new ideas had either first appeared in the 1950s or else become more prominent in the overall synthesis, they were integrated easily with older themes. Flying saucers now became an integral part of the esoteric world-view, as did past-life regression. It was in 1956 that Morey Bernstein published his book *The Search for Bridey Murphy*, which claimed to describe how a young mother had, under hypnotism, recalled a previous life as an Irish peasant woman. This tale, which ignited a minor boom in amateur hypnotism, is the direct ancestor of many later works on reincarnation and channeling.[6]

Many key figures from the 1930s and 1940s remained active through the midcentury years and served as links with the later boom. William Dudley Pelley lived and published until 1965, and his books remained in print for decades afterwards.[7] Manly P. Hall headed his Philosophical Research Society into the 1970s, while occult and Theosophical presses are still producing the tracts of Paul Foster Case, Alice Bailey, and the Curtisses. Father Divine, who died in 1965, lived long enough to instruct the young Indianapolis preacher Jim Jones in the requirements for a spiritual leader with messianic pretensions: the Father taught Jones the style and rhetoric, but also reinforced the need to cultivate secular politicians. Jones went on to accomplish his own private apocalypse in the jungles of Guyana.

The leaders who now rose to prominence had usually served long apprenticeships in the older esoteric movements. One such was John Paul Twitchell, who founded the ECKANKAR movement in 1965, claiming to be the 971st ECK Master in an order of succession dating back many millennia. Twitchell's occult interests dated back at least to the late 1940s, when he had joined an offshoot of the Hindu-oriented Self-Realization Fellowship, and edited its magazine, *The Mystic Cross*. He later followed another Asian guru, Kirpal Singh, and joined the new Church of Scientology about 1958. Twitchell's career parallels that of Earl Blighton, who in 1968 founded the Holy Order of MANS, a New Age group that was a characteristic product of the hippie era (the term "MANS" signified the Gnostic concepts of *Mysterion/ Agape/Nous/Sophia*, or Mystery-Love-Mind-Wisdom). Blighton, like Twitchell, had a long record of associations with esoteric movements over the decades, including spiritualism, Freemasonry, rosicrucianism (AMORC), Theosophy, and Yoga.[8]

Contrary to appearances, the older cults did not simply vanish in the Eisenhower years, and a few of the movements founded in the 1920s and 1930s survived to enjoy unprecedented success in the later era. Among the most persistent were those preaching mystical nationalism and racial pride. Elijah Muhammad lived until 1975, long enough to see his Nation of Islam become a real intellectual and spiritual force among African Americans, though increasingly the Nation's idiosyncratic ideas were supplanted by a more orthodox and nonracial Islam. The Black Muslims provided the focus of the most intense national cult scare to rage between the Second World War and the Charles Manson affair. In July 1959, a five-part television documentary on the Nation of Islam, entitled "The Hate That Hate Produced," created consternation among white observers. *Time* remarked on the "cold black hatred" of the "black supremacist" sect, which then had some seventy thousand known "cultists." As C. Eric Lincoln points out, this was the first time that a black cult leader was presented as a serious menace, rather than as a ludicrous figure, as had been the fate of Father Divine.[9] Despite its hostile tone, this media response promoted the Muslim movement among black Americans who were being radicalized by the contemporary conflicts over civil rights. The adherence of world heavyweight boxing champion Cassius Clay, renamed Muhammad Ali, gave the Nation of Islam a presence and influence that survived until they were squandered in internal warfare following the assassination of Malcolm X.

Believers embraced other forms of nationalist religion in both the early and the later years of the century. The Rastafarians retained the old Garveyite veneration for Ethiopia. Their ideology crystallized at the time of the coronation of Ethiopian emperor Haile Selassie in 1930, and the movement flourished in Jamaica.[10] Following the easing of immigration restrictions in the 1960s, Caribbean migrants brought these ideas to American cities, where they acquired a cachet through their association with reggae music, marijuana, and popular culture, and even influenced many young white people.

Another controversial racial movement was Identity Christianity, which holds that the white races of northern Europe are the descendants of the lost tribes of Israel and thus the authentic heirs of the people of the Old Testament. The idea began with the British Israel believers of the nineteenth century, whose beliefs included mystical notions concerning the Great Pyramid. These concepts were gradually transformed into more aggressively anti-Semitic directions and gained favor among followers of American demagogues like Pelley and Gerald L. K. Smith. Identity theories developed a following in California and Oregon, and especially in Los Angeles, where there was overlap with Silver Shirt activities. In 1953, the book *Apostles of Discord* reported on the ultraright Identity sects and ministries scattered throughout the United States. The movement made further strides during the 1960s and 1970s with the emergence of sects like the Aryan Nations, the Church of Jesus Christ—Christian, the Christian Defense League, and the Covenant, the Sword and the Arm of the Lord. One of the more influential political/religious sects, the Posse Comitatus, boasted a former Silver Shirt as its cofounder. Today, Christian Identity remains a powerful component of ultraright ideology, with a strong influence on neo-Nazi and Ku Klux Klan groups, as well as survivalists and militia members.[11]

### From New Age to New Age

Some of the older generation of New Age prophets retained their devoted followings. When seekers of the 1970s bought books to guide their spiritual quest, they were usually rediscovering the thinkers and prophets of thirty or forty years earlier, including Theosophists like Krishnamurti, G. I. Gurdjeff (who first came to America in 1924), and P. D. Ouspensky.[12] Also venerated was Charles Fort, the source for a vast body of lore concerning UFOs and inexplicable events, which he collected between 1910 and 1932. The scientific study of extrasensory perception dates from J. B. Rhine's 1934 book of that name. From a quite different context, it was in 1932 that the memoir *Black Elk Speaks* introduced a White audience to the riches of Native American spirituality and shamanism, and Black Elk's words proved a major inspiration to many hopeful White imitators in the 1960s and beyond. Another guru whom seekers were likely to encounter was Aldous Huxley, whose book *The Doors of Perception* alerted a new generation to the mystical effects of psychedelic drugs. Though drugs seemed to be a distinguishing feature of the new mystical consciousness of the 1960s, their use had a long history in the occult world, and drugs had played a key role in Aleister Crowley's rituals at least since the opening years of the century. His intimate familiarity with the topic is evident from his 1922 novel, *Diary of a Drug Fiend*. Huxley himself had lived in southern California since the late 1930s, and he undertook his experiment with mescaline in 1953.[13] Once again, what seem to be the most radical departures of the 1960s have parallels in the earlier New Age.

The I AM tradition also prospered. After the death of Guy Ballard in 1939, his movement was continued in diminished form by his wife Edna, who continued publishing the familiar tracts and revelations from the Saint-Germain Press in Santa Fe, New Mexico. She died in 1971, but the torch of the Ascended Masters had already passed into new hands. In 1958, Mark Prophet claimed that he had been contacted by the Ascended Master El-Morya to carry on the work of the Great White Brotherhood (El-Morya had also been the spiritual guide claimed by Madame Blavatsky). On his death in 1973, the mission was carried on by his wife, Elizabeth Clare Prophet, a prolific author whose works, like *The Lost Years of Jesus*, were sold in mass-market bookstores. The

Prophets' movement eventually became the Church Universal and Triumphant, which claimed several thousand adherents.[14] Though not a direct continuation of I AM, resemblances with the earlier movement are striking, in the central role played by the Count of Saint-Germain and the language of "the I AM Presence." Mrs. Prophet also inherited the Ballards' rightist and superpatriotic ideology: in 1986, fearing imminent global catastrophe, the church moved to a compound in Montana, equipped with substantial nuclear shelters.

In a few cases, modern-day groups assert still older chains of affinity with America's mystical past. One example was the metaphysical group formed in Detroit in the 1950s by Neva Dell Hunter, who claimed to serve as the medium for a spirit-guide: this guide in turn was in contact with the shade of New Thought founder Phineas Quimby, who had died in 1866. Under this august guidance, Dr. Hunter moved her operation to New Mexico in 1963. Her Quimby Center became the nucleus of Southwestern College, which evolved from an occult center to a wide-ranging therapeutic, mystical, and metaphysical operation, based in Santa Fe. Whatever one thinks of the idea of channeling, such activities do indeed represent an authentic inheritance from Quimby and his contemporaries, and they are, in that sense, very much in his spirit.[15]

Another figure of enduring influence was the clairvoyant Edgar Cayce, the "sleeping prophet," who founded his Association for Research and Enlightenment (ARE) in 1931. Cayce drew extensively on the traditions of Theosophy, while his career as a mystic healer was much influenced by the New Thought tradition dating back to Quimby. Though Cayce died in 1945, the publishing boom in his works did not reach full momentum until the late 1960s. By 1970, ARE had 12,000 members, and over a thousand study groups discussed Cayce's works. Membership grew to 32,000 by 1981, and the group became a focus for New Age activism and experimentation.[16] The association is one of several groups providing an institutional continuity to older occult traditions, surviving long enough to exploit the new opportunities offered by emerging technologies in the 1980s and 1990s. Most recently this has meant the Internet, which has become a fertile ground for all religions, both marginal and mainstream.

The deep roots of the modern esoteric tradition are further indicated by the Cosmic Consciousness movement, which traced its origins to the writings of Richard M. Bucke, the friend and executor of Walt Whitman. Bucke achieved a mystical illumination in 1872, and his 1901 book, *Cosmic Consciousness*, used the teachings of Jesus, the Buddha, and various mystics over the centuries to describe how the believer could be raised to a higher plane of cosmic existence.[17] Nevertheless, it was not until the early 1920s that the idea became an organized movement through the efforts of Dr. Walter Russell and his wife, Lao. The tradition received a new life in the 1950s and 1960s, when Lao Russell's prophetic warnings of the horrors of war won her a following in the Vietnam era.

### Voices From Space

Also recalling nineteenth-century influences was *The Urantia Book*, a vast (two-thousand-plus page) account of the history of the galaxy and the solar system. According to the work's official history, it was channeled in 1934 to 1935 by Wilfred Kellogg, a member of the Seventh-Day Adventist family that made its fortune with breakfast cereals. *Urantia* was eventually published in 1955 under the editorship of William Sadler, who had originally worked with the Victorian Adventist leader Dr. John Kellogg.[18] The *Urantia Book* reflected the continuing cultist fascination with the vastness of the universe and suggestions of many inhabited worlds beyond earth. These extraterrestrial themes were scarcely novel, as they featured heavily in Mormonism and in Black Muslim mythology, and true believers found accounts of starships in the OAHSPE Bible of the 1880s.

These pseudoscientific precursors all contributed to the emerging corpus of unidentified flying object lore, which developed following a rash of alleged sightings in 1947. Interest in UFOs existed on the borderland between fringe science and the occult, and the whole concept reflects the long-familiar attempt of marginal religious believers to claim objective scientific validity for essentially occult ideas. Groups of the 1930s had been fascinated with mystic rays and radio analogies, while the Black Muslims had their apocalyptic Mother Plane. One early exponent of UFO theories was science fiction author and occult believer Raymond Palmer, who in the early 1940s had recorded the visions of a welder who was believed to have recovered racial memories of Atlantis and Lemuria. Palmer went on to found *Fate* magazine, and an early issue included a pioneering account of the first flying-saucer sighting over Mount Rainier, ghostwritten by himself. A new genre of flying-saucer books followed from about 1950 onwards, reaching a climax during the nervous years of the Korean War.

Unidentified flying objects would soon be seamlessly integrated into the occult worldview alongside Atlantis and Great Pyramid theories, so that many believers replaced the old supernatural Ascended Masters with supposedly material alien intelligences. (The merger of UFO belief with Atlantis was in turn accomplished through the extravagant Bermuda triangle mythology of the 1970s.) The first UFO-oriented religious movement was the Aetherius Society, formed in 1956, but several other study groups and churches followed in the coming decades. Most were influenced by Robert Heinlein's 1961 science fiction novel *Stranger in a Strange Land*, in which a human raised by Martians forms a messianic cult on earth. The book excited the alternative and occult subcultures in the 1960s and 1970s, much as *Zanoni* had done a century previously. Charles Manson named one of his sons for Valentine Michael Smith, the book's Martian messiah, and the book also intrigued the founders of Heaven's Gate, the UFO-oriented group that carried out a mass suicide in San Diego in 1997.[19]

Among the new religious leaders influenced by both science fiction and the older New Age was L. Ron Hubbard. Like Palmer, Hubbard began his career as a science fiction writer, and in the mid-1940s, he was associated with Jack Parsons and the Crowleyan lodge based in Pasadena, where he was involved in the attempt to incarnate the Moonchild. In 1950, Hubbard published what he presented as a groundbreaking psychological system in his book *Dianetics*, and in 1954, the Founding Church of Scientology was opened in Washington, D.C.[20] Hubbard found an early advocate in the editor of the flagship science fiction magazine, *Astounding*. Hubbard's cosmology resembled the Theosophical view, which portrayed spiritual evolution occurring on countless worlds over many aeons and implied that past lives could be recalled. His system described the Thetans, immortal godlike beings trillions of years old, who incarnated repeatedly in new lives. The Thetans created the universe, but allowed themselves to become enmeshed in it, falling into the world of Matter-Energy-Space-Time. Through the auditing processes offered by Hubbard's church, an individual would be able to reascend to this lost divine status.[21]

### Witches and Satanists

The influence of earlier movements is particularly evident in the whole "occult explosion" of the late 1960s and in the rise of ritual magic and witchcraft. One major trend of the last three decades has been the rise of various forms of neopaganism, which apart from their own intrinsic significance, have had a huge influence on feminist religious thought in Christianity and Judaism. Modern Wiccans claim descent from the supposed witch movement of early modern times and view the witch-hunts of those years as an almost successful holocaust against their distinctive religion. In reality, though, the pagan movement dates from the publication in 1954 of Gerald Gardner's *Witchcraft Today*, which in turn relied heavily on the writings of Margaret Murray from the 1920s.[22] It also owes something to the ideas of earth-magic and ley-lines invented by Alfred Watkins's 1925 book *The Old Straight Track*, while much of the movement's Goddess spirituality is taken directly from Robert Graves' antiquarian fantasy, *The White Goddess* (1948). Neopaganism is strictly a development of the mid-twentieth century.

American Satanism is an equally modern and artificial creation. The movement's history conventionally begins on Walpurgis Night 1966 with the foundation of Anton LaVey's Church of Satan in San Francisco, which in turn spawned various breakaway groups, like the Temple of Set.[23] Here too, we can witness a process of evolution which dates back to the formation of Crowley's *Ordo Templi Orientis* lodges in the First World War era, but the main influences on LaVey were literary, including the works of Dennis Wheatley and H. P. Lovecraft. Ironically, Lovecraft himself was a thoroughly secular-minded materialist, who among other things ghostwrote for the archdebunker Harry Houdini, and whose own store of occult knowledge was mainly drawn from the *Encyclopedia Britannica*. Nevertheless, Lovecraft's writings were seen as arcane texts for occultists of the 1960s and beyond, who imagined that he was exposing authentic secret traditions. LaVey's *Satanic Rituals* (1972) created an entire ritual for the "Call to Cthulhu," which is included in a chapter on "The Metaphysics of Lovecraft." Lovecraft's stories also describe a fictional occult text called the *Necronomicon*, but its spurious quality did not prevent publishers producing at least two ostensible editions of the work in the 1970s. Both appeal particularly to high school Satanists, among whom these ersatz occult traditions quickly developed an authentic history. Contemporary ritual magic is heavily indebted to the work of Aleister Crowley and of the Golden Dawn before him.[24]

Though the numerical following of the occult sects was tiny, their potent presence in popular culture was neatly symbolized by the inclusion of Crowley's portrait on the cover of the 1967 Beatle album, *Sergeant Pepper's Lonely Hearts Club Band*. The following year, Dennis

Wheatley's best-known black magic novel was filmed as *The Devil Rides Out*, in a production that offered the fullest and most accurate depictions of Western ritual magic ever put on screen (its American title was *The Devil's Bride*): this film led to many imitators and also promoted a revival in Wheatley's novels. Occult and black magic ideas found their way into the contemporary lyrics of British rock bands, and thereby into the later genre of heavy-metal music. Also significant in promoting popular awareness of the occult were films like *Rosemary's Baby* (1968), *The Exorcist* (1973), and *The Omen* (1976): Anton LaVey appeared briefly as the Devil in *Rosemary's Baby*. When youthful cliques of the 1980s and 1990s claimed to be practicing Satanists, virtually all their ideas, practices, and slogans derived from these popular culture treatments, ultimately from Crowley, but a Crowley viewed through the imaginative lenses of Wheatley and LaVey.

Appropriately, the whole notion of teenage cult Satanism, which was such a nightmare for parents, teachers, and clergy in the 1980s, first appeared in a purely literary guise in the work of Robert Bloch. Bloch's 1960 story "Sweet Sixteen" accepts that the new generation of violent juvenile delinquents are "psychopaths," but suggests that this word is a medical euphemism for what earlier generations would have called demonic possession. Gradually, the youngsters acknowledge their diabolical parents and adopt overtly satanic rituals, complete with the Black Man and the Sabbat, and "the sacrifice bit." According to the story, this augured "a wave of Satanism and Black Magic which will put the Middle Ages to shame."

## The Cult Explosion

Though the various occult and esoteric ideas were rarely new, they did receive much greater public exposure in the 1960s; more important, they reached a national rather than a regional audience. The formation of new religious groups was a continuing process through the twentieth century, but in the decade after 1965, the rate of group formation accelerated and new manifestations attracted far more public attention than hitherto. There were several reasons for this new "cult explosion." Many of the older groups had been confined to particular locales, notably in southern California, and had received only sporadic attention from the national media. Though the post-1965 groups often had Californian roots, the growth of television meant that their doings were transmitted instantly across the nation, providing publicity for their ideologies and simultaneously arousing concern about the "cult problem." It now became vastly easier for cults to gain national audiences, not to mention national enemies. Also, while members of the older cults did not generally stand out in a crowd, the new sects were often ostentatious in their distinctive clothing, sometimes their adoption of Asian styles, and their aggressive proselytizing. The formal membership rolls of these new movements only represent the tip of a large iceberg of unaffiliated followers who dabbled in various movements, and who maintained a lively interest in what would generally be called New Age belief (see Table 8.1).

The upsurge of new spiritual movements reflected other social trends of these years, which were causing a fundamental reassessment of other national institutions. The baby boom was entering its young adult years in the late 1960s, so that religions, like businesses, found themselves dealing with an experiment-minded youth market of unprecedented scale and purchasing power. Though the range of options available in the religious marketplace might not have changed too substantially, the audience of potential consumers had expanded enormously. Widespread drug experimentation also aroused intense curiosity about spirituality and alternative realities, a trend that reached its height with the growing popularity of psychedelic drugs from the mid-1960s. This helps explain the interest in monistic South Asian religions in these years. On the negative side, bad experiences with psychedelics had by the early 1970s left a substantial population in need of a support system.

Meanwhile, social and political dislocation disrupted traditional institutions and family links, and inspired a thirst for alternative structures, for new forms of sexual relationship and communal living. After the decline of the Vietnam protest movement from its peak in 1970, political radicalism could no longer offer an acceptable channel for activism. This recalled the transition from the politically active second decade of the century, the era of Wobblies and socialists, of feminists and sexual radicals, to the conservative (and cult-rich) 1920s. Recalling other eras of religious and political excitement, the 1970s were also a golden age of conspiracy theories, which initially focused on the recent political assassinations but spilled over into rejection of "establishment" science and official explanations of UFOs. According to sociological theories of religion, widespread social dislocation, disaffection, and anomie are likely to ignite a countermovement based on personal faith, an emphasis on supernatural intervention, and a quest for de-

Table 8.1
Chronology of New Religious Movements, 1965–1980

1965*    Swami Bhaktivedanta arrives in United States, founder of ISK-
         CON.
         ECKANKAR.

1966     Church of Satan.

1967     Jesus People movement.

1968     Metropolitan Community Church.
         Holy Order of MANS.
         Beginning of David Berg's ministry, precursor of Children of God.

1969     Healthy-Happy-Holy Organization.
         Church of Armageddon (Love Family/Love Israel Family).
         Tibetan Nyingma Meditation Center (Berkeley, CA).
         Alamo Foundation ministry.

1971     First *est* seminar.
         Guru Maharaj Ji arrives in United States, founder of Divine Light
         Mission.

1973     Raelian movement.

1974     Naropa Institute of Boulder, CO.

1975     Temple of Set.

Source: Adapted from Timothy Miller, ed., *America's Alternative Religions* (Albany:
State Univ. of New York Press, 1995).
* Except where otherwise noted, dates refer to foundation of movement named.

pendable sources of authority, so is not surprising to find a rapid growth of small sects and communal groups during the early 1970s.[25]

In other historical settings, these circumstances might have led to a revival within the better-established Christian churches, but this option was scarcely open to spiritual seekers in the late 1960s. The mainline Protestant churches were dominated by liberal perspectives that emphasized social action to the point of viewing personal spirituality as a selfish distraction, while conservative and evangelical bodies were hostile to every aspect of the new youth culture, identifying it only with drugs, long hair, rock music, and radical politics. In previous eras like the 1840s and 1890s, a powerful spiritual hunger had often found answers in the Roman Catholic Church, but Catholics, too, found themselves ill-suited to provide absolute answers. In the aftermath of the second Vatican Council, which met from 1963 through 1965, the Church entered a period of bitter internal conflict and self-doubt, together with a sharp decline of mystical, liturgical, and communal traditions which would now have to be sought elsewhere. No reasonable person looked to the Catholic Church of the early 1970s as a rock of certainty. Though some Christian churches would ultimately find a strong following among the baby boomers, that development seemed far from likely during the 1970s.

It was, like the 1920s, a great age for magi and messiahs. Alan Watts, who did so much to inspire the new interest in mysticism, provided a tongue-in-cheek commentary on the time in his essay on the "trickster guru." This offers complete instructions for the would-be messiah seeking to attract and convert followers at a time when millions were "searching desperately for a true Father-magician" (a footnote cited the precedents of Mother-magicians like Mary Baker Eddy, Helena Blavatsky, Aimee Semple McPherson, Alice Bailey, and Annie Besant). "The first step is to frequent those circles where gurus are especially sought, such as the various cult groups which pursue Oriental religions or peculiar forms of psychotherapy, or simply the artistic and intellectual milieux of any great city." Subsequently, a persona can be projected: "when some student asks, 'Where did you get all this,' well, you just picked up a thing or two in Turkestan, or 'I'm quite a bit older than I look,' or say that 'Reincarnation is entirely unlike what people suppose it to be.' "[26] Though written as an extended joke, the article is all too convincing in its portrait of the available opportunities for gurus and messiahs—whether tricksters or otherwise.

Other factors helped ensure that new religions could arise and prosper without the threat of official intervention. From the early 1960s, the federal courts showed a new determination to enforce the First Amendment separation of church and state, thus ensuring that nothing like the repression of the Second World War years could ever be repeated. A series of Supreme Court cases from 1962 to 1963 prevented public schools participating in official prayer or any other exercise of religion, while cases involving small religious sects were determined with unprecedented sympathy towards the rights of minorities. The case of *Sherbert v. Verner* (1963) involved a Seventh-Day Adventist declared ineligible for unemployment compensation after he was dismissed for his refusal to work on Saturdays. The Court determined that although a balance must exist between the state interest and a private right, the state must show a compelling interest before taking any action to regulate religion and such regulation must use the least restrictive measure available. The 1971 decision in *Lemon v. Kurtz-*

*mann* prescribed strict criteria for any law, state or federal, which had the effect of regulating religious practice. The legal environment created by *Sherbert* and *Lemon* removed any danger of state intervention even with the most unpopular fringe religions.

Other decisions expanded the definition of religion to include groups whose status might otherwise have been questionable because they lacked traditional worship styles or liturgies. In 1965, the Supreme Court broadened the definition of religion for purposes of draft exemption to groups lacking any orthodox belief or structure, provided they held "a sincere and meaningful belief occupying in the life of its possessor a place parallel to that filled by the God of those admittedly qualified for the exemption" (*U.S. v. Seeger*). By analogy, the status of religion could not be denied to groups that did claim a set of recognizably religious beliefs and practices, like the Unification Church or Krishna Consciousness (ISKCON), nor could it be denied to therapy sects like Scientology or UFO-oriented groups. This recognition would insulate movements from later efforts to regulate any so-called pseudoreligions.

## Strands of Belief

Some of the beneficiaries of the new spiritual enthusiasm were the deep-rooted groups already remarked on above, but other traditions were authentically new to American society. The new religions that attracted the most immediate attention were the Asian imports, chiefly of Indian origin, but also Japanese, Tibetan, and Korean. The Theosophical movement and its successors had already sown the ground for these Asian influences, but the reform of American immigration law in 1965 permitted an unprecedented influx of Asian gurus and religious entrepreneurs. The new movements included ISKCON, the Divine Light Mission of Guru Maharaj Ji, and the followers of Meher Baba and Bhagwan Shree Rajnesh. In the public mind, the definitive guru was the Maharishi Mahesh Yogi, who was anointed by his association with the Beatles and who led the Transcendental Meditation movement, TM. Several of the new sects followed the Indian Sant Mat tradition, a North Indian-based school that emphasizes the role of the living guru: this was the origin of movements like the Divine Light Mission, ECKANKAR, and MSIA, the Movement of Spiritual Inner Awareness.[27] The Buddhist-inspired movements, meanwhile, developed from the Beat Generation's interest in Zen (Alan Watts's book, *The*

*Way of Zen*, appeared in 1957, Kerouac's *Dharma Bums* the following year). J. Gordon Melton suggests that of some 370 new religious movements founded in the period 1961 to 1979, around 18 percent could be classified as Asian in character.[28]

Though founded in Korea, the Unification Church led by Sun Myung Moon claimed a place within the Christian tradition, albeit one far-removed from the Western consensus. According to his system, the world fell in consequence of Lucifer's seduction of Eve, and the consequent failure of Adam to fulfill his divine potential. The world thus fell under the control of Satan, from which successive generations have struggled to reclaim it. True restoration requires a messiah, who cannot be Jesus Christ because he failed to fulfill his destiny by taking a female consort. In the present age, the messiah has arisen in the form of Moon, who is also the perfect Adam. However bizarre in terms of orthodox Christian theology, Moon's ideas have many parallels in the traditions of Gnostic and esoteric Christianity, and it should probably be seen as a near Christian sect rather being bracketed with other Asian movements. The Unification Church made its first American converts as early as 1959, and it spread rapidly during the early 1970s.

Another potent element of the new cult milieu was the therapy sect, which offered believers the chance to achieve their full human potential through personal growth and self-actualization by taking total responsibility for one's actions. The prototypical movement of this kind was est (Erhard Seminar Training), in which intense and often grueling sessions forced followers to confront a new view of reality.[29] The borderline between religion and therapy is often hard to define in such settings, and there would be long debate over the claims of Scientology to church status. In the American legal setting, however, religious status offered so many material advantages, especially in the form of tax exemption, that many groups were tempted to stress their spiritual aspects. In turn, critics viewed therapy sects as cultlike because of the analogies between their demanding training techniques and those of the overtly religious groups. One controversial organization was the Process, which has been termed a deviant psychotherapy cult and which in the 1980s acquired a worse reputation when it was (falsely) accused of being a homicidal satanic-sacrifice ring.[30]

Still another facet of the religious upsurge occurred among Christian groups with the rise of independent churches and religious fellowships not necessarily affiliated with any particular church or denomination. In the late 1960s, a portion of the youth subculture became Jesus People or Jesus Freaks, and the organizations they formed would take very different courses over the coming years. A few would grow into thriving Christian denominations, among the most important of which were the Calvary Chapel and its later offshoot, the Vineyard Fellowship.[31] Others took less orthodox courses, giving exalted roles to charismatic leaders and attempting to separate followers from their friends and families; these groups would be among the earliest targets for anticult critics. The most controversial of such ministries included the Alamo Foundation, The Way International, the Love Family, and the Children of God.

## Numbers

It is all too easy to find books and articles from the 1970s and 1980s that present the cults as a major challenge to traditional American religious patterns. These works suggest that America's young people were joining cults in vast numbers and that the growth of Asian-influenced groups in particular marked a quite revolutionary shift in spiritual consciousness. These charges were misleading and vastly exaggerated the scale and influence of the new sects.[32]

During the anticult agitation of the late 1970s, claims were commonly heard that the number of active cultists ran into the millions. Writers variously suggested cult populations between one and three million, around 1 percent of the national population, and a handful gave figures in the tens of millions. In 1995, Singer and Lalich suggest that "between two million and five million Americans are involved in cults at any one time."[33] In 1979, a Senate inquiry was told that "since the early 1970s, more than ten million Americans have embraced cult activities." Anticult activist Rabbi Maurice Davis spoke of "two million victims and four million parents, and a country bewildered and frightened and ashamed."[34] The news media eventually settled on the estimate of two to three million cultists, which had the virtue of being easily remembered and which conveyed the impression of a suitably vast menace. Endlessly quoted from source to source, its origins never questioned, the figure acquired the status of revealed truth.

However, even figures in the low millions are counterintuitive, and the most authoritative source on the membership of cults and alternative religions, J. Gordon Melton, estimated the range between 150,000 and 300,000. This far lower estimate seems credible when we realize that most of the dozen or so cults frequently mentioned in the media had only a few thousand devotees apiece, and the vast majority of other bodies would be lucky to count their members in the hundreds. Only a handful gained American followings in the tens of thousands: this was the case with The Way International, Scientology, the neo-pagans, and the Association for Research and Enlightenment. Even the Unification Church, often portrayed as the most insidious of the cults, has never had more than seven or eight thousand members in the United States. Though exact figures are controversial, the Krishna Consciousness movement may have had no more than three thousand American initiates at its height and the Children of God two or three thousand, while we can suggest strengths in the midthousands for the Divine Light Mission and the Church Universal and Triumphant.[35] Curiously, very few of the anticult texts even mention the Black Muslims or the Mormon polygamist groups, both of which can claim numbers far in excess of these other well-publicized organizations. The two to three million figure seems to belong to that family of wildly inflated guesstimates that so often characterize claims about emotive social issues, matters like drugs, serial murder, or missing children.

The conflict over numbers could be resolved if we assume that the few notorious cults were just the tip of a very large iceberg of several thousand bizarre sects, and this is exactly what some writers do claim. One text argues that there might still be three to five thousand active cults in the 1990s and that "over the past two decades, as many as twenty million people have been involved for varying periods of time in one or another of these groups."[36] Steve Allen, by no means an uncritical observer, suggested in 1982 that "there are now more than a thousand cults in the United States, with an estimated combined membership around the two million mark." In 1977, a Jewish text on *Kids in Cults* suggested that "in the United States today, there are approximately one million people, most of them between eighteen and twenty-five, who have abandoned their traditional American lifestyles in order to become members of one of the approximately five thousand religious sects and cults in America."[37]

If the Children of God or the Hare Krishnas really had several thousand obscure counterparts, then we might be able to credit the figure of two or three million active cultists, but these statistics, too, are far higher than other sources suggest. One of the best scholarly attempts to quantify "cultish" groups found an active total of only some five hundred in the late 1970s, and the great majority of these were tranquil and respectable bodies, often splinters of old established movements like Theosophy and spiritualism.[38] Only a handful would conceivably qualify as the "destructive cults" of media mythology.

Either someone's statistics about cult activity are in grave error or, more likely, very different phenomena are being observed. As always, everything depends on definitions, and the high figures cited for the number of cults were produced by simply assuming that all new or small religious movements were automatically cultlike. In reality, only a tiny fraction of the new organizations were anything like as antinomian, confrontational, and downright bizarre as, say, the Children of God. To take some counterexamples, both Calvary Chapel and the Vineyard Fellowship fell into the category of enthusiastic new religious movements formed in these years, though neither could remotely be classified as cults. Nor were the vast majority of the Asian-derived sects. Only the most intolerant of fundamentalist critics could describe all non-Christian movements as *ipso facto* cults.

Even if we could agree on the number of cults, there are grave difficulties in trying to estimate the total number of individuals who passed through these groups, not least that the same individuals often joined several sects and communes over a period of several years in what is sometimes termed the phenomenon of "circulating saints." Both the fringe religions and their enemies have a common agenda in making the sects look as large as possible for diametrically opposite rhetorical ends: the sects wish to prove their success and wide influence, the anticult groups seek to portray the cult problem in the most threatening terms possible. In 1959, the hair-raising television documentary on the threat posed by the Nation of Islam placed the movement's membership at 250,000, which was an overestimate of some 260 percent. Another anticult polemic in 1980 credited the Church of Scientology with three million members in the United States, but in 1993, a major survey of religious affiliation found only 45,000 American Scientologists.[39]

In short, the estimate of two to three million cultists seems to take account of everyone who had ever passed through a fringe sect or therapy movement, with the implication that even such a passing contact transformed the individual into a full-fledged cultist, who had renounced all contact with family and mainstream society, who lived in a compound or collective housing, and who was systematically brainwashed by cult leaders. We should recall here the division of types of cult groups, which range all the way from audience or client cults, which attract the casual grazer, to cult movements, which demand far more time and commitment. Even in the latter, by no means all converts remained within the group indefinitely: contrary to the stereotype of infallible cult-brainwashing techniques, many recruits simply deserted after a year or two, losing interest or becoming disillusioned. Millions of Americans in the 1970s had some ephemeral experience with a group that some described as a cult, just as they might have experimented with illegal drugs, but as in the case of drugs, the cult contact was for only a tiny minority an enduring or life-transforming experience.

Nor were cults, however defined, as ubiquitous a threat as was sometimes claimed. Certainly the marginal groups developed more of a national presence than in earlier years, but they retained their main centers in certain regions, above all in the West. This is indicated by Stark and Bainbridge's scholarly study that found some five hundred alleged cults (taking the term in a very broad sense). Tracing the headquarters of the various movements in the 1970s, the authors found that by far the largest number of cults was based, unsurprisingly, in California, which had a third of all cult centers, but if we allow for population size, the highest concentrations of cult headquarters were actually in Nevada and New Mexico. A total of 223 cult centers, or 44 percent, were based in just six western states, namely California, Arizona, Colorado, Nevada, New Mexico, and Oregon, a distribution pattern that would have made excellent sense to an observer in 1920. Conversely, in the 1970s as in the 1920s, cults were as poorly represented in the American South as they were abundant in the West and Southwest. As Sikh leader Yogi Bhajan boasted of his own group's New Mexico headquarters, "God is everywhere, but His address is in Española."[40]

## Born Again

However sensational at the time, the growth of marginal religious movements and cults must be put in perspective: these groups were neither as large nor as omnipresent as media accounts suggested, and involvement in them was by no means as all-consuming or obsessive. Nor was this situation terribly new. If we take the loose criterion for cult affiliation that critics used in these years, then the 1970s were scarcely more cultish than other periods, as for example the 1930s, when several million people had at least some contact with movements like I AM, Psychiana, or the Oxford Group, to say nothing of their many competitors.

For all the outpouring of books and news articles on the cult threat—the "cult seduction" of American youth—the most significant trends of the 1970s and 1980s were located in a quite different area of the religious spectrum. The fact that controversial cults were attracting some tens of thousands of mainly young people attracted vastly more media attention than the concurrent movement of millions into strict and ultraconservative Protestant and Pentecostal sects, which symbolized the real transformation of American religion in these years. Ultimately, these churches would also attract many of the boomers who had flirted with New Age and occult ideas some years before. These far-reaching changes proceeded scarcely noted by the mass media, which received a rude wake-up call following the surge of evangelical support for Jimmy Carter's presidential campaign in 1976. When Carter announced that he had been born again, an experience claimed by tens of millions of Americans, news commentators scrambled to find the meaning of the mysterious term, initially reporting the belief as if it were as bizarre as snake handling.[41]

Though little recognized in the mass media, evangelical and fundamentalist traditions remained strong through midcentury and received an enormous boost from the Billy Graham crusades, the first of which was launched in Los Angeles in 1949.[42] Between 1965 and 1985, the growth of evangelical and Pentecostal religious sentiment was indicated by radical changes in the structures of church membership nationwide, in the rapid growth of conservative sects and denominations, and the precipitous decline of liberal groups that had once flattered themselves as constituting the religious mainstream, churches like the Episcopalians, United Methodists, Presbyterians, Lutherans, and United Church of Christ. The reversal of fortune is suggested by comparing the (Pentecostal) Assemblies of God with the liberal United Church of Christ: between 1960 and 1987, the Assemblies of God grew from about half a million members to 2.2 million, while in the same period, the United Church of Christ shrank from 2.3 million to 1.7 million.[43] Though the liberal mainline churches somewhat stemmed their rate of decline in the 1990s, their remaining members still tended to be far older than those of the growing conservative sects. Other winners from this era were the small sects that evangelicals themselves had long denounced as intolerable cults. According to the National Survey of Religious Identification the Jehovah's Witnesses claimed 1.4 million members in the United States by the early 1990s and the Seventh-Day Adventists, 670,000 (Christian Science membership stagnated at around 214,000).

Figures for the Latter-Day Saints are more controversial, but at least four million American adherents seems a reasonable estimate, making the Mormon church considerably larger than several of the old so-called mainline bodies.

Though sensational groups like the Hare Krishnas and the Unification Church attracted so many column-inches in the newspapers of the 1970s, these movements were numerically insignificant when set aside the thriving new Protestant sects. A similar imbalance affects African American denominations, as groups like the Nation of Islam (with perhaps thirty thousand members today) have regularly grabbed headlines denied to vast and respectable organizations like the National Baptist Convention of the USA and the National Baptist Convention of America, each of which has several million followers. To put this in perspective, the National Baptist Convention—USA has roughly one affiliated *church* for every individual adherent of the Nation of Islam. Though they remain barely known to most white Americans, these African American Baptist churches both rank among the nation's largest.

To take a concrete symbol of the gulf between perception and reality, we might note the experience of the Willow Creek Community Church in Illinois, one of a new generation of megachurches that has excited such interest among evangelicals.[44] Sunday attendance at Willow Creek runs at about fifteen thousand, which would theoretically provide about enough seating capacity to accommodate the peak American strength of the Unification Church, the Children of God, and ISKCON. And though Willow Creek has been unusually successful, many thousands of other evangelical churches blossomed in these same years. If there was a new spiritual awakening in the 1970s, it was predominantly a Christian and evangelical event, and as in previous epochs, the cults existed on the edges of this core reality.

# NINE

# Cult Wars
## 1969–1985

The path of the cults leads to Jonestown.
Rabbi Maurice Davis

However misleadingly, religious change from the late 1960s onwards was perceived by Americans as a threat to their youth. In response to the supposed cult explosion, an anticult movement developed, which enjoyed great success in projecting its distinctive interpretation as the dominant view accepted by the mass media and the general public.[1] Between 1976 and 1981, America experienced an anticult Reaction phase as intense as any in its history.

Most of the cult stereotypes that thrived in these years would have been instantly recognizable to newspaper readers of the 1930s or the 1880s. The I AM case had popularized the idea of cultists blindly obeying prophets and gurus of dubious mental stability, who repaid this devotion by exploiting their followers and rending them from their families; the stories of both I AM and Mankind United had linked the cults to financial gangsterism. The House of David affair was only one of several incidents to raise the sexual danger posed by cults to female members, especially to very young girls. Also familiar was a xenophobic concern about the invasion of American society by foreign, particularly Asian, ideas. Nor would earlier critics have been too surprised by the new theories about the underhanded means by which individuals were recruited to odd fringe sects. While in the seventeenth century such a puzzling change could be blamed on witchcraft and on Mesmerism or hypnotism in the nineteenth, the fashionable explanation was now phrased in terms of brainwashing and mind control, an idea that permitted converts to be "deprogrammed" to what their families considered religious normality. The transition from hypnotism to brainwashing represented little more than a change in name for the same underlying concept. Though few of the anticult themes of the 1970s were truly new, some had not been so heavily emphasized in earlier cult scares. The cults of the 1970s were seen as much more likely to engage in violence against critics or dissenters, and the new rhetoric also placed an unprecedented emphasis on the cult threat to children.

In each case, there were genuine instances of aberrant behavior within the movements themselves, but a truthful foundation was all but obscured by a vast superstructure of myth, distortion, and hype. A charge against one group joined the snowballing repertoire of accusations in the general anti-cult mythology, and would subsequently be deployed against any other cult. When members of one sect attacked a critic with a rattlesnake, the image became a standard item in the arsenal of anti-cult horror stories, with the suggestion that this extreme behavior typified all fringe cults. By the late 1970s, the cults were tainted by the still more frightening image of mass suicide. As has been said of drug-related stories, we must always be on our guard against "the routinization of caricature—worst cases framed as typical cases, the episodic rhetorically recrafted into the epidemic."[2] By such rhetorical means, cultists were transformed from an older image of harmless crackpots to a new and more virulent picture of brainwashed potential assassins, who posed a real threat to the nation's stability.

## Mind Control and Brainwashing

A critical turning point in popular views of the cults was the murder series committed by the followers of Charles Manson in 1969, and the sensational trial that took place over the following year.[3] The Manson Family was at best tangentially connected to any other groups of this era, and it is arguable whether it can be described as a cult in any religious sense: it had no systematic belief or theology beyond a general regard of Manson as charismatic leader, whether Jesus or Satan. However, the Manson example established in the public mind certain images of the baneful cult. According to the cliché, a figure with messianic pretensions lives in a secluded compound surrounded by gullible young followers, whom he sexually exploits. The leader absolutely controls the minds and behavior of his devotees, who can be induced to commit any criminal or violent act, even murder. Within a few years, similar charges of mind control were being made against other fringe religions, especially those which were in this time period (1969–71) growing out of the Jesus Freak movement.

Several of these Christian-oriented groups in particular were identified as dangerous cults. The oldest established was The Way International, which was originally founded as a radio ministry in 1942 by Dr. Victor Paul Wierwille, a clergyman of the Evangelical and Reformed Church. By the 1970s, it had established a communal headquarters in Ohio. Despite these solid credentials, The Way was attracting vehement criticism by the 1970s. Defecting members reported the use of of mind control techniques, and rumors circulated that the group was accumulating weapons.[4] The Alamo Foundation began in 1969 as a ministry to hippies and young people on the streets. It soon faced familiar charges that members were being held in "virtual slavery," forced to work without pay and cut off from all family ties. Similar allegations were made against Seattle-based Love Family, or Church of Armageddon, which was founded in the same year. This group, headed by "Love Israel," likewise required its members to sever connections with their existing families. Another lightning rod for accusations was the Children of God, founded by David Berg as a southern California ministry to Jesus Freaks. In 1969, fearing that California would fall prey to a natural catastrophe, Berg (now "Moses") moved his followers to other states and began circulating the prophetic revelations he claimed to have received. By 1971, there were perhaps a hundred Children of God communes around the world, with a total membership of two to three thousand. Through the 1970s, the major targets of anticult groups included, invariably, Children of God, the Unification Church, and ISKCON, as well as, according to taste, some combination of the Alamo Foundation, the Love Family, The Way International, Synanon, the Church of Scientology, and the Divine Light Mission.[5]

According to a growing perception of cult behavior, young and vulnerable recruits were being subjected to intensive conditioning that amounted to brainwashing, a concept that had become familiar from the experiences of American prisoners during the Korean War. The concept of brainwashing was popularized in Robert J. Lifton's *Thought Reform and the Psychology of Totalism* and in fictional treatments like Richard Condon's 1959 book, *The Manchurian Candidate*, which was filmed in 1962.[6] Brainwashing was firmly associated with Asian villains, and the idea had a particular resonance for Americans of the 1970s, following the disastrous end of the Vietnam War and revelations about the mistreatment of U.S. prisoners of war. The Korean origins of the Moon organization gave popular credibility to charges that the sect might employ dastardly "Oriental" tactics against American youngsters.

Theories about brainwashing were much in the news in the mid-1970s following official investigations into misdeeds by U.S. intelligence agencies and the reopened investigation of the traumatic domestic assassinations of the 1960s. According to conspiracy speculations, which reached their height between about 1974 and 1977, the FBI and CIA had tried to create "programmed assassins" to remove political enemies. The linkage between cults and so-called programmed assassins was enhanced when in September 1975, Lynette "Squeaky" Fromme, an alumna of the Manson group, attempted to assassinate President Gerald Ford. In 1974, the kidnapping and apparent conversion of Patty Hearst by a terrorist cell showed how mind-control techniques could induce an innocent person to carry out violent acts. Those under control were often called "zombies," a term that evoked bygone anticult allegations.[7]

## The New Cult Threat

Critics were troubled by the means through which young people were initially recruited or converted into cult movements. The stereotype held that recruits were not consciously or knowingly joining a particular sect, but were pulled into it unwittingly through a deceptively titled front group. The Unification Church generated an impressive range of such fronts, which allowed a potential convert to be drawn into ever closer social and emotional ties with existing members. Once fully converted to the new cult, recruits were utterly cut off from the outside world except in stringently controlled and supervised circumstances, and their lives were virtually owned by the movement. In many groups, the transfer of absolute love and loyalty to the new sect was symbolized by rituals of initiation and even of renaming. Converts gave all their property and time to the movement, for whom they became slaves. In a typical attack on Children of God activities in California in 1971, an evangelical group charged that young recruits were "taught UN-CHRISTIAN DOCTRINES, guarded at all times, with fearfulness shaking their bodies, no sleep, no food . . . they are bussed to Arizona, taught in a hypnotic state, kept away from the sunlight, and filled with wickedness."[8]

Cult leaders were depicted as megalomaniacs who either genuinely believed their own exalted claims or cynically exploited the devotion of their followers. Whatever the case, the leaders and a few select allies lived in extreme luxury, while devotees were starved and subjected to forced labor. Anticult critic Rabbi Maurice Davis explicitly compared the new cults to German Nazism. In his view, a group like the Unification Church (the "Moonies") was "1. a totally monolithic movement with a single point of view and a single authoritarian head; 2. replete with fanatical followers who are prepared and programmed to do anything their master says; 3. supplied by absolutely unlimited funds; 4. with a hatred of everyone on the outside; 5. with suspicion of parents, against their parents. . . . I tell you, I'm scared."[9]

Anticult rhetoric stressed sexual threats, especially when it was learned that the Children of God were using sex ("flirty fishing") as a means of luring new members. By 1973, well-documented stories implicated this group in rape, adult-child sex, and child pornography, activities justified by an antinomian ideology that demanded believers explore the worst vices in order to prove their freedom from sin. The movement transferred its headquarters beyond American jurisdiction and began a series of wanderings, which over the years would take it through various European capitals. In consequence, the group's founder, David Berg, came to symbolize the most extreme forms of cult exploitation.[10] Charges of polygamy and sexual abuse were directed against other leaders, including Tony Alamo.[11] These tales acquired a new weight in an age when women's groups were drawing attention to all aspects of male sexual violence and exploitation. Like the references to zombyism, this element recalled earlier attacks on fringe religions, in this case the feminist attacks on polygamy a century before.[12]

Another target was Synanon, founded by Chuck Dederich to help drug addicts rehabilitate themselves. By the early 1970s, the group grew ever closer to the cult stereotype, demanding total conformity from members, who were required to "redistribute" their spouses in a ceremony of mass divorce and remarriage. Fearing external attack, the new authoritarian regime purchased an arsenal, and members trained in martial arts. The separation from the outside world became absolute, with increasing tension between members and rivals. "There were stories of Synanon hit-men threatening enemies and splittees. Beatings, muggings, threats, an ex-member's dog found hanging from a rope."[13] In one memorable incident of cult intimidation, a neighbor who had criticized the group was bitten by a rattlesnake that had been placed inside his mailbox.

In a few cases, peripheral religions seemed to be aiming at grandiose schemes of political domination. The most egregious was the Unification Church, which in the late 1970s controlled a corporate empire worth some $200 million and had extensive political ties. Pastor Jim Jones briefly made his People's Temple a potent political force in northern California and was hoping to extend its influence to Los Angeles. Democratic politicians accepted Jones's financial contributions and benefited from his solid voting bloc, which probably was the deciding factor in San Francisco's 1975 close-run mayoral elections.[14] Other groups attracted scandal by building arsenals either to intimidate rivals and critics or for more far-reaching political goals: in 1978, for example, ISKCON members were accused of accumulating weapons.[15]

## Deprogrammers

Like the cults themselves, the anticult movement became a visible presence in the early 1970s. Activism originated with a number of *ad hoc* organizations drawn from the families of converts, with the goal of rescuing the supposed victims of cult deception. Among the first was the Parents Committee to Free Our Sons and Daughters from the Children of God Organization, later FREECOG. This group and its successors used an appealing rhetoric of family restoration, using names like Love Our Children or Citizens Engaged in Reuniting Children.[16] The family groups developed rapidly, forming a national network to pressure the media and political leaders.

The family groups encountered the difficulty that converts rarely wanted to be saved from their new environments, but this only led to an ever firmer conviction that cult recruits had indeed been subjected to brainwashing, or "psychological kidnapping." If that was the case, then families thought themselves justified in using similar countermeasures, so that brainwashing would be defeated through "deprogramming." There soon arose a whole profession of deprogrammers, who would, for a fee, kidnap the convert and restore his or her proper mind-set. Deprogrammers presented themselves as skilled professionals who could speak with expertise about the range of cults and their techniques, so the news media regularly resorted to these individuals as authoritative sources about the cult problem. Obviously, deprogrammers had a vested interest in making the cults appear as predatory as possible in order to justify their own existence.[17]

The first deprogrammer was a California social worker named Ted

Patrick, who was active as early as 1971. He was the source for many of the most extreme claims about the cult menace and about the means required to combat it. He asserted that cults in contemporary America "are increasing by the day; and they are one of the most dangerous threats in the history of this country."[18] In 1974, he declared starkly, "In certain areas, the Constitution is outdated. Freedom of religion, this part of the Constitution is nothing but a license to kill, lie, and steal, and do everything under the sun as long as you've got a non-profit organization and say you're a church. But this part of the Constitution should be changed, and then know what these people are doing." Patrick's claims often sound occult in their own right, as when he stated that cult conversion took place by a kind of supernatural mental influence: "We know of people that can put their hand over a coffee table and that table will rise up without touching them and they can walk it all over the room. This is a mental energy that comes from the body—the brain wave—out through the fingertips and the eyes." Through such "energies," he claimed to have personally reconverted in only an hour or two cultists who had been involved for several years in groups like ISKCON.[19] For Patrick, all cult conversions were in effect kidnappings and required appropriate countermeasures: without deprogramming, cults "make it impossible for the person to think throughout the rest of their lives."[20]

Deprogramming won the support of some therapists, who provided the scientific justification for the whole concept of brainwashing and deprogramming. Psychiatrists listed the pathological symptoms found in ex-cult members, which had presumably been inflicted upon them by the traumatic cult experience. Cult converts were "often deluded, hallucinating, and confused in a highly manipulative environment, in their altered states of consciousness. Their minds are split."[21] Other commentators, though, argued that these symptoms were observed in cult members who had been deprogrammed and that this process had itself provided the trauma, which caused subsequent difficulties.[22] In the face of sharp controversy, the National Council of Churches issued a statement in 1974 that condemned deprogramming, at least for adults.

## The Anticult Movement

In addition to families, deprogrammers, and therapists, religious groups joined the anticult crusade. The Christian and particularly evangelical critique was the oldest aspect of the movement, and the turn-of-the-century antiheresy tradition revived in the 1970s. Christian writers differed from the more secular-minded activists in that they were unabashedly offering a correct spiritual prescription for America, and one that was both Christian and evangelical: there was no pretense here of recognizing religious pluralism. One active anticult organization was the Spiritual Counterfeits Project, itself an offshoot of the Jesus People movement. The title is interesting in its own right in suggesting that religions could easily be distinguished between "counterfeits" and others which were, presumably, "genuine." Evangelical writings tended to condemn cults as variants of "Eastern religion," an inaccurate term suggesting that the diverse traditions of East and South Asia were all somehow related and shared similar characteristics of fatalism and superstition. In 1976, a typical text published by the Campus Crusade for Christ offered a guide through "the mindfields of Eastern mysticism: TM, Hare Krishna, Sun Moon, and others."[23]

The new religious polemic was in marked contrast to that of the earlier years of the twentieth century, when moderates had denounced enthusiastic cults in order to promote the internal harmony and moderation of the "mainstream" churches. By the 1980s, however, cult exposés were used for the quite opposite reason, for furthering the ideological views of fundamentalists. The most active anticult activists came from small Christian sects of fundamentalist or Pentecostal bent, who drew attention to the cult menace in order to substantiate their apocalyptic claims about the imminence of the End Times. The rise of false messiahs and satanic rings demonstrated the reality of evil and the Antichrist, and thereby discredited those moderates who showed themselves soft on issues like the existence of the devil and the Second Coming. Evangelicals viewed the whole New Age movement as a satanic Trojan horse, a view that would be popularized in the 1980s in the popular religious novels of Frank Peretti.[24]

In addition to Christian evangelicals, Jewish activists fought what they saw as attempts to prey on Jewish youngsters, to convert them to other religions, including Christianity.[25] Moreover, some of the more controversial cult leaders were accused of anti-Semitic activities or rhetoric, including Holocaust denial. The conversion issue was particularly sensitive during the 1970s due to growing Jewish fears of assimilation and intermarriage, and some dire predictions warned that the American Jewish population would shrink dramatically in coming decades. The cults did indeed make inroads among Jewish teens and young adults.

Though estimates vary widely, Rudin and Rudin suggest that "perhaps 20 percent of Hare Krishnas are Jewish. Jews constitute as much as 30 percent of Divine Light mission membership, and there are many Jews in Scientology."[26] Jewish organizations particularly condemned movements like Jews for Jesus, which proclaimed Jesus as messiah, while retaining Jewish customs and ritual life. The overall threat to Jewish life may well have been exaggerated, and surveys of rabbis found no evidence of mass conversions, but the cult issue focused broader fears.[27]

For Jewish opponents of conversion, there was little to choose between different forms of evangelistic efforts among Jewish youngsters, whether the groups responsible were authoritarian and suspect cults or well-recognized Protestant denominations. This anticonversion approach potentially threatened to cause conflicts with Christian organizations, many of which disapproved of efforts to proselytize Jews, but would still resist any formal restrictions on evangelism. However, a broad interfaith consensus could be achieved if the conversion issue could be framed as part of the wider and commonly acknowledged cult problem.[28] In the Jewish context, therefore, the problem was framed in terms not just of cults but of "cults and missionaries," and regional Jewish organizations formed a variety of commissions and task forces on this dual theme. Merging these twin issues was a rhetorically valuable way in defusing potential hostility from Christian churches. Moreover, presenting messianic Jews as part of a cult served to discredit a movement that saw itself as a legitimate part of Judaism.

A final component of the anticult movement was drawn from the cultists themselves, in the form of individuals who had left the movements, either willingly or through the efforts of deprogrammers, and who now devoted themselves to fighting the cults with all the wonted zeal of the former convert. This was by no means a new historical phenomenon: Shakespeare had noted how "the heresies that men do leave/are hated most of those they did deceive," and through the centuries, defectors from particular religions had distinguished themselves by their fanatical zeal against their former friends and colleagues. In the American context, the alleged former priest or nun had been a staple of anti-Catholic hysteria from the time of Maria Monk and Charles Chiniquy, and metaphors of "jumping over the wall" and "finding our way out," were familiar in controversial literature. The nineteenth-century Shakers had found their worst enemy in ex-member Mary Dyer, and Mrs. Eddy's nemesis was her old colleague Josephine Woodbury. Hell hath no fury like a disciple scorned. The cult defector genre proliferated in the 1970s, and defector testimony was priceless because it claimed to offer a firsthand glimpse of life within highly secretive organizations.[29] As so often in the past, however, defectors also frequently magnified both their role in the movement they had forsaken and its evil qualities. One much-quoted polemic from these years was the 1972 book *The Satan Seller*, by evangelical Mike Warnke, which is at the least a vastly exaggerated account of his career as a satanic high priest.

This diverse anticult movement now began to form national structures. It coalesced into organizations like the Citizens Freedom Foundation (1974), which in turn evolved into the Cult Awareness Network (1986); in 1979, the American Family Foundation was formed to assist former cult members. There was also a Council on Mind Abuse, COMA. The broad movement gave birth to a range of magazines, like the *Cult Observer, Cultic Studies Journal, CAN News*, and *FOCUS News*. Activists disseminated their views through seminars, letter-writing campaigns, and a large body of books and pamphlets. Religious groups in particular tried to forewarn potential recruits by lesson programs and pamphlets that explored likely conversion scenarios.

## Critiquing the Critics

The anticultists did not lack critics, particularly among the so-called cults they were targeting, but also from academic observers. One effective countercharge was that the zeal of the emerging anticult coalition ironically made it indistinguishable from the worst cult stereotype. The anticult mythology did have its apocalyptic elements. According to cult foes, society was facing a literally diabolical challenge from evil pseudomessiahs whose occult powers could only be counteracted by the good magic of the deprogrammers: this was a thought-world little removed from that of Mesmerism or, perhaps, of I AM. The notion of an anticult group becoming cultlike in its own regard was scarcely new. In the nineteenth century, the Know-Nothings, opposed to the machinations of secret societies, had themselves organized as a secret society with its own mystic words and countersigns, while the Ku Klux Klan achieved its greatest success in the 1920s on the strength of its own variant of anticultism, namely, its attack on the Catholic Church. Like these earlier parallels, the new movement offered a complex and uncompromising belief-system that was quite intolerant of rival or dissenting views.

At several points, too, the anticultists were making assumptions that were far more questionable than might be suggested by their instant acceptance by the mass media. The fundamental notion of cult brainwashing should have aroused more controversy than it did. Though intensive psychological conditioning can profoundly change behavior, it is far from certain that the conditions existing in cult settings could be described in anything like these terms. When authors described the sinister methods used to induce and maintain personality change, they were often describing practices like repetitive chant and movement, which are commonly used in religious systems, including large sections of Eastern Orthodox Christianity and even American Protestant revivalism. To quote psychologist Paul Verdier, "The trance-like states that cult activities produce in the cult's members are the result of rhythmic bodily movement and of dirge-like chanting of nonsense syllables which have no action-evoking potential."[30] If the cults were wrongheaded and dangerous on these grounds, so were most religions worldwide.

Still, brainwashing was a convenient explanation for families unable to comprehend how their offspring could have become so hostile to their parents and to their former values: one person's salvation is another's insanity. The families found themselves in precisely the same position as the relatives of converts throughout history, of Victorian Protestants whose daughters had become nuns or Shakers, of Catholics whose sons had abandoned the priesthood to marry Protestants, of Jews whose children defected to Christianity, of evangelicals whose relatives spoke in tongues.[31] The difference in the 1970s was that the grievance could be framed in psychological terms, and a therapeutic label could be applied to the thuggery necessary to reclaim the errant child.

Also questionable was what we might call the underlying myth of the seduction narratives. According to many family accounts, promising young people loyally attached to their families were drawn away into cults, where their personalities were subverted by communal living, where they practiced degraded group sex, and where their very lives might be threatened by odd religious practices (in one 1972 incident, two members of the Love Family died from the effects of sniffing the inhalant, toluene). The problems with this picture become clear when we recall the chronology. Most of the cult recruits were baby boomers, in their teens and early twenties in the very disturbed years between about 1968 and 1973 when traditional family cohesion was under attack from many directions. The multifaceted cultural divisions of these years involved politics and drugs, gender and sexuality, long hair and eccentric clothing, and other matters of lifestyle. Long before the cults attracted the slightest attention, a thriving youth culture was experimenting with communal living and alternate forms of sexuality, as well as drug use and mystical spirituality.[32] To suggest that boomers needed cult leaders to order them to sever relations with their parents was to demonstrate amnesia about the social trends of the Nixon years, when a popular slogan advised the young, "If you can't turn your parents on, turn on them." Many young people were living a hand-to-mouth existence on the streets years before this pattern of life was taken over by some of the new religious communities. To a large extent, the cults were being blamed for their cultural association with the lifestyle of the late 1960s.

The anticult critique of the late 1970s was part of a general conservative reaction against the hedonism of the 1960s, which was also expressed in other contemporary moralistic campaigns. Many aspects of the social liberation of the late 1960s had deeply disturbed conservatives, but it was politically impossible to try and reverse these changes directly. Large sections of the public had accepted the libertarian argument that consenting adults should be permitted to pursue their own individual paths, even if that involved hitherto illegal behavior involving drugs, pornography, sexual experimentation or homosexuality. The libertarian view could, however, be challenged by transferring the threat from consenting individuals to innocent parties, especially to children, who could not give consent. Thus morality activists of the late 1970s campaigned not against sexual vice in general, but specifically against child pornography and prostitution, and not against homosexuality, but against child molestation. A movement against drugs in general would have been futile at a time of pervasive middle-class usage of cocaine and marijuana, but a vigorous assault could be mounted against the drug PCP, which found its chief market among young teenagers.[33]

In the religious area, similarly, the argument against cults and fringe religions was that their adherents lacked real freedom either to join or remain within the movements, whether because of their youth or because of the deceptive high-pressure tactics used to achieve conversion: contrary to appearances, recruits were not consenting adults. During the 1979 Dole hearings on cults, Rabbi Maurice Davis said he was "here to protest against child molesters. For as surely as there are those who lure children with lollypops in order to rape their bodies, so, too, do these lure children with candy-coated lies in order to rape their minds."[34] Furthermore, following the rhetoric of the time, the cults were attacked for abusing and corrupting the children of members. Whether in the areas of sex, drugs, or cults, the various movements to reverse the radical 1960s followed a broadly similar chronology, and all likewise reached their high-water mark between 1977 and 1979.

The anticult literature can also be criticized for making grossly excessive claims about the impact of a few specific groups, while ignoring other religious trends. In the countless books and articles appearing on the cult menace of the 1970s, very few paid any attention to groups other than those that mainly affected middle-class white youngsters (one rare exception was the mixed-race People's Temple, of Jonestown fame). Some accounts suggested that nonwhites were simply not vulnerable to cult attractions: Rudin and Rudin claim that "blacks and Hispanics are too street-smart to join movements that promise instant happiness." A more plausible explanation is that anticult investigators were just paying no attention to the very active religious fringe sects that appealed to African Americans, Asian Americans, and Hispanics because these movements were of little interest to the presumed "mainstream" (white) audience of the mass media, who were only concerned with the threat to their own youngsters. An equally plausible case of a cult menace could be made concerning those groups that appealed to black Americans, namely the Nation of Islam and its offshoots and local groupings like the Florida-based Yahwehs, besides other Christian and Christian-derived sects.[35] The anticult movement was highly selective in its choice of enemies.

## Cult Wars

From the mid-1970s, anticult views gained an impressive national influence as they were forcefully presented in political circles and in the mass media. In 1974, a subcommittee of the California state senate held a hearing on "the impact of cults on today's youth," an event demonstrating the distinctive directions in which the anticult groups sought to take the debate. Not all the witnesses were unequivocal enemies of the new religions, and the committee attempted to offer some time to representatives of the accused groups. Still, a series of irate and tearful family members complained of atrocities blamed on the Alamo Foundation, Children of God, and the Love Family. The senators heard of cult members being torn from their families and placed in conditions of physical coercion and intimidation. Deprogrammer Ted Patrick was cheered when he declared that "the groups we are talking about are not religious groups. These are plain old crooks . . . con artists."[36] The same year, State of New York's Charity Frauds Bureau undertook a searching investigation of the Children of God, publicizing charges of draft evasion, tax fraud, polygamy, incest, and child sexual abuse.[37] By 1976, a presidential election year, the family movements gained the sympathetic attention of national politicians. U.S. Senator Bob Dole held informal federal hearings at which family members and defectors presented their cases against the cults, which were widely reported in the news media. Meanwhile, Senator Walter Mondale investigated charges of child abuse within the cults, and San Francisco Representative Leo Ryan became an active opponent of Jim Jones's People's Temple group.

In 1976, too, the mainstream media declared open season on the cults. *Time* published a devastating account of "The Darker Side of Sun Moon," charging him among other things with massive personal corruption, megalomania, and the practice of ritual sex. Meanwhile, stories of cult busting and deprogramming appeared in mass-market magazines like *Seventeen*, *Woman's Day*, and *Good Housekeeping*. These accounts generally told how some young person was "rescued" or "escaped" from the clutches of an evil or destructive cult and reunited with a loving family. One example of this genre appeared in *Esquire* in 1978 under the characteristic title of "Rescuing David from the Moonies."[38]

In the late 1970s, the Unification Church played the starring role in such attacks. This movement featured as villain in books like *Crazy for God*, *Life among the Moonies*, *Lord of the Second Advent*, and *Escape from the Moonies*. The 1979 book *Hostage to Heaven* tells of "four years in the Unification Church by an Ex-Moonie and the mother who fought to free her." These titles further illustrate how the derogatory term "Moonie" became a standard term for members of this denomination, in a way that would have been inconceivable for any of the insulting epithets that could be applied to, say, Catholics or Jews. Another study, *Moonwebs*, became the basis for the 1981 movie *Ticket to Heaven*, an unabashed manifesto for deprogramming.[39] Children of God exposés were almost as common, as were general accounts of the "cult seduction" of American youth. A few high-profile cases involved celebrities: in 1982, comedian Steve Allen published a memoir of his son's recruitment to the Love Family.[40]

Cults became a pervasive presence in popular culture. The theme appeared in all kinds of films and television programs; in fictional dramas of rescue and defection, but also in comedies like *Mork and Mindy*. These stories often depicted the cult leaders as suffering revenge or humiliation from outraged families: in 1979, the comedy film *Serial* culminated with the father of a cult member turning a motorcycle gang loose on the headquarters of a Moonie-like group. In *Airplane* (1980), a pilot beats and forcibly silences the infuriating cult recruiters, Moonies, Jews for Jesus, and others, who block his way through an airport.

### Obedient Unto Death

By 1978, cult-related scandals were accumulating rapidly. Between 1976 and 1978, congressional hearings into the Koreagate scandals linked the Unification Church to a bewildering network of influence peddling and political corruption.[41] Meanwhile, in Philadelphia police became engaged in a dangerous standoff with the mainly black MOVE sect, which had fortified its headquarters, and in December 1978, Chuck Dederich of Synanon pleaded *nolo contendere* to charges of conspiracy to murder.[42] About this time, the followers of Ervil LeBaron were engaged in a homicidal campaign to establish him as the leader of the various Mormon polygamist sects, crimes that ended with his conviction in 1979.[43] Meanwhile, the Church of Scientology was engaged in a bitter war with the U.S. government, in which church members purloined thousands of documents from the Internal Revenue Service and Justice Department relating to the organization's request for tax-exempt status. In 1977, a small army of FBI agents raided Scientology headquarters in Los Angeles and Washington, D.C., seizing a hundred thousand pages of documents. Though courts delivered mixed verdicts about the legality of the raids, by 1978, eleven senior church officials went on trial for a variety of serious federal charges for what the prosecution described as a crime "of a breadth and scope previously unheard of."[44]

These earlier incidents paled into insignificance besides the Jonestown events of November 1978, in which murders and mass suicides claimed some nine hundred lives, including that of Congressman Ryan. The Jonestown affair was one of the major global news stories of the decade and radically changed the whole social environment for the new religions. In the following months, half a dozen books appeared with titles like *Guyana Massacre, Hold Hands and Die!*, and *The Suicide Cult*, while cult exposés of all sorts poured forth from publishers, and in 1980, *Guyana Tragedy* supplied the inevitable television-movie depiction of the disaster.[45] In the subsequent furor, anticult ideology gained instant credence. Surely, only brainwashed zombies could have killed themselves and their families in such an appalling way. Thereafter, a comparison to Jonestown or Jim Jones was guaranteed to escalate the threat-potential of even the tiniest unorthodox sect. As two of the leading anticult advocates write, "after Jonestown, much of the skepticism and doubt disappeared." The mere name "Jonestown" epitomized a mythology of desperate fanaticism quite as much as "Mountain Meadows" had for anti-Mormons a century before. Patricia Ryan, daughter of the murdered congressman, became a leading anticult spokesperson, and in 1990 she became president of the Cult Awareness Network (CAN). The depth of the trauma was suggested by the wave of news stories and documentaries commemorating the twentieth anniversary of the tragedy in 1998, which provided a new platform for media warnings against the continuing evils of cults.[46]

### Banning the Cults?

In the late 1970s, the cult problem achieved a far higher profile than at any time since the Second World War, and there were demands for legislation to curb unorthodox religion. In 1979, Senator Dole again chaired a hearing on the cult phenomenon. Though ostensibly an information-gathering event, witnesses at this second event included deprogrammers Ted Patrick and Joel Alexander, anticult writers Flo Conway and Jim Siegelman, and law professor Richard Delgado, who had recently published a law review piece justifying deprogramming efforts.[47] Members of the Senate Finance Committee suggested limiting the tax exemption granted to fringe religions by seeking a clearer and more restrictive definition of "church." By 1980, measures to investigate cults were under consideration in the legislatures of New York, Illinois, Maryland, and California. In Maryland, as was typical elsewhere, a committee was proposed to investigate recruiting techniques, fund-raising practices, and brainwashing allegations, in a measure backed by a number of cult defectors, including former Unification Church member Steve Hassan. In a memorable encounter, one legislator recalled the Jonestown events when he asked a representative of the Moon organization if his organization passed out "Kool-Aid cocktails" to followers.[48]

There were sporadic attempts to prohibit or regulate deviant religions or "pseudoreligions," to require that would-be recruiters fully disclose their identity and purposes, and even to require a cooling-off period before conversions were permitted. Despite the paniced atmosphere, these overambitious measures were doomed. Dissident voices expressed concern about government defining religious orthodoxy when such proposals were floated during the 1979 Dole hearings. The Unification Church might have been expected to denounce any potential inquisition, but so did figures representing the Baptist and United Church of Christ traditions, while many mainline churches subscribed to a warning against the effects of this "potentially flamboyant hearing." One Maryland legislator asked if the proposed investigation of cults would include his wife, who had spent several years as a Catholic nun.[49]

Trying to secure a consensus definition of religion has caused despair among many scholars of spiritual experience, so the difficulties of drafting such a law proved insuperable.[50] If there are pseudoreligions, there must be true religions, but which ones are they? What exactly is a harmful or eccentric doctrine? What forms of authority are unduly onerous or intrusive? What types of sexual expression are unorthodox? And how does one condemn one offending faith without stigmatizing virtually all beliefs except the blandest varieties of liberal Christianity and Judaism? Enough churches and religious bodies recognized that such a law would give certain specified bodies a legally established status within American society, and the language could be taken to condemn almost any religious body. These issues had already appeared in several legal cases, which had generally been resolved in the favor of the so-called cults. In 1977, for instance, charges of unlawful imprisonment and mind control were filed against members of the Hare Krishna sect, but a New York judge found that ISKCON was a bona fide religion and that followers were free to pursue their chosen lifestyle.

Proposals to restrict conversions threatened to entangle secular governments with the definition of religious orthodoxy, and the questions raised were nightmarish. Would new legislation penalize or prohibit conversions between faiths? Might conservatorship orders be issued against Jews who accepted Christianity or Christians who became Mormons? Also divisive here was the issue of "deception." A familiar complaint of Jewish organizations was that messianic believers were not in fact Jews and were practicing deception when they so described themselves in order to win over potential converts: on the other hand, messianic believers themselves had no doubts about their own Jewish identity. A law specifying how groups must identify themselves to potential recruits might achieve the goal of one religious tradition, of specifying who was and was not a Jew. Similarly, could a Mormon or a Jehovah's Witness be prosecuted for claiming to be a Christian? There was no shortage of evangelical writers who felt that neither sect qualified for authentic Christian status.

Another threat to religious freedom involved efforts by parents' groups to secure legal control of their adult offspring who had converted to one of the unpopular sects. This action was justified on the grounds that the children's actions in joining a cult showed a loss of responsibility equivalent to that caused by serious mental illness, defective intelligence, or extreme old age. The conservatorship process caused an adult child to revert for legal purposes to the status of a minor, unable to perform certain key social functions, and temporary orders offered the opportunity to remove a person from a cult setting, through police intervention if need be. Conservatorship orders were issued in California from the mid-1970s. In an important 1977 case, orders were issued granting conservatorships for five members of the Unification Church aged from twenty-one to twenty-six, though the decision was overturned on appeal, in a decision sufficiently broad to discourage future measures of this kind.[51]

Over the following years, proposals to revive and expand the conservatorship principle were introduced in several states, especially New York, where controversy reached a height in 1980 and 1981.[52] The proposed Lasher Amendment to that state's mental health law provided for the appointment of a conservator for any person who "has become closely and regularly associated with a group which practices the use of deception in the deprivation and isolation from family or unusually long work schedules and that such person . . . has undergone a sudden and radical change in behavior, lifestyle, habits and attitudes, and has become unable to care for his welfare and that his judgment has become impaired to the extent that he is unable to understand the need for such care."[53] The measure, which encapsulates anticult thinking, passed all the necessary legislative stages before being vetoed by Governor Hugh Carey.

The conservatorship principle was well established for adults who had been medically diagnosed as lacking proper control of their actions, and who were therefore vulnerable to "artful and designing persons," but in the new cases, the grounds for assuming a pathological condition were controversial. Much religious behavior does not conform well to

accepted standards of rationality. We might think that a natural candidate for conservatorship would be an enthusiastic convert to a sect
who sold all he or she had, gave the proceeds to the poor, and decided
ever after to live without taking thought for the morrow, but that
person would be literally following the instructions of Jesus. And why
should the principle only be used with overtly religious groups? The
process of change experienced by, say, participants in a U.S. Marine
boot camp is similar to the worst charges made against the repressive
cults.[54] Like the move to label pseudoreligions, the expansion of conservatorship raised thorny issues, which would have damned any new
law had it ever come before the federal courts.

### Armistice

Concern about cults peaked at the end of the 1970s with the legal and
ethical battles concerning deprogramming and conservatorships, but
shortly afterwards, the whole cult issue dropped out of media coverage
with remarkable suddenness and swiftly faded from the minds of legislators. At first sight, this change was remarkable because the stream
of sensational cult-related stories continued to flow unabated, and some
of these instances were quite as spectacular as those of the 1970s. There
was no shortage of new and interesting copy for the media. What was
new, however, is that both the legal and the demographic environment
had changed to make cults appear less threatening, and the claims of
the anticult activists less convincing.

By the mid-1980s, the cults that had recently attracted so much
concern were stagnating or actually disintegrating. Some were reeling
from legal problems, which often resulted from decisive actions by the
federal government. The Reagan administration, which took office in
1981, was dedicated to implementing the demands of moral conservatives in matters like child sexual abuse and illegal drugs, and it equally
showed itself very hostile to fringe religions. One of the last cult scandals of the older type occurred in Oregon, where the Indian leader
Bhagwan Shree Rajneesh had established a communal settlement
known as Rajneeshpuram and threatened to stage a political takeover
of the neighboring town.[55] His followers were also accused of plotting
more violent solutions, including poisoning the local water supply. The
*Oregonian* newspaper led a counterattack, and in 1985 the federal government acted forcefully by arresting and deporting the Bhagwan. The
commune collapsed shortly afterwards. Also about this time, Sun

Myung Moon was finally jailed on tax evasion charges. The Children of God had been on the run since the mid-1970s, and the Love Family commune dissolved some years later.[56]

In some cases, the suppression of the fringe groups involved actual bloodshed. In the 1984/85 era, federal authorities reacted to the terrorist campaign initiated by neo-Nazi groups inspired by Christian Identity thought and "Aryan" ideology, and by 1987 through 1988, a dozen leaders of the Identity movement were on trial for conspiracy to overthrow the U.S. government. Though these actions were not specifically directed against religious cults, the suppression of the various terrorist cells provided bad publicity for all types of dissident groups living in remote compounds. Meanwhile, the Philadelphia police launched a bloody attack on the West Philadelphia headquarters of MOVE, killing eleven and effectively wiping out the whole urban neighborhood in which the house was located. With the authorities demonstrating such a proactive stance, there was little need for independent anticult activists and entrepreneurs.

Meanwhile, the anticult movement itself came under attack, with growing attacks on the legality of deprogramming and its attendant crimes of kidnapping and forcible detention. By 1981, coercive actions had been condemned by a number of Christian anticult leaders, and the Citizens Freedom Foundation abandoned its support for the practice, though this still left the door open to forms of persuasion and "exit counseling." By the early 1990s, several leading deprogrammers were facing criminal charges, in cases that were extensively publicized by Scientologists and other old enemies. Most prominent among the fallen anticult leaders was Ted Patrick, sentenced to prison in 1980 for false imprisonment and kidnapping. In a 1992 case, a kidnapping attempt that targeted the wrong woman led to imprisonment for another deprogrammer. Scientologists also led a successful assault on CAN, launching multiple discrimination suits after hundreds of its adherents were denied membership. The litigation weakened CAN, which received a terminal blow when in 1995, a Pentecostal believer was awarded $1.8 million in legal damages resulting from a deprogramming.[57] CAN declared bankruptcy, and its name and assets were acquired by Scientologists, who continued to operate the organization from their very different ideological perspective. By then, Scientology itself had gained a new respectability, due in part to its popularity with film stars and media people, and the church finally achieved its long-sought tax-exempt status in 1993.

Demographic change played a role in altering the religious environment. The hippie culture that had provided a population vulnerable to cult temptations was a distant memory by the early 1980s, and the boomers themselves were at an age where they were themselves settling down with families and children of their own. It was unlikely that a relatively rooted individual with a secure lifestyle would suddenly defect to a commune. Certainly cult atrocity stories remained alive and well in the 1990s, with recurrent stories about young people being seduced to join totalistic fringe movements. Among the movements most often cited were the International Churches of Christ, which grew out of the Boston Church of Christ founded in 1979 and which attracted the same accusations that had earlier been levied against Unificationists.[58] In addition, the media reported critically on groups like the Brethren, the Ramtha channeling movement, and many individual gurus.[59] But the frequency of such stories was tiny compared to the incessant diatribes of the late 1970s, and the movements themselves were never depicted as anything like so pervasive a threat.

It seemed that both cults and their organized opponents would wither together, but the same factors that ended one scare also generated a new and related one, opening the way to a new emphasis on the cult threat to the children of the boomers. Just as older fears were subsiding. So the new nightmare of satanic or ritual abuse was emerging to galvanize a fading anticult movement, and this new menace dominated discussions of cults in the decade following 1984. Though the cult wars of the 1970s seemed to have ended in a de facto armistice, the claims and accusations of these years would enjoy a long afterlife and would influence official action and public debate up to the present day.

# TEN

# Devil Cults and Doomsday Cults
## 1980–2000

May Grace come, and may this world pass away. Hosanna to the God
of David.
   The *Didache*, 10: 6

If the 1970s were characterized by a generalized panic over cults,
later decades would be more specifically concerned over particular
aspects of the religious fringe, namely satanic movements in the
1980s and doomsday cults in more recent years. Both targets differed
widely from earlier movements like the Unification Church or ISK-
CON; the newly conceived threats were far less obvious than their
predecessors. As in the 1930s, a period of Reaction moved inexorably
into one of Speculation.

   While it was easy to document misdeeds by the controversial cults
of the 1970s, the careers of later satanic groups were much more shadowy, and many observers would now accept that the whole satanic
nightmare of the 1980s was based upon bogus claims and fabrications.
The doomsday cults are harder to dismiss in that many assuredly did
die in the confrontation at Waco and in movements like the Solar
Temple and Heaven's Gate, although the interpretation of these deaths
is still open to debate. The whole notion of "cult mass suicide" must
be treated with skepticism, and at least some incidents of mass fatalities
were not the suicides they initially seemed. As in the case of devil
worship, the mass media interpreted these events through the eyes of
anticult critics, who have a vested interest in presenting their enemies
as more threatening and sinister than the available evidence would
suggest.

The new anticult crusades were pervasively shaped by the rhetoric about marginal sects that had emerged in the 1970s. This anticult mythology was the source for the most alarming ideas: that at least some fringe movements were active in ritual murder and sacrifice and that they sexually abused children on a vast scale. Though all these ideas were questionable, the resulting wave of charges against suspect groups would have an enormous impact on the general public and on policymakers. Adding the terrifying possibility of mass suicide to the mythic repertoire of cult critics radically changed public attitudes to the necessity of intervening in the activities of small religious bodies. Led to expect that certain deviant behaviors would occur, the public was likely to support forceful action to protect the innocent members of these groups. The danger in such circumstances is that such official action risks provoking rather than preventing violent confrontation, and the events at Waco offer grim testimony to the consequences of the anticult mythology in shaping official behavior.

## Cults That Kill

During the 1980s, the American mass media presented stories about the doings of alleged satanic groups that harked back to the witch trials of seventeenth-century Europe. The modern devil-worship cults were said to be many thousands strong (some said millions), with representatives secretly placed in schools and public institutions, and their activities were monstrously depraved. In 1988, a work targeted at law-enforcement professionals linked Satanists to "the murders of unbaptized infants, child sexual abuse in day-care, rape, ritual abuse of children, drug trafficking, arson, pornography, kidnapping, vandalism, church desecration, corpse theft, sexual trafficking of children and the heinous mutilation, dismemberment and sacrifices of humans and animals. . . . [They are] responsible for the deaths of more than 60,000 Americans each year, including missing and runaway youth."[1]

These sensational allegations can ultimately be traced to two originally discrete trends of the late 1970s, which grew out of, respectively, the Manson murders and Jonestown. While the Manson case inspired tales of ritual murder gangs, Jonestown contributed the idea that extreme child abuse was a cult characteristic. Putting the two elements together gave rise to suggestions that secretive cults killed thousands of victims each year and sexually abused children in ritualistic settings. Though such claims seem ludicrous in retrospect, they were very familiar in the decade after 1984, the years of what some have called the "Satanic Panic." As in the 1930s, well-documented cult scandals escalated into wild allegations of devil worship and ritual murder.

Ritual murder theories emerged from journalistic speculations about the cult environment of Charles Manson. The notion of "killer cults" gained support from other murders of the early 1970s carried out by young people associated with the alternative culture of the time who used occult or satanic jargon.[2] In 1971, Ed Sanders's book, *The Family*, placed Manson in the context of the numerous occult and mystical movements then flourishing in northern California. One story linked Manson to the Church of the Process, a connection that the group would staunchly contest in the courts: Sanders "allude[d] to the existence of a sort of modern Thuggee or Satanic underground, in which he claim[ed] The Process to have been a central organizing factor."[3] By the mid-1970s, Manson-inspired legends had given rise to a lively folklore about itinerant Satanic cults kidnapping and murdering on a regular basis, and these themes found their way into movies like *Race with the Devil* (1975).

The concept of cult sacrifice also resurfaced in the context of the Black Muslims. A series of killings of whites by blacks in California in 1973 and 1974 (the "zebra murders") was associated with a clandestine splinter of the Black Muslims, the Death Angels, which is supposed to have claimed hundreds of white victims across the United States. The Death Angels of the 1970s, and some successor groups in the next decade, appear to have used the same terminology as the secret teachings of Wallace Fard, which reportedly spoke of the murder of four white devils as the price of admission to paradise. Though the scale of the Death Angels phenomenon is debatable, at least some racial murders did indeed have a religious purpose.[4]

By 1980, police departments across the country were exploring the possible existence of violent ritualistic and satanic cults. Also about this time, journalistic investigations of the Son of Sam killings in New York City proposed that these crimes were not, as they appeared, the unassisted work of the convicted offender David Berkowitz, but should rather be attributed to a much larger satanic cult, possibly thousands strong. Rumors said that the network might have national ramifications, tied to the Church of the Process and possibly to the Crowleyan occult group, the *Ordo Templi Orientis*. Similar rumors circulated about other celebrated murder series, like the Atlanta child murders of

1980–81, and by 1981 local investigators and theorists were beginning to form links and exchange ideas.

The idea of "cults that kill" reached its fullest and most outrageous expression with a 1988 book of that name, detailing the activities of murder gangs inspired by Satanism, witchcraft, and Santería.[5] Together, these groups were said to claim the lives of some fifty thousand Americans each year, which would represent approximately twice the number of recorded homicides in the same timespan. The human sacrifice concept seemed amply confirmed by reports of the murderous gang operating in Matamoros, Mexico, that was exposed in 1989.[6] Though subsequent investigation showed that this group was chiefly inspired by an extreme sexual sadism, the crimes were initially interpreted as a manifestation of Satanism, voodoo, or "Hispanic witchcraft." Antisatanic theories were popularized through seminars aimed at law enforcement personnel. Such theorizing could not fail to have its effect in the real world: in 1985, authorities in Lucas County, Ohio, embarked on a massive excavation of what was believed to be the cemetery of a local sacrifice cult, where over fifty bodies were reputedly buried. Needless to say, nothing out of the ordinary was found.

### Ritual Abuse

The Satanism idea also drew on claims about the extreme physical and sexual maltreatment said to be inflicted upon children in cult groups. The massacre of children at Jonestown excited the interest of police officers and journalists, who would later become important writers on "cult" activities. Kenneth Wooden's 1981 book, *Children of Jonestown*, pioneered the notion of cults "ritualistically abusing" young people; he even suggests, "Babies, born into cults, their births unregistered, are reported to have died of unnatural causes and to have been buried in secrecy, like pets."[7] Wooden's position as a television reporter and producer gave him a unique platform from which to disseminate his concept of cult abuses. In 1980, the book *Michelle Remembers* drew attention to the developing idea of ritualized child abuse and explicitly alleged that the cults involved were satanic in nature. The pseudonymous Michelle described memories she claimed to have recalled during therapy in the late 1970s, when she reported sexual and physical atrocities inflicted on her as a child in Vancouver in the early 1950s. This text would shape all subsequent narratives of ritual child abuse and also legitimized the theory that traumatic events could lie dormant until resurfacing during therapy. Appropriately, given the long record of racial stereotypes in shaping cult scares, the Michelle story draws heavily on charges that were originally leveled against violent West African secret societies of the 1950s, such as the Leopard Men.[8]

The various strands of speculation—about Satanism, cult violence, and ritual abuse—merged as a result of one of the most notorious criminal cases of the decade, the mass abuse case at McMartin preschool, which was first reported in the media in 1984. Not for the first time, a cult scare erupted from southern California. According to prosecutors, hundreds of small children attending this school had been sexually abused by a ring of teachers, often in ritualistic settings involving robes, pentacles, and church altars. Though the McMartin case is now generally recognized as spurious, this affair generated fears that satanic rings lurked behind the walls of preschools and day-care institutions across the country. There would be many subsequent investigations, and a number of equally unfounded criminal charges, with the most outrageous instances occurring at Bakersfield (California), Jordan (Minnesota), Edenton (North Carolina), Martensville (Canada), and Wenatchee (Washington).

The origins of the ritual abuse scare have been analyzed so extensively over the last few years that the affair needs only brief discussion here.[9] Essentially, the charges were based on statements that therapists elicited from impressionable children, often only four or five years of age, who responded to repeated leading questions by generating answers designed to please their interrogators. Therapists and prosecutors then collaborated to transform impossible claims into specific allegations of ritualistic sex abuse. Charges that children were being abused in these circumstances won support from an improbably large and diverse coalition of interest groups who would normally have had next to nothing in common: one study notes that the idea found adherents among "social workers, therapists, physicians, victimology researchers, police, criminal prosecutors, fundamentalist Christians, ambitious politicians, anti-pornography activists, feminists, and the media."[10]

Among the most important groups supporting the charges were therapists active in the recovered memory movement, in which tens of thousands of self-defined survivors believed that they were recalling ritualistic abuse committed against them when very young. The recovered memory trend became so influential as literally to beggar belief. There were two basic options: either North America had for many years been the home of a complete alternative satanic religion, which killed or molested many thousands of victims each year, or there was something radically wrong with the therapeutic techniques producing this remarkable evidence. The latter explanation became ever more probable when no evidence could be produced for the far-reaching allegations, and some specific defector accounts could be entirely debunked. Though the more extreme satanic theories did achieve some respectful notice in the mass media in the late 1980s, the tide of opinion soon changed, and by about 1993, the normal media response to a mass abuse or recovered memory case was one of deep suspicion and hostility to the therapists involved. Also in these years, the slow-grinding judicial appeal process began overturning most of the convictions handed down during the late 1980s, in what was already being presented as the latest American witch-hunt.

Though the ritual abuse idea was a novelty of the mid-1980s, the concept grew directly out of the older anticult movements, and the problem was phrased in terms of cult and ritual abuse. A familiar figure from earlier debates was the cult defector, newly renamed the survivor, who seemed to expose such vital information from within the secret organization itself. The ritual abuse genre that began with *Michelle Remembers* received new contributions: Lauren Stratford's *Satan's Underground* (1988), Judith Spencer's *Suffer the Child* (1989), and a host of others, all by self-described survivors.[11]

Another example of continuity from the anticult rhetoric of the 1970s was in the theory of brainwashing, which had provided the justification for the original deprogramming movement. The mind-control idea now evolved to suggest that satanic cults deliberately inflicted torture in order to traumatize a child, with the intention of creating the multiple personalities that therapists claimed to discover in their adult patients. Alternatively, mind control could be used to force the victim to bury memories of abuse. Satanic brainwashers were said to instill deep programming patterns in the minds of their subjects, patterns that could be revived in later life, as when the cult required a programmed assassin. Antisatanic writings of these years usually include lengthy bibliographies of works on brainwashing and mind control, often derived from the anti-CIA exposés of the mid-1970s. Sometimes, the revival of older anticult rhetoric was explicit: a 1995 text on ritual abuse and satanic mind control was entitled *Psychic Dictatorship in America*, as an *hommage* to Gerald Bryan's 1940 attack on I AM.[12]

By the early 1990s, a few therapeutic institutions with a particular interest in multiple personality and recovered memory therapy were diagnosing supposed cult assassins and programmed brides of Satan with astonishing frequency. Critics charged that such diagnoses were spurious and further noted that these techniques were especially likely to find florid types of mental illness in patients with rich insurance plans, who would require years of treatment until those benefits were exhausted. The fact that virtually none of the alleged survivors were black may be a comment on the continuing racial differential in benefit plans.

### Weird Tales

Quite as unconvincing as the psychological diagnoses were the historical accounts that the antisatanic movements offered of the cult phenomenon. Though therapists disdained any need to corroborate the stories coming from their patients, it was disturbing to find such elaborate stories of powerful satanic cults dating back to the 1930s or 1940s when observers at the time had observed no such phenomenon. Though journalists of this era had enthusiastically exposed all manner of strange and perverse cults, they had turned up nothing approximating ritual abuse, even as rumor. While cult leaders had been accused of exploiting young girls, their victims were young teenagers, not the toddlers of the ritual abuse mythology.

Yet modern-day therapists continued to find such recollections in their elderly patients. A popular recovery text, *The Courage to Heal,* tells the story of a woman who claimed that she had as a child been the victim of a cult led by the "town leaders, business-people and church officials" of "an upper middle class town in the Midwest" in the mid- or late 1930s. The woman described being "abused in rituals that included sexual abuse, torture, murder, photography and systematic brainwashing through drugs and electric shock." By the age of twelve, she was a "breeder," bearing children for the cult to sacrifice. Another older survivor reported "near total involvement of the entire village where she grew up on the affluent North Side of Chicago, Illinois, during the 1930s. Her parents . . . as well as Christian ministers, policemen, lawyers and socialites were involved" in a cult active in human sacrifice and Black Masses.[13] Assuming they were not purely imaginary, what could these cults have been?

Through rhetorical necessity, some writers tried to find precedents for ritual abuse charges by delving into older anticult theories, but the results were absurd. Some evangelical books reasserted the truth of the charges made in the original witch trials, while others revived the ancient conspiracy charges against the Illuminati.[14] In the 1994 text, *Safe Passage to Healing*, the author claims that "reports of cult practices are as old as recorded history and as recent as today's news," though the past events used to illustrate this statement are generally regarded as spurious. These precedents include the Catholic convent described by Maria Monk in her 1836 farrago. We are told, incredibly, that "ritual cannibalism was practiced by . . . some early Christian sects," while Goya "documented sexual sacrifice cults in his painting *Witches Sabbath*."[15]

There is no evidence for the genuine existence of any American cult vaguely resembling any of those described in survivor accounts from *Michelle* to the present day, which must of itself cast grave doubt on the authenticity of such stories. Having said this, the "recovered" tales do have numerous parallels in the literature of the 1930s and 1940s, which give almost identical accounts of secret cults in rural villages and suburban communities, which are dominated by cliques of clandestine devil worshipers. The difficulty for ritual abuse theorists is that, without exception, all these stories are fictions and are found in the works of Robert Bloch, August Derleth, and H. P. Lovecraft. What the modern anticult activists are postulating is a real-life Order of Dagon, a nonfictional Church of the Starry Wisdom. These same pulp authors of bygone days also provide the parallels, and perhaps the ultimate sources, for other aspects of the satanic mythology of the 1980s. The image of the serial killer or serial murder ring carrying out satanic sacrifices is directly traceable to Bloch's 1943 story, "Yours Truly, Jack the Ripper." In more senses than one, modern accounts of Satanism and ritual abuse are works of fantasy fiction, nothing more than weird tales.

## Doomsday Cults

By the early 1990s, the baroque confection of Satanism was encountering severe difficulties. Ritual abuse cases were collapsing apace, while media investigations were steadily producing more evidence of error and malfeasance by investigators and therapists. By 1993, most media reports on ritual abuse or satanic cults involved cases in which innocent individuals were falsely accused on the strength of ludicrous and unsubstantiated evidence, and the antisatanic theorists were being pilloried. But at the very time that satanic atrocities were finally encountering a needed degree of skepticism, the cult wars were threatening to reignite because of new and irrefutable evidence of serious violence and sexual exploitation involving fringe religious groups.

From the end of the 1980s, there were several reported cases of polygamist messiahs with apocalyptic expectations who carried out violent acts against either disciples or rivals. And though these stories were treated with nothing like the fervor of older cult stories, they were publicized in the press and the television magazine programs, usually under headlines that prominently featured the language of cults. In 1988, the followers of a Mormon polygamist killed by police retaliated by bombing a Utah church. Also from the fundamentalist Mormon tradition was Jeffrey Lundgren, whose followers carried out the sacrificial killings of several suspected traitors within the group in 1989.[16] The polygamous commune founded by Canadian cult leader Roch Thériault ended in scandal in 1989 after one of his wives died during his attempt to perform brutal amateur surgery: similar "treatments" had already caused the mutilation of other compound members. The magazine *MacLean's* described this as a "Cult of Horror . . . the most bizarre and violent group in the history of Canadian crime."[17] Also exposed at this time was the Yahweh sect in Florida, a messianic black Jewish group which was involved in at least a dozen murders, as well as widespread financial criminality.[18]

These affairs were dwarfed by four incidents occurring between 1993 and 1997 that drew worldwide attention.[19] These were, respectively, the siege of the Branch Davidian group at Waco, Texas (February–March 1993); the violence linked to the Order of the Solar Temple in Switzerland, France, and Canada in 1994 and 1995, in which seventy members perished; the terrorist attacks associated with the Japanese Aum Shinrikyo movement, which included nerve gas attacks on the Tokyo subway (March 1995); and the Heaven's Gate incident in San Diego, in which thirty-nine believers killed themselves (March 1997). Together, these episodes claimed over two hundred lives, and law enforcement agencies asserted that the respective groups had the means and the potential to cause destruction on a far wider scale. Observers of Aum Shinrikyo drew analogies to world conquest conspiracies normally thought to be the preserve of James Bond novels. The long-running debate on the relationship between cults and violence escalated in seriousness.[20] Reporting on so-called doomsday cults became a mainstay of the media, just as satanic cults had been a decade before.

## Waco

As the first of these spectacular incidents, the Waco affair would be
uniquely important in rekindling the anticult movement. Like so many
other fringe movements, the Davidian sect grew out of the sectarian
atmosphere of Los Angeles in the late 1920s, when preacher Victor
Houteff offered his new scriptural interpretation of the coming End
Times. Among other things, he denounced the Seventh-Day Adventist
Church for its laxity and for excessive compromise with the sinful
world.[21] By 1935, the new sect moved to a communal headquarters at
Waco, Texas, where the membership reached some fifteen hundred by
the 1950s. The Mount Carmel settlement remained under the patri-
archal rule of one family from the 1950s through the 1980s, but at
that point, a new force arrived on the scene in the form of Vernon
Howell, a young preacher with an astonishing command of Scripture.
Howell acquired the messianic persona of "David Koresh," a name that
refers to both the biblical King David and Cyrus as a royal representative of God: recall that the title had been taken by at least one earlier
leader, Cyrus Teed, who led his "Koreshans" at the turn of the century.
Though the media and law enforcement assert simply that he "claimed
to be Christ," Howell in fact preached a subtler doctrine in which a
messianic role was occupied by several individuals through history,
among whom Jesus was only one, and David Koresh might well be
another.

The new Koresh ruled the sect autocratically and, like many cult
leaders before him, allowed himself free access to the female members
of the group. He also faced opposition from a rival who regarded himself as the rightful heir to the Davidian regime. Through the late 1980s,
battles between the two factions were bitter and occasionally involved
firearms. By 1993, the Waco sect had amassed a sizable collection of
weapons, though the justification for this arsenal is uncertain. Some
believe that the Davidians were training to fight the forces of evil in
the coming Apocalypse, while law enforcement authorities have
charged that the weapons might have been intended for terrorist violence. As the sect supported itself by legally trading weapons, the supposed arsenal might more properly be called a commercial inventory.

The turning point in the Davidian story occurred on February 28,
1993, and ensuing events are so hotly debated that the different ver-
sions are best recounted separately. According to the federal government, the Davidians were in possession of illegal automatic weapons,
and so the Bureau of Alcohol, Tobacco, and Firearms (ATF) staged a

raid in order to seize them. Federal forces encountered armed resistance in which several ATF agents and a number of Davidians were killed. A siege ensued, in which the main responsibility for negotiating an end to the standoff passed from ATF to the FBI. Despairing of a peaceful end to the crisis, on April 19 federal agents moved against the compound with armored vehicles. This provoked the Davidians to begin fires with the deliberate purpose of committing mass suicide, and in the ensuing blaze, some eighty Davidians were killed, including Koresh himself.[22]

This official version of the case was bitterly contested. Some interpretations even proposed that the final catastrophe was a massacre deliberately undertaken by federal authorities, who purposely set the fires and machine-gunned survivors. It was this version of affairs that led to Waco becoming an apocalyptic symbol for the extreme right wing. The conflict provided a potent battlecry for white supremacist groups deeply imbued with premillenarian theology, often in Christian Identity guise. Remembering Waco became a basic creed for the militias, survivalists, and paramilitary groups dedicated to resistance against the Beast and One-Worldism. The massive bombing of the federal office building in Oklahoma City occurred precisely two years after the Waco inferno as an act of direct vengeance.[23]

While the more extreme conspiracy theories of the event cannot be supported, there is a fair consensus that the Waco siege was appallingly mishandled by federal authorities and that a major reason for their bungling lay in a reliance on misleading cult stereotypes. The initial raid at Waco now appears to have been justified by false claims about the nature of the compound, which was variously portrayed as the center of an illegal drug laboratory and as a hive of child sexual abuse. The charges about automatic weapons stemmed from "deprogrammed" former Davidians working with anticult leaders. As the ATF failed to follow legal procedures before carrying out its paramilitary operation against the Davidians, many believe that sect members were legally and ethically justified in using armed force to resist these invaders.

Crucially for our interpretations of cult behavior, the final "mass suicide" was probably no such thing. Though some individual members might have killed themselves during the final assault, the great majority of the Davidians died as a direct result of fires started when armored vehicles broke into the buildings, injecting highly flammable gas and knocking over heating devices. This alternative explanation recalls the circumstances of the MOVE siege in Philadelphia some years earlier, which similarly ended in a catastrophic fire, but in which the authorities were immediately condemned for their reckless disregard of human life. In addition, technical evidence contradicts FBI assertions that no federal forces were using firearms in the final assault at Waco.[24] Apparently, the attack was supported by a number of federal agents using automatic weapons, which may well have killed some Davidians. If not a deliberate massacre, then the Waco affair is a monument to official mendacity and incompetence.

### Trusting the Experts

Throughout the long siege, federal policy was shaped by certain fundamental notions about the nature of the Davidian sect, and at every point, these ideas were influenced by the experts on whom the government had decided to rely, namely the anticult experts who were veterans of the controversies of the 1970s. In selecting its advisers, the authorities faced the difficulty in that anyone described as a "cult expert" automatically has certain preconceptions about the nature of the phenomenon with which they are dealing. While other scholars knew more about the Davidians and other fringe groups, most refused to use polemical language about cults and rejected simplistic efforts to treat all such movements as part of a single problem. By definition, the sources sympathetic to marginal religions were not consulted, so that the government was left to choose entirely from a limited and self-defined pool of theorists.

According to the FBI's chosen advisors, the Davidians were a classic cult, and this idea seemed self-evident to the mass media, which from the first days of the crisis never referred to the Koresh group by any other name. Some stories embellished the title a little more, as when the *New York Times* referred to "a renegade offshoot of the Seventh Day Adventists," a phrase that suggests that the schism was a recent breach by an erratic or criminal element.[25] Presumably, no writer would refer to Lutherans and Episcopalians as renegade offshoots of the Roman Catholic Church. At no point did federal authorities take seriously the religious aspirations of the Davidians or of their "Bible babble." From the first, the only dilemma faced by FBI negotiators was whether Koresh was delusional or if he was a con man who was merely using religion: how could any cult leader be treated as honest or sincere, especially one who "claimed to be Christ?" The media concurred unquestioningly: one ABC reporter spoke of "the power of this madman [Koresh] . . . his skills at manipulation and mind control, powerful skills, frightening skills."[26]

But to speak incessantly of a cult (as opposed to a church or a small denomination) consistently suggested that this group was infected with all the sins associated with that word. Specifically, the term meant that sect members were not in the compound voluntarily, but were prisoners of Koresh and a few of his lieutenants: this harks back to the "psychological kidnapping" theories of earlier years. This perception would be crucial in forming the tactics of the following siege, in which the FBI used methods that properly belonged to a hostage situation, such as bombarding the compound with loud noises through the night in order to destabilize and intimidate the imagined kidnappers. Equally disturbing was the style of the final assault with tanks, again designed to overwhelm and terrify. If, however, the anticult view was wrong, then these tactics would have the effect of disorienting the whole community, both leaders and members, and eliminating any chance of a peaceful conclusion. The authorities left no stone unturned in devising ways of confirming the sect members in their belief that Armageddon was inevitable and that violence was the only possible outcome. It is scarcely surprising that observers discerned a malevolent official plot to provoke suicide or bloody confrontation. As later writers note, "For the Branch Davidians, no one was a hostage. The only rescue they needed was from the government itself."[27]

The standard anticult themes pervade the official interpretation of Waco. Apart from the idea of cult members as hostages, we also find the emphasis on child victims, which had emerged in ritual abuse accusations. Throughout the siege, the supposed abuse of the Davidians' children was a constant theme in the statements of the Cult Awareness Network and related groups. Invoking the child abuse was rhetorically important in order to justify intervention against unpopular religious groups. As happened in the 1980s, although a contemporary audience probably will not dispute the right of an individual to join the most authoritarian and exploitative of cults, cult opponents are more effective when they shift the grounds of their assault to those members who cannot give such full consent, the children recruited or assaulted by a particular group. Thus Satanism is assailed not as a revolt against the divine order but as an organized form of child molestation, and the destruction of the Davidians was justified by the notion that young members were being abused and had to be rescued even at the risk of their lives. To quote one immediate justification for the assault on

Waco, "babies were being beaten."[28] After Waco, James R. Lewis suggested that we should be at least as concerned about the implications of the "destructive anti-cult" as about the "destructive cults" they denounce.[29]

### Cult Suicide

The image of mass suicide proved decisive in impelling the Justice Department to attack. One criminologist had advised authorities that "[i]f we waited longer, the chances of suicide or some other tragic end were more likely." The media were already citing the Jonestown precedent in the first reports of the February shootout.[30] The whole concept of mass suicide is, however, a relatively late addition to the cult stereotype, though it rapidly became an integral component. As *Time* suggested after the Heaven's Gate affair, "suicide cults have entered the category of horrors that no longer qualify as shocks."[31] This charge virtually never appears in earlier cult scares, not in the time of the Mormons, the early Black Muslims, I AM, or any of the older militant movements (though obviously, the snake handlers of the 1940s were facing a high risk of death or injury).

The mass suicide notion had ancient origins in the context of fanatical groups like the Jewish rebels at Masada and the Circumcelliones in Roman North Africa. It was this latter and relatively obscure reference that gave rise to the first American reference to a mass cult suicide, which appeared in a 1955 mystery story by Edward D. Hoch. Hoch's "Village of the Dead" tells of a bizarre cult formed in a western town by a leader named Axidus the Prophet, who persuades his seventy or so followers to kill themselves en masse by throwing themselves over a cliff. Axidus was the name of the historical leader of the Circumcelliones, who is being imitated by the fictional modern-day cult leader.[32]

The first actual event of this kind, the Jonestown affair of 1978, owed nothing to such religious influences, but derived from New Left political rhetoric. Jim Jones admired the Black Panthers, who espoused what Huey Newton termed revolutionary suicide, the doctrine that a hopeless struggle against overwhelming odds would detonate mass revolutionary action.[33] The Panthers were in turn influenced by the Algerian anticolonial struggle of the 1950s, as reflected in the revolutionary film *The Battle of Algiers*. The suicide idea does not appear to have influenced pre-Jonestown cults, if we exclude questionable charges from defectors who claimed that the Unification Church had ordered them to kill themselves rather than face deprogramming (these allegations only surfaced after the Guyana incident).

Although the idea was new in 1978, the concept of "cult suicide" was so widely accepted because it so perfectly encapsulated all the images that had been developing over the previous decade: stereotypes of blind obedience, disregard of self and family, violent tendencies, and a preparedness to follow any orders issued by a deranged messiah. The idea became so well established that soon mass suicide seemed a probable outcome of cult extremism. The image of cult suicide was reinforced by the gradually changing use of the phrase "doomsday cult," which was the title of John Lofland's 1966 scholarly study of the Unification Church. Though the "doomsday" term originally implied groups obsessed with the idea of apocalypse, it became subtly transformed to describe movements like Aum Shinrikyo, which undertook armed violence or revolutionary action in order to provoke the End Times. The phrase now entered the vernacular, so that by 1995, the U.S. media generally described Aum Shinrikyo simply as "the Japanese Doomsday Cult."[34]

Doomsday cult language came close to making millenarian expectation *ipso facto* a token of cultlike behavior and even a warning symptom of likely mass suicide. The "doomsday" label was applied indiscriminately to those who prophesied catastrophe no less than those who tried to provoke it, even to those like the Davidians who had Armageddon visited upon them. The terminology made possible a kind of grim comedy of errors in which official expectations would lead a sect to become more paranoid and defensive, which would in turn cause even more official nervousness and intervention. There are few limits to the force that can be levied against any group once it has been designated a doomsday cult, a self-fulfilling title if ever there was one. Invoking the specter of mass suicide almost ensures that mass deaths will ensue. In the months following Waco, other secluded religious groups like the Church Universal and Triumphant expressed fears that they might be the next to be thus labeled, perhaps to face the same consequences as the Davidians.

### Apocalyptic?

The Waco precedent shaped public reaction to the diverse doomsday cults, ironically perhaps, because conventional Christian apocalyptic belief had little or nothing to do with the later groups. Heaven's Gate remains the only authenticated case of a cult mass suicide on American soil, and the ideology driving this group was concocted from New Age ideas and UFO speculation. The group emerged in the early 1970s under the leadership of Marshall Applewhite and Betty Lu Nettles, who respectively took the names Bo and Peep. Both were interested in UFO speculations, and Peep also incorporated some biblical teachings into their emerging movement (though after Applewhite died in 1985, her New Age approach remain unchallenged).

During the 1970s and 1980s, the followers of Bo and Peep increasingly developed the structures of a cult. They formed a communal family, which required strict regimentation of daily activities. The group also fell under Gnostic influence, as the leaders declared the body a troublesome vehicle, which should be shed in order to achieve a higher state of existence or consciousness. Devoted male followers accepted surgical castration in order to separate themselves from worldly temptation. After several changes of location, the group moved to Rancho Santa Fe, a mansion in San Diego, from which it advocated its views through the Internet. A crisis developed in 1997 with news of the approach of the spectacular Hale-Bopp comet: this was believed to be concealing an alien starship, which would take the Heaven's Gate followers home. In March, the members chose to escape the confines of planet Earth by taking cocktails of phenobarbitol and alcohol. However well it exemplifies standard images of cults, it is debatable whether the Heaven's Gate movement was motivated by any distinctively religious motives, as opposed to pseudoscience or science fiction: it had little to do with any known apocalyptic traditions.[35]

Other so-called doomsday groups were equally removed from Christian apocalyptic writing. Aum Shinrikyo offered a bizarre synthesis of Hinduism and Buddhism, with some trace Christian elements. The Solar Temple group was perhaps the strangest instance of all. Its beliefs combined occult and rosicrucian beliefs with an interest in homeopathic medicine and ecology: none of these strands has historically been associated with violent or suicidal impulses. Like many occult enthusiasts through the centuries, movement leader Luc Jouret was fascinated with the martyred Knights Templar of the fourteenth century, and he joined a movement claiming descent from that group before founding his own temple in 1984. Under the leadership of Jouret and Joseph DiMambro, the Solar Temple possessed perhaps five hundred members in Europe and North America. The group came to international attention in October 1994 with the discovery of over fifty bodies in Switzerland and Canada; more deaths would follow over the next three years.

The interpretation of the Solar Temple deaths remains controversial. Some at least certainly were suicides, the motives for which can be found in the group's writings and the opinions of survivors, which together suggest that members were dying in order to be reborn in a superior state, perhaps in another solar system. But not all died voluntarily. In the initial incident, many of the dead had been shot repeatedly, some were beaten or drugged, and several died with their hands bound. We should be speaking not of mass suicides, but of multiple murder-suicides. A Swiss police chief investigating the affair described the theory of mass suicide as "pure cinema."

The motives for this grotesque violence remain unclear, but we should take account of political and financial factors, as well as spiritual. Over the years, the Solar Temple had enjoyed a bizarre international career, including connections to money-laundering activities, right-wing terrorism, and intelligence movements; some members were involved in extensive fraud and financial manipulation. A spectacular event like the mass deaths naturally attracts a plethora of conspiracy theories and fabrications, but the criminal activities of Jouret and particularly DiMambro are documented in reputable media sources like the *New York Times* and *MacLean's*. Based on such credible accounts, we know that in just one recent international arms deal, DiMambro had used the Solar Temple as a front for illegal international transactions amounting to $95 million. The Solar Temple leaders operated in a deeply dangerous environment in which violence is commonplace, and many potential enemies might have had motives for striking at the group. We should perhaps regard the Solar Temple as an egregious example of corporate or organized crime rather than a doomsday cult.[36]

For all the uncertainties about the motives for violence, the media immediately branded these groups with the familiar Christian-derived imagery of "apocalyptic" and "millenarian" belief. All were, of course, "cults," inextricably linking that word with extreme and irrational violence. Following the Heaven's Gate suicides, the *New York Times* headlined a "cult suicide," and specifically reported on the action by "a millenarian cult."[37] After the first Solar Temple mass deaths in October 1994, even the outlets that knew of the group's criminal connections leapt to the conclusion that this was simply "another Jonestown." *MacLean's* headline read, "Apocalypse Now," while *Time* announced, "Once again, mass death in an apocalyptic sect . . . an episode in cult pathology to put beside Jonestown and Waco." As they seemed unnecessary, alternative explanations remained unexplored.[38]

The suicide stereotype was used to discredit other apocalyptic-thinking sects, even those that displayed no violent tendencies. When ABC's *Nightline* discussed the Solar Temple incident in October 1994, its two main commentators were anticult activists Cynthia Kisser and Steve Hassan, who both presented this exceptionally odd group as if it were typical of the cult phenomenon: Hassan even compared the organization to the Jehovah's Witnesses. Similar generalizations were expressed once more during 1998–1999 when the American "Concerned Christians" sect relocated from Colorado to Israel, to await the imminent millennium (curiously, this group had itself begun in the early 1980s as a militant anticult movement, growing out of an impassioned campaign against the supposed evils of Satanism). Rumor suggested that the group was plotting acts of violence, but by far the most damning charge against it was that this was a doomsday sect.[39]

If sects fascinated by ideas of apocalypse were in future to be cast as doomsday cults, then this had consequences for a very wide range of religious bodies, mainly, but not entirely, among Protestant Christians. While it is a familiar complaint that virtually any abuse can be justified by twisting Scripture, the concept of imminent apocalypse is deeply embedded in the earliest records of the words of Jesus and his followers, who told believers to separate from an evil world on the eve of destruction. Jesus himself instructed that no one could be his disciple if he did not "hate his own father and mother and wife and children and brothers and sisters, yea, and even his own life."[40] Christians are depicted in these texts as a small and hated minority, condemned by a society in thrall to the forces of evil, though the righteous will see their vindication with the violent fall of all earthly structures. In the meantime, believers should cleave only to each other in new communities of love: "Save yourselves from this corrupt generation."[41] The densest concentration of such texts is found in the phantasmogorical language of the Book of Revelation, in which Christians inhabit a doomed world ruled by the Beast and the Whore of Babylon, who murder the saints. A voice from heaven tells believers to "[C]ome out of her, my people."[42] Christianity may be the oldest extant doomsday cult, and it has never lost that strand of belief.

After Waco, the ever malleable cult terminology expanded to include apocalyptic or end-times beliefs of the sort held by tens of millions of American believers, many of whom share the Davidian expectation that

Christians would in the last days have to take up literal rather than spiritual arms to resist the Antichrist. A tradition therefore became cultish not by evolving new or radical religious interpretations, but by retaining ideas that would have seemed quite orthodox to most generations throughout American history.

# ELEVEN

# Teeming with Faith

*Turn up the sod of every vital religious group and you will find dreams, visions, and what the followers believe to be telltale traces of the divine. Whenever these came along, they were interpreted as holy whisperings or wild hallucinations, depending on the point of view.*
Marcus Bach, *They Have Found a Faith*

The escalating charges against religious cults make it ever more difficult to arrive at a consensus about their overall impact, but at least some groups have had long-term effects that are by no means as harmful as we might imagine from all the polemic about doomsday cults. Some fringe religious movements succeed in becoming mainstream churches or denominations, while others diffuse their ideas through the better established churches and sometimes through society at large. In either case, cults should be seen as the laboratories or proving grounds for religious innovation, out of which can come much creativity, in addition to some harm. The religious fringe has left a heritage far more substantial—and significant—than just Shaker furniture. This diverse contribution must be taken into account when we formulate responses to emerging religious movements.

## Towards Respectability

The formation of cults and new religious movements is a continuous and even inevitable process, as believers find that existing churches cannot respond rapidly enough to new social and spiritual trends. In the American context, the pace of change is accelerated by the influx of new ethnic groups, most of which bring with them their own distinctive spiritual traditions. Successive polemics against cults do not, however, lead us to recognize this cyclical pattern because cult critics invariably demonstrate shock and outrage that deviant organizations should arise in that given time and place. Often this reaction is expressed by contrasting the modernity and scientific advance of that society to the supposed primitivism of the new religious groups: how could a society as technologically advanced as that of the 1990s (or 1940s or 1890s) produce such monstrous throwbacks as these idolatrous cults? This constant sense of surprise is in itself rather surprising; even a slight degree of historical perspective shows us that new and unorthodox sects have always arisen, have always been treated by critics in more or less the same way, and have cyclically recurred and will recur ad infinitum. It is rhetorical necessity that leads opponents to declare that the cults of a given decade are always unprecedented, always more shocking and bizarre than earlier groups (a claim then supported by generalizing from a few extreme examples of sectarian misbehavior). Likewise, the present and future strength of the new sects is always portrayed in the most exaggerated terms. Not only are the cults always with us, but at least in public perceptions, the cult problem is always worse than it has ever been.

The religious margin is the seedbed of new churches and mainstream organizations. Though the great majority of new religious groups do not succeed in growing to become major denominations, at least some do make this transition.[1] Ultimately, all existing Protestant denominations began as new, radical sects, with the exception of a few groups like Episcopalians and Lutherans, who from their earliest days were accorded the status of an established church by a particular nation-state. Baptists, Methodists, Quakers, and Pentecostals all began their respective histories as suspicious and unpopular, yet each over time made the transition to respectability.

Some religious traditions have grown rapidly in both numbers and social acceptance in very recent times. The growth of the Latter-Day Saints is very striking; the Mormon rate of growth in its first century-and-a-half has exceeded that of early Christianity itself. Just as dramatic has been the expansion of American Islam since the 1960s, to the extent that there will be more Muslims than Jews in the United States within a decade or so (in this case, much of the growth is attributable to immigration rather than domestic conversions). Not long ago, Islam was regarded as a highly deviant belief-system for Americans, but today it is a well-established component of the religious scene: there are Muslim chaplains in the U.S. military, and imams have led the invocation at the opening of congressional sessions. The modern story of American Buddhism is quite as impressive. A century or so can make all the difference between renegade status and orthodoxy. There is no such thing as a successful or enduring cult: we simply start to call it a church (however incongruous it may be to apply the Christian-derived concept of "church" to Muslim or Buddhist communities).

This sect-church cycle has long been familiar to scholars of religion, who note that the achievement of respectability is by no means an unmixed blessing. In 1902, William James noted how a new movement arises in response to a charismatic impulse, a sense of divine inspiration, but as it becomes more established and respectable, the new church becomes "a staunch ally in every attempt to stifle the spontaneous religious spirit."[2] Newly respectable churches demonstrate their status by a determined effort to suppress still newer religions, rather as the Pentecostals and other fundamentalist denominations of the 1970s took the lead against the "cult problem." It would have amazed an observer of a century ago to find the present-day Latter-Day Saints Church launching an active ministry to preserve its young people against eccentric religions. We might speculate that in another half-century, the Unification Church and the Krishna Consciousness movement will be equally conservative and integrated into the social mainstream, and they will be struggling to prevent their restless adherents deserting to unorthodox upstart sects. Already in the 1990s, the Vineyard broke with some of its congregations that had adopted the extreme revivalism associated with the so-called "Toronto Blessing," whose adherents brayed and laughed as outrageously as their eighteenth-century precursors.

Many of the problems associated with cults can be attributed to their newness, the fact that they are still in the process of acquiring the structures that characterize established churches. Bismarck famously remarked that neither sausage nor legislation should be observed in the making, as both processes are inevitably messy and unsavory. Perhaps the same principle holds true of new religions. J. Gordon Melton has argued that the fact of newness goes far towards explaining much of the violence connected with cults. Unlike established denominations, fringe religions tend to have younger and more inexperienced leaders, and lack accepted means of transferring authority, making violent internal conflicts more likely.[3] This is especially true when leaders claim charismatic authority for their rule. Other kinds of violence arise from conflicts between the cults and their neighbors, who persecute the believers for their unorthodox views and practices.

Older churches may be more tranquil, but they do not share the charisma or the sense of divine inspiration that are so commonplace in the small sects. For better or worse, established churches are so integrated into the social mainstream that any kind of conflict or persecution is unthinkable. Unpalatable as this concept might be in the aftermath of Waco, the same factors that make some cults prone to violence are just the elements that make these movements exciting and spiritually vigorous. The more integrated they become, the more churchlike, the less violence will occur. But then there will be a need for still newer and more radical bodies to meet spiritual hungers, and the cycle will begin afresh.

## Oddity and Orthodoxy

The long-term development of the small sects can make the process of religious change seem like a uniquely ferocious Darwinian struggle, in which most new life perishes swiftly, and only a handful of uniquely hardy organisms survive to compete. Certainly many so-called cult groups perish within a decade or two; most of the controversial bodies of the 1970s have already vanished. The success or failure of small sects should not be measured entirely by their ability to evolve into larger denominations, however, as new movements can attain great influence without the formal adherence of millions of card-carrying recruits. Some of the major religious transformations of the last century have originated on the margins, associated with no specific sect. We might for instance observe the spread of ideas of reincarnation and karma, together with associated traditions like meditation and yoga. In the early twentieth century, all of these were associated with Theosophy and the New Thought groups, as well as countless groups following individual swamis. Though none of these individual organizations has any sizable membership today, the theories have entered the religious mainstream. The small movements and cults thus succeeded in developing and preaching ideas that found a response among a mass public, who accepted the specific ideas without feeling the need to adhere to any one movement. In this instance, too, new religious movements served as a conduit for the importation of ideas and themes from a once-exotic foreign culture.

The cults' role as spiritual laboratories is most evident when we look at issues connected with gender, where radical sects pioneered ideas that have entered the core of Christian belief and practice. The original pathbreaking sects have since dwindled or vanished, but their ideas survive and triumph. From the late eighteenth century, a few of the most radical movements preached that God was Father and Mother, containing both genders. One of the distinguishing oddities of the Shakers was praying to God as Father and Mother. Decades later, the Christian Science version of the Lord's Prayer began with the appeal to "Our Father, Mother God, all-harmonious, Adorable One." A theology of the divine Feminine can also be traced in Mormonism, and the dual Fatherhood/Motherhood of God was preached at the New Thought convention of 1900. Even the Adventist David Koresh prayed to "Our Father and Mother."[4] Such ideas were common across large portions of the sectarian landscape.

Standard cult exposés cited these beliefs as final proof of the utter silliness, and perhaps depravity, of the sects. The Christian Science version of the Lord's Prayer was a favorite quotation in such works, presumably because tampering with such a central religious artifact was so unthinkable. For Louis Binder, writing in 1933, the concept of the Motherhood of God was bizarre because it mistakenly ascribed gender to the deity, an error that Binder clearly did not believe was present when an orthodox believer prayed to God as "He" and "Father." Only marginally less shocking, the cults demonstrated their disregard for common sense and conventional decency by accepting the spiritual authority of women and ordaining women as clergy or religious officials. As we have seen, women either founded or played a key role in many of the new American religions of the last century or so, and anticult critic Walter Martin saw "the female teaching ministry" as a cult characteristic that had led to "confusion, division and strife." Female leadership violated St. Paul's explicit order that women were to "learn in silence with all subjection."[5]

The cult oddities of the 1920s became the religious orthodoxies of the 1990s. By the end of the twentieth century, most Protestant denominations ordained female clergy (including bishops), and women rabbis were commonplace. Protestant, Catholic, and Jewish traditions were all revolutionized by the "fomenting feminism" so crucial in "reshaping normative religious styles."[6] One epoch-making change was in the spread of gender-neutral terminology in scriptural translation and liturgies, and phrases like "Our Father and Mother" became quite common. Many Christian clergy now prefer to replace the venerated phrase

"Father, Son and Holy Spirit" with a more inclusive "Creator, Redeemer, and Sanctifier." In reciting the creed, a congregant can attract disapproving glares for inadvertently including the once-standard assertion that Jesus came down from Heaven "for us *men* and our salvation" (my emphasis). In this matter, the small sects were dismissed as cults because their doctrines were premature and simply ran too far ahead of the religious consensus.

Nor was the relationship between the cults and the churches merely a matter of coincidental parallel development. Feminist Christian and Jewish theologians explicitly drew on the insights of women-oriented fringe movements such as Wicca and neopaganism. During the 1980s, feminist thealogy ("goddess study," rather than "god study") cultivated goddess traditions, and Rosemary Radford Ruether's book *Women Church* (1985) proposed a wholesale reorganization of the institutional church on the model of spontaneous grassroots communities, which she called "covens."[7] Such borrowings sometimes caused consternation among the traditionally minded, as in 1993 when two thousand women attended a Minneapolis conference entitled "Re-Imagining," sponsored by the Presbyterian and Methodist churches. The gathering included a feminist eucharist involving milk and honey, and prayers were offered to Sophia, the feminine Wisdom of God, who was treated as more or less divine in her own right. Although the event ignited a firestorm in the sponsoring churches, the ideas were unusual only in the undiplomatically frank way in which they were presented on this occasion. Mainline churches normally tended to express far more concern about diehards who threatened to secede rather than accept innovations like female ordination and gender-neutral language: it was the conservatives who were reduced to the status of a cantankerous sect.

## The Jesus of the Cults

The cults also ran ahead of the churches in their explorations of esoteric Christianity. In the last quarter century, many Christian thinkers have been intrigued by the new gospels and apocryphal texts discovered at Nag Hammadi in Egypt in 1945, which became available in accessible translations in the 1970s. The value of these texts is debated, but they have been widely taken to suggest that early Christianity was far more complex and diverse than had often been supposed. Some New Testament scholars portray one such text, the *Gospel of Thomas,* as a Fifth

Gospel, at least equal in importance to the better known canonical works. The Jesus of these Gospels is a distinctly New Age figure, who speaks in a style reminiscent of Zen *koan*: the Nag Hammadi texts contain references to magic spells, ritual dances, meditation practices, and mystical sexuality, and women characters play a vital role throughout the documents. This vision had its impact on many mainstream believers, especially feminists, who felt that they were rediscovering a whole suppressed side of the Christian tradition.

Although this appears to be an example of a wholly new influence on Western religious belief, most of these interpretations long predate the Nag Hammadi discoveries. Madame Blavatsky drew on the scholarship on Gnostic and early Christian heresy that was available in her own day, and her Ascended Masters owed much to the Gnostic image of the heaven-sent Redeemer. Esoteric ideas were made familiar through successive "channelings" of Jesus since the late nineteenth century and books like Dowling's *Aquarian Gospel of Jesus the Christ.* Also since Victorian times, occult and Theosophical writers have assumed that Jesus acquired his mystical teachings from the Jewish sect of the Essenes. This fringe belief became more respectable following the discovery of the Dead Sea Scrolls about the same time as the Nag Hammadi find, and many scholarly books have since explored the possible Essene connections to early Christianity.[8] While esoteric believers in 1910 or 1940 would have been delighted to have their image of Jesus validated by authenticated ancient texts, they would scarcely have been surprised by such findings.

In other ways, too, a modern-day church member is likely to have more sympathy with the fringe believers of earlier eras than with their mainstream critics. Theosophists evolved their ideas of human brotherhood at the height of the era of imperialism and white racial supremacy, a time when their respectful attention to non-European spiritual traditions was profoundly countercultural, and denounced accordingly. In retrospect, the Theosophists have won their case. Although a syncretistic view of the ultimate truth of all the great religions was once highly unpopular and definitely cultish, this idea is now much more acceptable than the then orthodox Christian exclusivism.

For the mainline churches at least, this acceptance of the validity of other faiths also extends to primal and pagan traditions, with their greater reverence for Mother Earth. The extent of this ideological change became dramatically apparent in 1987, when the leading clergy of all the major Christian denominations in the Pacific Northwest,

including Roman Catholics, Lutherans, and Methodists, issued a declaration to the Native peoples of the region formally apologizing for
"the destruction of traditional Native American spiritual practices."
The declaration not only defended Native American practices, but asserted, "The spiritual power of the land and the ancient wisdom of
your indigenous religions can be, we believe, great gifts to the Christian
churches. . . . May the God of Abraham and Sarah, and the Spirit who
lives in both the cedar and Salmon People, be honored and celebrated."
If not exactly a new orthodoxy, both pantheism and nature religion
have moved from the outer reaches of American religious thought to
somewhere near the center.[9]

In political matters, too, modern-day mainliners are much more
likely than hitherto to adopt policies radically opposed to those of government. They now have a far better understanding of the motives of
the Jehovah's Witnesses, Mennonites, and the other sects that have
long resisted the demands of uncritical patriotism and war fever, even
when this position invited persecution and ostracism. In the aftermath
of the Vietnam war, of successive anti-nuclear campaigns, and the protest movements against U.S. military interventions in Central America
in the 1980s, many Catholics and Protestants have espoused the practice of civil disobedience.

Another religious style that has spread from the margins is the charismatic movement. In the early twentieth century this represented the
most bizarre extreme of worship, and many critics would have had
serious difficulty in describing it as Christian. Pentecostalism was dismissed as a matter of psychopathology rather than theology. Nevertheless, the movement ultimately became a major force in global Christianity, and according to some estimates, Pentecostals today represent
the second largest branch of Christianity, after the Roman Catholic
Church. Dismissive phrases like "holy rolling" are rarely heard today
because since the 1960s the mainline churches themselves have been
swept by charismatic revivals. Many otherwise unexceptional Catholic
parishes foster charismatic prayer groups and retreats, and the practice
has become widespread across denominational frontiers.[10] Predominantly white churches have also tried, with varying degrees of success,
to adapt into their own practice patterns of music and style that once
only characterized African American congregations. A less spectacular
manifestation of changing worship styles has been the growth in mainline churches of customs like liturgical dance. While we can scarcely
say that all liberal Christians have somehow become Shakers, the re-

ligious periphery has contributed some obvious, and occasionally dramatic, influences.

## The Secular Realm

In other matters, the "cultic" influence is not perceived as distinctly religious. One enormously significant social trend of the late twentieth century has been the twelve-step movement, which affected tens of millions of Americans both inside and outside religious denominations. In addition to the familiar Alcoholics Anonymous, the same recovery model was extended to narcotics users, sex addicts, the adult children of alcoholics, and a variety of "survivor" movements. The cult connection would certainly surprise most participants in these meetings, but in fact the AA idea emerged in the 1930s from the model of the Oxford Group, "Buchmanism," from which it derives the practice of intimate confession in group settings.[11] Ten of the famous twelve steps are appropriated directly from Oxford Group practice.

Other modern health concerns have their roots on the religious fringe. At least since the early nineteenth century, emerging religious movements have generally been enthusiastic about various dietary reforms, some of which have long ago ceased to be merely fads. This interest was particularly marked in the Adventist tradition, notably in the writings of Ellen G. White. By the early twentieth century, Adventists avoided alcohol, tobacco, and meat, and they have upheld these restrictions through decades in which they were marked as blatant cranks. Adventist Dr. John Kellogg developed his cereal business in part to ensure that the faithful could obtain their nourishment without partaking of meat. Adventist periodicals were expressing concern about the health dangers of cholesterol long before the concept had made any impact whatever on the general public.[12] This deviant population provided an ideal control group for researchers exploring the effects of eating red meat and smoking, and the resulting studies produced ample evidence that Adventists tended to live far longer than their non-Adventist neighbors. By the 1970s, Adventist principles were being enthusiastically embraced by the mainstream population, and "food faddists" appeared a lot less foolish than they once had. By the end of the century, tobacco companies were well on their way to being stigmatized quite as thoroughly as had been the most eccentric cults.[13]

Marginal religious groups have long been active in alternative kinds of medicine and spiritual healing, beliefs that today have gained a mass audience. In the 1920s, authors like Mencken and Morris Fishbein regarded chiropractic as one of the grossest manifestations of cult pseudoscience, yet a 1998 survey showed that about 16 percent of Americans have resorted to this method at some point in their lives. The same survey showed that the national figure for Americans using herbal health products is 17 percent, 5 percent for homeopathy, 13 percent for high-dose vitamins, 2 percent for acupuncture (Californians, however, use these techniques at about double the national rate). Another national poll at this time showed that those using alternative treatments "were much more likely than others to agree with the statement: 'The health of my body, mind and spirit are related, and whoever cares for my health should take that into account.' " Individual New Thought sects may be thin on the ground, but the ideology is by no means extinct.[14] By the late 1990s, alternative medicine represented an American industry worth $18 billion annually, if we take into account the money spent on herbal supplements, homeopathy, naturopathy, osteopathy, herbal medicine, acupuncture, and traditional Chinese medicine. The United States had two hundred professional homeopaths in 1970, but three thousand by 1998. Therapeutic touch (energy healing) has tens of thousands of practitioners in North America.

The usefulness of these medical techniques remains open to debate, and numerous lawsuits throughout the century have resulted from the deaths of patients, especially children, who were denied access to orthodox medical facilities. Still, the fact that alternative methods were being explored provided a useful social experiment. During the 1980s, mainstream practitioners found something else of value from the fringe when concern about possible AIDS contamination of the blood supply sparked a new interest in methods developed by Jehovah's Witness institutions for altogether avoiding the use of blood in surgery.

## Cults in the Courts

In matters like diet and health, fringe religions struggled for years to popularize their views, and they would presumably rejoice at their success. In other areas, though, the influence of the sects stems from legal controversies that at the time were regarded as disastrous. Nevertheless, successive conflicts over the rights of marginal religions have done much to define the law and constitution in this country, with effects far beyond the religious sphere, as strictly defined.

The issue of freedom of religious belief and practice is scarcely likely to come before the courts in the context of large bodies like the mainstream churches. Attempts to regulate small and unpopular groups, however, have been richly productive of litigation. Offering numerous possible areas of conflict with the secular law, sects like the Amish, Mennonites and Seventh Day Adventists have featured far more heavily in legal history than might be expected from their overall numbers. Often, the repercussions of these legal cases have reached far beyond the realm of religious organizations; American free speech law was transformed by the Jehovah's Witness cases that occurred between 1938 and 1948. Libertarian decisions like *Cantwell* went directly against the principles affirmed in speech cases during the previous few decades, in which the unpopular movements in question had been communist, socialist, or syndicalist. In contrast, the courts were more prepared to defend speech in matters of religious liberty, a point that also emerged from the *Ballard* case in these years. The most restrictive precedents concerning antisubversive speech would not be overturned until the 1960s, but the Jehovah's Witness cases did succeed in limiting the zeal of local authorities to curb the heretical and obnoxious; most important, they established the idea that the defense of free speech was a proper and necessary function of the federal government.

By continually pressing the boundaries of tolerance, and doing so in the name of religious liberty, new and emerging denominations have found themselves in the vanguard of constitutional development. If the states are the laboratories of democracy, then the sects and cults play a like role for the freedom of religion. Religious freedom cases have been important arenas for symbolic conflicts concerning the status of new social and ethnic groups, essentially determining their integration into the American mainstream. Such conflicts determine how far the so-called Judaeo-Christian tradition will stretch to accommodate new social groups, whose aspirations are often bound up with fringe religions. One striking demonstration of this flexibility came in 1993, when the activities of an Afro-Cuban Santería sect led the U.S. Supreme Court to redefine the limits of tolerated behavior by legitimizing animal sacrifice. The case was memorably named *Church of Lukumi Babalu Aye v. Hialeah* (1993).

The character of Native American identity has repeatedly been debated in legal cases arising from religious practices like ritual peyote use. When in 1990 the U.S. Supreme Court permitted states to penalize peyote users, the decision (*Employment Division of Oregon v. Smith*) provoked a political firestorm, as Christian and Jewish leaders of all ideological shades demanded legislation to protect the free exercise of religion. Congress responded with a sweeping law, the Religious Freedom Restoration Act, (RFRA), which the Supreme Court subsequently struck down. The issues arising from *Smith* and RFRA continue to be of pressing interest for constitutional scholars, and the wider controversy largely shaped American debate over the legal position of religion throughout the 1990s. Marginal religions generate mainstream law.

New and controversial religions will assuredly continue to emerge in the coming decades, and our response to them should take account of this history of cultural and social innovation. A new cult might well be asking useful questions that the religious mainstream has scarcely yet formulated, though it might not be possible for decades to identify which of the new trends are likely to have the most impact, for good or ill. Though specific sects might be defeated and destroyed, it is very unlikely that their ideas will be obliterated: marginal religious theories are amazingly resilient.

The long history of cult controversies also suggests that we should exercise great care in accepting the negative charges likely to be made against any new denomination. Some emerging sects are attacked for what appear to be excellent reasons, for instance when a movement is tainted by child maltreatment or tendencies to extreme violence, and such allegations are substantiated in some instances. On the other hand, we now have over a century of case studies to show how frequently groundless or exaggerated charges have been made, often on the basis of deeply ingrained stereotypes and well-used rhetorical scripts. When considering allegations against suspect fringe movements, evidence must be sifted very critically, with a view to detecting any agendas that might be generating dubious charges. Meanwhile, the fact that anticult beliefs are very widely held is no guarantee whatever of their authenticity. If that point was not sufficiently established by the anti-Jewish blood libel and the enduring legends of the secret cemeteries below Catholic convents, then the recent scare over satanic and ritual abuse should provide added confirmation. Even so, anticult movements are as perennial as cult scares, and it is equally unlikely that they will ever fade away.

Cult scares will recur as long as new religious movements emerge and established groups care sufficiently about their own beliefs to criticize the newcomers. Cult booms and cult scares proceed in tandem, each in their way reflecting the common social and religious passions of an age. Cult panics are an effective barometer of religious commitment and inquiry in a particular society; we might even argue that the more intense the panic, the greater the vigor. It is the society that lacks cults and cult panics that has most to fear about the state of its religious life.

# Notes

## ABBREVIATIONS

ASR     *American Sociological Review*
CC      *Christian Century*
JAF     *Journal of American Folklore*
JAP     *Journal of Abnormal Psychology*
LAT     *Los Angeles Times*
LD      *Literary Digest*
NYT     *New York Times*
WP      *Washington Post*

## ONE

1. Robert S. Fogarty, *The Righteous Remnant* (Kent, OH: Kent State Univ. Press, 1981); Anthony Sterling, *King of the Harem Heaven* (Derby, CT: Monarch Books, 1960), 137; Charles W. Ferguson, *The Confusion of Tongues* (Garden City, NY: Doubleday, 1928), 49–62.
2. Ferguson, *The Confusion of Tongues*, 4. Works used throughout this book include J. Gordon Melton, *Biographical Dictionary of American Cult and Sect Leaders* (New York: Garland, 1986); J. Gordon Melton, *Encyclopedia of American Religions*, 5th ed. (Detroit: Gale Research, 1996).
3. A. James Rudin and Marcia R. Rudin, *Prison or Paradise?* (Philadelphia: Fortress Press, 1980), 14, 16; Flo Conway and Jim Siegelman, *Snapping*, 2d ed. (New York: Stillpoint Press, 1995); Margaret Thaler Singer and Janja Lalich, *Cults in Our Midst* (San Francisco: Jossey-Bass, 1995), 31–37; Madeleine Landau Tobias and Janja Lalich, *Captive Hearts, Captive Minds* (Alameda, CA: Hunter House, 1994); John J. Collins, *The Cult Experience* (Springfield, IL: Charles Thomas, 1991).
4. Julius Friedrich Sachse, *The German Pietists of Provincial Pennsylvania* (Philadelphia: privately printed, 1895); Herbert Leventhal, *In the Shadow of the Enlightenment* (New York: New York Univ. Press, 1976); Jon Butler, "The Dark Ages of American Occultism," in *The Occult in America*, ed.

Howard Kerr and Charles L. Crow (Urbana: Univ. of Illinois Press, 1983), 58–78; Jon Butler, *Awash in a Sea of Faith* (Cambridge, MA: Harvard University Press, 1990); John L. Brooke, *The Refiner's Fire* (New York: Cambridge Univ. Press, 1994).

5. Martin E. Marty, *Modern American Religion II: The Noise of Conflict* (Chicago: Univ. of Chicago Press, 1991), 264.

6. There is an important chapter on "Cult Membership in the Roaring Twenties" in Rodney Stark and William S. Bainbridge, *The Future of Religion* (Berkeley: Univ. of California Press, 1986), 234–62. See also J. Gordon Melton and James V. Geisendorfer, *A Directory of Religious Bodies in the United States* (New York: Garland, 1977), which quantifies the new groups emerging in respective eras. Robert Galbreath, "Explaining Modern Occultism," in Kerr and Crow, eds., *The Occult in America*, 21. Robert T. Handy, "The American Religious Depression," *Church History* 29 (1960): 3–16; though contrast Joel Carpenter, *Revive Us Again* (New York: Oxford Univ. Press, 1997).

7. The quote about "overrun with messiahs" is from Ferguson, *The Confusion of Tongues*, 1; "pottin' from the bushes" is taken from Sinclair Lewis, *It Can't Happen Here* (New York: New American Library, 1970), 47.

8. Marty, *Modern American Religion II: The Noise of Conflict*, 12.

9. Ferguson, *The Confusion of Tongues*, 7.

10. Stark and Bainbridge, *The Future of Religion*, 26–27.

11. Barry A. Kosmin and Seymour P. Lachman, *One Nation Under God* (New York: Harmony Books, 1993), 15–17; James R. Lewis and J. Gordon Melton, eds., *Perspectives on the New Age* (Albany: State Univ. of New York Press, 1992).

12. Louis R. Binder, *Modern Religious Cults and Society* (Boston: R. G. Badger, 1933), 17; for the "cult racket," see Milton S. Mayer, "Unmasking the Silver Shirts," *Real American*, June–July 1934, 8–13. Read Bain, "Sociology and Psychoanalysis," *ASR* 1, no. 2 (1936): 203. The "cult" Bain was describing in this instance was psychoanalysis.

13. For issues of definition, see James T. Richardson, "Definitions of Cult," *Review of Religious Research* 34 (1993): 348–56; Thomas Robbins, *Cults, Converts, and Charisma* (Newbury Park, CA: Sage, 1991); Marc Galanter, *Cults: Faith, Healing, and Coercion* (New York: 2d ed, Oxford Univ. Press, 1999).

14. Singer and Lalich, *Cults in Our Midst*, 10.

15. Anson D. Shupe, ed., *Wolves Within the Fold* (New Brunswick, NJ: Rutgers Univ. Press, 1998); Philip Jenkins, *Pedophiles and Priests* (New York: Oxford Univ. Press, 1996).

16. H. Richard Niebuhr, *The Social Sources of Denominationalism* (New York: Henry Holt, 1929); Ernst Troeltsch, *The Social Teaching of the Christian Churches* (New York: Macmillan, 1931); Liston Pope, *Millhands and Preachers* (New Haven: Yale Univ. Press, 1942); Bryan Wilson, *Religious Sects* (New York: World University Library, 1970). For the Continental scholars who formulated these theories, another critical division was that churches had some degree of official support or legal privilege, while sects

did not, so that in some respects, the whole division is not really appropriate for the American setting. For the idea of greedy groups, see Lewis A. Coser, *Greedy Institutions* (New York: Free Press, 1974).

17. The threefold division is from Stark and Bainbridge, *The Future of Religion*. The phrase about "something new and different" is from Rudin and Rudin, *Prison or Paradise?* 14.

18. Since I reject the popular distinction between cults and sects, I will not observe the difference in this book. The distinction is also ignored by European scholars and in the common usage of most European languages. See for example Massimo Introvigne, *Le Nuove Religioni* (Milan: Sugarco, 1989); Jean-Marie Abgrall, *La Mécanique des Sectes* (Paris: Éditions Payot, 1996).

19. Stan Cohen, *Folk Devils and Moral Panics* (Oxford: Blackwell, 1972); Erich Goode and Nachman Ben-Yehuda, *Moral Panics* (Oxford: Blackwell, 1994); Philip Jenkins, *Moral Panic* (New Haven: Yale Univ. Press, 1998).

20. Elizabeth Puttick and Jo Campling, *Women and New Religions* (New York: St. Martin's Press, 1997); Susan J. Palmer, *Moon Sisters, Krishna Mothers, Rajneesh Lovers* (Syracuse: Syracuse Univ. Press, 1995); Catherine Wessinger, ed., *Women's Leadership in Marginal Religions* (Urbana: Univ. of Illinois, 1993); Ursula King, *Women and Spirituality*, 2d ed. (University Park, PA: Penn State Press, 1993); Mary Farrell Bednarowski, "Women in Occult America," in Kerr and Crow, eds., *The Occult in America*, 177–95. Nor is this female emphasis solely a Western characteristic: nineteenth-century Japan likewise witnessed the rise of important new movements founded by plebeian women and practicing spiritual healing. One, Tenrikyo, bears many resemblances to Christian Science and other American sects of the same era.

## TWO

1. Robert N. Bellah and Frederick E. Greenspahn, eds., *Uncivil Religion* (New York: Crossroad, 1987); David H. Bennett, *The Party of Fear*, 2d ed. (New York: Vintage, 1995).

2. For military messiahs in the Bible, see Acts 5:36–37 (RSV). Norman Cohn, *Pursuit of the Millennium*, 3d ed. (London: Paladin, 1970).

3. Thomas Edwards, *Gangraena* (London, 1646); Jerome Friedman, *Blasphemy, Immorality, and Anarchy* (Athens: Ohio Univ. Press, 1987).

4. Joseph J. Kelley, *Pennsylvania: The Colonial Years 1681–1776* (Garden City, NY: Doubleday, 1980), 221. Sydney E. Ahlstrom, *A Religious History of the American People* (New Haven: Yale Univ. Press, 1972). For the European reaction against religious enthusiasm in these years, see Hillel Schwartz, *The French Prophets* (Berkeley: Univ. of California Press, 1979); Michael Heyd, *Be Sober and Reasonable* (Leiden, Netherlands: E. J. Brill, 1995).

5. Jenny Franchot, *Roads to Rome* (Berkeley: Univ. of California Press, 1994); *Harvard Journal* April 16, 1934; John T. McGreevy, "Thinking on One's Own," *Journal of American History* 84 (1997): 97–131.

6. In *The Truth About the Catholic Church* (Girard, KS: Haldeman Julius,

1926), former monk Joseph McCabe recounted many scandals involving drunkenness and sexual license, while as late as 1962, former priest Emmett McLoughlin published his study of *Crime and Immorality in the Catholic Church* (New York: Lyle Stuart, 1962). David G. Bromley, ed., *The Politics of Religious Apostasy* (Westport, CT: Praeger, 1998).

7. Marcus Bach, *They Have Found a Faith* (Indianapolis: Bobbs-Merrill, 1946), 14; Donald L. Kinzer, *An Episode in Anti-Catholicism* (Seattle: Univ. of Washington Press, 1964).

8. David Brion Davis, "Some Themes of Counter-Subversion," in *From Homicide to Slavery* (New York: Oxford Univ. Press, 1986), 137–54.

9. Bennett, *The Party of Fear*.

10. M. Aikin, *Memoirs of Religious Impostors* (London: Jones and Co., 1822).

11. Fawn Brodie, *No Man Knows My History*, rev. ed. (New York: Vintage, 1971), 230–31; Bruce Kinney, *Mormonism: The Islam of America* (New York: Fleming H. Revell, 1912); Gary L. Ward, ed., *Mormonism I: Evangelical Christian Anti-Mormonism in the Twentieth Century* (New York: Garland, 1990); Fuad Sha'ban, *Islam and Arabs in Early American Thought* (Durham, NC: Acorn, 1991).

12. Jon Butler, "The Dark Ages of American Occultism," in *The Occult in America*, ed. Howard Kerr and Charles L. Crow (Urbana: Univ. of Illinois Press, 1983), 58–78; Jon Butler, *Awash in a Sea of Faith* (Harvard University Press, 1990); Anne Braude, *Radical Spirits* (Boston: Beacon, 1991); Robert L. Moore, *In Search of White Crows* (New York: Oxford Univ. Press, 1977); Arthur Wrobel, ed., *Pseudo-Science and Society in Nineteenth-Century America* (Lexington: Univ. Press of Kentucky, 1987). For the British experience, see Alison Winter, *Mesmerized* (Chicago: University of Chicago Press, 1998).

13. Paul E. Johnson and Sean Wilentz, *The Kingdom of Matthias* (New York: Oxford Univ. Press, 1994).

14. Mary Marshall (i.e., Mary M. Dyer), *The Rise and Progress of the Serpent from the Garden of Eden to the Present Day* (Concord, NH: 1847). The quote is from 147; the use of electricity is described on 184–85; Mesmerism on 221. Mary M. Dyer, *A Portraiture of Shakerism* (Concord, NH: 1822). Lawrence Foster, *Religion and Sexuality* (New York: Oxford Univ. Press, 1981).

15. Though see chapter three below for William Oxley, *Modern Messiahs and Wonder Workers* (London: Trubner and Son, 1889).

16. Isaac Kramnick and R. Laurence Moore, *The Godless Constitution* (New York: Norton, 1996).

17. Kathleen Egan Chamberlain, "The Native American," in *Religion in Modern New Mexico*, ed. Ferenc M. Szasz and Richard W. Etulain (Albuquerque: Univ. of New Mexico Press, 1997). James Mooney, *The Ghost Dance* (North Dighton, MA: JG Press, 1996).

18. Mark Twain, *Roughing It* (Chicago: F. G. Gilman, 1872); J. H. Beadle, *The History of Mormonism* (Toronto: A. H. Hovey, 1873); Gary L. Bunker and Davis Bitton, *The Mormon Graphic Image, 1834–1914* (Salt Lake City: Univ. of Utah Press, 1983).

19. *The Mormon Menace, being the confession of John Doyle Lee, Danite, an official assassin of the Mormon church under the late Brigham Young* (New York: Home Protection Publishing, 1905); *Mormonism Unveiled; or, The life and confessions of the late Mormon bishop, John D. Lee. . . . Also the true history of the horrible butchery known as the Mountain Meadows massacre* (St. Louis: Bryan, Brand, 1877); Juanita Brooks, *The Mountain Meadows Massacre*, rev. ed. (Norman: Univ. of Oklahoma Press, 1970); T. B. H. Stenhouse, *The Rocky Mountain Saints* (Salt Lake City: Shepard Book Co., 1904).

20. Ann Eliza Young, *Wife No. 19, or The Story of a Life in Bondage* (Hartford, CT: Dustin, Gilman, 1875); Jennie Anderson Froiseth, ed., *The Women of Mormonism* (Detroit: C. G. G. Paine, 1882). The book *Life in Mormon Bondage* discussed here was basically a reprinting of *Wife No. 19* and was published by Philadelphia's Aldine Press in 1908. The quotation from the Massachusetts paper is from Ann Taves, "Sexuality in American Religious History," in *Retelling U.S. Religious History*, ed. Thomas A. Tweed (Berkeley: Univ. of California Press, 1997), 45.

21. Fanny Stenhouse, *Tell It All: The Story of a Life's Experience in Mormonism* (Hartford, CT: A. D. Worthington, 1877); Fanny Stenhouse, *An English woman in Utah. . . . Including a full account of the Mountain Meadows massacre, and of the life, confession and execution of Bishop John D. Lee* (London: S. Low, Marston, Searle and Rivington, 1882).

22. Taves, "Sexuality in American Religious History," 45.

23. For Fruitlands, see Anne C. Rose, *Transcendentalism as a Social Movement* (New Haven: Yale Univ. Press, 1981), 125–28; Louis J. Kern, *An Ordered Love* (Chapel Hill: Univ. of North Carolina Press, 1981). Charles Nordhoff, *The Communistic Societies of the United States* (London: J. Murray, 1875), 287–98.

24. The survey of hostile press reports is from Spencer Klaw, *Without Sin* (New York: Penguin, 1993), 163; the Syracuse paper is quoted in ibid., 245.

25. Harry Houdini, *A Magician Among the Spirits* (New York: Harper, 1924), 187–88; Charles E. Rosenberg, *The Trial of the Assassin Guiteau* (Chicago: Univ. of Chicago Press, 1976).

26. Herbert W. Schneider and George Lawton, *A Prophet and a Pilgrim* (New York: Columbia Univ. Press, 1942); "Respiro," *The Man, the Seer, the Adept, the Avatar*, 2d ed. (London: E. W. Allen, 1897); Thomas Lake Harris, *Brotherhood of the New Life* (Santa Rosa, CA: Fountain Grove Press, 1891). The quote from the *Wave* is from Schneider and Lawton, 556.

27. Barbara Goldsmith, *Other Powers* (New York: Knopf, 1998); Howard Kerr, *Mediums, and Spirit-Rappers, and Roaring Radicals* (Urbana: Univ. of Illinois Press, 1972); Houdini, *A Magician Among the Spirits*.

28. Houdini, *A Magician Among the Spirits*.

29. "In every case with but one exception" is from Houdini, *A Magician Among the Spirits*, 195; *Preliminary report of the Commission appointed by the University of Pennsylvania to investigate modern spiritualism* (Philadelphia: J. B. Lippincott, 1887); Reuben Briggs Davenport, *The*

*Death-Blow to Spiritualism* (1888; New York: G. W. Dillingham, 1897); Elijah Farrington and C. F. Pidgeon, *Revelations of a Spirit Medium* (St. Paul, MN: Farrington, 1891); David P. Abbott, *Behind the Scenes with the Mediums* (Chicago: Open Court, 1907); William Jackson Crawford, *Hints and Observations for those Investigating the Phenomena of Spiritualism* (New York: E. P. Dutton, 1918).

30. Arthur H. Barrington, *Anti-Christian Cults* (Milwaukee: Young Churchman, 1898), 29–30.

31. Peter Washington, *Madame Blavatsky's Baboon* (New York: Schocken Books, 1995); K. Paul Johnson, *Initiates of Theosophical Masters* (Albany: State Univ. of New York Press, 1995); K. Paul Johnson, *The Masters Revealed* (Albany: State of New York Press, 1994); Joscelyn Godwin, *The Theosophical Enlightenment* (Albany: State Univ. of New York Press, 1994); Michael Gomes, *The Dawning of the Theosophical Society* (Wheaton, IL: Theosophical Society, 1987); Bruce F. Campbell, *Ancient Wisdom Revived* (Berkeley: Univ. of California Press, 1980); Robert S. Ellwood, "The American Theosophical Synthesis," in Kerr and Crow, eds., *The Occult in America*, 111–34. The quote is from Blavatsky, in K. Paul Johnson, "Imaginary Mahatmas," *Gnosis* 28 (summer 1993): 28. Blavatsky made an enormous contribution to the Western mythology depicting Tibet as a mystic paradise: see Donald S. Lopez, *Prisoners of Shangri-La* (Chicago: Univ. of Chicago Press, 1998).

32. Cited in Barrington, *Anti-Christian Cults*, 101. Edmund Garrett, *Isis Very Much Unveiled: Being The Story Of The Great Mahatma Hoax* (London: *Westminster Gazette*, 1894). For other contemporary attacks on Theosophy, see Aidan A. Kelly, ed., *Theosophy II* (New York: Garland, 1990).

33. *Poor Little Edith Freeman: The Victim of a Father's Fanaticism!* (Philadelphia: Barclay and Co., 1879).

34. For campaigns by the *Brooklyn Eagle*, see *The Emmanuel Movement: A Brief History of the New Cult* (Brooklyn: *Brooklyn Daily Eagle*, 1908); William H. Muldoon, *Christian Science Claims Un-Scientific and Un-Christian . . . Eddyism, its healings and fallacies investigated* (Brooklyn: *Brooklyn Daily Eagle*, 1901); and chapter 3 below for the paper's attacks on Pastor Russell and the Watch Tower Society.

35. Robert S. Fogarty, *All Things New* (Chicago: Univ. of Chicago Press, 1990); Donald E. Pitzer, ed., *America's Communal Utopias* (Chapel Hill: Univ. of North Carolina Press, 1997); Timothy Miller, *The Quest for Utopia in Twentieth-Century America: 1900–1960* (Syracuse University Press, 1998).

36. Martin E. Marty, *Modern American Religion I: The Irony of It All* (Chicago: Univ. of Chicago Press, 1986), 243–44.

37. "This Hollow World: Koreshans," *Newsweek*, December 6, 1948, 26; Elmer T. Clark, *The Small Sects in America* (New York: Abingdon, 1949), 147–50; Hugo Hume, *The Superior American Religions* (Los Angeles: Libertarian Publishing, 1928); Fogarty, *All Things New*; James E. Landing, "Cyrus Reed Teed and the Koreshan Unity," in Pitzer, ed., *America's*

*Communal Utopias,* 375–95. For expectations concerning Ann Lee, see Marshall, *The Rise and Progress of the Serpent.*

38. Josephine Woodbury, *War in Heaven,* 3d ed. (Boston: Samuel Usher, 1897), 43.

39. Stewart H. Holbrook, "Oregon's Secret Love Cult," *American Mercury,* February 1937, 167–74. The *American Mercury* was H. L. Mencken's publication, and it delighted in exposing the follies of the fringe religions.

40. Anthony Sterling, *King of the Harem Heaven* (Derby, CT: Monarch Books, 1960), 63; Robert S. Fogarty, *The Righteous Remnant* (Kent, OH: Kent State Univ. Press, 1981), 37–40.

41. The account of "outrages" at Point Loma is from Emmett A. Greenwalt, *The Point Loma Community in California* (Berkeley: Univ. of California Press, 1955), 67–76; "the disciples of spookism" is quoted in Carey McWilliams, "Cults of California," *Atlantic,* March 1946, 105–10.

## THREE

1. Louis R. Binder, *Modern Religious Cults and Society* (Boston: R. G. Badger, 1933), 46.

2. The New Testament reference to false Christs is Mark 13:22. William Oxley, *Modern Messiahs and Wonder Workers* (London: Trubner and Son, 1889); Frederick W. Peabody, *A Complete Exposé of Eddyism or Christian Science* (Boston: n.p., 1901); James Vincent Coombs, *Religious Delusions* (Cincinnati: Standard Publishing, 1904); William C. Irvine, *Heresies Exposed,* 3d ed. (New York: Loizeaux Brothers, 1921). The first edition was published in 1917 under the title *Timely Warnings;* the second edition was published in 1919 as *Modern Heresies Exposed.* Arthur H. Forster, *Four Modern Religious Movements* (Boston: Richard G. Badger, 1919).

3. Laurence A. Waddell, *The Buddhism of Tibet: Or, Lamaism with its mystic cults, symbolism and mythology* (London: W. H. Allen, 1895).

4. Marvin Dana, "Voodooism," *Metropolitan Magazine* 29 (1908): 529–38.

5. For the Ghost Dance example, see Frederick M. Davenport, *Primitive Traits in Religious Revivals* (New York: Macmillan, 1905), 35–36; Arthur H. Barrington, *Anti-Christian Cults* (Milwaukee: Young Churchman, 1898). In order to avoid confusion about early uses of the word "cult," I should note that modern editions of J. H. Noyes's *History of American Socialisms* bear the title *Strange Cults and Utopias of Nineteenth Century America* (New York: Dover, 1966). Though a loose bibliographical citation can make it appear that this particular "cults" title dates back to 1870, in fact this phrase was only applied to the text in the 1960s.

6. Emmett A. Greenwalt, *The Point Loma Community in California* (Berkeley: Univ. of California Press, 1955), 52–56; Steven F. Walker, "Vivekananda and American Culture," in *The Occult in America,* ed. Howard Kerr and Charles L. Crow (Urbana Univ. of Illinois Press, 1983), 162–76; Richard Hughes Seager, *The World's Parliament of Religions* (Bloomington: Indiana Univ. Press, 1994).

7. Lisa Lowe, *Immigrant Acts* (Durham, NC: Duke University Press, 1996). For the Japanese threat, see Barbara Tuchman, *The Zimmermann Telegram*

(New York: Ballantine, 1979); Alexander Saxton, *The Indispensable Enemy* (Berkeley: Univ. of California Press, 1971).

8. George Bedell Vosburgh, *Christian Science Examined: Mary Baker G. Eddy, "The New Cult"* (Denver: Denver Printing and Publishing, 1906); *The Emmanuel Movement: A Brief History of the New Cult* (Brooklyn: Brooklyn Daily Eagle, 1908); John E. Brown, *In the Cult Kingdom": Mormonism, Eddyism and Russellism* (Siloam Springs, Ark: International Federation Publishing, 1918); Charles E. Locke, *Eddyism: Is it Christian? is it scientific? how long will it last?* 12th ed. (Los Angeles: Grafton Publishing, 1911); Peabody, *A Complete Exposé of Eddyism*; Herbert M. Wyrick, "Seven Religious Isms" (1940), reprinted in Aidan A. Kelly, ed., *The Evangelical Christian Anti-Cult Movement* (New York: Garland, 1990).

9. Jan Karel Van Baalen, "The Gist of the Cults" (1944), reprinted in Kelly, ed., *The Evangelical Christian Anti-Cult Movement*; Jan Karel Van Baalen, *The Chaos of Cults*, 5th ed. (1938, Grand Rapids, MI: Eerdmans, 1946); Walter R. Martin, "Division of Cult Apologetics," in *The Rise of the Cults* (Grand Rapids, MI: Zondervan, 1955); Walter R. Martin, *The Kingdom of the Cults* (1965; Minneapolis: Bethany House, 1992); Anthony A. Hoekema, *The Four Major Cults* (Exeter, England: Paternoster Press, 1963).

10. The phrase about "they take Biblical Christianity" is from Walter R. Martin, *The New Cults* (Santa Ana, CA: Vision House, 1980), 11; "pointedly contradictory to orthodox Christianity" is quoted in J. Gordon Melton, *Encyclopedic Handbook of Cults in America*, rev. ed. (New York: Garland, 1992), 338.

11. Van Baalen, *The Chaos of Cults*, 17.

12. Charles W. Ferguson, *The Confusion of Tongues* (Garden City, NY: Doubleday, 1928), 1.

13. Kelly, ed., *The Evangelical Christian Anti-Cult Movement*, 336.

14. Martin E. Marty, *Modern American Religion I: The Irony of It All* (Chicago: Univ. of Chicago Press, 1986).

15. Ibid., 225.

16. "Hunt for Happiness," *Nation*, January 17, 1923, 59–60.

17. C. Alan Anderson, *Healing Hypotheses* (New York: Garland, 1993); Gail T. Parker, *Mind Cure in New England from the Civil War to World War I* (Hanover, NH: Univ. Press of New England, 1973).

18. Gaius Glenn Atkins, *Modern Religious Cults and Movements* (London: G. Allen and Unwin, 1923), 123; Charles W. Ferguson, *The Confusion of Tongues* (Garden City, NY: Doubleday, 1928), 160; Wyrick, *Seven Religious Isms*; Melton, *Encyclopedic Handbook*, 30; Stephen Gottschalk, *The Emergence of Christian Science in American Religious Life* (Berkeley: Univ. of California Press, 1973); Robert L. Moore, *Religious Outsiders and the Making of Americans* (New York: Oxford Univ. Press, 1985); Stuart E. Knee, *Christian Science in the Age of Mary Baker Eddy* (Westport, CT: Greenwood Press, 1994); Paul K. Conkin, *American Originals* (Chapel Hill: Univ. of North Carolina Press, 1997); Willa Cather and Georgine Milmine, *The Life of Mary Baker G. Eddy and the History of Christian Science*, ed.

by David Stouck (Lincoln: Univ. of Nebraska Press, 1993). For the Shakers and healing, see Mary Marshall (Mary Dyer), *The Rise and Progress of the Serpent from the Garden of Eden to the Present Day* (Concord, NH: the author, 1847), 94.

19. Mark Twain, *Christian Science* (1907, New York: Oxford Univ. Press, 1996), 49.

20. The New Thought movement took its name from the title of the magazine *New Thought*, founded in 1894. Charles S. Braden, *These Also Believe* (1949, New York: Macmillan, 1963), 128; Charles S. Braden, *Spirits in Rebellion* (Dallas: Southern Methodist Univ. Press, 1963); A. W. Griswold, "New Thought: A Cult of Success," *American Journal of Sociology* 40 (1934): 309–18; Marcus Bach, *They Have Found a Faith* (Indianapolis: Bobbs-Merrill, 1946), 222–54; Ferguson, *The Confusion of Tongues*, 214–30; Melton, *Encyclopedic Handbook*.

21. Hugh D'Andrade, *Charles Fillmore: Herald of the New Age.* (New York: Harper and Row, 1974). Braden, *These Also Believe*, 153.

22. Ralph Waldo Trine, *In Tune with the Infinite, or, Fullness of Peace, Power, and Plenty* (New York: Dodge, 1910).

23. The description of Fillmore's *Modern Thought* is from Bach, *They Have Found a Faith*, 227; William James, *Varieties of Religious Experience* (New York: Penguin Classics, 1985), 94. The remark about "American psychology on dress parade" is from F. Lynch, "Religion Run Riot," *Review of Reviews* (November 1929): 112ff. The comment about "American independence" is from Hugo Hume, *The Superior American Religions* (Los Angeles: Libertarian Publishing, 1928), 65.

24. Lynch, "Religion Run Riot."

25. Atkins, *Modern Religious Cults and Movements*, 327.

26. Sinclair Lewis, *Main Street* (New York: Penguin Twentieth Century Classics, 1995), 79, 119, 278.

27. Braden, *These Also Believe*, 180.

28. Josephine Woodbury, *War in Heaven*, 3d ed. (Boston: Samuel Usher, 1897), 53; Josephine C. Woodbury, "The Book and The Woman," *Arena*, May 1899, 558.

29. "Modern Witchcraft," *Independent*, October 14, 1909, 888–90; Peabody, *A Complete Exposé of Eddyism*; Fred Lieb, *Sight Unseen* (New York: Harper, 1939); Braden, *These Also Believe*, 182; Woodbury, *War in Heaven*, 38; Martin Gardner, *The Healing Revelations of Mary Baker Eddy* (Buffalo: Prometheus, 1993).

30. The *McClure's* series was published as *The Life of Mary Baker G. Eddy and the History of Christian Science*, with Georgine Milmine cited as sole author: however, the most recent edition of the book credits it jointly to Cather and Milmine. The Christian Science Church would campaign equally vigorously against E. F. Dakin, *Mrs. Eddy — Biography of a Virginal Mind* (New York: Scribner's, 1929).

31. Gilbert V. Seldes, *The Stammering Century* (New York: John Day, 1928), 387; Atkins, *Modern Religious Cults and Movements*, 171; Twain, *Christian Science*, 23, 67. The "official publication" involved Bliss Knapp, *The*

*Destiny of the Mother Church*: (Christian Science Publication Society, 1991). Controversy was all the more fierce because publication of the Knapp book was required if the church was not to lose a multimillion dollar bequest.

32. Woodbury, "The Book and The Woman," 550–70; the quote is from 570. *Arena* had recently acquired as associate editor Horatio W. Dresser, author of *A History of the New Thought Movement* (New York: T. Y. Crowell, 1919). For other attacks on Eddy from this period, see "Modern Witchcraft"; Gillian Gill, *Mary Baker Eddy* (Reading, MA: Perseus, 1998), 471–80.

33. The reference to "hunger for power" is from Twain, *Christian Science*, 210; ibid., 83 for the "other papacy," and ibid., 211 for "Satanic considerations." H. L. Mencken, "Hooey From the Orient," in *A Mencken Chrestomathy* (New York: Knopf, 1962), 355–57.

34. Binder, *Modern Religious Cults and Society*, 77.

35. H. L. Mencken, "Christian Science," in *A Mencken Chrestomathy*, 343–46.

36. "Hunt for Happiness," 60; Gary L. Ward, ed., *Christian Science: Controversial and Polemical Pamphlets* (New York: Garland, 1990).

37. The attack of the San Diego clergy on Theosophy is from Emmett A. Greenwalt, *The Point Loma Community in California* (Berkeley: Univ. of California Press, 1955), 52–56. The San Francisco reference is from Woodbury, *War in Heaven*, 32. I. M. Haldeman, "Theosophy or Christianity," and other pamphlets reprinted in Aidan A. Kelly, ed., *Theosophy 2* (New York: Garland, 1990).

38. Barrington, *Anti-Christian Cults*, 82. Annie Besant, *Is Theosophy Anti-Christian?* (Chicago: Rajput Press, 1904), 16.

39. "Hunt for Happiness."

40. Sinclair Lewis, *Elmer Gantry* (New York: Signet Classic, 1980), 222–24.

41. Ferguson, *The Confusion of Tongues*, 64–65; Jerry Bergman, ed., *Jehovah's Witnesses II: Controversial and Polemical Pamphlets* (New York: Garland, 1990); M. James Penton, *Apocalypse Delayed* (Toronto: Univ. of Toronto Press, 1985). Conkin, *American Originals*.

42. Walter Martin, *The Kingdom of the Cults* (1965; Minneapolis: Bethany House, 1992), 39–40.

43. Philip Jenkins, "Spy Mad," *Pennsylvania History* 63 (1996): 204–31.

44. Greenwalt, *The Point Loma Community in California*.

45. Ferguson, *Confusion of Tongues*, 365.

46. Vinson Synan, *The Holiness-Pentecostal Tradition*, 2d ed. (Grand Rapids, MI: W. B. Eerdmans, 1997); Conkin, *American Originals*.

47. The reference to "numberless creeds" is from *LAT*, April 18, 1906; the British criticism is quoted from Grant Wacker, "Travail of a Broken Family," *Journal of Ecclesiastical History* 47 (1996): 511.

48. Grant Wacker, "Hell-Hatched Free Lovism," *Christian History* 58 (1998): 28–30.

49. *LAT*, April 18, 1906.

50. Quoted in David D. Daniels, "They Had a Dream," *Christian History* 58

(1998): 19; James R. Goff, *Fields White Unto Harvest* (Fayetteville: Univ. of Arkansas Press, 1989).

51. Wacker, "Travail of a Broken Family," 514–15.

52. Edith Blumhofer, *Restoring the Faith* (Urbana: Univ. of Illinois Press, 1993).

53. Binder, *Modern Religious Cults and Society*; Carey McWilliams, "Cults of California," *Atlantic*, March 1946, 108; Ferguson, *The Confusion of Tongues*, 394–413; Daniel M. Epstein, *Sister Aimee* (New York: Harcourt Brace Jovanovich, 1993); Edith Blumhofer, *Aimee Semple McPherson* (Grand Rapids, MI: Eerdmans, 1993); "Sister Aimee" *CC*, October 11, 1944, 1159–60.

54. The linkage between Aimee and Point Loma is suggested by McWilliams, "Cults of California." Lewis, *Elmer Gantry*, 185, 210.

55. Quoted in Ted Olsen, "American Pentecost," *Christian History* 58 (1998): 16–17. For analogies between modern-day New Age and Pentecostal groups, see Phillip C. Lucas, "The New Age Movement and the Pentecostal/Charismatic Revival," in *Perspectives on the New Age*, ed. James R. Lewis and J. Gordon Melton (Albany: State Univ. of New York Press, 1992), 189–211.

56. Michael Barkun, *Religion and the Racist Right* (Chapel Hill: Univ. of North Carolina Press, 1994).

57. Lewis, *Elmer Gantry*, 208; though see David Edwin Harrell, *All Things Are Possible* (Bloomington: Indiana Univ. Press, 1975).


FOUR

1. J. Gordon Melton, "How New Is New?" in *The Future of New Religious Movements*, ed. David G. Bromley and Phillip E. Hammond (Macon, GA: Mercer Univ. Press, 1987), 46–56. Phillip C. Lucas suggests that the late-twentieth-century New Age differs fundamentally from its predecessors because "the movement's socio-political views and values, including its emphasis on individual freedom and self-empowerment, its willingness to innovate and experiment, and its acceptance of planetary, as opposed to an ethnocentric or national, perspective, all resonate with identifiable thematic currents in modern society." "The New Age Movement and the Pentecostal/Charismatic Revival," in *Perspectives on the New Age*, ed. James R. Lewis and J. Gordon Melton (Albany: State Univ. of New York Press, 1992), 189–211. To the contrary, I argue that all these characteristics are found in the New Age movements of the first half of the twentieth century and, indeed, the closing years of the nineteenth.

2. Robert L. Moore, "The Occult Connection?" in *The Occult in America*, ed. Howard Kerr and Charles L. Crow (Urbana: Univ. of Illinois Press, 1983).

3. For Buddhism, see Rick Fields, *How the Swans Came to the Lake* (Boulder, CO: Shambhala, 1981); Thomas A. Tweed, *The American Encounter with Buddhism, 1844–1912* (Bloomington: Indiana Univ. Press, 1992); Stephen R. Prothero, *The White Buddhist* (Bloomington: Indiana Univ. Press,

1996); Charles S. Prebish and Kenneth K. Tanaka, eds., *The Faces of Buddhism in America* (Berkeley: Univ. of California Press, 1998); Thomas A. Tweed and Stephen Prothero, eds., *Asian Religions in America* (New York: Oxford Univ. Press, 1999). For Theosophy, see *The Theosophical Movement, 1875–1950* (Los Angeles: Cunningham Press, 1951), 10; Robert S. Ellwood, *Alternative Altars* (Chicago: Univ. of Chicago Press, 1979); Robert S. Ellwood, "American Theosophical Synthesis," in Kerr and Crow, eds., *The Occult in America*, 111–34.

4. The quote about "the first heathen is from Charles W. Ferguson, *The Confusion of Tongues* (Garden City, NY: Doubleday, 1928), 300; Steven F. Walker, "Vivekananda and American Culture," in Kerr and Crow, eds., *The Occult in America*, 162–76; Richard Hughes Seager, *The World's Parliament of Religions* (Bloomington: Indiana Univ. Press, 1994); *Vedanta in Southern California* (Hollywood: Vedanta Press, 1956). Soyen Shaku, *Zen For Americans* (New York: Barnes and Noble, 1993), is a reprint of a series of lectures delivered by a Japanese Buddhist abbot visiting the United States in 1905–6.

5. Gaius Glenn Atkins, *Modern Religious Cults and Movements* (London: G. Allen and Unwin, 1923), 226; Catherine Wessinger, "The Vedanta Society and the Self-Realization Fellowship," in *America's Alternative Religions*, ed. Timothy Miller (Albany: State Univ. of New York Press, 1995), 173–90. For bogus swamis, see *LD*, January 15, 1898, 81.

6. Isabel Cooper-Oakley, *The Count of Saint-Germain* (1912; Blauvelt, NY: Rudolf Steiner Publications, 1970), 160. For Lytton's impact on German occultism, see Nicholas Goodrick-Clarke, *The Occult Roots of Nazism* (Wellingborough, UK: Aquarian Press, 1985).

7. Charles Piazzi Smyth, *Our Inheritance in the Great Pyramid* (London: A. Strahan, 1864).

8. Richard Ellis, *Imagining Atlantis* (New York: Knopf, 1998); William P. Phelon, *Our Story of Atlantis* (San Francisco: Hermetic Book Concern, 1903). Phelon's book was reprinted in 1937 under the full title of *Our Story of Atlantis: Written down for the Hermetic Brotherhood and the Future Rulers of America* (Quakertown, PA: Philosophical Publishing, 1937); Ignatius Donnelly, *Atlantis: The Antediluvian World* (New York: Harper, 1882).

9. Ronald Decker, Michael Dummett, and Thierry Depaulis, *A Wicked Pack of Cards* (New York: St. Martin's Press, 1997).

10. Massimo Introvigne, *Il Cappello del Mago* (Carnago, Italy: Sugarco, 1990); Ellic Howe, *The Magicians of the Golden Dawn* (London: Routledge Kegan Paul, 1972). Frances A. Yates, *The Rosicrucian Enlightenment* (London: Routledge Kegan Paul, 1972); Moore, "The Occult Connection?" 157. The first work to use "occultism" in this sense seems to be A. P. Sinnett's *The Occult World* (London: Trubner, 1881).

11. Manly Palmer Hall, *An Essay on the Fundamental Principles of Operative Occultism* (Los Angeles: Hall Publishing, 1926).

12. Manly Palmer Hall, *An Encyclopedic Outline of Masonic, Hermetic, Qabbalistic and Rosicrucian Symbolical Philosophy* (1928; Los Angeles: Phil-

osophical Research Society, 1959); Isidor Kalisch, ed., *Sepher Yezirah*, 8th ed. (1877; Ancient Mystical Order Rosae Crucis [AMORC], 1968).

13. Franz Hartmann, introduction to *Secret Symbols of the Rosicrucians*, also known as *Cosmology, or, Universal Science, Cabala, Alchemy, containing the mysteries of the universe regarding God* (Boston: Occult Publishing, 1888).

14. Manly P. Hall, *The Lost Keys of Freemasonry*, 4th ed. (New York: Macoy Publishing and Masonic Supply Co., 1931).

15. Hartmann, introduction to *Secret Symbols of the Rosicrucians*,

16. E. E. Slosson, "Revival of Witchcraft," *Independent*, July 9, 1921, 3–4.

17. By 1936, the number had again fallen to 28,000. Carl A. Wickland, *Thirty Years Among the Dead* (Los Angeles: National Psychological Institute, 1924).

18. Charles W. Ferguson, *Fifty Million Brothers* (New York: Farrar and Rinehart, 1937); Mark Carnes, *Secret Ritual and Manhood in Victorian America* (New Haven: Yale Univ. Press, 1989); Lynn Dumenil, *Freemasonry and American Culture, 1880–1930* (Princeton: Princeton Univ. Press, 1984); Albert Pike, *Morals and Dogma of the Ancient and Accepted Scottish Rite of Freemasonry* (Charleston: 1871); Albert Pike, *Lectures of the Arya* (1873; Louisville, KY: Standard Printing, 1930); Hargrave Jennings, *The Rosicrucians*, 3d ed. (London: John C. Nimmo, 1887).

19. Joel Carpenter, *Revive Us Again* (New York: Oxford Univ. Press, 1997), 102–5; Nesta H. Webster, *World Revolution* (London: Constable, 1921).

20. Emmett A. Greenwalt, *The Point Loma Community in California* (Berkeley: Univ. of California Press, 1955); J. Gordon Melton, "The Theosophical Communities," in *America's Communal Utopias*, ed. Donald E. Pitzer (Chapel Hill: Univ. of North Carolina Press, 1997), 375–95; Peter Washington, *Madame Blavatsky's Baboon* (New York: Schocken Books, 1995), 111; Carey McWilliams, "Cults of California," *Atlantic*, March 1946, 105–10; Kevin Starr, *The Dream Endures* (New York: Oxford Univ. Press, 1997), 98–102; Nat Freedland, *The Occult Explosion* (New York: Berkley Medallion, 1972), 80; Aleister Crowley, *The Confessions of Aleister Crowley*, ed. John Symonds and Kenneth Grant (New York: Hill and Wang, 1970), 847.

21. The remark about "It was through Point Loma," is from McWilliams, "Cults of California," 106. There is an excellent survey of the southern California religious fringe in Carey McWilliams, *Southern California Country* (New York: Duell Sloan Pearce, 1946), 249–73. Alice Bailey, *Letters on Occult Meditation*, 2d ed. (New York: Lucis, 1926); Alice Bailey, *The Reappearance of the Christ* (New York: Lucis, 1948).

22. John P. Deveney, *Paschal Beverly Randolph* (Albany: State Univ. of New York Press, 1997). For the nineteenth-century tradition, see Hartmann, *Secret Symbols of the Rosicrucians;* J. Gordon Melton, ed., *Rosicrucianism in America* (New York: Garland, 1990).

23. For the twentieth-century revivalists, see H. Spencer Lewis, *The Ancient and Mystical Order Rosae Crucis in the United States of America* (American Supreme Council, Ancient and Mystical Order Rosae Crucis, 1915);

*The Rose Cross College* (Quakertown, PA: Rosicrucian Foundation, 1917); R. Swinburne Clymer, *The Rosicrucians in America* (Quakertown, PA: Rosicrucian Foundation, 1934); Rosicrucians Foundation, *The Order Militia Crucifera Evangelica* (Quakertown, PA: Rosicrucian Foundation, 1935).

24. H. Spencer Lewis, *The Symbolic Prophecy of the Great Pyramid* (San Jose, CA: Supreme Grand Lodge of AMORC, 1936); Phelon, *Our Story of Atlantis*; Max Heindel, *Rosicrucian Christianity* (Oceanside, CA: Rosicrucian Fellowship, 1909–1910); Max Heindel, *The Rosicrucian Cosmo-Conception; or, Mystic Christianity* (Oceanside, CA: Rosicrucian Fellowship, 1911); Max Heindel, *Teachings of an Initiate* (Oceanside, CA: Rosicrucian Fellowship, 1927).

25. The quote about Evangeline Adams is from Melton, "How New Is New?" 50. Paul Foster Case, *An Introduction to the Study of the Tarot* (New York: Azoth, 1920); Paul Foster Case, *The True and Invisible Rosicrucian Order*, 3d ed. (San Marino, CA: 1933); Baird T. Spalding, *Life and Teaching of the Masters of the Far East*, 5 vols. (Santa Monica, CA: DeVorss, 1935–64).

26. Jessie L. Weston, *From Ritual to Romance* (Cambridge: Cambridge Univ. Press, 1920).

27. Rudolf Steiner, *The Submerged Continents of Atlantis and Lemuria* (Chicago: Rajput Press, 1911); Wishar S. Cerve, *Lemuria: The Lost Continent of the Pacific* (San Jose, CA: Rosicrucian Press, AMORC College, 1935); Lewis Spence, *The Problem of Lemuria* (London: Rider, 1932). The quotation about the Garden of Eden is from James Churchward, *The Lost Continent of Mu* (New York: Ives Washburn, 1931); the quote about "treading the same road" is from Churchward, *Cosmic Forces as They Were Taught in Mu* (New York: Ives Washburn, 1934), 21. The Lemurian Fellowship is described in *The Theosophical Movement, 1875–1950* (Los Angeles: Cunningham Press, 1951), 307.

28. Hall, *Encyclopedic Outline.*

29. Harriette A. Curtiss and F. Homer Curtiss, *The Key of Destiny* (1923; Washington, DC: Curtiss Philosophic Book Co., 1933), 190–91, 203.

30. The quotation about "the philosophy of Christian psychology" is from an advertisement in the endpapers of Curtiss and Curtiss, *The Key of Destiny.* The quote about Jesus as avatar is from Harriette A. Curtiss and F. Homer Curtiss, *Letters from the Teacher*, Vol. 2 (Washington, DC: Curtiss Philosophic Book Co., 1924), 212. See also F. Homer Curtiss, *Letters from the Teacher (of the Order of the 15.) Transmitted by Rahmea, Priestess of the Flame* (Denver: Curtiss Book Co., 1909). The following books are all by Harriette A. Curtiss and F. Homer Curtiss: *The Voice of Isis* (Los Angeles: Curtiss Book Co., 1912); *Realms of the Living Dead* (Philadelphia: Curtiss Philosophic Book Co., 1917); *The Key to the Universe* (New York: E. J. Clode, 1917); *The Temple of Silence* (San Francisco: Curtiss Philosophic Book Co., 1920); *The Message of Aquaria*, 2d ed. (San Francisco: Curtiss Philosophic Book Co., 1923).

31. Curtiss and Curtiss, *The Key of Destiny*, 168–211; the "very powerful number" is from 168.

32. For Newbrough, see Lee Priestley, *Shalam* (El Paso: Texas Western Press, 1988).

33. Alice Bailey, *Discipleship in the New Age* (New York: Lucis, 1944); Paul Foster Case, *The Great Seal of the United States: Its History, Symbolism, and Message for the New Age* (Santa Barbara, CA: J. F. Rowny, 1935); Corinne Heline, *The New Age Bible Interpretation* (Los Angeles: New Age Press, 1938).

34. Leon Landsberg, quoted in Steven F. Walker, "Vivekananda and American Culture," 165.

35. T. Swann Harding, "Adele and the Swami, and I," *Nation*, June 22, 1927, 693–94. For the seasonal migration of the swamis, see Ferguson, *The Confusion of Tongues*, 3, 297–320.

36. Kevin Starr, *Material Dreams* (New York: Oxford Univ. Press, 1990), 135–6; Gregory H. Singleton, *Religion in the City of Angels* (Ann Arbor, MI: UMI Research Press, 1978); Tamar Frankiel, *California's Spiritual Frontiers* (Berkeley: Univ. of California Press, 1988); Robert V. Hine, *California's Utopian Colonies* (New Haven: Yale Univ. Press, 1953).

37. Frederick S. Miller, *Fighting Modern Evils That Destroy Our Homes* (Chicago: 1913), 219–20.

38. McWilliams, "Cults of California," 107.

39. Stephen Fox, "Alternative Spiritual Communities," in *Religion in Modern New Mexico*, ed. Ferenc M. Szasz and Richard W. Etulain (Albuquerque: Univ. of New Mexico Press, 1997); Frank Ryan, *The Forgotten Plague* (Boston: Little, Brown, 1993); Barbara Bates, *Bargaining for Life* (Philadelphia: Univ. of Pennsylvania Press, 1992); Arrell M. Gibson, *The Santa Fe and Taos Colonies* (Norman: Univ. of Oklahoma Press, 1983); Chris Wilson, *The Myth of Santa Fe* (Albuquerque: Univ. of New Mexico Press 1997).

40. These data are all drawn from the important discussion in Rodney Stark and William S. Bainbridge, *The Future of Religion* (Berkeley: Univ. of California Press, 1986), 234–62.

41. Quoted in Starr, *Material Dreams*, 135–36. See Miller, *Fighting Modern Evils That Destroy Our Homes*, 224, for the Mazdaznan movement.

42. H. L. Mencken, *A Mencken Chrestomathy* (New York: Knopf, 1962), 291.

43. The passage about "the hills of Krotona" is from Jane Levington Comfort, *From These Beginnings* (New York: Dutton, 1937); "Courses were given . . ." is from McWilliams, "Cults of California," 107; for the Krotona group's vegetarian cookbook, see James R. Lewis, ed. *Theosophy I* (New York: Garland, 1990), 65–126.

44. Sidney Kirkpatrick, *A Cast of Killers* (New York: Dutton, 1986).

45. Quoted in Gerald B. Bryan, *Psychic Dictatorship in America* (Los Angeles: Truth Research Publications, 1940), 129–30.

46. Louis R. Binder, *Modern Religious Cults and Society* (Boston: R. G. Badger, 1933), 62.

47. Nathanael West, *Day of the Locust* (New York: New Directions, 1969), 142; for the Agasha Temple of Wisdom, see William Eisen, *Agasha, Master of Wisdom* (Marina del Rey, CA: DeVorss, 1977).

48. Ferguson, *The Confusion of Tongues*, 312–20; Catherine Wessinger, "The Vedanta Society and the Self-Realization Fellowship," in Miller, ed., *America's Alternative Religions*; "Way of Cults," *Newsweek*, May 7, 1956, 102–3; Eugene D. Fleming, "California Cults and Crackpots," *Cosmopolitan*, May 1959, 80–84. For the Ramakrishna centers, see Wendell M. Thomas, *Hinduism Invades America* (New York: Beacon, 1930), 287.

49. Betty Lewis, *Holy City* (Santa Cruz, CA: Otter B. Books, 1994).

50. McWilliams, "Cults of California," 105–10; R. DeWitt Miller, "Southern California Riddle," *American Mercury*, May 1956, 99–102; Fleming, "California Cults and Crackpots." The quote about "hothouse of cockeyed sectarianism" is from "Mighty I AM," *Time*, February 28, 1938, 32. The remark about the Sinclair campaign is from Kevin Starr, *Endangered Dreams* (New York: Oxford Univ. Press, 1996), 137–38.

51. John Gunther, *Inside USA*, rev. ed. (New York: Harper, 1951), 62–63.

52. Frank B. Robinson, "In Defense of Psychiana," *American Mercury*, 52 (1941): 505–6; Frank B. Robinson, *Life Story of Frank B. Robinson* (Moscow, ID: Review Publishing, 1934); Frank B. Robinson, *Gems of Spiritual Truth*, rev. ed. (Moscow, ID: Psychiana, 1947); Frank B. Robinson, *The Strange Autobiography of Frank B. Robinson, Founder of Psychiana*, rev. ed. (Moscow, ID: Psychiana, 1949); Marcus Bach, "The Life and Death of Psychiana," *CC*, January 1957, 11–14.

53. Charles S. Braden, *These Also Believe* (1949; New York: Macmillan, 1963); Marcus Bach, *Strange Sects and Curious Cults* (New York: Dodd, Mead 1961), 154–75.

54. Robinson, "In Defense of Psychiana"; Rich Roesler, "Mail Order Religion: Moscow, Idaho, once was home to a booming religion known as Psychiana," *Spokane Spokesman Review*, September 3, 1996; "Mail Order Faith Enjoys Revival," *Idaho Statesman* (Boise) September 17, 1996.

55. F. S. Mead, "Lunatic Definition of Religion: Rapid Expansion of Crackpot Religions," *American Mercury*, February 1941, 167–75; J. Kobler, "Shepherd of Moscow, Idaho," *Colliers* 111, February 20, 1943, 46+.

56. William Dudley Pelley, *The Greater Glory* (New York: A. L. Burt, 1919); William Dudley Pelley, *"Seven Minutes in Eternity," with Their Aftermath* (New York: Robert Collier, 1929); William Dudley Pelley, *The Door to Revelation: An Autobiography* (Asheville, NC: Pelley Publishers, 1939); William Dudley Pelley, *The Golden Scripts* (Indianapolis: Fellowship Press, 1941); William Dudley Pelley, *Earth Comes: Design for Materialization* (Indianapolis: Fellowship Press, 1941); Donnell Byerly Portzline, "William Dudley Pelley and the Silver Shirt Legion of America" (Ed. D. diss., Ball State Univ., 1966); John McIntyre Werly, "The Millenarian Right: William Dudley Pelley and the Silver Legion of America" (Ph. D. diss., Syracuse Univ., 1972); Leo P. Ribuffo, *The Old Christian Right* (Philadelphia: Temple Univ. Press, 1983); Michael Barkun, *Religion and the Racist Right* (Chapel Hill: Univ. of North Carolina Press, 1994).

57. William Seabrook, *Witchcraft: Its Power in the World Today* (New York: Harcourt, Brace, 1940); Arthur H. Fauset, *Black Gods of the Metropolis* (Philadelphia: Univ. of Pennsylvania Press, 1944), 56.

58. The "great Christian Army" is quoted in Ferguson, *Fifty Million Brothers*, 113.
59. Eckard V. Toy, "Silver Shirts in the Northwest," *Pacific Northwest Quarterly* 80 (1989): 139–46.
60. Godfre Ray King, *Ascended Master Light* (Chicago: Saint Germain Press, 1938); Godfre Ray King, *Unveiled Mysteries* (Chicago: Saint Germain Press, 1939). The following account draws heavily on Bryan, *Psychic Dictatorship in America*; "Mighty I AM"; H. G. McGaughey, "Another One in Los Angeles," *CC*, August 31, 1938, 1039.
61. McGaughey, "Another One in Los Angeles"; "Mighty I AM."
62. This account of sources is based on Bryan, *Psychic Dictatorship in America*, 106–16, which lists the following works: Will L. Garver, *Brother of the Third Degree* (1894); Frederick S. Oliver, *A dweller on two planets, or, The dividing of the way, by Phylos, the Thibetan* (1905); Maude Lesseur Howard, *Myriam and the Mystic Brotherhood* (1915); Marie Corelli, *The Secret Power* (1921); Lillian E. Roy, *The Prince of Atlantis* (1929); Spalding, *Life and Teaching of the Masters of the Far East*.
63. Bryan, *Psychic Dictatorship in America*, 134.
64. Quoted in Mead, "Lunatic Definition of Religion," 171.
65. Bryan, *Psychic Dictatorship in America*, 19.
66. Fred Lieb, *Sight Unseen* (New York: Harper, 1939), 63. For the distribution of I AM centers, see "Mighty I AM."
67. McWilliams, "Cults of California," 105–10.

## FIVE

1. Elmer T. Clark, *The Small Sects in America* (New York: Abingdon, 1949), 125.
2. Arthur H. Fauset, *Black Gods of the Metropolis* (Philadelphia: Univ. of Pennsylvania Press, 1944); Raymond Julius Jones, *A Comparative Study of Religious Cult Behavior Among Negroes* (Washington, DC: Howard University, 1939). Larry Murphy, J. Gordon Melton, and Gary L. Ward, eds., *Encyclopedia of African American Religions* (New York: Garland, 1993).
3. Wilson J. Moses, *Black Messiahs and Uncle Toms*, rev. ed. (University Park, PA: Penn State Press, 1993), 123–41; Joseph R. Washington, *Black Sects and Cults* (Garden City, NY: Doubleday, 1972).
4. Claude McKay, "There Goes God: The Story of Father Divine and His Angels," *Nation*, February 6, 1935, 151–53; Ira Reid, "Let Us Prey," *Opportunity* 4 (1926): 274–78.
5. John P. Nugent, *White Night* (New York: Rawson, Wade, 1979), 13; Sara Harris, *Father Divine, Holy Husband* (Garden City, NY: Doubleday, 1953); Kenneth E. Burnham, *God Comes to America* (Boston: Lambeth Press, 1979); Robert Weisbrot, *Father Divine and the Struggle for Racial Equality* (Urbana: Univ. of Illinois Press, 1983); Jill Watts, *God, Harlem USA* (Berkeley: Univ. of California Press, 1992).
6. The quote about Sayville is from McKay, "There Goes God," 151. L. Levick, "Father Divine Is God" *Forum*, October 1934, 217–21; R. A.

Parker, *The Incredible Messiah* (Boston: Little Brown, 1937); S. McKedway and A. J. Liebling, *God in a Rolls-Royce* (New York: Hillman-Curl, 1936).

7. Marcus Bach, *They Have Found a Faith* (Indianapolis: Bobbs-Merrill, 1946), 162–88; Charles S. Braden, *These Also Believe* (1949; New York: Macmillan, 1963), 12; the remark about the Father's statistical mood is from F. S. Mead, "Lunatic Definition of Religion: Rapid Expansion of Crackpot Religions," *American Mercury*, February 1941, 167.

8. Hadley Cantril and Muzafer Sherif, "The Kingdom of Father Divine," *JAP* 33 (1938): 163.

9. Sinclair Lewis, *It Can't Happen Here* (New York: New American Library, 1970), 47.

10. Marcus Bach, *Strange Sects and Curious Cults* (New York: Dodd, Mead 1961), 126.

11. Both quotes are from Fauset, *Black Gods of the Metropolis*, 56, 59.

12. Braden, *These Also Believe*.

13. This account is based on Fauset, *Black Gods of the Metropolis*, 22–30; Elmer T. Clark, *The Small Sects in America* (New York: Abingdon, 1949), 122–24.

14. Fauset, *Black Gods of the Metropolis*, 112.

15. Douglas Frantz and Brett Pulley, "Harlem Church Is Outpost of Empire," *NYT*, December 17, 1995.

16. Fauset, *Black Gods of the Metropolis*, 115.

17. Elly M. Wynia, *The Church of God and Saints of Christ* (New York: Garland, 1994); Clark, *The Small Sects in America*, 120–22, 151; Fauset, *Black Gods of the Metropolis*, 31–40; Mead, "Lunatic Definition of Religion," 167–75.

18. The Black Jews of Harlem were founded by J. Arnold Ford, who is not to be confused with the Muslim prophet, Wallace Fard: Howard Brotz, *The Black Jews of Harlem* (New York: Schocken, 1970); Moses, *Black Messiahs and Uncle Toms*, 186–87.

19. Fauset, *Black Gods of the Metropolis*, 41–51; Robert A. Hill, ed., *The FBI's RACON* (Boston: Northeastern Univ. Press, 1995), 536.

20. Charles W. Ferguson, *Fifty Million Brothers* (New York: Farrar and Rinehart, 1937), 33–34, 189–202; William Muraskin, *Middle Class Blacks in a White Society* (Berkeley: Univ. of California Press, 1975); William H. Grimshaw, *Official History of Freemasonry Among the Colored People in North America* (New York: Negro Univ. Press, 1969).

21. Wynia, *The Church of God and Saints of Christ*, 15.

22. Hill, ed., *The FBI's RACON*, 92, 535.

23. Louis R. Binder, *Modern Religious Cults and Society* (Boston: R. G. Badger, 1933), 61.

24. Hill, ed., *The FBI's RACON*, 88–93, 538–40, 545–47; Claude Andrew Clegg, *An Original Man* (New York: St. Martin's Press, 1997).

25. This account is based on Erdmann D. Beynon, "The Voodoo Cult Among Negro Migrants in Detroit," *American Journal of Sociology* 43 (1937–38): 894–907. The quote is from 900.

26. Quoted in C. Eric Lincoln, *The Black Muslims in America*, 3d ed. (Grand Rapids, MI: Eerdmans, 1994), 70.

27. This account is based on Clegg, *An Original Man*. Martha F. Lee, *The Nation of Islam* (Lewiston, NY: E. Mellen Press, 1988).

28. William Seabrook, *Adventures in Arabia* (1927; New York: Blue Ribbon, 1930), 203.

29. Kathleen M. O'Connor, "The Islamic Jesus," *Journal of the American Academy of Religion* 66 (1998): 493–532; Malise Ruthven, *Islam in the World* (London: Penguin, 1991), 203–26.

30. Beynon, "The Voodoo Cult Among Negro Migrants in Detroit," 899, 903; Clegg, *An Original Man*, 30–36.

31. Quoted in Clegg, *An Original Man*, 33, 37.

32. Beynon, "The Voodoo Cult Among Negro Migrants in Detroit."

33. Fauset, *Black Gods of the Metropolis*, 104.

34. Alfred Métraux, *Voodoo* (London: Sphere, 1974); Joseph M. Murphy, *Working the Spirit* (Boston: Beacon, 1994).

35. Marvin Dana, "Voodooism," *Metropolitan Magazine* 29 (1908), 536–37; Sir Spenser St. John, *Hayti; or, The Black Republic* (1884; London: F. Cass, 1971). J. Austin, "Worship of the Snake: Voodooism in Haiti Today," *New England Magazine*, 12, June 1914, 170–82. Bach, *Strange Sects and Curious Cults*, 71.

36. Richard A. Loederer, *Voodoo Fire in Haiti* (New York: Literary Guild, 1935), 16–19.

37. William Seabrook, *The Magic Island* (New York: Harcourt, Brace, 1929); the quote is from William Seabrook, *No Hiding Place* (Philadelphia: Lippincott, 1942), 368. Though Seabrook's account of Haiti was widely criticized as fictitious, it received some confirmation from Zora Neale Hurston's 1938 book, *Tell My Horse: Voodoo and Life in Haiti and Jamaica* (New York: Perennial Library, 1990). For examples of the more outrageous sexual imagery in accounts of voodoo, see Rosita Forbes, "Priestess of the Impossible," *Country Life*, September 1935, 51–52.

38. Faustin Wirkus and Taney Dudley, *The White King of La Gonave* (Garden City, NY: Doubleday, Doran, 1931); Faustin Wirkus and H. W. Lanier, "Black Pope of Voodoo," *Harpers*, December 1933/January 1934, 38–49, 188–98; Seabrook, *The Magic Island*, 171–84.

39. L. Saxon, "Voodoo," *New Republic*, March 23, 1927, 135–39; Joseph J. Williams, *Voodoos and Obeahs* (New York: Dial Press, 1933); Joseph J. Williams, *Psychic Phenomena of Jamaica* (New York: Dial Press, 1934); J. L. Maddox, "Modern Voodooism," *Hygeia*, February–March 1934, 153–56 and 252–55; John Houston Craige, *Cannibal Cousins* (New York: Minton, Balch, 1934); H. P. Davis, "Sunlight on Voodoo Mysteries," *Travel*, May 1939, 34–37. Bryan Senn, *Drums of Terror: Voodoo in the Cinema* (Baltimore: Midnight Marquee Press, 1998).

40. "Cuban Authorities Battle Cult Practicing Kidnapping and Human Sacrifice" *LD*, January 2, 1937, 29.

41. "Only at dead of night" is from Loederer, *Voodoo Fire in Haiti*, 16–19, and ibid., 252–53 for the remark about zombies.

42. Lothrop Stoddard is quoted in Hans Schmidt, *The United States Occupation of Haiti, 1915–1934* (New Brunswick, NJ: Rutgers Univ. Press, 1995), 142. The remark about the "African mentality" is quoted in Loederer, *Voodoo Fire in Haiti*, 15, 258; Marcus Bach, *Strange Altars* (Indianapolis: Bobbs-Merrill, 1952); Métraux, *Voodoo*.

43. Mary Alicia Owen, *Voodoo Tales, as told among the Negroes of the Southwest* (1893; New York: Negro Univ. Press, 1969). Rod Davis, *American Voudou* (Denton: University of North Texas Press, 1998).

44. Dana, "Voodooism," 529.

45. For the serial murder wave of the early twentieth century, see Philip Jenkins, *Using Murder* (Hawthorne, NY: Aldine De Gruyter, 1994), 35.

46. Newbell Niles Puckett, *Folk Beliefs of the Southern Negro* (1926; New York: Dover, 1969), 167–310; the quote is at 190–91. Robert Tallant, *Voodoo in New Orleans* (New York: Macmillan, 1946); Robert Tallant, *The Voodoo Queen* (New York: Putnam, 1956); Zora Neale Hurston, *Mules and Men* (1935; New York: Perennial Library, 1990). Jason Berry, *The Spirit of Black Hawk* (Jackson: Univ. Press of Mississippi, 1995); David C. Estes, "Ritual Validations of Clergywomen's Authority in the African-American Spiritual Churches of New Orleans," in *Women's Leadership in Marginal Religions*, ed. Catherine Wessinger (Urbana: Univ. of Illinois Press, 1993), 149–71; Davis, *American Voudou*.

47. Hurston, *Mules and Men*, 183–85, 191–211; Zora Neale Hurston, "Hoodoo in America," *JAF* 44 (1931): 317–417.

48. M. Lea, "Two Head Doctors," *American Mercury* October 1927, 236–40.

49. E. Granberry, "Black Jupiter: A Voodoo King in Florida's Jungle," *Travel*, April 1932, 32–35.

50. Williams, *Voodoos and Obeahs*.

51. "Cuban Authorities Battle Cult Practicing Kidnapping and Human Sacrifice"; William Seabrook, *Witchcraft: Its Power in the World Today* (New York: Harcourt, Brace, 1940), 306.

52. Cornell Woolrich, "Music from the Big Dark," in *Cults!* ed. Charles G. Waugh and Martin H. Greenberg (New York: Barnes and Noble, 1983), 146–47, 162.

SIX

1. The magicians' campaign has obvious echoes in recent years in the debunking efforts of sceptics like the Amazing Randi. See Carl Sagan, *The Demon-Haunted World* (New York: Ballantine, 1996).

2. Compare Charles Lefebure, *The Blood Cults* (New York: Ace, 1969).

3. Dashiell Hammett, *The Dain Curse* (New York: Knopf, 1929), 20; E. H. Smith, "Crooks of Ghostland," *Saturday Evening Post*, April 24, 1920; Thomas F. Coakley, *Spiritism: The Modern Satanism* (Chicago: Extention Press, 1920); Joseph McCabe, *The Fraud of Spiritualism* (Girard, KS: Haldeman-Julius, 1927); William Seabrook, *Witchcraft: Its Power in the World Today* (New York: Harcourt, Brace, 1940), 369–79.

4. Harry Houdini, *A Magician Among the Spirits* (New York: Harper, 1924),

66–78; Bernard M. L. Ernst and Hereward Carrington, *Houdini and Conan Doyle* (New York: A. and C. Boni, 1932).

5. Julien J. Proskauer, *Spook Crooks!* (New York: A. L. Burt, 1932), 9; Joseph Dunninger, *Houdini's spirit exposes from Houdini's own manuscripts, records and photographs* (New York: Experimenter Publishing, 1928).

6. Proskauer, *Spook Crooks!* 161–67.

7. Ibid., 115–30.

8. "afflicted by its healers" is from Morris Fishbein, *The New Medical Follies* (New York: Boni and Liveright, 1927), 13; the other examples cited are from ibid., 25–26. H. L. Mencken, *A Mencken Chrestomathy* (New York: Knopf, 1962), 346–50.

9. F. S. Mead, "Lunatic Definition of Religion: Rapid Expansion of Crackpot Religions," *American Mercury*, February 1941, 167–75; "Way of Cults," *Newsweek*, May 7, 1956, 102–10.

10. Betty Lewis, *Holy City* (Santa Cruz, CA: Otter B. Books, 1994), 43.

11. Louis R. Binder, *Modern Religious Cults and Society* (Boston: R. G. Badger, 1933), 62.

12. Elmer T. Clark, *The Small Sects in America* (New York: Abingdon, 1949), 227–28.

13. Quoted in Carey McWilliams, "Cults of California," *Atlantic*, March 1946, 110. H. T. Dohrman, *California Cult* (Boston: Beacon Press, 1958), 2.

14. "Profit's Prophet," *Time*, May 21, 1945; Dohrman, *California Cult*, 50–53.

15. Jonathan Ned Katz, *Gay/Lesbian Almanac* (New York: Harper Colophon, 1983); 335; Philip Jenkins, *Moral Panic* (New Haven: Yale Univ. Press, 1998.)

16. Philip Hoare, *Oscar Wilde's Last Stand* (New York: Arcade, 1998).

17. The "Eve" reference is quoted in Catherine Wessinger, "The Vedanta Society and the Self-Realization Fellowship," in *America's Alternative Religions*, ed. Timothy Miller (Albany: State Univ. of New York Press, 1995), 185. "What has come over our women?" is from Frederick S. Miller, *Fighting Modern Evils That Destroy Our Homes* (Chicago: 1913), 215, 220.

18. Miller, *Fighting Modern Evils That Destroy Our Homes*, 200, 203.

19. The quote about the "fire-eyed Oriental" is from Miller, *Fighting Modern Evils That Destroy Our Homes*, 218; "the mother of the new messiah" is ibid., 224.

20. Seabrook, *Witchcraft*, 354–60.

21. Miller, ed., *America's Alternative Religions*, 278.

22. John Oliphant, *Brother Twelve* (Toronto: McClelland and Stewart, 1991).

23. Ibid., 153–54.

24. Cecilia Rasmussen, "Laying Bare the Nature of Nudism," *LAT*, July 12, 1998.

25. Hammett, *Dain Curse*, 122.

26. Ibid., 43–44.

27. Miller, *Fighting Modern Evils That Destroy Our Homes*, 222. The 1911 case of the disputed will is quoted in Catherine Wessinger, "The Vedanta Society and the Self-Realization Fellowship," 185.

28. The "academic observer" is Frederick M. Davenport, *Primitive Traits in Religious Revivals* (New York: Macmillan, 1905), 238: this book is also a major source for the central significance of hypnotism in religious movements. W. T. Root is quoted from his "The Psychology of Radicalism," *JAP* 19 (1924–25), 344. Theodore Schroeder, "Revivals, Sex and Holy Ghost," *JAP* 14 (1919–20), 34–47. Nicole Hahn Rafter, ed., *White Trash* (Boston: Northeastern Univ. Press, 1988).

29. Gary Silver, *The Dope Chronicles* (San Francisco: Harper and Row, 1979), 172–73. For a case study of insanity linked to spiritualism, see Edward E. Mayer, "A Case Illustrating So-called Demon Possession," *JAP* 6 (1911–12), 265–78.

30. Houdini, *A Magician Among the Spirits*, 181–82.

31. Gerald B. Bryan, *Psychic Dictatorship in America* (Los Angeles: Truth Research Publications, 1940), 191.

32. Louis R. Binder, *Modern Religious Cults and Society* (Boston: R. G. Badger, 1933), 58–60; Rodney Stark and William S. Bainbridge, *The Future of Religion* (Berkeley: Univ. of California Press, 1986), 173–77. Simon Stone, "The Miller Delusion: A Comparative Study of Mass Psychology," *American Journal of Psychiatry* 91 (1934): 593–623; Read Bain, "Sociology and Psychoanalysis," *ASR* 1, no. 2 (1936): 214; Hadley Cantril and Muzafer Sherif, "The Kingdom of Father Divine," *JAP*, 33 (1938): 147–67; "Snake Handling Cultists Resemble Other Groups," *Science News Letter*, August 17, 1940, 103. Stefan Zweig, *Mental Healers: Franz Anton Mesmer, Mary Baker Eddy, Sigmund Freud* (1932; New York: F. Ungar 1962). J. E. Hulett, Jr., "The Kenny Healing Cult," *ASR* 10, no. 3 (1945): 364–72.

33. Binder, *Modern Religious Cults and Society*, 109.

34. Claude Andrew Clegg, *An Original Man* (New York: St. Martin's Press, 1997), 96–97.

35. Carleton F. Brown, "The Long-Hidden Friend," *JAF* 17 (1904): 89–152; Helen R. Martin, *Sabina: A Story of the Amish* (New York: Century, 1905). The appearance of the *JAF* in 1888 indicates the growing interest in American folklore traditions at the end of the nineteenth century: Elizabeth C. Seip, "Witch-Finding in Western Maryland," *JAF* 14 (1901): 39–44.

36. A. Monroe Aurand, *An Account of the Witch Murder Trial* (Harrisburg, PA: Aurand Press, 1929); Arthur H. Lewis, *Hex* (New York: Trident, 1969). For contemporary periodical coverage, see D. Nichols, "Witches Win in York," *Nation*, January 23, 1929, 98–100; W. Hichens, "Waylaying the Witchdoctor," *Fortune*, January 31, 1929, 93–99; O. P. White, "Gobble'uns 'll Git You," *Colliers* 83, February 9, 1929, 8–9; "York County's Other Side," *LD*, May 4, 1929, 52–56; E. E. Slosson, "Revival of Witchcraft," *Colliers* 83, May 25, 1929, 48; M. Widdemer, "Goblins That Got Us," *Mentor*, September 1929, 38–41; T. Kenyon, "Witches Still Live," *North American*, November 1929, 620–26; "Witchcraft Disease," *LD*, May 27, 1930, 27; N. Hibschman, "Witches and Wills," *North American*, November 1930, 622–27. Before the York case, witch beliefs were regarded as

marking a culture as irredeemably primitive and superstitious: see "Witches Burned in Mexico" *LD*, March 29, 1919, 32.

37. "Witchcraft Murders," *LD*, January 5, 1929, 24–25; for Pennsylvania witchcraft, compare Raube Walters, *The Hex Woman* (New York: Macaulay, 1931); D. E. Starry, "Witchcraft in my Backyard," *Travel*, August 1943, 22–23+. For Seabrook, see Lewis, *Hex*, 116.

38. A. Monroe Aurand, *The Realness of Witchcraft in America* (Lancaster, PA: Aurand Press, n.d.)

39. A. Hamilton, "Witchcraft in West Polk Street," *American Mercury* January 1927, 71–75; John R. Crosby, "Modern Witches of Pennsylvania," *JAF* 40 (1927): 304–9; A. P. Hudson and P. K. McCarter, "The Bell Witch of Tennessee and Mississippi," *JAF* 47 (1934): 45–63; S. P. Bayard, "Witchcraft-Magic and Spirits on the Border of Pennsylvania and West Virginia," *JAF* 51 (1938): 47–59; Vance Randolph, *Ozark Superstitions* (New York: Columbia Univ. Press, 1947); J. R. Aswell, "Kate Was an Old Rip," *American Mercury*, August 1953, 49–54.

40. "Witchcraft Still Earning Millions," *LD*, October 31, 1936, 7; Seabrook, *Witchcraft*, 301.

41. "How Witches Weave Their Spells Today," *LD*, April 26, 1930, 41–42; Marc Simmons, *Witchcraft in the South West* (Lincoln: Univ. of Nebraska Press, 1980); "Broomless Bruja," *Time*, April 29, 1946, 28.

42. Margaret A. Murray, *The Witch Cult in Western Europe* (Oxford: Clarendon, 1962); Margaret A. Murray, *The God of the Witches* (Oxford: Clarendon, 1970).

43. Murray, *The Witch Cult*, 49, 253. The quote is from Charles W. Upham, *Lectures on Witchcraft* (Boston, 1832), 53. For the "delusion," see Samuel G. Drake, *The Witchcraft Delusion in New England* (Roxbury, MA: W. E. Woodward, 1866); John Metcalf Taylor, *The Witchcraft Delusion in Colonial Connecticut, 1647–1697* (New York: Grafton Press, 1908). Hawthorne's "Young Goodman Brown" could be read as describing a genuine witch cult, though the standard reading is that the story involves a fantasy or delusion.

44. For modern political parallels, see L. Price, "Witchcraft Then and Now," *Nation*, October 4, 1922, 331–33. R. Dann, "Salem Witchcraft Delusion," *Scholastic*, May 12, 1941, 12+; Marion L. Starkey, *The Devil in Massachusetts* (1949; Garden City, NY: Doubleday 1969).

45. "How Witches Weave Their Spells Today."

46. Herbert S. Gorman, *The Place Called Dagon* (New York: George H. Doran, 1927); see the discussion in H. P. Lovecraft, "Supernatural Horror in Literature," in *H. P. Lovecraft's Book of Horror*, ed. Stephen Jones and Dave Carson (New York: Barnes and Noble, 1993), 43.

47. "The Call of Cthulhu" was written in late 1926 and appeared in *Weird Tales* in 1928. Among the genuine esoteric sources cited by Lovecraft is W. Scott-Elliot, *The Story of Atlantis and The Lost Lemuria* (1925; London: Theosophical Publishing House, 1930.)

48. *The Case of Charles Dexter Ward* was written in 1927, though not pub-

lished in *Weird Tales* until 1941. "The Dreams in the Witch-House" appeared in *Weird Tales* in 1933.

49. Henry Kuttner, "The Graveyard Rats," reprinted in *Devils and Demons*, ed. Marvin Kaye (New York: Doubleday, 1987), 253.

50. Fred Lieb, *Sight Unseen* (New York: Harper, 1939), 165.

51. J.-K. Huysmans, *Down There* (New York: A and C. Boni, 1924); A. E. Waite, *Devil Worship in France* (London: G. Redway, 1896).

52. Seabury Quinn, "Satan's Stepson," *Weird Tales: 32 Unearthed Terrors*, ed. in Stefan R. Dziemianowicz, Robert Weinberg, and Martin H. Greenberg (New York: Bonanza, 1988), 115–60; E. Hoffmann Price, "The Stranger from Kurdistan," in *Devil Worshipers*, ed. Martin H. Greenberg and Charles G. Waugh (New York: DAW, 1990), 233–40.

53. Betty May, *Tiger Woman* (London: Duckworth, 1929).

54. Quoted in John Symonds, *The Great Beast* (London: Mayflower, 1973), 225–26.

55. For Crowley in New York, see William Seabrook, *Witchcraft*, 216–32; for Los Angeles, see Russell Miller, *Bare-Faced Messiah* (New York: Henry Holt, 1988), 113–30; Michael Staley, "Sorcerer of Apocalypse," in *Apocalypse Culture*, ed. Adam Parfrey (Portland, OR: Feral House, 1990), 172–92; Aleister Crowley, *The Confessions of Aleister Crowley*, ed. John Symonds and Kenneth Grant (New York: Hill and Wang, 1970), 844–49.

56. For the "houmfort," see Staley, "Sorcerer of Apocalypse," 179; Miller, *Bare-Faced Messiah*.

57. Symonds, *Great Beast*, 255; May, *Tiger Woman*.

58. Jules Michelet, *Satanism and Witchcraft* (New York: Walden, 1939). For the Yezidis, see Joseph Isya, *Devil Worship* (Boston: Richard G. Badger, 1919); William Seabrook, *Adventures in Arabia* (1927; New York: Blue Ribbon, 1930); Seabrook, *Witchcraft*; or Montague Summers, *Witchcraft and Black Magic* (New York: Rider, 1945). Elliott O'Donnell, *Strange Cults and Secret Societies of Modern London* (New York: E. P. Dutton, 1935).

59. Wheatley was not the only author exploring this territory: a child sacrifice is central to the Satanic ritual described in Charles Williams's 1930 novel *War in Heaven*, which has added significance given Williams's own background in the Order of the Golden Dawn.

60. Seabrook, *Witchcraft*, 82–88, at 83. William Seabrook, *No Hiding Place* (Philadelphia: Lippincott, 1942), 367–70. For the church in Toledo, David G. Bromley and Susan G. Ainsley, "Satanism and Satanic Churches," in Miller, ed., *America's Alternative Religions* 403–4; "Way of Cults," 102–10.

61. Ray A. Williamson, *Living the Sky* (Boston: Houghton Mifflin, 1984), 218–20. The Pawnee case was also popularized by a discussion in Frazer's *Golden Bough*. The extent of human sacrifice among North American Native cultures remains a controversial topic, but recent work suggests that both ritual sacrifice and cannibalism were common in some regions at particular times: see Christy G. Turner and Jacqueline A. Turner, *Man Corn: Cannibalism and Violence in the Prehistoric American Southwest* (Salt

Lake City: Univ. of Utah Press, 1999). The argument has also been convincingly made that the lynchings of African-American men in the early twentieth century fulfil all the classic definitions of human sacrifice: see Orlando Patterson, *Rituals of Blood* (Washington, DC: Civitas/Counter-Point, 1998).

62. Abraham G. Duker, "Twentieth Century Blood Libels in the United States," in *Rabbi Joseph H. Lookstein Memorial Volume*, ed. Leo Landman (New York: KTAV Publishing House, 1980), 85–109; Leonard Dinnerstein, *Anti-Semitism in America* (New York: Oxford Univ. Press, 1994).

63. "The Murdering Jews," in *The Canadian Nationalist* (Winnipeg: 1934); *Jewish Ritual Murder in San Diego* (London: Brown and Burrowes, 1933); Arnold S. Leese, *My Irrelevant Defence* (London: Imperial Fascist League, 1938), 53–54; Donald S. Strong, *Organized Anti-Semitism in America* (Washington, DC: American Council on Public Affairs, 1941); George J. Mintzer and Newman Levy, *The International Anti-Semitic Conspiracy* (New York: American Jewish Committee, 1946), 28.

64. "Nine Are Indicted in Cult Slaying," *NYT*, April 5, 1933; Elmer T. Clark, *The Small Sects in America* (New York: Abingdon, 1949), 98. Another oft-told tale concerning human sacrifice in backwoods communities involved the Oklahoma-based Sacred Followers, who supposedly tried to sacrifice a virgin to prevent the feared catastrophe associated with Halley's Comet on its appearance in 1910: see George Johnson, "Comets Breed Fear, Fascination, and Web Sites," *NYT*, March 28, 1997.

65. Steven Nickel, *Torso* (Winston-Salem, NC: John F. Blair, 1989), 154.

66. For the "Sabbat," see Owen F. McDonnell, "Bolber Tells of Starting Practice as Witch Doctor Here in 1931," *Philadelphia Inquirer*, August 5, 1939; Owen F. McDonnell, "Bolber Tells of Cures He Effected in Philadelphia With His Witchcraft," *Philadelphia Inquirer*, August 7, 1939. Other stories by McDonnell in this 1939 *Inquirer* series included "Witchcraft in Philadelphia Revealed by Bolber in Own Story of His Life," August 3; "Bolber Tells Story of his Witchcraft Knife," August 4; "Bolber Says Petrillo Lost $1000 By Trying to Be a Witch Doctor," August 8; "Bolber Tells of Ousting Ghost," August 9. See also Seabrook, *Witchcraft*, 21; George Cooper, *Poison Widows* (New York: St. Martin's Press, 1999).

67. May, *Tiger Woman*, 176; Crowley, *The Confessions of Aleister Crowley*, 364, 755.

68. Jenkins, *Using Murder*.

## SEVEN

1. Carey McWilliams, "Cults of California," *Atlantic*, March 1946, 108.

2. Fred Lieb, *Sight Unseen* (New York: Harper, 1939), 65–66.

3. Gerald B. Bryan, *Psychic Dictatorship in America* (Los Angeles: Truth Research Publications, 1940), 53–54.

4. Ibid., 187.

5. Ibid., 15.

6. McWilliams, "Cults of California," 109; John Gunther, *Inside USA*, rev. ed. (New York: Harper, 1951), 63.

7. Marcus Bach, *They Have Found a Faith* (Indianapolis: Bobbs-Merrill, 1946), 126 and 123–61 passim; Charles S. Braden, *These Also Believe* (1949; New York: Macmillan, 1963), 410; Herbert M. Wyrick, *Seven Religious Isms*, 1940, reprinted in *The Evangelical Christian Anti-Cult Movement*, ed. Aidan A. Kelly (New York: Garland, 1990), 55; Charles W. Ferguson, *The Confusion of Tongues* (Garden City, NY: Doubleday, 1928), 89–109.

8. Philip Jenkins, *Hoods and Shirts* (Chapel Hill: Univ. of North Carolina Press, 1997); House Special Committee on Un-American Activities, *Investigation of Un-American Activities in the United States: Hearings on H. Res. 282 (The Dies Committee)*, 75th Congress, 3rd sess./76th Congress 1st sess. (Washington, DC: Government Printing Office, 1940), 12: 7201–7333.

9. H. T. Dohrman, *California Cult* (Boston: Beacon Press, 1958), 43.

10. Betty Lewis, *Holy City* (Santa Cruz, CA: Otter B. Books, 1994).

11. J. Kobler, "Shepherd of Moscow, Idaho: Psychiana," *Colliers* 111, February 20, 1943, 46ff.

12. Claude Andrew Clegg, *An Original Man* (New York: St. Martin's Press 1997), 84–108.

13. United States v. Ballard, 322 U.S. 78 (1944); "Religious Liberty and Fraud," *CC*, May 10, 1944, 583–85, Braden, *These Also Believe*.

14. John L. Spivak, *Shrine of the Silver Dollar* (New York: Modern Age Books, 1940).

15. Jerry Bergman, ed., *Jehovah's Witnesses II: Controversial and Polemical Pamphlets* (New York: Garland, 1990). The *Reader's Digest* quote is from Walter R. Martin, *The Kingdom of the Cults* ( 1965; Minneapolis: Bethany House, 1992), 33.

16. The main cases in the Witnesses' struggle with the civil authorities are Lovell v. City of Griffin, GA, 303 U.S. 444 (1938); Cantwell v. State of Connecticut, 310 U.S. 296 (1940); Minersville School District Chaplinsky v. Gobitis, 310 U.S. 586 (1940); Chaplinsky v. State of New Hampshire, 315 U.S. 568 (1942). D. R. Manwaring, *Render Unto Caesar* (Chicago: Univ. of Chicago Press, 1962).

17. John T. Noonan, *The Lustre of Our Country* (Berkeley: Univ. of California Press, 1998).

18. Marcus Bach, *They Have Found a Faith* (Indianapolis: Bobbs-Merrill, 1946), 24; Martin E. Marty, *Modern American Religion III: Under God Indivisible* (Chicago: Univ. of Chicago Press, 1996), 217; Jerry Bergman, "The Adventist and Jehovah's Witness Branch of Protestantism," in *America's Alternative Religions*, ed. Timothy Miller (Albany: State Univ. of New York Press, 1995), 43; William Kaplan, *State and Salvation* (Toronto: Univ. of Toronto Press, 1989).

19. F. S. Mead, "Lunatic Definition of Religion: Rapid Expansion of Crackpot Religions," *American Mercury*, February 1941, 173.

20. These cases are West Virginia State Board of Education v. Barnette, 319 U.S. 624 (1943); Saia v. People of State of New York, 334 U.S. 558 (1948).

Martin E. Marty, *Modern American Religion II: The Noise of Conflict* (Chicago: Univ. of Chicago Press, 1991), 356.

21. Martha S. Bradley, *Kidnapped From That Land* (Salt Lake City: University of Utah Press, 1993), 86, for the Mormon rejection of "cultists." "Polygamist in Utah Gets Five Year Term," *NYT*, December 5, 1943; "Fifty Taken in Raids to End Polygamy," *NYT*, March 8, 1944; "Fundamentalist Polygamists," *Newsweek*, March 20, 1944, 86; "Fundamentalist," *Time*, March 20, 1944, 55.

22. The governor is quoted from Bradley, *Kidnapped From That Land*, ix. Gladwin Hill, "Arizona Raids Polygamous Cult: Seeks to Wipe Out Its Community," *NYT*, July 27, 1953; "Wider Polygamy Charged," *NYT*, July 29, 1953; "Cult Women Evacuated," *NYT*, August 2, 1953; "Big Raid," *Newsweek*, August 3, 1953; "Great Love-Nest Raid," *Time*, August 3, 1953, 16; "Lonely Men of Short Creek," *Life*, September 14, 1953, 35–39; J. Cary, "Untold Story of Short Creek," *American Mercury*, May 1953, 119–23.

23. The cartoon is reprinted in Bradley, *Kidnapped From That Land*. James Brooke, "Utah Struggles With a Revival of Polygamy," *NYT*, August 23, 1998; Timothy Egan, "The Persistence of Polygamy," *New York Times Magazine*, February 28, 1999, 51–53.

24. David L Kimbrough, *Taking Up Serpents* (Chapel Hill: Univ. of North Carolina Press, 1995); Dennis Covington, *Salvation on Sand Mountain* (Reading, MA: Addison Wesley, 1994); Thomas G. Burton, *Serpent-Handling Believers* (Knoxville: Univ. of Tennessee Press, 1993); Weston LaBarre, *They Shall Take Up Serpents* (Minneapolis: Univ. of Minnesota Press, 1962).

25. "Snake Defiers Jailed," *NYT*, August 1, 1940; "Snake-Bitten Child Remains Untreated," *NYT*, August 3, 1940; "Snake at Service Bites Three Cultists," *NYT*, August 6, 1940.

26. "Holiness Faith Healers: Virginia Mountaineers Handle Snakes to Prove Their Piety" *Life*, July 3, 1944, 59–62; "They Shall Take Up Serpents," *Newsweek*, August 21, 1944, 88–89; J. Kobler, "America's Strangest Religion" *Saturday Evening Post*, September 28, 1957; Deborah Vansau McCauley, *Appalachian Mountain Religion* (Urbana: Univ. of Illinois Press, 1995); "Snake Handling Cultists Resemble Other Groups" *Science News Letter*, August 17, 1940, 103; J. A. Womeldorf, "Rattlesnake Religion," *CC*, December 10, 1947, 1517–18; A. W. Taylor, "Snake Handling Cults Flourish," *CC*, October 29, 1947, 1308.

27. "This Hollow World: Koreshans," *Newsweek*, December 6, 1948, 26.

28. Wyrick, *Seven Religious Isms*, 51.

29. Charles S. Braden, "Why Are the Cults Growing?" *CC*, January 12–February 2, 1944; Charles S. Braden, "Learning From the Cults," *CC*, February 9, 1944, 169–70;.

30. Braden, *These Also Believe*, ix. Graham White and John Maze, *Henry A. Wallace* (Chapel Hill: Univ. of North Carolina Press, 1995), 271.

31. Fritz Leiber's *Conjure Wife* was first published in 1943 in magazine form; Fritz Leiber, *Conjure Wife* (Boston: Gregg Press, 1977).

32. August Derleth, "Night Train to Lost Valley," in *Devil Worshipers*, ed. Martin H. Greenberg and Charles G. Waugh (New York: DAW, 1990), 131–47.

33. Shirley Jackson was not arguing for the literal existence of such secret pagan cults, and she herself had no doubts about the standard liberal view of the Salem affair: she agreed that early witchcraft was a pure delusion. Shirley Jackson, *The Witchcraft of Salem Village* (New York: Random House, 1956).

34. Boucher's "Compleat Werewolf" is a favorite in horror anthologies: Greenberg and Waugh, eds., *Devil Worshipers*, 54–113.

35. *Magic Inc.* was originally published in *Unknown* in 1940, as "The Devil Makes the Law."

EIGHT

1. Marilyn Ferguson, *The Aquarian Conspiracy* (Los Angeles: J. P. Tarcher, 1980); William G. McLoughlin, *Revivals, Awakenings, and Reform* (Chicago: Univ. of Chicago Press, 1978); Harvey Cox, *Turning East* (New York: Simon and Schuster, 1977); John Godwin, *Occult America.* (Garden City, NY: Doubleday, 1972); Nat Freedland, *The Occult Explosion* (New York: Berkley Medallion, 1972); Daniel Logan, *America Bewitched* (New York: Morrow, 1974).

2. Wendell M. Thomas, *Hinduism Invades America* (New York: Beacon, 1930). Wouter J. Hanegraaff, *New Age Religion and Western Culture* (Albany: State Univ. of New York Press, 1997); Robert S. Ellwood, *The Fifties Spiritual Marketplace* (New Brunswick, NJ: Rutgers Univ. Press, 1997); Marcus Bach, "In the Church's Backyard," *CC*, January 8, 1958, 45–46; Richard Mathison, *Faiths, Cults, and Sects of America* (Indianapolis: Bobbs-Merrill, 1960); Martin E. Marty, *Modern American Religion III: Under God Indivisible* (Chicago: Univ. of Chicago Press, 1996); J. Gordon Melton, "How New Is New?" in *The Future of New Religious Movements*, ed. David G. Bromley and Phillip E. Hammond (Macon, GA: Mercer Univ. Press, 1987).

3. Roger Finke and Rodney Stark, *The Churching of America, 1776–1990* (New Brunswick, NJ: Rutgers Univ. Press, 1992), 239.

4. "Way of Cults," *Newsweek*, May 7, 1956, 102–10; William R. Catton, Jr., "What Kind of People Does a Religious Cult Attract?" *ASR* 22, no. 5 (1957): 561–66; Eugene D. Fleming, "California Cults and Crackpots," *Cosmopolitan*, May 1959, 80–84. The early 1950s witnessed an apparent upsurge of witchcraft-related media stories, but virtually all these were in fact related to the political witch-hunt of the day, in which Salem analogies were so commonly drawn.

5. H. T. Dohrman, *California Cult* (Boston: Beacon Press, 1958), 97; Fleming, "California Cults and Crackpots," for the number of cults in southern California. Several major studies of cults and fringe belief appeared in the 1950s, including Ralph Lord Roy, *Apostles of Discord* (Boston: Beacon

Press, 1953), and Leon Festinger, Henry W. Riecken, and Stanley Schacter *When Prophecy Fails* (Minneapolis: Univ. of Minnesota Press, 1956).

6. Morey Bernstein, *The Search for Bridey Murphy* (Garden City, NY: Doubleday, 1956). Milton V. Kline, ed. *A Scientific Report on The Search for Bridey Murphy* (New York, Julian Press, 1956).

7. William Dudley Pelley, *Why I Believe the Dead Are Alive*, 3d ed. (Noblesville, IN: Soulcraft Chapels, 1954); William Dudley Pelley, *The Golden Scripts* (Noblesville, IN: Fellowship Press, 1973).

8. David C. Lane, *The Making of a Spiritual Movement* (Del Mar, CA: Del Mar Press, 1983); Phillip C. Lucas, *The Odyssey of a New Religion* (Bloomington: Indiana University Press, 1995).

9. Claude Andrew Clegg, *An Original Man* (New York: St. Martin's Press, 1997), 125–27; "Black Supremacists," *Time*, August 10, 1959, 24–25; "Black Supremacy Cults in the United States: How Much of a Threat?" *U.S. News & World Report*, November 9, 1959, 112–14; Alex Haley, "Mr. Muhammad Speaks," *Readers Digest*, March 1960, 100–104; Nat Hentoff, "Elijah in the Wilderness: Temples of Islam," *Reporter*, August 4, 1960, 37–40; "Despair Serves Purposes of Bizarre Cults," *CC*, August 10, 1960, 917; Louis E. Lomax, *When the Word Is Given* (Cleveland: World, 1963); C. Eric Lincoln, *The Black Muslims in America*, 3d ed. (Grand Rapids, MI: Eerdmans, 1994), 103.

10. Leonard E. Barrett, *The Rastafarians*, rev. ed. (Boston: Beacon, 1988).

11. Michael Barkun, *Religion and the Racist Right* (Chapel Hill: Univ. of North Carolina Press, 1994); Leo P. Ribuffo, *The Old Christian Right* (Philadelphia: Temple Univ. Press, 1983); Roy, *Apostles of Discord*; Kenneth S. Stern, *A Force Upon the Plain* (New York: Simon and Schuster, 1996); Kevin Flynn and Gary Gerhardt, *The Silent Brotherhood* (New York: Signet, 1990).

12. Peter Washington, *Madame Blavatsky's Baboon* (New York: Schocken Books, 1995).

13. John G. Neihardt, *Black Elk Speaks* (New York: W. Morrow, 1932); Aldous Huxley, *The Doors of Perception* (New York: Harper & Row, 1990). John Symonds, *The Great Beast* (London: Mayflower, 1973). Crowley's *Diary of a Drug Fiend* appeared in an American edition (New York: Dutton, 1923). Huxley himself depicted the southern California mystical ambience in his 1939 novel, *After Many a Summer Dies the Swan* (New York: Harper Colophon, 1983).

14. Jay Kinney and Richard Smoley, "War on High," *Gnosis* (fall 1991): 32–37.

15. Stephen Fox, "Alternative Spiritual Communities," in *Religion in Modern New Mexico*, ed. Ferenc M. Szasz and Richard W. Etulain (Albuquerque: Univ. of New Mexico Press, 1997); Michael F. Brown, *The Channeling Zone* (Cambridge, MA: Harvard Univ. Press, 1997).

16. Thomas Sugrue, *Such Is the Kingdom* (New York: Henry Holt, 1940); Thomas Sugrue, *There Is a River* (New York: Henry Holt, 1956); Phillip C. Lucas, "The Association for Research and Enlightenment," in *America's Alternative Religions*, ed. Timothy Miller (Albany: State Univ. of New

York Press, 1995), 355; Michael York, *The Emerging Network* (Lanham, MD: Rowman and Littlefield, 1995); K. Paul Johnson, *Edgar Cayce in Context* (Albany: State Univ. of New York Press, 1998).

17. Richard M. Bucke, *Cosmic Consciousness* (Philadelphia: Innes, 1905).

18. Martin Gardner, *Urantia: The Great Cult Mystery* (Buffalo: Prometheus, 1992).

19. Frank Scully, *Behind the Flying Saucers* (New York: Holt, 1950); Donald E. Keyhoe, *The Flying Saucers Are Real* (New York: Fawcett, 1950); John Mack, *Abduction* (New York: Scribner's, 1994); C. D. B. Bryan, *Close Encounters of the Fourth Kind* (New York: Knopf, 1995); James R. Lewis, ed., *The Gods Have Landed* (Albany: State Univ. of New York Press, 1995).

20. Russell Miller, *Bare-Faced Messiah* (New York: Henry Holt, 1988); L. Ron Hubbard, *Dianetics* (New York: Hermitage House, 1950).

21. Jon Atack, *A Piece of Blue Sky* (New York: Carol Publishing 1990); Miller, *Bare-Faced Messiah*; Roy Wallis, *The Road to Total Freedom* (New York: Columbia Univ. Press, 1977); Paulette Cooper, *The Scandal of Scientology* (New York: Tower Publications, 1971).

22. Margot Adler, *Drawing Down the Moon*, 3d ed. (New York: Penguin/ Arkana, 1997); Ellen Evert Hopman and Lawrence Bond, *People of the Earth* (Rochester, VT: Destiny Books, 1996); James R. Lewis, ed., *Magical Religion and Modern Witchcraft* (Albany: State Univ. of New York Press, 1996), especially the chapter by James W. Baker, "White Witches," 171–92; York, *The Emerging Network*; Loretta Orion, *Never Again the Burning Times* (Prospect Heights, IL: Waveland Press, 1995); Aidan Kelly, *Crafting the Art of Magic* (St. Paul: Llewellyn, 1991); J. Gordon Melton, *Magic, Witchcraft, and Paganism in America* (New York: Garland, 1982); Susan Roberts, *Witches, USA* (New York: Dell, 1971); J. Kobler, "Out for a Night at the Local Cauldron: British Witches," *Saturday Evening Post*, November 5, 1966, 76–78.

23. S. Alexander, "Ping is the Thing—A LaVey's New Satanic Religion," *Life*, February 17, 1967, 31; Arthur Lyons, *Satan Wants You* (New York: Mysterious Press, 1988); Massimo Introvigne, *Il Cappello del Mago* (Carnago Italy: Sugarco, 1990).

24. Kenneth Grant, *The Magical Revival* (London: Muller, 1972).

25. Steven M. Tipton, *Getting Saved from the Sixties* (Berkeley: Univ. of California Press, 1982).

26. Alan Watts, "The Trickster Guru," in *The Essential Alan Watts* (Berkeley, CA: Celestial Arts, 1977), 4–5.

27. J. Gordon Melton, *Encyclopedia Handbook of Cults in America*, rev. ed. (New York: Garland, 1992).

28. Finke and Stark, *The Churching of America, 1776–1990*, 240. Teresa Watanabe, "Buddhism Flourishing in Southland," *LAT*, November 14, 1998.

29. Steven Pressman, *Outrageous Betrayal* (New York: St. Martin's Press, 1993); Tom Zito, "Lampooned Personality," *WP*, November 4, 1978. Analine M. Powers, *Silva Mind Control* (New York: Garland, 1992); Gini Graham Scott, *Cult and Countercult* (Westport, CT: Greenwood, 1980).

30. William S. Bainbridge, *Satan's Power* (Berkeley: Univ. of California Press, 1978).

31. Ronald M. Enroth, Edward E. Ericson, Jr., and C. Breckinridge Peters, *The Story of the Jesus People* (Exeter: Paternoster, 1972); Donald E. Miller, *Reinventing American Protestantism* (Berkeley: Univ. of California Press, 1997).

32. Robert L. Moore, *Religious Outsiders and the Making of Americans* (New York: Oxford Univ. Press, 1985), 121–127.

33. Flo Conway and Jim Siegelman, *Snapping*, 2d ed. (New York: Stillpoint Press, 1995). Barbara Underwood and Betty Underwood, *Hostage to Heaven* (New York: Clarkson Potter, 1979), 283; *The Cult Awareness Network* (Los Angeles: *Freedom Magazine*, 1995); Margaret Thaler Singer and Janja Lalich, *Cults in Our Midst* (San Francisco: Jossey-Bass, 1995), 12.

34. Jackie Speier, in *Transcript of Proceedings: Information Meeting on the Cult Phenomenon in the United States (Dole Hearings)* (Washington, DC: Ace-Federal Reporters, 1979), 25; Rabbi Davis in ibid., 79.

35. This listing is adapted from J. Gordon Melton, "How New Is New?" in *The Future of New Religious Movements*, ed. David G. Bromley and Phillip E. Hammond (Macon, GA: Mercer Univ. Press, 1987); Miller, ed., *America's Alternative Religions*. For ISKCON, see E. Burke Rochford, *Hare Krishna in America* (New Brunswick, NJ: Rutgers Univ. Press, 1985); Faye Levine, *The Strange World of the Hare Krishnas* (New York: Fawcett, 1974).

36. Singer and Lalich, *Cults in Our Midst*, 5.

37. In Aidan A. Kelly, ed. *Cults and the Jewish Community* (New York: Garland, 1990), 163. Compare Steve Allen, *Beloved Son* (Indianapolis: Bobbs-Merrill, 1982).

38. Rodney Stark and William Sims Bainbridge, *The Future of Religion* (Berkeley: Univ. of California Press, 1986).

39. A. James Rudin and Marcia R. Rudin, *Prison or Paradise?* (Philadelphia: Fortress Press, 1980); Walter R. Martin, *The New Cults* (Santa Ana, CA: Vision House, 1980).

40. Stark and Bainbridge, *The Future of Religion*; Finke and Stark, *The Churching of America, 1776–1990*. The quote from Yogi Bhajan is from Fox, "Alternative Spiritual Communities," 148.

41. William C. Martin, *With God on Our Side* (New York: Broadway, 1996).

42. Joel Carpenter, *Revive Us Again* (New York: Oxford Univ. Press, 1997).

43. Finke and Stark, *The Churching of America, 1776–1990*, 249.

44. Lynne Hybels and Bill Hybels, *Rediscovering Church* (Grand Rapids, MI: Zondervan, 1995).

## NINE

1. Dave Hunt, *The Cult Explosion* (Irvine, CA: Harvest House, 1980).

2. Craig Reinarman and Harry G. Levine, eds., *Crack in America* (Berkeley Univ. of California Press, 1997), 24.

3. Ray Stanley, *The Hippy Cult Murders* (New York: Mcfadden-Bartell, 1970).

4. For the origins of these charges, see J. Gordon Melton, *Encyclopedic Handbook of Cults in America*, rev. ed. (New York: Garland, 1992), 315–21; Sandra G. Boodman, " 'The Way' Recruiters Are Active in D.C., Tidewater," *WP*, October 13, 1981.

5. Lee Hultquist, *They Followed the Piper* (Plainfield: Logos International 1977); Christopher R. Evans, *Cults of Unreason* (London; Harrap, 1973); John W. Drakeford, *Children of Doom* (Nashville: Broadman, 1972).

6. Paul Andre Verdier, *Brainwashing and the Cults* (North Hollywood, CA: Wilshire Book Co., 1977); Ronald M. Enroth, *Youth, Brainwashing, and the Extremist Cults* (Grand Rapids, MI: Zondervan, 1977); Flo Conway and Jim Siegelman, *Snapping*, 2d ed. (1978; New York: Stillpoint Press, 1995); Lowell D. Streiker, *Mind-Bending: Brainwashing, Cults, and Deprogramming in the '80s* (Garden City, NY: Doubleday, 1984); Thomas W. Keiser and Jacqueline L. Keiser, *The Anatomy of Illusion* (Springfield, IL: Thomas, 1987); Robert J. Lifton, *Thought Reform and the Psychology of Totalism* (New York: W. W. Norton, 1961).

7. Walter H. Bowart, *Operation Mind Control* (New York: Dell, 1978); John D. Marks, *The Search for the Manchurian Candidate* (New York: Times Books, 1979).

8. Quoted from Drakeford, *Children of Doom*, 95. Hultquist, *They Followed the Piper*; Lowell D. Streiker, *The Cults Are Coming!* (Nashville: Abingdon, 1978); Sophia Collier, *Soul Rush* (New York: William Morrow, 1978); Robert Connor, *Walled In* (New York: New American Library, 1979); Joel A. MacCollam, *Carnival of Souls* (New York: Seabury Press, 1979); A. James Rudin and Marcia R. Rudin, *Prison or Paradise?* (Philadelphia: Fortress Press, 1980); John G. Clark et al., *Destructive Cult Conversion* (Weston, MA: American Family Foundation, 1981); Steve Allen, *Beloved Son* (Indianapolis: Bobbs-Merrill, 1982).

9. Davis is quoted from Ronald Enroth, "The Seduction Syndrome," in *Youth, Brainwashing, and the Extremist Cults*, 157.

10. Deborah Davis and Bill Davis, *The Children of God* (Grand Rapids, MI: Zondervan, 1984); Ruth Gordon, *Children of Darkness* (Wheaton, IL: Living Books, 1988); David E. Van Zandt, *Living in the Children of God* (Princeton: Princeton Univ. Press, 1991); Miriam Williams, *Heaven's Harlots* (New York: Eagle Brook, 1998).

11. "Evangelist, Guilty of Tax Evasion, is Jailed," *NYT*, June 12, 1994.

12. Compare Jennie Anderson Froiseth, ed., *The Women of Mormonism* (Detroit: C. G. G. Paine, 1882).

13. Allen, *Beloved Son*, 191; William F. Olin, *Escape from Utopia* (Santa Cruz, CA: Unity Press, 1980).

14. John P. Nugent, *White Night* (New York: Rawson, Wade, 1979).

15. Nori J. Muster, *Betrayal of the Spirit* (Urbana: Univ. of Illinois Press, 1997); John Hubner and Lindsey Gruson, *Monkey on a Stick* (San Diego: Harcourt Brace Jovanovich, 1988).

16. Anson D. Shupe, David G. Bromley, Donna L. Oliver, *The Anti-Cult*

*Movement in America* (New York: Garland, 1984); James A. Beckford, *Cult Controversies* (London: Tavistock, 1985).

17. Anson D. Shupe and David G. Bromley, *The New Vigilantes* (Beverly Hills: Sage Publications, 1980); David G. Bromley and Anson D. Shupe, *Strange Gods* (Boston: Beacon Press, 1981); David G. Bromley and James T. Richardson, eds., *The Brainwashing/Deprogramming Controversy* (New York: Edwin Mellen Press, 1983); Anson D. Shupe and David G. Bromley, *A Documentary History of the Anti-Cult Movement* (Arlington: Center for Social Research, Univ. of Texas at Arlington, 1985). Anson D. Shupe, *Anti-Cult Movements in Cross-Cultural Perspective* (New York: Garland, 1995).

18. *Transcript of Proceedings: Information Meeting on the Cult Phenomenon in the United States (Dole Hearings)* (Washington, DC: Ace-Federal Reporters, 1979), 63.

19. All quotes are from *Hearing on the Impact of Cults on Today's Youth, Senate Select Committee on Children and Youth* (California State University, Northridge California, August 24, 1974) (Sacramento, CA: Committee on Children and Youth, 1974), 53–58.

20. *Transcript of Proceedings (Dole Hearings)*, 63; Ted Patrick and Tom Dulack, *Let Our Children Go!* (New York: Dutton, 1976), 198–99; Ted Patrick, "Interview," *Playboy*, March 1979, 53–58.

21. John Clark, in *Transcript of Proceedings (Dole Hearings)*, 40.

22. *The Cult Awareness Network: Anatomy of a Hate Group* (Los Angeles: *Freedom Magazine*, 1995).

23. Pat Means, *The Mystical Maze* (San Bernardino, CA: Campus Crusade for Christ, 1976); Alan W. Gomes, *Unmasking the Cults* (Grand Rapids, MI: Zondervan, 1995); Bob Larson, *Larson's New Book of Cults* (Wheaton, IL: Tyndale House, 1989); Richard Abanes, *Cults, New Religious Movements, and Your Family* (Wheaton, IL: Crossway Books, 1998); Dave Breese, *Know the Marks of Cults*, rev. ed. (Eugene, OR: Harvest House, 1998).

24. Caryl Matrisciana, *Gods of the New Age* (Eugene, OR: Harvest House, 1985); Texe W. Marrs, *Dark Secrets of the New age* (Westchester, IL: Crossway Books, 1987); Lowell D. Streiker, *New Age Comes to Main Street* (Nashville: Abingdon Press, 1990); John Ankerberg and John Weldon, *Cult Watch* (Eugene, OR: Harvest House, 1991); Ron Rhodes, *The Culting of America* (Eugene, OR: Harvest House, 1994).

25. *The Challenge of the Cults* (Philadelphia: Jewish Community Relations Council of Greater Philadelphia, 1978); Shea Hecht and Chaim Clorfene, *Confessions of a Jewish Cultbuster* (Brooklyn: Tosefos Media, 1985).

26. Rudin and Rudin, *Prison or Paradise?* 101.

27. Jan Hoffman, "Inside Jews for Jesus," *New York*, April 28, 1986; Ellen Kamentsky, *Hawking God* (Medford, MA: Sapphire Press, 1992). For the impact on the Jewish community, see "Cultists Held No Threat to Jews," *WP*, March 25, 1977; Gary D. Eisenberg, ed., *Smashing the Idols* (Northvale, NJ: J. Aronson, 1988).

28. Aidan A. Kelly, ed., *Cults and the Jewish Community* (New York: Garland, 1990).

29. Christopher Edwards, *Crazy for God* (Englewood Cliffs, NJ: Prentice-Hall, 1979); Allen Tate Wood and Jack Vitek, *Moonstruck* (New York: William Morrow, 1979); Steve Hassan, *Combatting Cult Mind Control* (Rochester, VT: Park Street Press, 1988).

30. Verdier, *Brainwashing and the Cults*, 23; Conway and Siegelman, *Snapping*. The issue of brainwashing continues to incite scholarly controversy: though largely discredited in recent years, the concept has recently been revived and has predictably been much attacked: see Benjamin Zablocki, "Exit Cost Analysis," *Nova Religio* 1, no. 2 (1998), and the debate with David Bromley in the same issue; Charlotte Allen, "Brainwashed!" *Lingua Franca*, December 1998/January 1999, 26–37.

31. Compare Grant Wacker, "Travail of a Broken Family," *Journal of Ecclesiastical History* 47 (1996): 519.

32. William Hedgepeth and Dennis Stock, *The Alternative* (New York: Collier, 1970); Richard Fairfield, *Communes USA* (Baltimore: Penguin, 1972).

33. Philip Jenkins, *Moral Panic* (New Haven: Yale Univ. Press, 1998); Philip Jenkins, *Synthetic Panics* (New York: New York Univ. Press, 1999).

34. Marjorie Hyer, "Cults Hearing Noisy, Tense," *WP*, February 6, 1979.

35. Rudin and Rudin, *Prison or Paradise?* 98. Raymond E. Fowler, *The Cultic Seduction of Black Americans* (Fort Worth, TX: Black Evangelical Press, 1994).

36. *Hearing on the Impact of Cults on Today's Youth*, 53–55.

37. *Final Report on the Activities of the Children of God to Hon. Louis J. Lefkowitz, Attorney General of the State of New York* (Albany: Charity Frauds Bureau, 1974).

38. "The Darker Side of Sun Moon," *Time*, June 14, 1976, 50; Remsberg and Remsberg, "Why I Quit the Moon Cult," *Seventeen*, July 1976, 107ff; Marc Rasmussen, "How Sun Myung Moon Lures America's Children," *McCall's*, September 1976, 102ff; Ann Crittenden, "The Incredible Story of Ann Gordon and Rev. Sun Myung Moon," *Good Housekeeping*, October 1976, 86–88, David Black, "The Secrets of the Innocents," *Woman's Day*, February 1977, 166–75; Warren Adler, "Rescuing David from the Moonies," *Esquire*, June 6, 1978; Robert Friedman, "Cults: Are Teens Being Brainwashed?" *Seventeen*, May 1979, 178–79+.

39. Edwards, *Crazy for God*; Barbara Underwood and Betty Underwood, *Hostage to Heaven* (New York: Clarkson Potter, 1979); Josh Freed, *Moonwebs* (Toronto: Dorset, 1980); Steve Kemperman, *Lord of the Second Advent* (Ventura, CA: Regal Books, 1981); Deanna Durham, *Life among the Moonies* (Plainfield, NJ: Logos International, 1981); Susan Swatland and Anne Swatland, *Escape from the Moonies* (London: New English Library, 1982); E. Heftmann, *Dark Side of the Moonies* (Harmondsworth, England: Penguin, 1983); Willa Appel, *Cults in America* (New York: Holt, Rinehart, and Winston, 1983). David G. Bromley and Anson D. Shupe, *Moonies in America* (Beverly Hills: Sage Publications, 1979); Eileen Barker, *The Making of a Moonie* (Oxford: Blackwell, 1984).

40. Hultquist, *They Followed the Piper*; John Garvey, ed., *All Our Sons and Daughters* (Springfield, IL: Templegate, 1977); David Hanna, *Cults in*

*America* (New York: Belmont Towers Books, 1979); Carroll Stoner and Jo Anne Parke, *All God's Children* (New York: Penguin, 1979); Lowell D. Streiker, *The Cults Are Coming!* (Nashville: Abingdon, 1978); C. Elkins, *Heavenly Deception* (Wheaton, IL: Tyndale House, 1980); Una McManus and John Charles Cooper, *"Not for a Million Dollars"* (Nashville: Impact, 1980); Marcia R. Rudin, "New Target of the Cults: You," *50 Plus*, October 1981, 21–23. For a defense of the new movements, see Robert F. Corens, "One Man's Road to Krishna," *WP*, April 8, 1979; Ken Levitt and Ceil Rosen, *Kidnapped for My Faith* (Van Nuys, CA: Bible Voice, 1978); J. Gordon MelMAN and Robert L. Moore, *The Cult Experience* (New York: Pilgrim Press, 1982); Allen, *Beloved Son.*

41. Robert Boettcher and Gordon L. Freedman, *Gifts of Deceit* (New York: Holt, Rinehart, and Winston, 1980); House Committee on Standards of Official Conduct Korean Influence Investigation Hearing held in Washington, D.C. October 19, 1977–April 11, 1978, 95th Congress, 1st sess./ 2nd sess. (Washington DC: Government Printing Office, 1977–1978); Select Committee on Ethics of the United States Senate, *Korean Influence Inquiry: Executive Session Hearings held Mar. 14–August 7, 1978, 95th Congress, 2nd sess.* (Washington, DC: Government Printing office, 1978); Boettcher testimony in *Transcript of Proceedings (Dole Hearings),* 30–34.

42. Hizkias Assefa and Paul Wahrhaftig, *The MOVE Crisis in Philadelphia* (Pittsburgh: Univ. of Pittsburgh Press, 1990).

43. Scott Anderson, *The Four O'Clock Murders* (New York: Doubleday, 1993).

44. Quoted in Russell Miller, *Bare-Faced Messiah* (New York: Henry Holt, 1988), 348.

45. Charles A. Krause, *Guyana Massacre* (New York: Berkley, 1978); Marshall Kilduff and Ron Javers, *The Suicide Cult* (New York: Bantam Books, 1978); John Maguire and Mary Lee Dunn, *Hold Hands and Die!* (New York: Dale Books, 1978); Michael E. Knerr, *Suicide in Guyana* (New York: Belmont Tower Books, 1978); Jeannie Mills, *Six Years with God* (New York: A and W. Publishers, 1979); Stephen C. Rose, *Jesus and Jim Jones* (New York: Pilgrim Press, 1979); Nugent, *White Night*; George Klineman, Sherman Butler, and David Conn, *The Cult That Died* (New York: Putnam, 1980); Mark Lane, *The Strongest Poison* (Hawthorn Books, 1980); Ethan Feinsod, *Awake in a Nightmare* (New York: W. W. Norton, 1981); Kenneth Wooden, *The Children of Jonestown* (New York: McGraw Hill, 1981); Min S. Yee *In My Father's House* (New York: Holt, Rinehart, and Winston, 1981); James Reston, *Our Father Who Art in Hell* (New York: Times Books, 1981); Tim Reiterman and John Jacobs, *Raven* (New York: Dutton, 1982). Over the coming years, several more volumes provided a more considered examination of the career of Jim Jones and the broader implications for radical religion. See Kenneth Levi, ed., *Violence and Religious Commitment* (Univ. Park, PA: Penn State Press, 1982); Shiva Naipaul, *Journey to Nowhere* (New York: Simon and Schuster, 1981); John R. Hall, *Gone from the Promised Land* (New Brunswick, NJ: Transaction, 1987); John R. Chidester, *Salvation and Suicide* (Bloomington: Indiana Univ. Press, 1988);

Mary McCormick Maaga, *Hearing the Voices of Jonestown* (Syracuse: Syracuse Univ. Press, 1998).

46. The quote about "after Jonestown" is from Rudin and Rudin, *Prison or Paradise?* 8. For the commemoration of the Jonestown anniversary, see Tim Reiterman, "Remembering Jonestown," *LAT*, November 14, 1998; "Cults Remain Even After Jonestown," Associated Press story, November 14, 1998; Deborah Layton, *Seductive Poison* (New York: Anchor/Doubleday, 1998).

47. Richard Delgado, "Religious Totalism," *Southern California Law Review* 51 (1977); T. R. Reid, "Public Relations a Factor as Sen. Dole Opens Session," *WP*, February 6, 1979; Hyer, "Cults Hearing Noisy, Tense."

48. Stephanie Mansfield, "Panel Urged to Probe Cults," *WP*, March 14, 1980; Hassan, *Combatting Cult Mind Control*.

49. *Transcript of Proceedings (Dole Hearings)*; Reid, "Public Relations a Factor as Sen. Dole Opens Session"; Hyer, "Cults Hearing Noisy, Tense."

50. Larry D. Shinn, "Who Gets to Define Religion?" *Religious Studies Review* 19 (1993): 195–208.

51. Peter Collier, "Bringing Home the Moonies," *New Times*, June 10, 1977, 25–29; Delgado, "Religious Totalism."

52. Shupe et al., *The Anti-Cult Movement in America*.

53. Quoted in Barker, *The Making of a Moonie*, 128.

54. The Marine analogy is discussed, and rejected, in Margaret Thaler Singer and Janja Lalich, *Cults in Our Midst* (San Francisco: Jossey-Bass, 1995), 98–102.

55. Laura Parker, "Guru Recruits Drifters," *WP*, September 25, 1984; Hugh Milne, *Bhagwan: The God That Failed* (New York: St. Martin's Press, 1986); Rosemary Hamilton and Rosemary Lansdowne, *Hellbent for Enlightenment* (Ashland, OR: White Cloud Press, 1998).

56. Carlton Sherwood, *Inquisition* (Chicago: Regnery, 1991). For the Love Family, see Saundra Saperstein, "TM on Trial," *WP*, December 12, 1986. Tony Alamo would also be imprisoned in 1994.

57. This section is based on *The Cult Awareness Network*; also "The Cult Awareness Network," report on CBS's *60 Minutes*, December 28, 1997; Laurie Goodstein, "Plaintiff Shifts Stance on Anti-Cult Group," *WP*, December 23, 1996.

58. For the International Churches of Christ, see Jon Nordheimer, "Ex-Members Compare Campus Ministry to a Cult," *NYT*, November 30, 1994; Mary Geraghty, "Recruiting Tactics of a Religious Group Stir Campus Concerns," *Chronicle of Higher Education*, December 13, 1996; Randy Frame, "The Cost of Discipleship," *Christianity Today*, September 1, 1997, 64–66.

59. Nancy Clark and Nick Gallo, "Do You Believe?" *Family Circle*, February 23, 1993, 98ff. See also the television exposés of Gabriel of Sedona on "True Believers," *Dateline NBC*, February 24, 1998; or of the Brethren on "The Brethren," *Primetime Live*, March 25, 1998. Marybeth F. Ayella, *Insane Therapy*. (Philadelphia: Temple Univ. Press, 1998); Mark E. Laxer,

*Take Me For a Ride* (College Park, MD: Outer Rim Press, 1993); John Joseph Pietrangelo, *Lambs to Slaughter* (Tucson, AZ: J. Pietrangelo, 1994).

## TEN

1. Alan H. Peterson, foreword to *The American Focus on Satanic Crime*. Vol. 1 (South Orange, NJ: American Focus Publishing, 1988).

2. Philip Jenkins, *Using Murder* (Hawthorne, NY: Aldine De Gruyter, 1994); D. T. Lunde, *Murder and Madness* (New York: W. W. Norton, 1976); Robert Graysmith, *Zodiac* (New York: Berkeley, 1987).

3. R. N. Taylor, "The Process," in *Apocalypse Culture*, in ed. Adam Parfrey (Portland, OR: Feral House, 1990), 159; William S. Bainbridge, *Satan's Power* (Berkeley: Univ. of California Press, 1978); Maury Terry, *The Ultimate Evil* (New York: Bantam, 1987); Larry Kahaner, *Cults That Kill* (New York: Warner, 1988), 83; Carl A. Raschke, *Painted Black* (San Francisco: Harper and Row, 1990), 111–16; Ed Sanders, *The Family* (London: Panther, 1972), 125. Sanders's suggestion is supported by Vincent Bugliosi and Curt Gentry, *Helter Skelter* (New York: Norton, 1974).

4. Clark Howard, *Zebra* (New York: Berkley, 1980); Steven Barboza, *American Jihad* (New York: Doubleday, 1993); Claude Andrew Clegg, *An Original Man* (New York: St. Martin's Press, 1997), 297; Sydney P. Freedberg, *Brother Love* (New York: Pantheon Books, 1994).

5. Terry, *Ultimate Evil*, 172–81; Kahaner, *Cults That Kill*.

6. Gary Provost, *Across the Border* (New York: Pocket, 1989); Jim Schutze, *Cauldron of Blood* (New York: Avon, 1989); Clifford Linedecker, *Hell Ranch* (New York: Tor, 1990); Edward Humes, *Buried Secrets* (New York: Dutton, 1991).

7. Kenneth Wooden, *The Children of Jonestown* (New York: McGraw Hill, 1981), 205.

8. Michelle Smith and Lawrence Pazder, *Michelle Remembers* (New York: Congdon and Lattes, 1980); Philip Jenkins and Daniel Maier-Katkin, "Occult Survivors," in *The Satanism Scare*, ed. James T. Richardson, Joel Best, and David Bromley (Hawthorne, NY: Aldine De Gruyter, 1991), 127–44.

9. From a large literature on the Satanism scare of the 1980s, see Philip Jenkins, *Moral Panic* (New Haven: Yale Univ. Press, 1998); J. S. LaFontaine, *Speak of the Devil* (Cambridge: Cambridge Univ. Press, 1998); Debbie Nathan and Michael Snedeker, *Satan's Silence* (New York: Basic Books, 1995); Richard Ofshe and Ethan Watters, *Making Monsters* (New York: Scribner's, 1994); Robert D. Hicks, *In Pursuit of Satan* (Buffalo: Prometheus Books, 1991).

10. Nathan and Snedeker, *Satan's Silence*, 5.

11. Among the extreme statements of the satanic danger in these years, see John W. De Camp, *The Franklin Cover-up* (Lincoln, NE: AWT, 1991); James R. Noblitt and Pamela Sue Perskin, *Cult and Ritual Abuse* (Westport, CT: Praeger, 1995); Linda Blood, *The New Satanists* (New York: Warner, 1994); Jerry Johnston, *The Edge of Evil* (Dallas, TX: Word, 1989); Bob Larson, *Satanism* (Nashville: Thomas Nelson, 1989); Bob Larson, *In*

the Name of Satan (Nashville: Thomas Nelson, 1996); Judith Spencer, Satan's High Priest (New York: Pocket Books, 1998). For survivor memoirs, see Laura Buchanan, Satan's Child (Minneapolis: Compcare, 1994); Gail Carr Feldman, Lessons in Evil, Lessons from the Light (New York: Crown, 1993); Judith Spencer, Suffer the Child (New York: Pocket, 1989); Lauren Stratford, Satan's Underground (Eugene, OR: Harvest House, 1988). For an academic attempt to justify antisatanic claims, see Stephen A. Kent, "Deviant Scripturalism and Ritual Satanic Abuse," two part article in Religion 23, no. 3 (1993): 229, and 23, no. 4 (1993): 355.

12. Alex Constantine, Psychic Dictatorship in the United States (Portland, OR: Feral House, 1995).

13. Ellen Bass and Laura Davis, The Courage to Heal (New York: Harper and Row, 1988), 417; Peterson, The American Focus on Satanic Crime, 1:28.

14. Raschke, Painted Black.

15. Chrystine Oksana, Safe Passage to Healing (New York: Harper Perennial, 1994), 43.

16. Pete Earley, Prophet of Death (New York: Avon, 1993); Cynthia Stalter Sassé and Peggy Murphy Widder, The Kirtland Massacre (New York: Zebra, 1992).

17. MacLean's, February 8, 1993; Paul Kaihla, and Ross Laver, Savage Messiah (Toronto: Seal, 1994); Rod Colvin, Evil Harvest (New York: Bantam, 1992).

18. Freedberg, Brother Love.

19. James J. Boyle, Killer Cults (New York: St. Martin's Press, 1995); Brian Lane, Killer Cults (London: Headline, 1996).

20. David E. Kaplan and Andrew Marshall, The Cult at the End of the World (New York: Crown, 1996); D. W. Brackett, Holy Terror (New York: Weatherhill, 1996;) Senate Permanent Subcommittee on Investigations of the Committee on Governmental Affairs. Hearings on the Global Proliferation of Weapons of Mass Destruction, 104th Congress 1st. Sess., Washington, DC: Government Printing Office, 1996). J. Gordon Melton, Encyclopedic Handbook of Cults in America, rev. ed. (New York: Garland, 1992), 361–93; Thomas Robbins and Susan J. Palmer, Millennium, Messiahs and Mayhem (New York: Routledge, 1997).

21. William L. Pitts, "The Davidian Tradition," Bulletin—Council of Societies for the Study of Religion, November 1993, 99–101.

22. Dick J. Reavis, The Ashes of Waco (New York: Simon and Schuster, 1995); James D. Tabor and Eugene V. Gallagher, Why Waco? (Berkeley: Univ. of California Press, 1995); Stuart A. Wright, Armageddon in Waco (Chicago: Univ. of Chicago Press, 1995); James R. Lewis, ed., From the Ashes (Lanham, MD: Rowman and Littlefield, 1994); Clifford Linedecker, Massacre at Waco, Texas (New York: St. Martin's Press, 1993). NYT, headline "Apparent Mass Suicide Ends a 51 Day Standoff in Texas" over photos of the burning "cult compound," April 20, 1993.

23. Eugen Weber, Apocalypses (Cambridge, MA: Harvard University Press 1999); Richard H. Popkin and David S. Katz, Messianic Revolution (New York: Hill & Wang, 1999); Richard Abanes, End Time Visions (New York:

Four Walls Eight Windows, 1998); Mark Hamm, *Apocalypse in Oklahoma* (Boston: Northeastern Univ. Press, 1998); Paul Boyer, *When Time Shall Be No More* (Cambridge, MA: Harvard Univ. Press, Belknap Press, 1992).

24. Richard Leiby and Jim McGee, "Waco: Still Burning," *WP*, April 18, 1997. One major source for the events is the documentary film *Waco: Rules of Engagement.*

25. Sam Howe Verhovek, "Messiah Fond of Rock, Women, and Bible," *NYT*, March 3, 1993; "Fanning the Fires at Waco," *Freedom*, Church of Scientology, 1995, 14–16; Tabor and Gallagher, *Why Waco?*

26. The FBI opinions are based on interviews broadcast on PBS's *Frontline* special on Waco, October 17, 1995. For the ABC program, see Tabor and Gallagher, *Why Waco?* 124.

27. Tabor and Gallagher, *Why Waco?* 4.

28. Ellison and Bartkowski, in Wright, ed., *Armageddon in Waco*, 111–52.

29. Wright, ed., *Armageddon in Waco*, 109.

30. Quoted in an Associated Press report, "Expert Urged FBI to Make a Move," (*State College, PA*) *Centre Daily Times* April 21, 1993.

31. Richard Lacayo, "The Lure of the Cult," *Time*, April 7, 1997, 45–46; Bill Hoffmann and Cathy Burke, *Heaven's Gate* (New York: Harper, 1997).

32. Edward D. Hoch, "Village of the Dead," in *Cults!* ed. Charles G. Waugh and Martin H. Greenberg (New York: Barnes and Noble, 1983).

33. Huey P. Newton, *Revolutionary Suicide* (New York: Harcourt Brace Jovanovich, 1973).

34. John Lofland, *Doomsday Cult* (Englewood Cliffs, NJ: Prentice-Hall, 1996); Jane Allyn Hardyck and Marcia Braden, "Prophecy Fails Again," *Journal of Abnormal and Social Psychology* 65 (1962): 136–41. See also "Ukraine Police Arrest Leader of Doomsday Cult in Church," *NYT*, November 11, 1993; Ron Martz, "Focus on a Doomsday Cult," *Atlanta Journal Constitution*, November 5, 1995.

35. James R. Lewis, ed., *The Gods Have Landed* (Albany: State Univ. of New York Press, 1995); Brad Steiger and Hayden Hewes, *UFO Missionaries Extraordinary* (New York: Signet, 1997); Bill Hoffmann and Cathy Burke, *Heaven's Gate* (New York: Harper, 1997); William W. Zellner and Marc Petrowsky, eds. *Sects, Cults, and Spiritual Communities* (Westport, CT: Praeger, 1998).

36. Tom Post et al., "Mystery of the Solar Temple," *Newsweek*, October 17, 1994, 42–44; Bruce Wallace, "Twisted Legacy," *MacLean's*, October 24, 1994, 12–15; Massimo Introvigne, "Ordeal by Fire," *Religion* 25, no. 3 (1995): 267–83; James Walsh, "The Sunburst Sacrifices," *Time*, January 8, 1996, 45; Brenda Branswell, "Deadly Voyages," *MacLean's*, April 7, 1997, 46–47. The remark about "pure cinema" is from Barbara Demick, "Cult Deaths Seen as Mass Murder," *Philadelphia Inquirer*, October 7, 1994.

37. *NYT*, March 29, 1997.

38. Richard Lacayo, "In the Reign of Fire," *Time*, October 17, 1994, 59–60.

39. Anson D. Shupe, "Beware Alleged Experts' Doomsday Warnings," special issue of *Freedom* (Church of Scientology, 1995), 32. Gershom Gorenberg, "Tribulations," *New Republic*, June 14, 1999.

40. Luke 14:26; Mark 3:34; Matt 10:34–37.
41. Acts 2:40, 43–45; 2 Cor. 6:14, 17.
42. Rev. 18:4–5.

ELEVEN

1. David G. Bromley and Phillip E. Hammond, eds., *The Future of New Religious Movements* (Macon, GA: Mercer Univ. Press, 1987); Mary Farrell Bednarowski, *New Religions and the Theological Imagination in America* (Bloomington: Indiana Univ. Press, 1989).
2. William James, *Varieties of Religious Experience* (New York: Penguin Classics, 1985), 337.
3. J. Gordon Melton, *Encyclopedic Handbook of Cults in America*, rev. ed. (New York: Garland, 1992).
4. Hugo Hume, *The Superior American Religions* (Los Angeles: Libertarian Publishing 1928), 75–76). For the tradition of goddess and Heavenly Mother images in Mormonism, see Maureen Ursenbach Beecher and Lavina Fielding Anderson, eds., *Sisters in Spirit* (Urbana: University of Illinois Press, 1987); Janice Allred, *God the Mother, and Other Theological Essays* (Salt Lake City: Signature Books, 1997).
5. Walter Martin, *The Kingdom of the Cults* (1965; Minneapolis: Bethany House, 1992), 249–50.
6. Wade Clark Roof, *A Generation of Seekers* (San Francisco: Harper, 1993), 233. For a case-study of parish life after the feminist revolution, see Nora Gallagher, *Things Seen and Unseen* (New York: Knopf, 1998).
7. Rosemary Radford Ruether, *Women-church: Theology and Practice of Feminist Liturgical Communities* (San Francisco, Harper & Row, 1985). For the varieties of feminist spirituality, see Philip G. Davis, *Goddess Unmasked* (Dallas, Tex.: Spence Publishing, 1998); Cullen Murphy, *The Word According to Eve* (Boston: Houghton Mifflin, 1998); Cynthia Eller, *Living in the Lap of the Goddess* (New York: Crossroad, 1994); Cynthia Eller, "Twentieth Century Women's Religion as Seen in the Feminist Spirituality Movement," in *Women's Leadership in Marginal Religions*, ed. Catherine Wessinger, 2d ed., (Urbana: Univ. of Illinois, 1993), 172–95; Rosemary Radford Ruether, "The Women Church Movement in Contemporary Christianity," in *ibid.*, 196–210; Ursula King, *Women and Spirituality*, 2d ed. (University Park, PA: Penn State Press, 1993).
8. Robert S. Ellwood, "The American Theosophical Synthesis," in *The Occult in America*, ed. Howard Kerr and Charles L. Crow (Univ. of Illinois Press, 1983), 124–25. Nicholas Notovitch, *The Unknown Life of Jesus Christ from Buddhistic Records* (New York: G. W. Dillingham, 1894); Levi H. Dowling, *The Aquarian Gospel of Jesus the Christ* (Los Angeles: Royal Publishing 1908); Rudolf Steiner, *The Fifth Gospel: From the Akashic Record*, 3d ed. (London: Rudolf Steiner Press, 1995); Elizabeth Clare Prophet, *The Lost Years of Jesus* (Malibu, CA: Summit University Press, 1984).
9. "Public Declaration to the Tribal Councils and Traditional Spiritual Leaders of the Indian and Eskimo Peoples of the Pacific Northwest," Seattle, Washington, November 21, 1987, from World-Wide Web Site of Native-L

group. Catherine Albanese, *Nature Religion in America* (Chicago: Univ. of Chicago Press, 1988).

10. Harvey Cox, *Fire From Heaven* (Reading, MA: Addison Wesley, 1995); Richard Quebedeaux, *The New Charismatics* (Garden City, NY: Doubleday, 1976).

11. Charles Bufe, *Alcoholics Anonymous: Cult or Cure?* (San Francisco: See Sharp, 1991).

12. This section draws on Jerry Bergman, "The Adventist and Jehovah's Witness Branch of Protestantism," in *America's Alternative Religions*, ed. Timothy Miller (Albany: State Univ. of New York Press, 1995), 43.

13. Colin Spencer, *The Heretic's Feast* (London: Fourth Estate, 1993).

14. Terrence Monmaney and Shari Roan, "Hope or Hype?" *LAT*, August 30, 1998.

# Index